PENGUIN HANDBOOKS

THE PENGUIN BOOK OF PETS

Emil P. Dolensek, D.V.M., is the Chief Veterinarian for the New York Zoological Society (the Bronx Zoo) and Honorary Veterinarian for the New York City Police Department. He is a graduate of the Michigan State University Veterinary College and lives in New York.

Barbara Burn is an editor with a New York publishing firm. She has written a pet calendar and contributed to *The Whole Horse Catalogue* (1977) and, with her husband, Dr. Dolensek, is co-author of articles on pet care for *American Home Magazine*.

Bruce Buchenholz, the photographer, is the author of the award-winning *Doctor in the Zoo* (1974) and is at work on a photographic study of training animals.

A PRACTICAL GUIDE TO

ANIMAL-KEEPING

The Penguin Book of Pets

Originally published as
A PRACTICAL GUIDE TO
IMPRACTICAL PETS

EMIL P. DOLENSEK, D.V.M.,
and BARBARA BURN
Photographs by Bruce Buchenholz

PENGUIN BOOKS

Penguin Books Ltd, Harmondsworth,
Middlesex, England
Penguin Books, 625 Madison Avenue,
New York, New York 10022, U.S.A.
Penguin Books Australia Ltd, Ringwood,
Victoria, Australia
Penguin Books Canada Limited, 2801 John Street,
Markham, Ontario, Canada L3R 1B4
Penguin Books (N.Z.) Ltd, 182–190 Wairau Road,
Auckland 10, New Zealand

First published in the United States of America
under the title
A Practical Guide to Impractical Pets by
The Viking Press 1976
Published in Penguin Books 1978

Copyright © Bruce Buchenholz, Emil P. Dolensek,
and Barbara Burn, 1976
All rights reserved

LIBRARY OF CONGRESS CATALOGING IN PUBLICATION DATA
Dolensek, Emil P.
The Penguin book of pets.
First published in 1976 under title: A practical
guide to impractical pets.
Bibliography: p. 368.
Includes index.
1. Pets. 2. Wild animals as pets.
I. Burn, Barbara, 1940– joint author. II. Title.
[SF413.D58 1978]   636.08'87   77-11002
ISBN 0 14 046.318 6

Printed in the United States of America by
The Book Press, Brattleboro, Vermont
Set in VIP Garamond #3 and Helvetica

Except in the United States of America,
this book is sold subject to the condition
that it shall not, by way of trade or otherwise,
be lent, re-sold, hired out, or otherwise circulated
without the publisher's prior consent in any form of
binding or cover other than that in which it is
published and without a similar condition
including this condition being imposed
on the subsequent purchaser

CONTENTS

FOREWORD xi

PART ONE SELECTING A PET

1 ARE YOU A PRACTICAL PET OWNER? 3

2 EASY PETS 12

Mammals ———————————————————————— 13
MICE 17
RATS 19
HAMSTERS 21
GERBILS 23
CHINCHILLAS 25
GUINEA PIGS 26
RABBITS 28
CATS 33

Birds ——————————————————————————— 40
CANARIES 47
SMALL FINCHES 48
BUDGERIGARS 50
LOVEBIRDS 51
COCKATIELS 51
BEE BEE PARROTS 52

Reptiles and Amphibians ———————————————— 53
TURTLES 56
SNAKES 58
LIZARDS 62
SALAMANDERS 64
FROGS AND TOADS 65

Insects ——————————————————————————— 68
ANTS 69
CRICKETS 70
EARTHWORMS 71
BUTTERFLIES AND MOTHS 71
PRAYING MANTISES 72
SPIDERS 73

Fish ———————————————————————————— 74
BRINE SHRIMP 78
LAND HERMIT CRABS 78

3 DIFFICULT PETS 80

DOMESTIC ANIMALS 81

Mammals — 82
DOGS 82
FERRETS 90
HORSES, PONIES, AND DONKEYS 93
SHEEP AND GOATS 96
LLAMAS 99
PIGS AND COWS 99

Birds — 101
CHICKENS AND GUINEA FOWL 101
DUCKS 103
GEESE AND SWANS 105
PEACOCKS AND PHEASANTS 106
PIGEONS 107

Insects — 110
BEES 110

WILD ANIMALS 112

Mammals — 115
ARMADILLOS 115
OPOSSUMS 117
SQUIRRELS AND CHIPMUNKS 118
SKUNKS 120
THE RACCOON FAMILY 123

Birds — 130
PARROTS 130
MYNAH BIRDS 133
TOUCANS 134

4 IMPOSSIBLE PETS 135

ENDANGERED WILDLIFE 137

ADULT WILD ANIMALS 139

DANGEROUS ANIMALS 140

Mammals — 142
THE RODENT FAMILY 142
THE WEASEL FAMILY 144
THE CAT FAMILY 147
WILD DOGS 152
UNGULATES 156
BEARS 157
PRIMATES 157

Reptiles — 163
CAIMAN 163

Birds — 164
INJURED BIRDS 165
FREE-ROAMING PET BIRDS 167

PART TWO KEEPING A PET

5 HOW TO GET A PET— AND HOW NOT TO   173

PET SHOPS   176

BREEDERS   178

HUMANE SOCIETIES   180

GIFTS FROM FRIENDS   181

STRAYS AND BEGGARS   181

6 LEARNING TO LIVE WITH A PET   184

COMMUNICATING WITH YOUR PET—AND VICE VERSA   185

ADJUSTING YOUR HOUSEHOLD TO THE ANIMAL   190

ADJUSTING THE ANIMAL TO YOUR HOUSEHOLD   193

    Taming —— 193

    Training —— 197

    Equipment —— 203

    Surgery —— 205

ADJUSTING TO SPECIAL OCCASIONS   207

LEARNING TO LOVE YOUR PET   210

7 CARING FOR A PET   213

LIVING ARRANGEMENTS   213

    Enclosures for Large Mammals —— 215

    Cages —— 217

    Vivaria and Aquaria —— 222

FEEDING 225

    Commercial Foods —————————————————————— 232

    Fresh Food and Table Scraps ———————————————— 235

    Food Supplements ———————————————————————— 237

    The Importance of Water ———————————————————— 237

    Feeding Wild Birds —————————————————————— 238

    Feeding Wild Mammals ——————————————————— 240

GROOMING 241

    Mammals ———————————————————————————— 243

    Birds ——————————————————————————————— 251

    Reptiles ————————————————————————————— 251

EXERCISE 252

8 IN SICKNESS AND IN HEALTH 257

SELECTING A VETERINARIAN 257

CARE AND HANDLING OF A VETERINARIAN 259

HANDLING AN ANIMAL IN TROUBLE 262

PREVENTIVE MEDICINE 267

FIRST-AID TREATMENT 270

ANIMAL DISEASES THAT MAN CAN CATCH 272

9 GROWING YOUR OWN 277

NOT BREEDING 277

BREEDING MAMMALS 282

    The Pregnant Female ————————————————————— 282

    Care of Mother and Offspring ———————————————— 283

HAND-REARING BABY MAMMALS 285

BREEDING BIRDS 290

10 THE END OF THE AFFAIR 295

DEATH 296

LOST OR STOLEN 298

GETTING RID OF A PET 301

    Finding a New Home —— 301

    Selling —— 303

    Giving Away —— 303

    Releasing —— 305

EUTHANASIA 307

AFTERWORD 311

REFERENCE CHARTS 313

BIBLIOGRAPHY 368

INDEX 375

ACKNOWLEDGMENTS

It would be impossible to list every animal person who has, inadvertently or not, provided information and anecdotes for this book. The authors of various books and papers on the subject of animals and their care are listed in the bibliography or in the charts at the back of the book, but we would like to thank a few special people to whom we are particularly grateful for the time and encouragement by mentioning them here. Perhaps at a future date some of them will write animal books of their own; the stories and experiences they have to share would fill many volumes: Dore Ashton and family, Ed and Jackie Atkins, Caroline and Joe Atkinson, John Behler, Joseph Bell, Mary Bloom, Gretchen Buchenholz, William G. Conway, Martina D'Alton, Giuseppe di Campoli, William Decker, Jim Doherty, Ian and Christian Dolensek, Jack and Reiko Douglas, Robert Hendrickson, Karen and John Janiga, David Joslin, Catherine Kleinschmidt, the Bruce McWilliams family, Sherry Nelson, Aldo Pasera, Gail and Werner Rentsch, Jeanne Reynal and Thomas Sills, Tom Riddick, George Rose, Karen and Charles Sconce, Thelma Shaw, Frank and Louise Terry, Caroline Thompson, Catherine and Arthur Tyler, and Jack Winter.

FOREWORD

Not long ago in a pet shop I picked up a small booklet about the care and feeding of pet alligators. With attractive color photographs and enthusiastic descriptions of North American alligators and common caimans—the two species recommended as pets—the author made it abundantly clear that owning an alligator was a simple, inexpensive, and rewarding experience. A close reading made it even clearer, however, that the author was referring to baby alligators rather than full-grown specimens; the only hint that alligators might become impractical as pets was a chart near the end of the book indicating that a six-year-old alligator can reach a length of about seven feet and a weight of about 125 pounds. There was not a single piece of advice for the disenchanted alligator owner who finds that he cannot afford to give over half his living room to a glass cage in which to house the beast or to buy the pounds of fresh fish and beef liver needed each week to keep it alive and healthy. There may not be an army of full-grown alligators coursing through the sewer system of New York City as is often rumored, but there are undoubtedly a large number of unhappy people who have more than once felt like getting rid of their problems by flushing both alligator and booklet down the nearest toilet.

In order to avoid giving the impression that this book will be a similar exercise in encouraging animal lovers to adopt and care for unusual animals without a thought for the possible consequences, let me make the purpose of this book evident at the outset and explain what the title is all about.

First, some definitions. By "pet" we mean any animal that is kept for the enjoyment of its owner throughout the extent of the animal's natural life. (This definition eliminates the large category of animals that are kept for their usefulness to man—such as laboratory animals, laying hens, beef cattle, and guard dogs; it also eliminates such animals as the alligator, which is both an endangered species, and thus illegal to keep, and an impossible animal for the average householder to enjoy for its natural life.) All pets can be considered impractical to some degree, even the so-called easy ones, as they require a certain expenditure of time, money, and energy by the owner, on whom the animal is dependent. No matter how independent an animal may appear to be—the cat "who walks by itself" or the raccoon which relies on your garbage can for sustenance—the animal nevertheless turns to a human being in order to maintain its health and, in fact, its very life. By removing any animal from its natural habitat or disrupting its natural lifestyle—whether by taking in a wild animal or domesticating a whole species of them—we make ourselves responsible for supplying those needs that nature would otherwise provide.

The first and most obvious responsibility that we assume when we bring an animal into the house involves answering physical needs: nourishment, adequate living conditions, and health care (which includes regular cleaning, grooming, and exercise, as well as veterinary attention). The next area of responsibility—and one too often taken for granted—demands emotional or psychological commitment. Without its natural companions (a mate, members of its own species, and even predators, which serve an important role in any wild animal's life), an animal kept in captivity can become very dependent on its human companions for affection, simple company, or at least for some kind of relationship. It has been observed in many animals, for instance, that their natural psychological growth is retarded in certain ways by living with humans. Notice how a full-grown dog will show submissive, puppylike behavior toward its owner by wagging its tail, lowering its head, or flattening its ears, and otherwise indicating the dominance of the "master." A certain amount of this behavior in dogs is natural, as we have seen by observing wild canines, but a poodle that can't be out of the sight of its owner or that urinates on the floor when visitors arrive is definitely not behaving like a confident adult animal. Gavin Maxwell, in his book *Ring of Bright Water,* gives a moving account of living with otters in the west of Ireland and points out how much like babies his grown otters would behave—by demanding constant attention and protection against the natural elements to which they had never been conditioned. Even the most unresponsive animals must be attended to and controlled in some way if they are to adapt to a captive life— whether by caging or by training. It is generally true, however, that the more responsive the animal (and presumably the more enjoyable), the more emotionally demanding it can be for the owner.

Most people who have animals in their homes and many who are thinking about getting a pet are already aware of these aspects of keeping animals. But it is surprising how little we project into the future to consider the possible consequences of our tampering with another life, especially those of us who are pushovers for baby animals. Like the baby alligator, which is easy to keep and fun to watch, most baby animals grow up into adults that are not so easy and not so much fun. There are far too many sad stories about well-meaning families who have adopted orphaned raccoons or purchased exotic ocelot kittens only to find that the mature animals are suddenly capable of biting people, destroying the furniture, and becoming in other ways impossible to live with. How does one dispose of an animal that has suddenly become too difficult a pet? This question is asked not only by people who have made a mistake by impulsively selecting an animal before they have enough information about it, but also by those with, say, a family cat that regularly produces a litter of kittens, which can't be kept, of course, without increasing the cat population in the house to an "impractical" level? Giving away cute kittens may be easy and even fun at first, but eventually it becomes a nuisance, and sometimes kittens are simply destroyed at birth to save the owners trouble. Giving away a full-grown animal—particularly one that has proven difficult as a house pet—is an even tougher job; the local school or zoo may not want what you have suddenly developed a generous impulse to give them, and often the only solution is to destroy the animal. Many irresponsible people simply choose to abandon their pets, and city newspapers are full of reports of feral dogs and cats roaming the streets, creating health hazards, or attacking unsuspecting passers-by.

As I hope I am beginning to make clear, this book will not tell you how much fun it is to keep a wolf in your living room or how impressed the neighbors will be to find that you are loved by a spider monkey. There are many charming books that have been written about such rewarding experiences. Our task here is not quite so charming but rather more serious; as there is no single book written for the average animal lover incorporating information about pets of all kinds—mammals, reptiles, birds, fish, and even insects—we felt that a one-volume compendium dealing with the care and feeding of various kinds of animals would be both useful and interesting. I have found in my experience as a veterinarian that a family owning a couple of dogs and a cat or two is also likely to have a gerbil or may be willing to take in an injured or unwanted creature of some other species. I hope that this book will answer many of their questions, eliminating the need to purchase several different books (some of which have not, in fact, been written as yet). In addition to basic, up-to-date information about individual species, I have also included sections covering care and feeding, breeding, training, first-aid, and the most humane ways of getting rid of a pet that can no longer be kept. Because of limited space and the wide variety of animals considered here, these sections are in no way intended as comprehensive treatises but simply as general essays introducing the reader to material that is not always available to the public. I have included a bibliography to enable interested readers to explore further the various areas only touched upon in this book.

The first few chapters, however, are perhaps the most important because they elaborate what I have been stressing in these introductory remarks: the relative impracticality of keeping any animal as a pet and the serious responsibility that every pet owner must accept along with the animal itself. People own animals for many reasons, and every potential pet owner must examine his own reasons very carefully. Often I have felt that it was not the animal that was impractical but the owner; the love of animals may be a characteristic common to most pet owners but it is by no means the only prerequisite for the job. In fact, many well-meaning animal lovers have been known to kill their pets with kindness—by overfeeding, underdisciplining, and other forms of mistreatment brought about through simple ignorance of the animal's real needs.

Many kinds of animals have been kept in captivity as housepets, and it would be foolish of me to try to include all or even most of them in this book. Some non-native animals are now impossible to obtain in this country unless they are born here (and some that we do discuss may soon be impossible because of increasingly stringent importation laws), and many animals are simply not suitable for the average pet owner. But a goodly number of animals have been kept in or around the house with some degree of success, and most of them will be covered here. We have divided them into three main categories: easy pets, difficult pets, and impossible pets. I wish that space allowed me to make categories for owners, for they, too, can be classified as easy, difficult, and impossible. An immaculate housekeeper, for instance, might find the relatively undemanding cat impossible because it leaves fur around and scratches the upholstery, whereas some hardy soul might not turn a hair at a houseful of flying squirrels. But these are extremes and this book is not written for them, although the immaculate housekeeper might be happy with another sort of animal discussed here (an aquarium full of decorative, quiet, and furless tropical fish, perhaps).

All I hope to do here is to provide the average animal lover who has or who wants to keep a pet with some information so that he can make up his own mind as to what he can tolerate (or what can tolerate him). Much of this information is given in chart form at the back of the book where the animals are listed alphabetically. I hope the text and the photographs, as well as several illustrative anecdotes, will prove helpful. You will find that some of the charts and chapters include discussions of animals that I would not particularly recommend as housepets, but they are described here for two reasons: first, to illustrate to the uninitiated how demanding certain species may be; and, second, to answer some of the many questions that people already owning these animals may have. As a zoo veterinarian, I am constantly besieged by the owners of unusual or exotic pets for assistance that veterinarians in private practice often feel they are not qualified or are unwilling, for one good reason or another, to provide. Because my own responsibilities do not leave me the time to handle these cases, I must restrict my "treatment" by referring these owners to specialized books or papers and to other veterinarians or animal hospitals where such help can be obtained. Although I do not expect that the material in this book will solve all of these problems, it is my hope that at least some unfortunate situations can be avoided—particularly those in which the animal is likely to suffer even more than its owner; this is often the plight of wild-animal pets that have not been properly bred or conditioned to a life in captivity.

Our awareness and appreciation of wildlife is not increased by removing an animal from its natural surroundings, thereby disturbing the ecology of its environment, and by creating an artificial situation in which it can survive comfortably in the presence of human beings. It is true that the natural lifespan of a wild animal may be increased in captivity by the availability of medical attention, a steady supply of food, and the removal of predators. But this success is more often the result of expert care by specialists than it is of the enthusiasm and good intentions of pet owners. An animal in the home can be the source of enormous pleasure, and it can live a full and comfortable life under the proper conditions. Providing those conditions is not always an easy task but it is an essential one, demanding a full understanding of our responsibilities— not only to the individual animal but also to ourselves and to the world we live in.

EMIL P. DOLENSEK, D.V.M.

THE PENGUIN
BOOK OF PETS

PART ONE
Selecting a Pet

1 ARE YOU A PRACTICAL PET OWNER?

We are assuming that most readers of this book are interested in animals, and it is likely that many will consider themselves animal people, a label adopted proudly and often with good reason by many animal lovers. But being an animal lover or an animal person is no guarantee that you will make a good pet owner. Deciding for yourself whether you are or not depends a great deal on the kind of animal you have (or intend to get), and in later chapters we will look at various kinds of animals and their relative suitability. First of all, however, let's find out about your own suitability.

Pet keeping is a time-honored tradition, and many authorities believe that this tendency in humans has played an important role in our development as well as in that of certain domesticated species; the process that began as long as 20,000 years ago with the domestication of the dog. Most domestic animals are kept by man for their usefulness, but many have been kept and even bred in captivity for quite different reasons—mostly curiosity, scientific or otherwise. Curiosity has killed many more animals than the cat, as conservationists and humane societies keep telling us, but this is hardly a modern problem. Primitive tribes are known to have captured animals and kept them captive for no other reason than that they were valued as curiosities; some Australian aborigines today tie up wallabies, opossums, and even frogs and young birds in their camps, where many of them die because they are not properly fed or cared for. The Egyptians kept baboons because they were considered sacred and are supposed to have trained them to perform household chores such as tending gardens and waiting on table. Assyrian children kept hamsters in cages as playthings, and the Greeks and Romans collected enormous menageries and used tamed exotic beasts in various kinds of spectaculars for the amusement of the people.

Most of us would prefer to think that we are more civilized today—that we are less cruel or exploitative and definitely more concerned with the well-being of our animals. That *may* be the case, but the situation is by no means as clearcut as one might assume. Ask

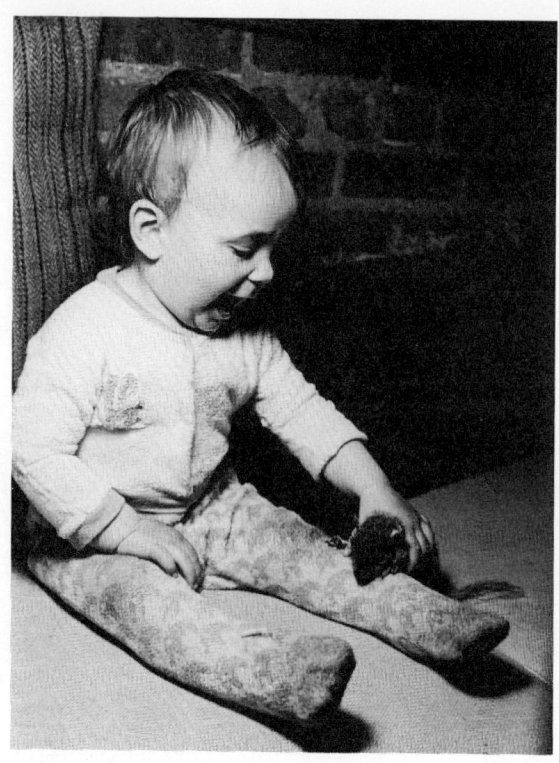

BABY SQUIRRELS MAY LOOK LIKE CUTE LITTLE TOYS FOR BABY HUMANS . . .

yourself why *you* want to keep an animal and try to answer the question as honestly as possible.

Is it because the animal is cute or beautiful or somehow irresistibly attractive? The urge to possess something for esthetic reasons is age old, though often best confined to obtaining inanimate objects, such as paintings or fine furniture. There need be nothing wrong with having a Siamese cat around the house as a decorative object because even if one is concerned only with its looks, one must necessarily keep it well fed and relatively content, and this is not a difficult undertaking. But if one feels that a Siamese cat is not quite enough and that only an ocelot or a squirrel monkey will do, one might reconsider one's motives. Are you interested in satisfying something other than your esthetic sense—your desire to impress the neighbors, for instance? Many people have been successful in keeping tame cheetahs and other exotic animals, and they genuinely enjoy their pets for more than the effect they make walking down the street, but these people are dedicated and very special indeed; for every one of them there are hundreds who have found the going too difficult and are hard put to find a humane way of getting the problem out of their hair or the house.

If you cannot resist the appeal of a playful kitten or puppy, fine, as long as you realize that the animal is going to become a less playful and possibly downright unattractive adult. Many cute animals grow into beautiful specimens, but many lose their interest value when they lose their baby fat and fuzz. Unbelievable as it may seem, I have been asked on a number of occasions by new kitten owners how much it will cost to have the animal destroyed when it reaches maturity and becomes more trouble than it is "worth" in amusement value. People who obtain kittens at the beginning of summer and then abandon them in the fall when the kids go back to school are no less irresponsible, though far greater in number.

Some people find themselves pet owners because an animal is hurt or apparently homeless and seems to need human attention. In many instances this concern for the animal's welfare is valid and admirable, but too often more harm than good is accomplished. It is also illegal in many states to confine wild animals for whatever purpose, and permits will be required, even if the confinement is for the good of the animal and not for the purpose of making it a pet, or selling it as such.

Baby animals found alone in the woods are usually not abandoned at all; deer, raccoons, and most animal parents will leave their

... BUT THEY AREN'T.

offspring briefly while they hunt for food or a new home, and the good Samaritan frequently creates orphans where none existed. Of course, many baby animals *are* abandoned by their parents—squirrels and birds may not always rescue babies that fall from the nest—and the human who is willing to hand rear or repair the animal himself and to return it to the wild when it is able to fend for itself is usually doing nature a service. But this service is frequently inadvertently ill rendered, and there are many professionals in rescue shelters or humane societies that can do a better job than the average person. Often baby animals may be replaced in their original nests (birds, for instance, cannot detect human odor and will usually readopt their own young), and injured animals are extremely difficult to handle or to save. Even under the care of experts, injured wild animals are not easy to help; if they are subdued enough to tolerate handling, they are probably so far gone that they cannot be saved. I am not saying that one should leave these creatures to suffer, but one should carefully consider whether help is, in fact, necessary or possible, and whether one can provide it or knows someone who can. This matter will be covered in greater detail in later chapters, but for the moment suffice it to say that this motivation for taking in an animal has nothing to do with keeping pets and should not be considered an excuse for doing so.

Many parents feel the need to keep an animal or two in the house for the sake of their children. It is true that this is an excellent way to teach children about responsibility and about the animal world in general or, rather, in particular. But consider the child and the animal: Is the child mature enough to take on full responsibility for another creature's life? Are *you* willing to take the ultimate responsibility yourself? If the child is demanding a pet because his friends have one or because he wants a toy to play with, think again, and while you're doing so, put the welfare of both child and animal at the top of your priorities. Many children have been bitten, scratched, or worse, and many animals have been tortured, destroyed, or given away as "vicious" because of ignorance and lack of supervision on the part of the parents.

Watching the natural life cycle of an animal or the birth of kittens or puppies can be an exciting educational experience for a child, but some families would be better off letting the local zoo, natural history museum, or classroom do the educating if the household is not suitable for keeping animals (and their offspring) for the full course of their lives. Humane societies are filled with unwanted kittens and puppies because of these home-taught courses in reproduction. Much has been written about the good psychological effect that animals have had on children who are disturbed or lonely for one reason or another, and miracles have been accomplished by puppies where expert psychiatrists have failed. But not all animals are suitable for this responsibility, and none can be effective if appropriate parental or professional guidance is lacking.

Many animals are kept as pets because they are excellent companions and there is no dismissing the importance of love and of being loved involved in pet keeping. A great many old (and not so old) people who are alone have found comfort in having some creatures that they can care for and that will care for them in return. As with children, however, the pet's welfare must also be considered, and along with love one must be prepared to give proper care and to tolerate the difficulties that owning any animal will entail. Therefore, the choice of the animal must be carefully considered. A person may truly love a cheetah and enjoy having such a wild, beautiful creature love him back, but there is no excuse for endangering a species and possibly oneself when the same quality of affection can be shared with an animal that can adapt far more readily to a human way of life. Possibly the love one receives from a wild animal removed from its natural habitat could more realistically be considered a dependency that in the wild the animal would not feel at all or would direct toward members of its own species.

Owning an exotic pet—or any wild animal—can be a beautifully rewarding experience and lots of people have written books to tell us so, but mere curiosity can be satisfied by reading those books or visiting the local zoo to see how the animal fares in captivity. The desire for a challenge can be satisfied more humanely—if one cannot simply resist the impulse—by going out into nature and trying to survive in the animal's habitat rather than forcing it to survive in ours. There is no question but that various endangered species have been rescued from extinction by being kept and bred in captivity, and many private individuals have contributed to that success. Their achievements, however, have not been easily gained and could not be matched by the average person, unless he is dedicated enough to devote most of his time, much of his money, and nearly all of his energy to the task. There has been a great deal of resistance by these special individuals to the existing and forthcoming federal and state laws preventing the importation of animals into the United States, the shipping of them between states, and the keeping of native wild animals in the home. Some of these laws were devised for reasons other than the prevention of the keeping of pets and seem unfair to those people qualified to house them, but they exist nonetheless and have, for the most part, done more good than harm. The point of all this discussion is not to make excuses for laws, however, but simply to emphasize the fact that curiosity about animals is not usually best satisfied by keeping them at home. Such a form of entertainment is no more civilized a form of behavior than it was for the Romans to watch how lions kill their prey in an amphitheater, were it a Christian or another lion.

Many of the motivations for keeping animals as pets are reasonable and justifiable, particularly if good motivations are taken in combination and are well balanced. Someone who loves animals, gets pleasure from their appearance and their behavior, is willing to care for them or to teach children to do the same, and is curious or interested enough to learn about their individual (and nonhuman) characteristics can be an excellent pet owner and an "animal person" deserving of the title. But someone who is lacking in any of these attitudes or carries them to excess without using common sense can be doing himself or the animal a great deal of harm. Making an animal live in a human environment rather than the one for which it is adapted is a form of slavery after all (ants and other social animals do it, too, so it's not exactly unnatural nor is it necessarily to be despised), and any potential pet owner should realize that and be aware of the consequences to himself, moral and otherwise.

Which brings us to the next group of questions any animal owner must ask: Can I tolerate the animal and can it tolerate me? Many people drawn to a cuddly pup in a pet-store window do not realize until they get the animal home that they are in fact physically incapable of tolerating it or that some member of the family cannot live in the same house with it. Allergies to fur are common, as are nervous reactions to the noise and general confusion caused by animals. Even the gentlest pup is going to have to be trained not to chew furniture and not to urinate on the rug, and even the tiniest parakeet can give a painful nip on the finger or drive one out of the house with its squawking.

In addition to physical stress, there is the more vague and less predictable area of psychological tolerance. Some people who are accustomed to a particular way of life or time schedule will find it very difficult to adjust their routines to accommodate a dog that needs walking, a cat that demands a special kind of food, or a bird whose cage may smell and look horrible if it isn't cleaned out daily. I know one woman who keeps at least twelve animals in her seven-room house, including a duck, several cats, the smallest of which rules the whole roost, a dog, two iguanas, a tiny monkey, and a baby gorilla. (She works for the local zoo, which is why she has such an odd assortment.) She loves them all and her life with them, but she can never take a vacation. She must be constantly alert to the demands of her various cohabitants (especially the gorilla who does not take naps, refuses to stay in the playpen, and thinks of her as his mother, who would, in nature, rarely let him out of her grasp), and she must tolerate a high degree of noise, damage to the furniture, general chaos, and odd looks from the neighbors. She has never had the same man to read the gas meter twice in a row and cannot give dinner parties, but she is popular enough with the neighborhood children who assume wrongfully that she cannot refuse the gift of whatever stray or unwanted pet they can manage to find for her.

I haven't even begun to mention the other difficult—though perhaps more obvious—factors involved in keeping one or more pets, such as the expense and the trouble of building appropriate housing and providing adequate living conditions. If you are considering the purchase of an animal or the acceptance of a gift, can you be sure that you will be able to support the animal for the rest of its life? Some rabbits have been known to live as long as ten years in captivity, and many dogs and cats live far longer than that. Are you prepared to find out what adequate living conditions are for such an animal and tolerate the expense, the effort, and the time involved? Consider not only the normal course of events but also possible emergencies. Veterinary bills can mount up rapidly, and the cost of boarding an animal (if it can tolerate such an arrangement) can also be a heavy burden if one wishes to take a vacation without one's pet.

Speaking of vacations, one should not forget the responsibility involved in feeding local wild animals—squirrels, raccoons, birds, and so on. Many of these creatures have become dependent on people who enjoy watching them come around but forget them entirely when they take off for a holiday. Some birds will die during the winter months when their source of food runs out; having failed to migrate south, as they would normally, because of the plentiful, unseasonable availability of seeds, they become incapable of fending for themselves in the deep snow and may die of the cold and of starvation. Raccoons are usually clever enough to find another house to raid when the pickings grow slim, but if they have become accustomed to human kindness they can be a real pest to less generous neighbors.

Normal daily care and emergency treatment aside, other responsibilities must also be considered. Some animals require special operations to make them adaptable to life with human beings. Male cats will spray urine creating a disagreeable odor on the furniture (or whatever they hit) if they are confined to an apartment, for instance, and any animal that hasn't been altered can produce offspring, wanted or not—mostly not. It is surely less cruel to deny an animal the right to reproduce than it is to allow the indiscriminate production of animals you do not intend to keep or place in good care. Furthermore, many female animals—including cats and dogs—will live far healthier, longer lives after spaying.

All animals—even the least responsive ones—will have to undergo some sort of adaptation to a life in confinement; this may be helped along by training, by adjusting to a diet, or by adapting to routines for eating, sleeping, being cleaned, and being examined for reasons of health. It is the owner's responsibility to see that such adaptation is made successfully.

I have touched upon only a few of all the possible contingencies of

MANY PEOPLE THINK THEY WOULD ENJOY AN EXOTIC BIRD AS A PET, BUT THERE ARE SEVERAL QUESTIONS A POTENTIAL PET-OWNER MUST ASK HIMSELF BEFORE TAKING ON THE RESPONSIBILITY.

owning a pet; there are as many of them as there are pets, as some of the anecdotes in the following chapters may suggest. It is difficult for even the most informed and farseeing individual to predict what lies ahead, but one should at least be aware that there are a lot of unforseen events in store—many of them enjoyable to be sure. It helps to be as fully prepared as possible and to be willing to cope with whatever comes along, as tolerantly as can be managed. If you

have read this chapter and asked yourself the necessary questions, answering them honestly to your own satisfaction, then you are ready to decide whether or not you are a practical pet owner. If you decide that you are, the next step is to determine what sort of pet you are willing to keep, or perhaps, more appropriately, what sort of pet will be willing to let you keep it.

2 EASY PETS

Are you the sort of person who wouldn't mind giving houseroom to a mouse or a snake or perhaps a collection of ants? If so, you're not the least bit peculiar, for these animals are among the easiest and most entertaining of pets—if, that is, they aren't camped in your kitchen or cellar but kept in a controlled environment that enables you to enjoy them on your own terms. Wild mice, poisonous snakes, and stinging ants have caused humans a lot of pain and problems over the centuries, but their domestic or harmless native cousins have helped to make up for the sins of the others by giving both pleasure and enlightenment to those who have taken the time to care for them. We have no exact figures on the number of pet animals now kept in the United States, but there must be many millions indeed; in 1975 there were over a hundred million dogs and cats accounted for, and many more that weren't. Most of these pets are of species that will be mentioned in this chapter, because they are easily and inexpensively obtained and they can be cared for in the average household with a minimum of time, money, and effort.

There are exceptions, of course. A rare breed of domestic cat can cost more than $500, and many well-heeled pet owners will spend a great deal every year on special food, lodging, and even clothing for their animals. Some people will find the negligible cost and effort involved in caring for a tiny hamster an unwelcome burden, while others will keep a large number of animals in the same house and think nothing of it. One couple I know raises birds, which kept singly or in pairs would certainly classify as easy pets, but they have over two hundred fifty birds housed in some two hundred different cages and their life style is, needless to say, completely ruled by the demands of their unusual household. Some neighbors of mine, on the other hand, live perfectly normal lives, yet at any given time they may be supporting an orphaned rabbit, a few transient swans, and an injured bird in addition to their regular family of geese, pigeons, dogs, and a pony. Somehow they manage to take all these boarders in their stride, and the place doesn't erupt in confusion and chaos every time yet another creature in need of comfort shows up.

For the most part, the animals that are kept successfully in the home are those familiar species that have lived happily in human surroundings for hundreds of years, providing their owners with rewards far above their demands. Although individual animals of the same species may vary considerably, just as their owners do, some useful generalizations can be made in terms of their characteristics and their potential as pets. Mammals may not be the easiest class of animals to adopt, but they are perhaps the most responsive as pets, and we might just as well begin with them.

MAMMALS

Cats and dogs are probably the first animals to come to mind when one thinks of pets, but small rodents, such as the mouse, white rat, hamster, gerbil, chinchilla, and guinea pig, are far easier to keep and care for in the home. They are not expensive to buy or support and they make wonderful pets, if treated properly. They can be housed comfortably in relatively small cages, handled with ease, and they require very little attention to live to ripe old ages (what "ripe old" means will vary from species to species).

Because of their high rate of mortality in nature—they have few defenses and many predators—these animals breed rapidly and readily. This is one of the reasons they are so popular in scientific laboratories. Although many animal lovers deplore the experimentation carried on in the medical and behavioral sciences, it is, ironically, because of this experimentation that these animals are available as housepets in such large quantity today, and it is thanks to them that we have learned so much about ourselves, our diseases, our heredity, and our behavior.

Most of these rodents can be obtained at reasonably low cost from pet stores, but one must be sure that the dealer is a reliable one and that his stock is healthy and well cared for. Breeders and laboratories are also sources, but unless you know exactly what you are looking for, a pet store is probably the best source for the average pet owner. Breeders will often charge premium prices for unusual varieties or pedigreed breeding stock, and laboratories often use animals that are not particularly suitable as pets.

Buying or accepting an animal from a friend is often the source of a good pet, but make certain that the animal you select is in good condition and that you may return it if in the first week or so the animal turns out to be unhealthy. The signs of good health are readily apparent: soft, silky coat; a strong, solid body; bright eyes; and freedom from blemishes on the nose, feet, ears, or fur. Although you may feel sympathy for the runt of the litter, avoid the weakest animal in the group; pick the liveliest and the most handsome individual you can find.

If you are interested in breeding, see that the pair you get is correctly sexed; I've heard lots of sad stories from disappointed owners whose pairs have failed to produce litters even under the most comfortable and conducive of surroundings, only to discover that each "pair" consisted of two males or females, compatible in many but not nearly enough ways.

Since all of these rodents are small and relatively active, it is best to keep them housed in cages most of the time. This will protect them as well as yourself, for when loose they can manage to disappear into parts of your house you never knew existed. The best cages are made of metal, which is easy to keep clean and offers no wood to tempt these natural gnawers. The size of the cage should accommodate the particular animal properly (see the charts for space requirements), but the construction for each species is similar. Wire-screen floors with removable trays below make daily cleaning a simple matter, but since these animals are natural burrowers, most will prefer floor litter or bedding of some sort to root around in; wood shavings, cat litter, sawdust, shredded paper, or any clean absorbent material will do. The metal cages are available in most pet stores, but inexpensive cages of wood and wire may be made at home (see Chapter 7), and for the smallest animals, glass aquarium tanks with wire-screen lids are also suitable. Be sure that you give the creature a place to retreat for peace and quiet; a small box of any unchewable material with a tiny hole for coming and going will be fine, and will also serve as a nesting box if you have a breeding pair. Shelves, climbing devices, exercise wheels, and the like are necessary furnishings for the small active animals to prevent the problems that can arise from boredom or lack of exercise.

The cage, which should have a secure latch, must be superficially cleaned daily, and a thorough cleaning should be undertaken at least once a week; this involves removing all the litter and food particles, scrubbing all surfaces of the cage with hot soapy water, and rinsing them carefully. Then the cage should be dried and fresh litter or bedding arranged within. (You will probably need a holding cage or box to keep the animal safe while you do your chores.)

One of the reasons rodents have been so successful as experimental animals is that they are susceptible to many diseases, some of which—paratyphoid for instance—can be very serious. Kept in the home under good, clean conditions and isolated from other animals and from parasites, they should remain relatively free from disease. A constant temperature range of 70° to 80°F. and a humidity no higher than 60 per cent will reduce the possibility of pneumonia and a condition common to newborn mice and rats known as ringtail. Regular, thorough cleaning of the cage and the occasional use of a disinfectant should keep mites, fleas, lice, and other disease carriers away. If these pests should appear, a rotenone-based flea powder or a

2 to 4 per cent Malathion powder brushed into the animal's fur should remove the problem, but you will also have to clean the cage thoroughly at the same time, discarding all flooring and nesting material. Cockroaches and bedbugs are more difficult to exterminate, as any big-city apartment dweller can tell you, but various effective solutions are on the market that can be sprayed around the outside of the cage (not inside or you'll exterminate the pet as well) to keep intruders away. Sturdy lids that can only be removed by human hands will keep larger pests (cats and dogs and human babies) from getting in or letting the animals out, but you should also take the precaution of quarantining or isolating all newcomers to your colony for a period of about three weeks to avoid letting in some trouble yourself. A complete examination of each of the incoming pets should also be made to uncover any obvious disease symptoms or external parasites.

If you find it difficult to keep the cage at the right temperature, a heating element may be used (though the animals should be able to escape the source to avoid being cooked). Do not put the cage in direct sunlight or in drafts. Some of these hardy creatures can tolerate varying degrees of hot and cold, but extremes or sudden changes will give them respiratory problems, and a constant cold temperature may make them sluggish or even send them into a state of hibernation.

All of these animals are herbivores and will survive happily on nuts and vegetables, although individuals will have particular tastes. Special pellets or chows are available commercially, and these are nutritionally complete and palatable (guinea pigs have their own pellets containing vitamin C, which they cannot synthesize but which they must have to avoid the onset of scurvy). Most pet and feed stores carry these pellets, but check the quality of those you buy, for they can quickly become musty; for this reason, purchasing in large quantities for one or two pets is not an economical measure. Nuts (in uncracked shells), seeds, lettuce, carrots, parsley, celery, apples, grapes, and even turnips, potatoes, small-size dog kibble, grains, and bread are all good staple foods for these rodents if served fresh and changed daily. Any or all of these items may be used to supplement a pellet diet, but take care not to offer too much of any single food or to introduce new food without some gradual conditioning. The best policy is to provide a varied diet and let the animal eat what it likes. Extras such as wheat-germ oil, milk, bird seed, citrus fruit, and even meat can also be given, although there are various schools of thought on their relative usefulness to the animal. The important point is that food be clean, fresh, and varied. Guinea pigs are prone to overeating, and their food intake should be controlled, but the smaller rodents have very high metabolic rates and should have access to food at all times.

Water should also be accessible, though the gerbil, for one, taking in most of its fluid through its food like the adaptable desert animal it is, may never seem to drink. Nevertheless, water should still be available all the time. Since small dishes can be overturned, the most practical way to provide water is in a gravity-flow bottle attached to the side of the cage. These are sold commercially, but they can be made easily at home (see Chapter 7).

Another item that should be on hand constantly is a small piece of unpainted hardwood to allow these rodents to keep their teeth uniformly trimmed. The four front teeth of animals in this toothy family continue to grow throughout their lives, and if they do not have sufficient opportunity to chew, their teeth can grow so long that they will have difficulty eating. A rat's incisors, for instance, may grow as much as six inches during three years of life. Be sure to make an occasional check on your pet's teeth and claws to see that they are not getting too long.

Some of the rodents are nocturnal, whereas others are more active during the day. Most of them, however, respond well to handling regardless of the time, and the more handling you give them, the more responsive they will be. All of them can be easily tamed and even trained somewhat if rewarded with bits of food. But they are naturally timid and need daily attention if their confidence is to be gained. Because they are easily frightened, even the tamest mouse or hamster may bite or scratch, so it is a good idea to avoid using sudden gestures or rough handling of any kind. Instead of sticking your hand into the cage (it's the animal's territory, after all), try to coax your pet out of its domain and into your hand or onto some neutral territory for playing or handling. Bred females are especially prone to nipping or even charging the hand that intrudes into their privacy, but one should learn to be gentle with all these animals, regardless of their condition.

Rodents can be safely and securely carried if you put your hands firmly around their bodies without applying any pressure; the smallest mice and gerbils should be lifted by the root (not the tip!) of the tail because they can be so easily damaged by crushing. It is probably a good idea to supervise children while they are handling their pets, at least until you are sure that they know what gentle handling is all about. Do not be alarmed if the animal bites you or your child; there is no danger of infection from a well-bred, well-cared-for domestic rodent, and the nip may even act as an effective bit of discipline for careless, rough hands.

As we all know, rodents are prolific breeders, and many owners enjoy observing the phenomenon of birth and the raising of offspring (a lot less involved than raising kittens and puppies), as well as the more sophisticated aspects of breeding such as the development of new strains or producing animals for sale. See Chapter 9 and the sections on the individual species you intend to breed, but keep in mind that after the youngsters mature, they will need cages of their own and all of the other amenities that respectable housepets deserve.

Mice

One of the oldest domesticated mammals on earth, and certainly the smallest, is the ordinary house mouse, scientifically known by the rather dignified name of *Mus musculus* (mouse little mouse). Around 10,000 years ago, when man in Asia first learned to cultivate and store grain, this species of mouse just happened to be native to that region and quickly gave up its life in the wild and moved in to share man's house and food. It has been there ever since, for better or worse, mostly better, for us as well as itself. Although widely regarded as a pest (and one of the reasons we domesticated the cat), the mouse has also been held in high esteem and deliberately bred in large quantities for various purposes: white mice were worshipped for centuries as gods, and mutant specimens of all sorts have been collected for fun, for show, and for science. The valuable experimental laboratory animals, which number some 27 million today and which have taught us an enormous amount about genetics, animal behavior, diseases, and the effect of chemicals on mammals, are direct descendants of the "fancies" bred originally as housepets in Japan in the seventeenth and eighteenth centuries.

Because mice breed at the drop of a hat and because they tend to inbreed naturally, it has been possible to develop numerous strains in a whole range of colors, shapes, personalities, and physiques, including white, yellow, red, spotted, Angora, hairless, fat, waltzing (from an inner-ear defect that upsets the balance and causes the mouse to whirl), diabetic, and even alcoholic. In spite of the variety, all of these types are members of the same species and a number of them make excellent pets—perhaps the easiest to keep of any animal. Wild mice, such as *Mus sylvaticus* (the field mouse) and *Mus minutus* (the harvest mouse), have also been kept as pets, but they are not generally as successful in captivity even if raised from infancy, for they almost invariably display an aggressive temperament and constantly attempt to escape from their cages. They will breed with domestic mice, given the chance, but because of their undesirable characteristics and because they carry a number of diseases and parasites in the wild state, one should take the utmost care to protect domestic mice from them.

The mouse is a tiny creature, weighing about an ounce and measuring up to eight inches from nose to tip of tail, yet it is remarkably alert, agile, and capable of living in all sorts of environments. Like its wild ancestor, the mouse is shortsighted and timid, but it hears and smells extremely well, and its whiskers enable it to sense shapes and spaces accurately, even at night. Although it prefers to remain undercover, the mouse can jump, climb, run swiftly, and even swim, and it can survive on almost any sort of food and very little fresh water. When food is scarce and the temperature is cool, the mouse goes into a dormant state, using up very little energy. All of these characteristics, together with a rapid reproductive rate, combine to make the mouse a highly adaptable animal and one of the world's most successful mammals. But because the mouse has many enemies, its lifespan in the wild is rarely more than a year and a half; however, in captivity—with favorable living conditions and no predators—a healthy mouse can live three or four years.

Favorable conditions are not difficult to provide; as we have already seen, cages are simple to set up and require a minimum of care. Mice are naturally fastidious; they do not need to be bathed but will groom themselves continually (especially when nervous, as a displacement reaction), by licking their fur or burrowing into flooring material. They will usually defecate in the area farthest from where they sleep and eat, so that if you will pile the flooring higher in this corner, you can remove the soiled portion daily without disturbing the rest of the cage. Female mice alone are odorless, but males in the cage will create a pretty strong smell if the cage is not cleaned regularly.

Mice are nibblers (one of the reasons they are difficult to exterminate with poison), and though food need not be elaborate or even particularly varied, it should be constantly available. Mice eat so little (4 to 5 grams a day) that they are inexpensive to feed. Domestic mice, with the exception of some special strains of laboratory mice, are mild mannered and easily become accustomed to handling. Although they are not particularly intelligent, they can be trained to eat from your hand and do simple tricks as long as food is used as a reward. Frequently handled mice bite very rarely—unlike some of the other small rodents—unless they are badly frightened.

If you simply want one or two mice and no more, be sure to select the odorless females; if you want to breed, buy a buck and two or three does, add a nesting box and bits of cotton to the cage, and be prepared for a rapid increase in your mouse population. Females should begin breeding at the age of about two months, and gestation is 19 to 21 days. Although a litter of as large as thirty has been recorded, the average is five to eight, and the doe can handle no more than twelve. She can conceive within 24 hours of the birth of the first litter, though implantation of the egg in the uterus may be delayed, and the second litter may not arrive for up to 26 days. During the nursing period, which lasts for about three weeks, the female cannot conceive again after the first day until the young are weaned. Hamsters have a shorter gestation (16 days), but they do not breed quite so frequently. A female mouse has been known to give birth to as many as seventeen litters in a single year, and it doesn't take much arithmetic to realize that well over 30,000 mice could be produced before the year is out if every mouse proves fertile and active. One pair alone could be responsible for one hundred thirty-five offspring. The mind boggles.

At birth mice are pink and hairless, and their eyes are tightly closed; but by the time they are ten days old, fur has grown in; and before two weeks have passed, their eyes are open. By the time they are weaned, they have begun to crawl out of the nest, though they are not ready to leave mama until they are about four weeks old and have had some helpful coaching on the facts of life from their parents (males will help out here). Because baby mice are fragile, it is not a good idea to handle them—or even do more than peek occasionally through the cotton—until their eyes are open. If any of the young appear to be defective or weak you may destroy them (a couple of drops of chloroform on some cotton will do the job humanely), and be sure to remove any dead babies you find. When the healthy offspring are out of the nest, determine the sex of each and place the males in separate cages; mice are territorial and the dominant buck will quickly dispose of rivals if there are any handy. To differentiate the sexes, simply lift the mouse by the nape of the neck; if it is a male, a tiny penis will be visible. Females can live peacefully (and unproductively) together or (productively) with a single buck. Overcrowding, however, can produce frantic behavior and may even cause tumors in distressed mice. And there you have it, an excellent home-grown object lesson in the dangers of overpopulation!

Rats

Nearly everything that we've said about the mouse is applicable to the rat, with three important exceptions: the rat is bigger, smarter, and has a universally terrible reputation. Although man has no one to blame but himself for the preservation—nay, the encouragement—of this species, it is true that the rat's bad reputation is well deserved. It is estimated that there is at least one rat on earth for every human being, which means that some five billion of them are out there raiding our food supplies, gnawing at our belongings, spreading our diseases, and deserting our ships. They are dangerous, destructive, and ubiquitous—just like us; even the word rat is rich in nasty connotations. But there is a good side to this bad character: the domestic version of the Norway rat (named for its seagoing tendencies and apparently blamed on Norway's maritime economy) has been as good to man as the other has been bad. With the help of the laboratory rat, we have managed to conquer polio and tuberculosis and are working toward victory over cancer, arthritis, and other diseases. Because the rat's reaction to various nutrients is surprisingly similar to our own, much of the original research into the value

IN SPITE OF ITS REPUTATION, THE DOMESTIC RAT CAN BE AN AFFECTIONATE, INTELLIGENT ANIMAL TO HAVE AROUND THE HOUSE ... OR THE NECK.

of vitamins and minerals in human nutrition was made possible by this cooperative creature. We have learned about operant conditioning and other aspects of psychology through behavioral experiments with the rat, and we have even sent the animal into outer space to scout for the astronauts. As if all that weren't enough, the rats have also rewarded us for years of free room and board by producing strains of gentle, affectionate companions for thousands of pet owners.

A rat can weigh ten times more than a mouse, and is nearly twice as long, yet it eats only about three times as much as a mouse does and needs a cage only slightly larger than its small cousin. Like mice, they thrive in clean, well-lighted, and ventilated surroundings with constant access to food and water. Their breeding habits are almost exactly the same as mice, although the breeding life of both male and female is somewhat shorter. Because rats are larger, however, and because they are apt to be far more responsive to handling, their chief interest as pets is not as breeding machines but as individuals, and one rat can be an ideal choice for the right pet owner.

Be sure that the rat you select is from one of the gentle, reliable strains, such as the White Animal Farm strain, which are rarely known to bite, and do handle it frequently so that it learns to know you. Do not pick up a rat by the tail but hold it gently around the body; also, try to avoid loud or sudden noises which can startle even

EASY PETS

the most docile rat. Actually, after the first few days with a friendly rat, you won't need any encouragement to play with it. There are few animals brighter or more attractive in personality than these; the intelligence that makes the rat capable of springing traps without getting caught enables it to learn all sorts of tricks. Many schoolteachers we have talked with even prefer rats to gerbils or hamsters because, instead of racing into obscure corners when they escape their cages or the hands of a child, the rats tend to stick around, following the children in their games and eventually returning to their cages where they know their food awaits them. Laboratory rats have been taught to recognize letters of the alphabet and to run complex mazes; a little patience, a bit of food, and some imagination on the part of the rat owner are all that are required—the rat will figure out the rest. Rats are as smart as dogs and cats and can be equally affectionate with people if they are treated nicely. A pet rat I had in veterinary school would sit patiently on my shoulder and nibble gently on my ear while I was looking through the microscope; if I kept at my work too long, the rat would run down my arm and curl up for a snooze in my lap and then run back up again when I was finished and ready for a game or two.

Like most interesting personalities, the rat's character is not indicated by his hue, and the "good rat" may wear a coat of several different colors. There are good black rats, and there are rats that come in gray, tan, red, blue, chocolate-brown, or banded colors (called wild agouti). The Irish rat is black with white feet and other markings, while the hooded rat is white with a colored marking that runs from shoulder to tail. Even the white rat can afford the breeder some variation by having black or pink eyes. But all this beauty is only fur deep and of interest primarily to rat fanciers and geneticists; what is of greater importance to most of us is the character underneath—one that deserves a good deal of respect even in the worst of situations and a generous helping of affection in the best.

Hamsters

The golden hamster is a common housepet today, but it has a most uncommon and interesting history. In 1930, a Palestinian zoologist discovered in the course of his research an ancient reference to "Syrian mice" which were kept by Assyrian children as caged pets. These "mice" had apparently been imported from the district of Chaleb, now Aleppo, where Professor Aharoni then went to find out whether the species still existed. He shortly turned up a few of the creatures—a mother and twelve babies in a burrow eight feet deep—and he took them back to Jerusalem with him. They multiplied rapidly, and in 1931 he sent a few to England for study. By 1938 hamsters had made their first appearance in the United States, where they quickly became popular as pets, and were used in laboratory research. They are undoubtedly more numerous in captivity than in their native state, where their numbers are kept under control by predators against whom they have few defenses. Besides the golden hamster, there are two other types: the dwarf hamster and the giant hamster, both found in Europe and Asia though the giant is most common in Saxony, Germany. The word hamster comes from the German verb *hamstern,* meaning to hoard—which is what hamsters do with extra food.

The golden hamster is the type most familiar to pet owners (and most of the millions now in captivity are direct descendants of Aharoni's original colony of thirteen), and it makes a charming pet indeed. It is usually reddish brown on the back and sides with a white or gray belly and a stumpy tail. The fur varies naturally in condition at different times of the year, and the skin is loose enough so that folds may be pulled several inches from the trunk. The cheek pouch is a characteristic hamster feature and can be distended some two inches when filled with food or nesting material. Although hamsters can be lifted by the ample scruff of the neck without feeling pain, they dislike rough handling of any sort and the safest method is to grasp them firmly but gently around the body.

Some people will tell you that the hamster can be a very mean character, but this reputation is based on its unusual fearlessness and an occasional desire to impress others (even large others) with its ferocity. Mature hamsters (particularly bred females) are not above nipping a nearby finger, but biting is a natural reflex in a startled animal and puncture wounds are rare. Frequent, gentle handling and the avoidance of sudden movements and noises are far more effective than gloves, for the hamster is essentially a tractable creature and easily tamed. Bites may also occur because of irritability caused by gastric distress or uncomfortable surroundings, as well as simply by the odor of food on the handler's fingers—all of which can be avoided with care and common sense. Most hamster aggression is actually directed at other hamsters, usually for reasons of sexual jealousy or maternal protectiveness, and many experts feel that virgin stock and males are the easiest to work with.

Unlike some rodents, hamsters do not seem to mind living alone; in fact, it is a good idea to keep individuals in separate cages until breeding is desired, because two hamsters are more than likely to fight with each other. The hamster is noted for its remarkable rate of reproduction, having the shortest gestation of any known animal (16 days), and maturity is reached in three months or less. One pair, breeding at full speed (which, incidentally, they are not apt to do), could theoretically be responsible for some one hundred thousand offspring in a single year.

The hamster, like the mouse and rat, does not need a large cage, but there should be plenty of room for exercise and for the animal to select separate areas for sleeping, eating, and eliminating. Being nocturnal, they are most active at night and will, if bored, kick their litter all over the place and pull at their cages; this is more for want of exercise than from a desire to escape. Daily exercise outside the cage or in an exercise wheel will keep them content and prevent a kind of paralysis that can develop without sufficient activity. Hamsters are clean and odorless, and their cages may be placed anywhere as long as there is little direct sunlight and good ventilation, though drafts are to be avoided. They will hibernate if the temperature is low but humidity is also a factor; the damper the atmosphere the more likely they are to suffer from disease or become dormant. Food and water should be available at all times for this active little creature; there is no danger in overfeeding because what they do not wish to eat they will simply *hamstern*.

Although hamsters have no natural diseases of their own, they can develop respiratory diseases if the cage is allowed to become damp or chilly. Listlessness, a swollen nose, sniffling, and sneezing should be treated with warmth, plenty of fresh bedding, and bits of bread or oatmeal soaked in water. Constipation may be caused by a steady diet of pellets unrelieved by vegetable supplements; lettuce (in small quantity), bits of fruit, rolled oats, or bread will relieve the problem in most cases. Hamsters kept in good, clean quarters and fed a balanced diet will remain healthy and hardy for as long as three years.

Gerbils

Considered an exotic pet a decade ago, the gerbil is now almost as common as its larger cousin the hamster. Gerbils are gray brown in color with long furry tails and large bright eyes, and because of that tail many people who cringe at the sight of a pet mouse or rat will find the gerbil irresistible. Many species are known in the arid areas of Asia, the Near and Middle East, and Africa, but only the Mongolian *Meriones unguiculatus* is widely sold in the United States as a household pet, since that was the variety imported in 1954 from northwest Manchuria for laboratory research. The gerbil is banned in some states because if allowed to run loose, this fertile and adaptable little rodent could potentially pose a threat to farmers; be sure to check your state's Department of Agriculture before you invest in a gerbil, especially if you are purchasing it out of state. Their natural lifespan in the wild is not more than about eighteen months, but they can live in the pampered environment of the home as long as four or five years.

Unlike hamsters, gerbils are very social (and apparently monogamous), and they should be kept in pairs or groups rather than singly. However, care should be taken when adult males are introduced for the first time. They are friendly creatures and easily tamed, biting only under the stress of fear or pain. Gerbils are extremely clever, and cages should be foolproof; they should also be roomy enough to provide space for exercise, and, as with the other rodents we have discussed, exercise wheels, ladders, shelves, and material for gnawing are desirable and necessary furnishings. Gerbils—being desert animals—are very efficient in their use of water, especially if greens are available; they produce little urine and their feces are dry, so that cages are odorless and easy to keep clean, needing thorough cleaning only every three weeks or so. Gerbils are adaptable to most temperatures but extremes of heat and cold, sudden changes in temperature, and high humidity should be avoided.

Again like the hamster, the gerbil is timid, curious, and responsive to frequent handling and stroking. They can quickly be coaxed to eat from your hand and to be picked up and carried about, but because they are quick and likely to jump unexpectedly, it is a good idea to hold them by the root of the tail until they are firmly cupped in the hand. Gerbils are diurnal and will sleep naturally at night, although, like rabbits, males have been known to carry on a surprisingly loud thumping activity in the wee hours, usually just before mating.

THIS MONGOLIAN GERBIL LOOKS QUITE AT HOME IN AN AQUARIUM TANK CONVERTED TO A DESERT CLIMATE.

This is, however, the loudest thing a gerbil does; its squ[eak is] extremely soft and unobtrusive.

Gerbil females in the wild are receptive to breeding only during certain seasons, but gerbils in captivity can breed at almost any time, even during the nursing period. Because the two sexes get along so well, you can leave the pair together at all times; gestation is about 25 days, and the average litter is five. Again, as with all small rodents, the female shouldn't be disturbed during and after the birth process. If she feels that you are looking too closely, she will move the cubs to a new nest or even eat them out of nervousness. However, she does not usually mind the presence of her mate. Gerbils, which are hairless at birth and remain so until the end of the first week, are weaned at about six weeks, though they will take solid food as early as three weeks and can remain with the mother indefinitely, since they do well in community groups. Once a pair has begun to breed, however, which can be as early as three months after birth, it is a good idea to put them into a separate cage, since a breeding male may be aggressive toward other males, even its own brothers, and because records will become progressively more difficult to keep.

The gerbil is remarkably free of endemic diseases, but they can become excessively nervous in strange surroundings and they may pick up respiratory infections if the climate is not to their liking. Skin disorders may be caused by dirty cages, and sores may appear on their tiny noses if they are able to thrust them through the bars of the cage. A mild antiseptic ointment will usually clear up the condition readily, but prevention is undoubtedly the best medicine.

Chinchillas

This elegant rodent, like the guinea pig, once ran wild in the mountains of Peru, Bolivia, Chile, and western Argentina but is now almost exclusively a domesticated animal, raised in large quantities in the United States for its beautiful silver fur. Unlike the mink, which is still hunted to some extent by trappers, the chinchilla has become rare in nature because of hunting, and most of the luxurious coats and accessories made of chinchilla pelts (as many as two hundred a coat) come from animals raised in captivity. Although the initial cost may be high (about $25 for a virgin animal*) chinchillas can be purchased from an occasional pet shop or directly from a breeder, and in terms of care, these lovely creatures are as easy and inexpensive to keep as their less exotic relatives.

Chinchillas can tolerate a rather wide range of temperature (40° to 75°F.) and, like the rabbit, can live happily out of doors during the warmer months, if care is taken to protect them from drafts and rain.

*This $25 price would apply only to culls, or animals a breeder determines unsuitable for breeding or for its fur; good breeding stock may cost as much as $250 apiece.

The cage should be furnished with water at all times, and should in addition to a sleeping box include a shallow pan of sand in which it can "dust" itself—a method of cleaning its long silky fur. Food, which can be constantly available or fed intermittently—at least once a day—should include timothy hay and commercial pellets, supplemented with moderate amounts of fresh greens, raw vegetables, and cup-up apples. Feces and uneaten food should be removed daily and, of course, thorough cleanings should be performed on a weekly basis. It is best to keep chinchillas in separate cages because they may act aggressively to each other.

Chinchillas breed readily in captivity, and the male and female can be placed together as maturity approaches at the age of about six months. Although multiple matings have been observed, chinchillas do not usually accept strange mates after the first breeding. Gestation is long—about 111 days—but the young, which average two to a litter, are well developed at birth and have open eyes. They are weaned in about 60 days. The males may remain with the females during this period; some breeders, however, remove them for a day or so when the babies are born. Unlike the unfortunate animals raised for their fur, chinchillas kept as pets can live at least five or six years and perhaps even longer with good care and no exposure to disease or injury.

Although not as bright as the rat or as docile as the guinea pig, the chinchilla is a lively, alert, and friendly creature. As with the gerbil and hamster, quick movements that surprise or startle it may provoke a bite in self-defense, but with proper handling they can be as cuddly as they look. Those who have an unsatisfied longing for an "exotic" animal but can't see themselves taking on all the problems—legal and otherwise—involved in owning an ocelot or one of the other breeds so prized for their beauty by furriers and pet owners alike may take special pleasure in owning a chinchilla, and have far less trouble.

Guinea Pigs

Guinea pigs are not from Guinea, nor are they pigs, and no one seems to know why they are called by the name, though they did originally enter England (where they are called cavies, for reasons known only to the English) on Dutch "guineaman" ships and they do squeal like swine and are squat in shape. Guinea pigs, in fact, originated in Peru, where they were first domesticated by the Incas for food, and where they may still be found wild in their natural habitat. As a result of a thousand years in domestication, guinea pigs can be bred in numerous shapes and sizes, colors and lengths of fur, the most common varieties being the English smooth-coated type, the Abyssinian rough-coat, and the long-haired Peruvian. Guinea pigs weigh as much as 3 pounds, though most average about a pound

THE NOBLE GUINEA PIG.

apiece, and they are very easy to keep as pets. They are relatively quiet (except for a rather admirable whistle), resistant to disease (however, in laboratories they can be infected with nearly anything), odorless, gentle, and pleasant to handle. Unlike the smaller rodents, guinea pigs are not particularly active or prolific, since in the wild they have few predators and the mountains of Peru are rich in the vegetation they need. They do not eat or hoard nuts or seeds but live on a diet of leafy plants and stems, and they are considered hardy and long-living. The gestation for a guinea sow is long—at least 70 days—and the litters are small and the weaners well developed at birth. Because of this low reproduction rate and larger size, guinea pigs are no longer so much in demand as laboratory animals, but these attributes are just what make the animal particularly suitable as a housepet.

Guinea pigs like thick bedding and covered sleeping boxes like the other rodents; they don't need exercise wheels (though shelves and perches may be used), since they are not acrobats. They do need the usual warm, clean, dry atmosphere, and in warm climates they may be kept in outdoor hutches, if protected against other animals (other pets and parasites) and the elements. They are diurnal and like daylight, but cool shade should be provided as a refuge against the sun. Their milder, less hyperactive behavior makes them more responsive to handling, or at least a lot easier to hang on to, and they are rarely prone to bite or scratch.

Like the other rodents, guinea pigs need gnawing material for their teeth and scratching material for their nails. The long-haired varieties will also require occasional grooming or combing to prevent matting or tangles, but the short-haired type needs no more attention than a hamster or gerbil, which keeps itself well groomed without any help.

Guinea pigs eat much the same food as the other rodents—with a number of important exceptions. Because they cannot synthesize vitamin C, care should be taken to see that they receive it as a regular part of their diet, either by providing special guinea-pig pellets or by adding fresh greens, citrus fruit, or a vitamin supplement to their staple foods. They also like hay, which requires a good deal of chewing activity, and gives the animal a chance to wear down its teeth and discourages it from chewing on its own hair—a habit that many guinea pigs will take up if their teeth are not given enough to do. Salt should also be made available—in small blocks if possible—and, of course, water should be accessible always. During the summer, the guinea pig might be happy to have some mowed grass or dandelion greens, but as with all fresh vegetables, make sure they are thoroughly clean, unwilted, and free from insecticides and other poisons. (One nice treat for the pig would be to place its cage—if it has a wire-screen bottom—on the lawn during the summer, moving it from place to place as the animal mows.)

Root vegetables, such as beets, carrots, and turnips, are good during winter months, as is a nutritious mash made of grains cooked in milk or water, though this should be fed sparingly because it is very rich. Linseed or wheat-germ oil can be added to the food occasionally for the sake of the animal's coat and general condition. Diarrhea is rare but can be serious; if it occurs, be sure the animal has plenty of water, hay, and pellets, but withhold the lettuce and fresh foods. If it persists, consult a veterinarian. Minor injuries can be treated with an antiseptic cream, but any serious symptoms or accidents call for a veterinarian's care. Whatever you do, don't make the guinea pig a guinea pig for any experimental home remedies.

Rabbits

Although rabbits are not technically rodents (they are lagomorphs, which means shaped like a hare), they have much in common with the animals we have been discussing: they are fun and easy to keep; they are regarded as pests, especially by people with vegetable gardens; and they breed like, well, like rabbits. It has been said that one rabbit is a wonderful pet, two rabbits are a fascinating lesson in reproduction, and any more than that are an occupation. The Romans were known to have kept and bred rabbits in captivity, though not very successfully, since the rabbits would burrow under the walls of the hare gardens (hares are not burrowers and just jumped over); it was not until the Middle Ages that monks succeeded in domesticating the species, which they raised for food. (Curiously enough, the flesh of newborn or unborn rabbit was not

SOME RABBITS
NEED COMBING
AS WELL AS PETTING.
AN ANGORA RABBIT.

considered meat in those days and was thus acceptable for Lenten meals.)

Since that time, rabbits have been raised in large numbers in captivity, and a great many breeds have been developed in various shapes and sizes and colors, depending on whether they were to be used for meat, fur, laboratory stock, show breeds, or housepets. It is the last category that interests us, and many of the breeds—regardless of their original use—are wonderfully adaptable to home life with humans. The most popular breeds are the New Zealand rabbit (or albino), the smaller Dutch (in black, brown, blue, and gray), the huge Flemish (some weigh over 20 pounds), the tiny Polish (2 or 3 pounds), and the fancy fur breeds—the Angora, chinchilla, satin, silver fox, and rex. Some breeds are interesting for their shape rather than their size or color; the rare Lop has ears as long as 26 inches, and the Belgian hare is a long, lean type although it is by no means a hare. (A note on the difference between rabbits and hares: the two species are in the same lagomorph order, but they cannot interbreed and, in fact, they don't even get along with each other. Hares are surface animals with open nests, whereas rabbits prefer subterranean haunts;

MAMMALS

29

hares are far more difficult to keep in captivity—they need high ceilings and a number of other special conditions—where they are unlikely to breed and are not nearly so easy to tame.) Wild rabbits, though they may be perfectly easy to handle as youngsters, should for the most part be avoided as likely pets; they may carry diseases and retain wild temperaments that make it difficult for them to settle down in a confined environment. Domestic rabbits are so easy to get and so much safer that it's just not worth the risk of coaxing your local wild version into captivity and yourself into possible trouble.

Once you have chosen a breed, the source for your rabbit can be a pet shop, if it is a common type, or a breeder, who will probably charge more but will also throw in registration papers and a pedigree, which are of great importance to anyone who is seriously interested in breeding animals for sale or show. Just be sure the source is reliable and that the animal you select is healthy and lively.

Rabbit hutches come in all shapes and sizes. Breeders and laboratories use all metal wire cages, which can be ordered through pet shops; however, it is a simple matter to construct a wooden frame and attach wire windows, door, and floor. The floor should be made of a ½-inch-mesh hardware cloth to allow droppings to fall below the rabbit, unless the particular breed prefers a wooden floor and soft bedding. A wooden shelf is a good addition to any cage, though the rabbit may gnaw on the edges if they aren't protected with metal. Large rabbits need large hutches, but the ideal size for an average bunny is a floor space of 18 inches by 3 feet and a height of 18 inches. Rabbits should be kept in separate hutches, unless, of course, they are nursing babies. Young does can be kept together for a while, but bucks will fight and are much better off living by themselves. Although rabbits will do well indoors, they can also be kept outside even in bad weather as long as the hutch is protected by burlap or a tarpaulin to keep out the elements. Ventilation should be good, and the hutch must be kept dry, clean, and draft- and pest-free, with some shade against the sun and complete protection from other animals. A salt block will be appreciated by most rabbits, and, to keep their rodentlike teeth trim, a piece of hardwood is a necessity. Although most rabbits keep themselves well groomed and clean, some of the long-haired breeds may need help to keep their beautiful coats from getting matted. The hair is very fine and their skins are tender, so a brush or coarse comb should be applied with a great deal of care.

Now that rabbit pellets have been developed to provide these vegetarians with a complete diet, feeding is simplicity itself, but overfeeding should definitely be avoided. Unlike rodents, who will store what they do not use, rabbits will eat until they become pot bellied and sluggish, even ill. Carrots and green lettuce in quantity may give them diarrhea, but rabbits don't know this and will eat greens anyway. One rabbit I know was so taken with the lettucy green of a parrot's tail, which had been conveniently lowered into the hutch on which the bird was sitting, that he took a nice big bite and got—not diarrhea—but a good peck on the nose. Water can, and should, be available at all times from a spout or a heavy dish that can't be upset easily. If a rabbit refuses to eat for some reason, a small quantity of greens or some oats might perk up its appetite, but one should avoid making sudden food changes, and any persistent irregularity deserves the attention of a veterinarian. Because rabbits are naturally more active at night than during the day, it is a good idea to feed them in the evening or late afternoon. This may cause a certain amount of noise, but this shouldn't be a problem if the hutch is outside the house or in a room far from sleeping humans or other diurnal species.

Almost everyone knows that a rabbit shouldn't be picked up by its ears, everyone, that is, except very young children who should probably only be allowed to pet the animal. Rabbits can be lifted by the skin of the back as long as one hand supports the body and the ears are kept close to the neck. This seems to keep their sense of balance intact and they are less inclined to kick, scratch, or bite. Some breeds are more nervous than others, but all are easily tamed, and the best approach with a new rabbit is a gradual one, restricted to petting or stroking at first and eventually expanded to lifting and carrying about.

There have been volumes written on rabbit breeding both for scientific and commercial purposes, and I will give only some general guidelines here, though I believe that breeding tends to improve quantity at the expense of quality in pet rabbits. A house or yard full of rabbits requiring individual hutches (which will be necessary at least eight weeks after birth) can be fairly inconvenient, and you can't always count on being able to give away or sell your litter (though you may, of course, eat them if you can bear it). Nevertheless, breeding rabbits can be an absorbing occupation, an educational experience for children, and not a difficult matter, so long as you know what to expect and how to handle the situation.

In selecting a mate for your female rabbit, be sure to pick one of the same breed; if the quality of the line is good, you can breed rabbits of the same strain, since inbreeding can result in excellent animals as long as the two rabbits do not have the same faults. If you own only one of the pair, be sure that the other is free from disease and in good general condition so that your own animal is not infected. Newly purchased or borrowed rabbits should always be isolated from your other rabbits for at least three weeks before they are put together in the same room.

Rabbit does are polyestrus, meaning that they have multiple heat periods a year, and though ova develop continually, they are not released until sexual stimulation occurs. Therefore, breeding may take place at almost any time. A doe can normally have from four to five litters a year beginning at the age of six or eight months (larger rabbits mature more slowly than small or medium ones), but if you are planning on a single litter, the best time for breeding is the spring or warm months, particularly if the rabbits are kept outdoors. The doe should be taken to the buck's cage for mating, which should occur almost immediately. When the buck flops over in exhaustion, return the doe to her own cage. The pair can then be remated five or six hours later, to insure pregnancy, but the two must not be left together unsupervised, because they may fight. If the doe starts pulling out her own fur to make a nest within 17 to 22 days after mating, she is having a false pregnancy and should be remated at once. Nest making in true pregnancy does not occur until about four weeks after mating, or a day or two before the litter is kindled. About a week before you expect the doe to kindle, put a nesting box into the hutch with clean straw or wood shavings that she can mix with her own fur to make the nest. Don't disturb her during this period; however, you can check the nest box periodically after the babies are born to remove any dead newborns.

Young bunnies are born without fur, and their eyes remain closed for about ten days. Within a month they are fully furred and are old enough to leave the nest box and to nibble on pellets. Now is the time when you can start to handle and play with them. They can be weaned at six to eight weeks and removed to their own individual hutches. If you are interested in finding out what the sex of your young rabbits may be, simply press open the genital opening with thumb and forefinger; if the opening is a long slit, the animal is a doe, and if the opening is round, with a tiny penis, you've got a buck. If the doe should die while the babies are nursing, or if she should give birth to more than she can handle, it is possible to hand rear the babies although the job is tedious and time consuming (see Chapter 9).

Most veterinarians can identify and treat the diseases and parasites that afflict rabbits. No vaccines or preventive medical measures are necessary beyond an adequate diet and good, clean housing. External parasites (such as ear or skin mites) can be exterminated, either by the use of flea powder or by whatever your veterinarian recommends; the hutch will also need a complete cleaning if the problem is not to recur. Loss of appetite, dull eyes, rough coat, a hunched position, or prolonged diarrhea can indicate the presence of disease or internal parasites and a veterinarian should be consulted.

As with other animals, however, good care and freedom from contamination should prevent most trouble, and a healthy rabbit can remain so for as long as eight or ten years. Though they are not as responsive as dogs, as lively as hamsters, or as quiet as mice, rabbits do make very cuddly, comforting animals to have around. If you have enough patience, rabbits can be housebroken to a litter box and given freedom of the house instead of being confined to a hutch, although it is a good idea to keep the hutch on hand for sleeping quarters or unsupervised gnawing and burrowing (furniture legs and nice thick rugs can be tremendously appealing). Otherwise rabbits are no more troublesome than cats.

One rabbit habit not likely to be found in cats, however, could be potentially embarrassing to some sensitive souls; it provoked at least one amusing incident for a family I know. The parents had acquired a handsome buck bunny for their five-year-old daughter and successfully housebroke it, so that the animal was allowed to run free as a well-mannered member of the household. One evening when the family was gathered together in the living room, the rabbit suddenly found something sexually irresistible about the father's leg and soon began humping away energetically, in spite of papa's efforts to shrug off the problem and avoid comment. No such luck. The little girl quickly piped up and said, "Daddy, do you know what the rabbit needs?" Settling back in his chair and trying to remember how the old birds-and-bees story went, he answered as casually as he could, "No dear, what?"

"Glasses," she replied.

Cats

If volumes have been written about rabbits, entire libraries have been devoted to the subject of cats—their history, their personalities, their beauty, their care and feeding. A book has even been written for people who hate cats. Though there are many happy families who have lived in perfect harmony with both dogs and cats, the world does seem at times to be divided between cat people and dog people, with all the usual stereotypes that bigotries produce. Cat people, of course, are unmarried ladies or gentle souls of discriminating taste, while dog people are regular guys who are as outgoing and athletic as their animals. Anyone who has ever owned a Maine coon cat or a delicate chihuahua would be happy to provide stories to repaint those images, just as the owner of an affectionate tabby would be eager to point out the cool aloofness of a Doberman pinscher. Nonetheless, there are definite distinctions between the two species which can be noted without resorting to extremes or individual exceptions, though I must say that so far as I'm concerned, any true animal lover will appreciate the virtues of both equally.

There are surely as many cats living in close proximity to human beings throughout the world as there are dogs, but a lot of people will maintain that the cat has never been truly domesticated in the way that a dog has, that cats are generally less responsive and less intelligent, though easier to keep and not nearly so demanding.

There is some truth in these assumptions but not nearly enough. Unlike dogs, cats are not naturally social animals; they do not run in packs with dominant leaders, and it is simply not in their nature to behave submissively to other creatures. From the time they are weaned, cats learn to stalk their own food rather than passively accept it from their mothers as is the case with canines; in a wild state dogs will regurgitate gathered food for their young. Cats are hunters and they are independent, so it should not be surprising to see a small kitten attack a ball of yarn (it is certainly more entertaining than watching a puppy chew your slippers), nor should we expect gratitude for feeding an animal that assumes it has found the food through its own cleverness. These characteristics are what led us to domesticate the cat in the first place, for they have been wonderful hunters in man's behalf since the time of ancient Egypt.

Because there is little or no skeletal difference between the older species of domesticated and wild cats, it is difficult for zoologists to pinpoint exactly when cats joined man's household. It is fairly certain, however, that domestication took place in the Near East and Africa. The word "cat" is derived from the Arab word *qttah* or similar words in North African languages; "tabby" is apparently of Turkish origin; "puss" is supposed to come from the name of the Egyptian goddess Pasht. In any event, cats were domesticated relatively late in comparison with other animals, probably around 3000 B.C., although evidence is ambiguous. It is likely that the cat simply moved in and made its presence welcome by preying on pesty rodents; in gratitude, the Egyptians worshiped the animal, going so far as to prohibit the killing of cats and to mourn their deaths and mummify their bodies. From Egypt cats (and beautiful statues of cats) were introduced into Greece and eventually to Rome and then to Northern Europe, where their reputations deteriorated rather badly. During the fifteenth century, in fact, Pope Innocent VIII declared open war on cats, which were associated with the devil, witches, and other baddies and were therefore to be persecuted and burned. Atrocity stories about cats abounded at least into the nineteenth century, but, except for the annual appearance of the Halloween witch's pet and occasional black-cat superstitions, the animal's reputation is much improved as of the present day.

Because domestic cats could interbreed with local European wild cats, a number of different characteristics and colorings crept into the species *Felis catus*. Even today there is little difference between the domestic and wild varieties except in the color, pattern, and length of hair; the striped tabby is closest to the wild cat, though the blotched tabby—with bands of black arranged in a spiral or circle—is not found in wild cats. The most common kind of cat seen today in the United States is a descendant of this European domestic *Felis catus* and is called a domestic shorthair, which to most people is plain old "cat." Other breeds have been given more elegant geographic names, which are often misleading or inaccurate. The Abyssinian does not come from Abyssinia but is probably derived from a wild European type and simply needed an exotic name to become a desirable breed; it has a striking multicolored short coat of reddish and copper tones. Although most zoologists believe that the Persian and Angora long-haired breeds come from the mountainous areas of the Middle East, the only definite fact is that the long hair, which can require a great deal of care, is the result of selective breeding just as it is with Angora goats and rabbits. In India cats have been domesticated for at least 2000 years, and it is most likely that the elegant Siamese is a descendant of an Indian breed. In spite of the legends about cats guarding Siamese temples, the Siamese cat first appeared in Britain in the nineteenth century and is not much different skeletally from European and African cats; nevertheless, most experts agree that the breed has an Eastern if not Siamese origin because of its coloring and the kinked tail. Himalayan cats, which are long-haired with Siamese coloring, are probably the simple result of crossbreeding between Persian and Siamese cats. The beautiful dark-brown or blue Burmese cats do come from Burma, though the custom of keeping domestic cats there, as in India, may well have originated in Egypt, which brings us right back to the domestic shorthair, via a very circuitous route.

Another cat—the manx—is also appropriately named, since it was on the Isle of Man that this breed of tailless cats was established and is still carefully maintained. Tailless cats have been found all over the world, since taillessness is a simple mutation, apparently linked with long-leggedness. There is no exotic oriental origin for the manx breed, though cats with short tails have been found here and there in the Far East where the mutation has been fixed. The manx is actually an abnormal or crippled specimen and does not always breed true; many breeders have given up on them, because the shortened spinal cord may cause malfunctioning nerves in the animal, which also suffers from a reputation—not always deserved—for a bad temper.

America's only original breed is the Maine coon cat, which is also correctly named for its geographic origin. These cats have somewhat longer hair than the domestic shorthair, although they do not need frequent combing like the Persian (they are probably a crossbreed of the two); they come in almost any color, not necessarily striped or tiger, and their name is probably derived from the fact that they—like raccoons—seem to like being in high places. In fact, they are terrific climbers—as hunters in Maine whose dogs have treed them will attest—much to the dismay of apartment dwellers with nice long draperies.

There are many other breeds of domestic cat, most of them based on color types—such as the Russian and British blues, the Havana brown, and the tortoiseshell—or physical types—such as the rex (curly-coated) which is bred in various colors. And new breeds will undoubtedly be developed in due course, either as crossbreeds or as derivations from mutations like long tails, short tails, long necks, or long ears, with various kinds of markings. All you need, apparently, is a breeder's devotion, patience, and imagination, a good record book, and an atlas!

The care and breeding of cats seem to come naturally to most people who like cats; there are plenty of books on the subject, and anyone who owns a cat is delighted to pass along good advice (usually with a gift kitten) to a new owner. So we don't need to go into much detail here, but I would like to touch on a few general areas and straighten out a few misconceptions that persist in spite of all the sensible information around.

Most cats are given the run of the house wherever they are kept, and country and suburban cats are generally allowed outside as well. Because apartment cats do not usually come into contact with strange animals, they are often free of disease; nevertheless, it is always a good idea to have a cat inoculated against the prevalent feline diseases which can be carried on the clothes or shoes of an owner who has been in contact with an affected cat (see Chapter 8 and the cat chart). Free-roaming cats should also have rabies vaccine once a year, and I would also recommend the use of a collar (the safety type which stretches) with a tag giving the owner's address and telephone number. Cats vary in their roaming habits, and although, as natural hunters, they can often survive for quite a while on their own, without a collar they may simply be adopted by others or, worse, end up as strays at the local humane society, where they are likely to be destroyed. It is a good idea to make sure that your cat comes in and stays in every night; for this reason, evening is the best time to feed your cat, which will be sure to stick around or come in for the occasion.

Many people like to keep food in the cat's dish all day because cats are naturally intermittent eaters or nibblers, but I tend to prefer a regular feeding time because it is a good way of regulating the animal's diet, of feeding medication when required, and of seeing that the animal shows up on a regular basis. There is no harm in leaving dry pellets around (cats do not like these as a steady diet), but the more moist foods will become unappetizing after an hour or so and attract all sorts of unwelcome crawly creatures. Water should be available at all times, regardless of feeding schedules.

Like most successful species, cats will eat a great variety of things, for all their real or imagined likes and dislikes, and there is certainly nothing wrong with any good fresh meat or vegetable served in proper proportion and quantity—if the animal will eat it. Less is known about the nutritional needs of cats than dogs, for instance, but it is clear that while cats are carnivores, they need a balanced diet of more than just straight meat. Some of the commercial cat foods are satisfactory from a nutritional point of view, and others must be supplemented with meat and other foods if they are to be well balanced and palatable. Consult the chart and Chapter 7, or ask your veterinarian for advice.

If your cat supplements its own diet with mice or birds, be sure to see that it is examined once or twice a year for internal parasites (worms); this involves simply taking a fecal sample to your veterinarian and following his instructions. Feeding medication to a cat may be a touchy business, but after a bit of practice, giving pills is not difficult and can be a very useful trick to know. Most cat owners find that their animals will vomit from time to time; this may be caused by any number of things and is not usually serious unless it persists. Illness aside, vomiting may be a reaction to new types of food suddenly introduced into the diet, chewing on grass (or houseplants), ingesting fur and the subsequent development of furballs in the stomach, or simple nervousness. Frequent continued vomiting, like diarrhea, constipation, or refusal of food, are to be considered serious symptoms and a veterinarian should be called.

Other than being asked to provide sensible food and preventive medical care, the owner of a cat will find few real impracticalities beyond the problem of cleanliness and the perfectly natural feline habits of scratching things and producing kittens. Cats are by nature clean animals and easily housebroken. In fact, the mother cat will do the housebreaking job for you; most kittens take quickly to using a litter pan, and all you need to do is change the litter and clean the box frequently enough so that odor is not apparent. Short-haired cats will keep themselves impeccably groomed, but long-haired cats do require regular and careful combing to prevent both furballs and matting, which can demand professional attention if allowed to get out of hand. The amount of cat hair on furniture or rugs can't be completely controlled by grooming, because periodic shedding is natural and necessary. Frequent brushing may help keep down the quantity.

Beds for cats are optional equipment (most will prefer to sleep on their owners), but it is a good idea to have a warm place that the cat knows is its own. Another optional piece of cat furniture is a scratching post, which, unless a cat is taught how to use it, can be the most useless object in the house.

Contrary to popular opinion, cats *can* be trained to do various things, though they are not quite so eager to please as dogs are. Even people who maintain that their cats have never learned anything will find that the animal shows up regularly at suppertime or as the refrigerator door is opened; most cats will respond to their names if they are called by those names often enough and rewarded with a bit of food or an affectionate pat. If a cat refuses to acknowledge the presence of a scratching post, let alone its function, don't try to force the situation. Use some catnip to make the thing attractive and praise the cat lavishly every time it goes near the post; make it clear by frowning or a harsh word that the chair or the sofa is off-limits, and with patience, and luck, the cat might get the idea. Or get a nice scratchable log, which may be more interesting, and give the cat a reward every time it scratches there. Or get some leather upholstery, which is easy to keep clean anyway.

Just as grooming will not prevent shedding, so clipping a cat's toenails will not prevent scratching behavior; in fact, scratching may even be encouraged. It is possible to have a cat declawed, of course, which involves removing the entire nail and third phalange, but this is a painful procedure (even in young cats, which do, however, recover more quickly than older ones) and must be performed by a veterinarian. Many people feel that it is unnatural and cruel to remove a cat's natural means of defense, but declawed cats can still run normally and climb without claws and hiss ferociously if sufficiently offended. Nevertheless, an outdoor cat which spends much of its time hunting mice would be at some disadvantage without claws, but then that animal isn't the sort likely to bother the furniture much. It is really up to the owner to weigh the pros and cons; my feelings is that the operation is justified if the animal is likely to lose a good home, for which the loss of its claws may be a sensible sacrifice.

The subject of claws brings up the matter of tree climbing, which is often a source of distress to an inexperienced owner and to the local fire department if it has been called to save the animal. Since I have never seen or even heard of anyone seeing a cat skeleton in a tree, I can only assume that firemen are incredibly good natured and efficient or that cats are perfectly capable of getting down by themselves. With all due respect to firemen, however, I prefer the latter explanation.

One problem for which many novice cat owners may not be prepared is the animal's persistent but potentially dangerous habit of chewing on plants; some cats are only occasional chewers when they are bored or frustrated, but others may be obsessed with the idea of destroying every bit of greenery in the house. Some common houseplants, including the wandering Jew and the spiderplant, are not harmful, but many are: Jerusalem cherry, poinsettia, philodendron, elephant ear, mistletoe, oleander, azalea, English ivy, and a number of garden plants, such as lily of the valley, foxglove, delphinium, privet, boxwood, yew, and larkspur. If you allow your cat the run of the house or yard, be sure that you keep all potentially harmful plants out of reach; check with your local arboretum, the Department of Agriculture, or reference books, if you are not sure about the toxic nature of the plants you have. If the cat shows signs of poisoning (drooling, vomiting, diarrhea, or convulsions and paralysis), get it to the veterinarian without delay; if you know what substance it was that the cat ate, take that information or a sample along with you. A cat's reaction to a certain plant may or may not be serious, depending on the animal (just as some cats are more susceptible to catnip ecstasy than others), but if you see it eating some suspicious plant, to avoid trouble consult your veterinarian even before symptoms appear. Considerable trouble can also be in store for your plants if cats are allowed to chew on them; my own plants are hung from the ceiling and, although I am an enthusiastic gardener, I must admit that I try to encourage them not to grow so long that they become tempting for my gymnastic Siamese. A certain amount of roughage is good for cats, but it is best to try to incorporate it into their regular diet.

An enormous amount can be said about the breeding of cats—both for and against—but for the average cat owner who wants kittens, very little information is needed, since the average cat needs virtually no assistance. Cats will breed and deliver litters by themselves and all the owner need do is make sure that he provides a warm, dry place for the delivery, a watchful eye during the birth process, enough food to nourish her litter, and a sense of responsibility about the future of the kittens. If the cat for some reason cannot nurse her young, it is a simple if very time-consuming business to rear kittens on a dropper—but it can be done (see Chapter 9). The most sensible information I can give to owners of a new cat is to neuter it. Kittens are very cute and the birth and development of a litter is a fine educational thing for the children, but far too many kittens are destroyed each year for want of a good home. A few cats may be able to survive for a while without a good home because they can hunt or may be clever enough to find temporary quarters behind garbage-rich restaurants or supermarkets; however, these cats are not usually good citizens in the community and they will never live out all nine lives. Kittens will quickly become wild and even untamable, and many of these feral animals constitute a real health hazard to pet cats and even to people who try to handle them.

Many cat owners will automatically have their male cats castrated to eliminate the odor of the urine that toms spray on objects to demonstrate their sexual prowess or territorial rights, but I strongly recommend that female cats also be neutered unless the owner is a professional breeder.

Spaying may not be the most effective way of controlling cat populations, because it is an expensive and serious operation (like a hysterectomy) and some people are not willing to pay for it. But there are spay clinics in many communities and other birth control methods have been developed in recent years; some of them are now becoming available to veterinarians. Whatever method you use, however, the main point is that there is no good reason to leave a cat unneutered. Population control is an important factor, but psychological and physiological advantages are also gained by neutering. Male cats are less likely to roam, they do not spray, and they are less susceptible to bladder stones, fighting injuries, and automobile accidents. Neutered female cats do not go into heat, which can be a noisy, frustrating business for both cat and owner, especially if the local tomcats come around; and many conditions, such as uterine infection or tumors, can be avoided in later life.

And speaking of later life, cats in good condition and kept free of disease and injury may live as long as 15 or 20 years, repaying their thoughtful owners' efforts to provide good care with loyalty and affection—unobtrusive repayment at times, perhaps, and always given on the cat's own terms, but strong and persistent nevertheless.

BIRDS

A few decades ago, a caged bird was a familiar living-room sight, but in recent years the popularity of singing canaries and talking parrots has declined as rapidly as the popularity of tropical-fish aquaria has increased. This may reflect the fact that many people no longer like the idea of confining a beautiful winged creature to a small cage, but it also has been caused by the fear of disease and the severe restrictions on the importation of birds into the United States. At one time birds were imported in enormous quantities, many of them dying in the process, and with them came the threat of psittacosis—which can be transmitted to humans as a kind of pneumonia—and a source of concern to farmers who feared the damage that escaped exotic birds could do to their crops. Some non-native species, in fact, such as the English sparrow, the starling, and the monk parakeet, adapted so readily to the North American climate that they are considered real pests in some areas. The threat of psittacosis (or ornithosis, as it is more accurately called, since psittacine birds—the parrot family—are not the only carriers) has virtually disappeared, since it can be easily controlled with antibiotics, but the effects of Newcastle disease, often carried by imported birds, are still dreaded by poultry farmers. Since 1970, therefore, any individual wishing to bring a pair of birds into the country must prove that they have been in his possession for at least 90 days and must keep them in quarantine for at least 30 days after examination by a veterinarian. Commercial importers may bring in birds in quantity, but because of the cost of holding them in special quarantine stations for a month and because many birds die in transit, the resold birds are expensive. Canaries and parakeets raised in captivity in this country are perfectly safe to own, and many breeders here have been successful in maintaining a regular source of supply to pet shops. These and similar, easily raised species are the only birds that can be considered "easy" pets for the average household. Domestic birds generally require more care than these small cage varieties and will be discussed in a later chapter; exotic birds that do not breed in captivity and must be imported are both expensive and hard to get and must also be considered "difficult" pets. Because it is illegal to capture and confine wild birds in the United States (with a few exceptions), native species must be put into the impossible category, although they may provide a good deal of pleasure as "free-roaming pets" for conscientious people with backyard feeders. In spite of the fact that the number of species of birds that may be considered easy pets is therefore relatively small, the variety they offer in both appearance and personality is quite great. The most popular of these are the canaries, tiny finches, budgerigars, and certain small parrots, and even if they can't boast of exotic origin, they can make striking, if noisy, additions to the average household without causing too much trouble or costing too much money.

Whether you obtain your bird from a pet shop, a breeder, or a friend, be sure that the animal you select is in good condition, with a sleek plumage, bright eyes, and an alert, inquisitive manner. It is best to get a bird when it is young so that it may become more attached to you. Newly hatched parrots, canaries, and finches are blind and naked for the first month or so. After the first molt, which may take place at about a year, it is not easy to determine a bird's age, except that older birds tend to be less smoothly feathered and may be somewhat obese. Unless the male and female of the same species are differently colored, it is often very difficult even for experts to determine sex, except surgically or by behavior during breeding season—so don't necessarily trust the dealer's claim should he make one. Canaries during the breeding season can be distinguished because the male, which is somewhat bolder and thicker set than the hen, has a strong musical song while the hen cheeps quietly. Adult budgerigars can sometimes be differentiated by color, though this is not possible with many other members of the parrot family. Both sexes of psittacine birds, however, mimic equally well, so sex is really important only for breeding or, with some species, when housing more than one bird in a single cage.

If you have one bird and want to get another, be sure to isolate the newcomer for at least two weeks, inspecting the cage daily for signs of excessive molting or diarrhea which may indicate disease. (Normal droppings are target shaped, with a dark center composed of feces and an outer rim of white urine excretion.) Introduce the two birds gradually by placing them in nearby cages before putting them together; this will help avoid squabbling, though some of this may occur anyway until the two birds have worked out a relationship and established territory. It is usually a good idea to put the two birds together in a cage that is new to them both.

All of the birds to be discussed in this section are seed-eating cage birds, and they share many characteristics that determine care and feeding. Cages may be elaborate or simple, purchased or homemade, and detailed information is given in Chapter 7. Generally speaking, there are two different kinds of cages for birds: those intended for single birds or a pair and aviaries, which are larger flight cages for birds kept in groups. Whatever the type, the cage should be large enough so that the bird or birds can move about freely without being cramped in any way, and they should be kept scrupulously clean, free of drafts, and out of direct sunlight. The temperature of the room in which the cage is kept should be fairly constant at about 70°F., and the windows should be closed against drafts; plastic sheeting may be draped around any cage that must sit near a window although larger birds, if they can grab hold, may chew on it. Incandescent lighting will provide some heat, if the room cannot be kept warm otherwise. Though birds can become acclimated to higher or lower temperatures, they cannot tolerate sudden changes and drafts.

Cage furnishings may be as fancy as you like (again, see Chapter 7), but the most important thing is that they be easy to clean and indestructible. There should be at least two perches (so the bird can fly from one to the other); some species like them near the roof of the cage, others don't seem to care. Swings, toys, chains, bells, and mirrors will all help distract a bird and keep it from getting bored, but don't let this make you think that you can leave the animal alone all the time; it needs your company as much as it needs its daily food and cleaning. A girl I know used to have a small mirror attached to the side of the cage holding her small bee bee parrot which became so enamored of its "companion" that it was reluctant to attend to her talking lessons, but this may just have been an example of a bad student, for I'm sure the mirror didn't give it all that much attention back.

Droppings should be cleaned out once a day (removable trays beneath wire-mesh floors are particularly convenient), and the water and food dishes washed and dried before each daily refilling; the cage will need a thorough cleaning only about once a week, at which time every inch of the cage and its furnishings should be scrubbed with soap and water, rinsed, and dried. This will help keep the bird free of mites and bird lice, though some people like the insurance of a No-pest strip (hung at a distance from the cage since they can be toxic on contact) or a camphor block (commercially sold as a "bird protector"). The strips are best used for a short period of time (6 to 12 hours) in a confined area if they are to eliminate mites. Other larger pests (dogs, cats, and nosy humans) should be kept from poking fingers and noses in the cage and startling the bird (or damaging it), so the cage should be hung or supported somewhere safely out of reach. It is a good idea to do the feeding, watering, and cleaning chores at the same time each day, since birds become accustomed to a routine and become nervous if it is disturbed. They are also easily frightened by sudden movements or changes of any sort—such as a new dish or additions to the cage or a move to another room—so one should learn to move slowly and quietly and keep surprises to a minimum.

Because all of the birds in this chapter are seed eaters, they are all easy to clean up after, and commercial seed mixes are readily available and designed to satisfy the nutritional needs of the various species. Serious bird owners prefer to buy their seed unmixed and wholesale in large quantities, because it is cheaper, but the owner of a single bird or pair will find it easier to buy smaller bags, since seeds will become stale or infested if allowed to sit around for a long time. Canary mix, millet, and sunflower seeds are the most common seeds used, but birds also like fresh fruit and vegetables in small quantities, in addition to mineral and vitamin supplements. Oranges cut in half, apples, bananas, plums, cherries, cucumbers, celery, carrots, and leafy greens can all be offered in small daily portions; anything served should be fresh and removed before it has a chance to wilt or spoil. One couple we know gives their birds an occasional morning treat of scrambled eggs and toast, which sets the whole house squawking in delight. Other items such as egg biscuits, cookies, or bird crackers are also good as treats. Codliver oil or wheat-germ oil mixed with the seed is considered desirable by many bird owners (one teaspoon for each pound of seed), but the only other real necessity is grit, which is granite gravel, often mixed with ground oyster shell; the birds need the grit in order to digest their food. A piece of cuttlebone attached to the side of the cage is also useful in helping the bird keep its beak from getting too long and in providing calcium supplements.

Birds generally keep themselves pretty clean and do not need baths, though they may occasionally need to have their claws and beaks clipped or filed (best done by a professional), and some like a sprinkle of water on warm days or the chance to splash in a bowl of water. Exercise is good for most birds, and many people like to let their birds out of the cage once a day or so; caution should be used, however, and windows and doors kept closed. A few years ago, some friends of mine lost a pair of valuable peach-faced lovebirds and managed to set a whole neighborhood in lower Manhattan astir. During the summer, this couple likes to hang some of their cages on a clothesline in the back yard, moving them inside at night. One day the lovebirds found their door ajar, and they took off across the street to perch on a fire escape. The owners tried to get access to the adjoining apartment but the occupant called down, "Don't bother, I'll get 'em!" The moment he touched the fire escape, the birds took off again as if they had been electrocuted and flew farther north. A few minutes later, another neighbor called to say: "We've seen your birds; they're on Fourteenth Street now," and the chase continued, to no avail. Assuming the birds had gone forever or been adopted by someone with an open window, they went home but hung the cage on the clothesline, just in case. Sure enough, the next day, the birds were back in their cage eating out of their seed dishes, just like two well-trained homing pigeons.

Most birds can be conditioned to handling—the more they get, the better they like it, if treated properly. Any frightened—or even just curious—bird can give a sharp peck or bite with its beak, and many people who handle birds like to wear gloves to prevent injury, inadvertently caused or not. I tend to believe that gloves cause more problems than they prevent; if they are thick enough to cushion a peck, they are probably too thick to enable the handler to be gentle with the bird. Bird bones are extremely fragile, and even the slightest pressure applied in the wrong place can cause a fracture. The best way to prevent injury is to learn to hold a bird properly. In handling a new bird, or a bird whose behavior you do not know well, it is advisable to hold the head between thumb and index finger on each side of the beak, exerting slight but gentle pressure. In picking up a bird from a cage, it is necessary to move quickly but firmly (in an aviary, a net may be required); grasp the whole bird by the body, not one of the legs, and hold it firmly to prevent struggling, with the wings clasped against the body, the neck between the first and second fingers, the back against the palm, and the thumb and third finger encompassing the body. Do not put pressure on the bird's chest, and don't hold it any longer than necessary. Canaries are much less agreeable about this than budgies, which may even learn to like it. The ideal way to remove a bird from its cage is to train it to perch on your hand and carry it out; this takes patient, daily work (in short fifteen-minute sessions) until the bird becomes accustomed to your hand and gets the general idea when you press your finger against its breast, but it's well worth the trouble.

Birds can also be trained on the reward system to do various "tricks," but most cage-bird owners—except for those specializing in pigeons—are primarily interested in vocal training. Canaries are usually bought for the sake of their song, and birds of the parrot and starling (mynah) families are often obtained with the hope that elaborate vocabularies will suddenly develop. Although all of these birds do make a lot of noise, it isn't always produced in a desirable or convenient way. Some birds can be taught to talk, especially if acquired young; in training, the bird must be kept out of earshot of other birds (and radios and people), and one must patiently repeat the word being taught over and over again in short daily training sessions. As soon as one word is learned, you can begin on another, but do not be discouraged if the first word takes a long time and a lot of patience.

The best way to be sure you have a guaranteed songster or mimic is to get a bird that has already demonstrated its prowess with a previous owner. These birds are likely to cost more than unproven specimens, and they may take quite a while to adapt to you, but you'll be rewarded in due course if you treat them right. Parrots with vocabularies to make a sailor blush are rare except in stories about retired ministers and retiring spinsters, but since birds that mimic will pick up whatever they are taught without understanding a word, some can be surprising and delightful additions to a household. One family we know owns a small parrot that had lived with a woman who must have spent all of her time on the telephone, for its conversation is almost exclusively one-sided: "Yes? Oh, hello. Fine, thanks, and you? Oh really? Well, tell me *all* about it!" And another parrot makes party noises whenever its owner gets on the telephone, with everything from uproarious laughter to the tinkle of ice in glasses, much to the owner's embarrassment.

Many a disappointed canary owner, however, has found that its pet simply will not utter a note, and hours of "Polly want a cracker?" have been spent in vain on parakeets who are perfectly content to screech crackerless. Before you get a bird, therefore, be sure of at least two things: that you (and your neighbors) are prepared for bird noises of whatever sort and that you will be just as happy with the bird regardless of its vocal abilities. The reasons a bird cannot be taught to sing or talk are not always clear—sometimes vocalizations are limited because of a genetic trait, sometimes the living conditions are not conducive (particularly if the bird is one of a pair or group), sometimes sex has an influence. Male canaries are far more likely to sing than females, though there is no similar sexual difference in the vocal abilities of psittacine birds. Much research has been done recently in bird language, and the results are fascinating, though not always enlightening in practical terms for the frustrated bird owner who can probably never know all the variables involved in his own pet.

Whether or not the sound is a desirable one, most birds do make a lot of racket and can cause a real disturbance for the sensitive ear, but this usually occurs only during daylight hours. When the room—or cage, thanks to a draped cloth—is dark, most birds will become quiet; since birds seem to need at least 12 hours of sleep a day, it may be necessary for you to regulate its daylight hours in any case, the noise factor aside.

Most diseases among caged birds can usually be avoided by proper care and eliminating exposure to other animals, and some of these precautions will be discussed later in this chapter. There are, however, a number of symptoms that may result from psychological stress, and if an owner is sure that cleanliness, an adequate balanced diet, with water and grit, and controlled temperature are being provided, the problems may in fact be the result of some less obvious cause. Cages that are too large and open can be made more agreeable by the addition of plants or perches or shelter boxes, and nervous or easily frightened birds will usually become steadier. Some stereotyped behavior—such as repeated bowing or compulsive chewing—can be the result of a cage that is too small; birds will sometimes indulge in self-mutilation by plucking their feathers or nibbling at their toes if they are bored or stimulus starved. Highly social birds do not do well without others of their kind in the same or adjacent cages, although some individuals are more or less aggressive, particularly those with territorial tendencies, and may suddenly provoke fights or attack their cage mates even after a period of relative peace. Most parrots are prone to this kind of aggression and should be kept singly or in pairs; however, mates will sometimes turn on each other.

Injuries from fighting or from accidents usually take the form of broken legs or wings and cuts or abrasions. These may be mended at home if the injuries are not serious, but when in doubt call a veterinarian. If professional or expert help is not available, consult a good text on the subject of bird injuries; see also page 165, which deals with the care of injured wild birds.

All birds molt regularly (and should not be moved during these periods) so don't worry if you see feathers in the bottom of the cage once in a while; if the molting seems excessive to you and bare patches can be seen, and if you are sure the animal isn't doing the damage to itself, seek medical advice, for this may be a disease symptom. Birds are also susceptible to respiratory infection, external parasites, and various disease conditions, most of which can be prevented by good management and the lack of exposure to other birds.

Some birds breed readily in captivity—canaries, finches, lovebirds, and some of the small parrots—whereas others can be bred successfully only by experts. One of the most difficult aspects of breeding (covered in greater detail in Chapter 9) is making sure that a pair is correctly sexed. If you have a pair of the opposite sexes and wish to encourage breeding, be sure to place a nesting box in the cage and provide nesting material (most birds will enjoy this kind of privacy even if they have no intention of laying eggs). The best policy is to leave the birds in peace and avoid disturbing them except to check on the eggs; incubation times vary according to species and unless you are experienced, incubating the eggs yourself and rearing the babies can be a difficult task. But if you are successful, you have every reason to be as proud as the real parents, for you will have helped increase the population of some of the world's most beautiful creatures.

Canaries

These charming songsters have been kept as pets for centuries and are one of the most popular of all cage birds. The yellow canary is a descendant of a wild bird native to the forests of the Canary Islands. When the Spanish conquered the islands in the fifteenth century, they began a lively trade in these green birds, which had probably been kept in captivity by the inhabitants. Perhaps because the Spanish wished to keep a monopoly on the breeding of canaries, or because of the value of the male as a singer, the Spanish exported male birds only. In the late sixteenth century, however, a boat carrying a breeding cage was wrecked on the shores of Elba and the birds became feral on the island; since by that time the canary was already popular, the Italians took advantage of their presence and began breeding them on a large scale. By the eighteenth century, the birds were being bred all over Europe, and the most famous centers of breeding now are in some small towns in the Harz Mountains of Germany. Caged canaries are still popular in the Canary Islands, but many of these birds are, in fact, imported from Europe.

Canaries can be purchased at pet shops or through registered breeders, and there are many varieties from which to choose. The two most general types are song canaries and type canaries; the former are bred mainly for their song and the latter for their appearance, though many of these sing as well. Song canaries are either choppers or rollers; the chopper's song is louder, more boisterous, and more popular than the roller's, which is soft, mild, and delivered through a nearly closed beak.

These song birds are raised and trained carefully by fanciers, who enter them in contests, where they are expected to sing beautifully on cue (usually by exposing them to light) for 15 minutes or so. The type canaries, usually somewhat larger than choppers or rollers, which are about 5 inches in length, are raised purely for color and shape. Red factor canaries, the border fancies, and frosted breeds (with white tints on their feathers), are popular as are various others, such as the Norwich, Yorkshire, and American singers. Although the wild canary was a greenish bird, canaries are bred now in almost every color of the rainbow, not just the familiar "canary yellow," and some of them are extraordinarily beautiful.

Because canaries—like most birds—are particularly fragile and subject to illness or disturbance during molting season, which may last from July to October, it is best to buy a new canary during the winter or spring months. Females are worth less than males, and "unsexed" canaries are usually the former. It is difficult to tell the age of a canary unless it was banded as a youngster; they can live as long as fifteen years, though the average lifespan is eight years. Birds between one and four years are best for singing or breeding, and the younger the better if you intend to train them to sing.

Most adult nonbreeding canaries will do well on 50 per cent canary seed, 25 per cent rape seed, and 25 per cent millet, with occasional supplements of greens and vegetables and mashes (see chart). For optimal health, the addition of "condition food" or "song food" will supply extra protein, vitamins, and minerals. Special soft-food formulas may be necessary for breeding birds, and some experts believe that color may be improved or intensified by the addition of certain foods (such as carrots or greens) during molting season.

Small Finches

The order of Passeriformes (or perching) birds, to which the canary belongs, is a huge one with hundreds of species, several of which have been domesticated as cage birds for many years. They vary greatly in size, color, and behavior, and finch owners delight in their beauty and in the breeding of certain species. Most of them are social birds and prefer the company of at least one companion; a large number will do well in an aviary big enough to give each species its own territory. Most finches are seed eaters, but some will require insects or soft food, especially at breeding time, and will do well on canary seed, millet, and greens, with supplements of "condition food." Because of their relatively small beaks, the tiny birds prefer small seeds and will not touch rape seeds, for instance, which are a staple of the canary's diet. Most of the species that have been domesticated and that are available in this country through pet shops or breeders are relatively hardy, not messy or terribly noisy, and make delightful, easy pets to keep.

The most popular varieties come from the dry regions of Australia and the tropical areas of South America and Asia—and it is difficult to choose between them for beauty. The society or Bengalese finch has been domesticated for so long that its wild ancestor is unknown. Like many of the other finches, it is about 4½ inches long and has been bred in a wide variety of colors—mostly white with blotches of different colors. They breed easily in captivity though they are difficult to sex by color and are, in fact, often used as foster parents for finches that are difficult to raise.

The zebra finch of Australia is another popular cage bird of approximately the same size and with several color variations—white, gray, tan, buff, and cream. Unlike many species, the sex of the zebra finch can be determined by color—the males have red bills and chestnut flanks and cheeks. They too breed well in captivity, the females laying white eggs that take only about 12 days to hatch.

The Java sparrow is about 5½ inches long and is mostly gray with a red bill, white cheeks, and black tail. These are not as easy to breed as the zebra or society finches. All of these species are members of the Estrilidae family, as are the mannikins, waxbills (which are African and do sing, unlike many small finches), cordon blues, and cutthroat finches (which are apt to bully smaller birds and should be kept in separate cages or in pairs). The Ploceidae family includes weavers and bishops and the elegant whydah, which during breeding season is the most dramatic in appearance of all. The whydah cock's tail can reach a length of 15 inches and the feathers become deeper red on the chest and black on the back. After breeding, however, the male and female are rather drab in color and short tailed. The whydahs, incidentally, do not incubate their own eggs but leave this task to other birds, in whose nests the eggs are laid.

Other finches are the beautiful Lady Gouldian of Australia, the star finch, and the South American cardinals and warblers, not to be confused with the native North American species which cannot legally be kept in captivity. Although these small finches are not usually songsters like the canary, there is an advantage in that they are far less noisy and, like all seed eaters, relatively easy to keep clean. As social birds that thrive on the company of other birds, they do not tend to relate well to their owners, who find them attractive mainly because of their beauty and their interesting behavior patterns. One family we know in New York City owns about twenty finches, seven or eight species of them, and finds that each individual has a favorite spot in the aviary (most of them preferring to perch high up just under the roof) and even favorite companions, not always of the same species. There are occasional squabbles when territorial boundaries are forgotten or disregarded, but no serious injuries have resulted and peace is the rule. To encourage breeding, the owners leave bits of this and that—rope, string, and colored yarns—in the cage, and find that the weaver birds, true to their name, like to decorate wooden and plastic strawberry baskets that are hung from the sides of the cage. They will also make elaborate nests from fresh grass if the pieces are long enough.

The parrot family (Order: Psittacidae), from the small budgerigar to the huge macaw, is undoubtedly the most striking of all the cage birds. They are very beautiful and many of them are quite intelligent and even affectionate. Some can be taught large vocabularies, and one parrot I know, in addition to learning his musical scales, could even trill the bell song from *Lakmé*. Many species are difficult to get because of the importation laws and because they do not breed readily in captivity, but a number of parakeets and parrots are available through pet shops or breeders, even if they are now not as inexpensive as they once were. Most parrots, with the exception of the Loriinaes (lorikeets) and some others, are seed eaters and relatively hardy, but the following species are particularly recommended as "easy" birds because of their smaller size, their availability, and their proven success as pets.

Budgerigars

This bird, a native of Australia and known also as the grass parakeet,* is undoubtedly the most popular of all cage birds; it is certainly one of the easiest to keep and one of the most rewarding of pets. It is an interesting fact that the first budgie owner was an English convict, one Thomas J. Watling, a counterfeiter who spent his exile in Australia painting birds and, as it turned out, teaching at least one of them to talk.** He was subsequently pardoned and raised many of these little birds; however, it was not until some years later, in the nineteenth century, that they were exported to England where they were eventually bred in enormous quantities for the pet market.

Budgies are slender, long-tailed birds about 7½ inches long and have been bred in a variety of colors, including white and yellow, though the wild type is generally green with bars of a darker color, a yellow forehead and bib, and a blue and green tail. Immature birds are difficult to sex, but adults can sometimes be differentiated since the cere, or patch of bare thick skin at the point where the forehead joins the upper mandible, is blue in males and brown or pink in females, becoming deeper in color as the birds mature. Unlike canaries, budgies of both sexes are equally vocal, and some learn to talk quite well with patient training. It is generally true that a single budgie is more easily trained than a pair, since one bird will distract the other. These birds are far more apt to respond to their owners than canaries or other finches, and they can be made very tame, especially if handled from an early age. Budgies are also easy to breed, but they will breed only if two or three pairs are within sight or hearing distance of each other, not as solitary pairs. Nevertheless, a single budgie will do very well on its own and may live as long as fifteen years with good care.

Canary seed and millet make up the basic diet for budgies, which dehusk the seeds and swallow them whole; they discard the husk, usually by scattering it on the floor of the cage, but sometimes by simply leaving it in the seed dish. This habit, which is common to all seed eaters, will often make the seed dish look full, though it may be quite empty of nourishment; owners should be sure to check the dish daily. Like the other birds, budgies should have ready access to

---

*The term parakeet applies to a number of species of the Psittacidae order, found in Central and South America, Africa, Asia, Australia, and the offshore islands of these continents. Budgerigar is an Australian bush word meaning "pretty bird."

**Curiously enough, it was another convict—Robert Stroud, an American—who did much original research in the care and diseases of birds and became known as the "Birdman of Alcatraz."

water and grit, as well as a cuttlebone to keep their beaks trim. They will eat small amounts of vegetables and greens, as well as biscuits and mashes containing egg yolk, alfalfa meal, wheat germ, yeast, vitamins, etc. Budgies, as well as finches, will thrive with the regular supplement of "condition food" for vitamins and minerals; the packaged seed mixtures prepared by commercial firms usually contain all the nutrients needed by these relatively undemanding creatures. Vitamins may also be given by adding a commercial preparation to the water, though some birds will refuse to drink tainted water. Overfeeding will cause obesity in these small birds, particularly if they do not get enough exercise. Their cages need not be large, but they should be roomy enough to allow a certain amount of flight, and exercise outside the cage, together with handling by the owner, is also desirable.

Lovebirds

These natives of Africa are not as popular as the budgerigar, probably because they have a reputation for aggressive behavior, but if they are kept singly or in pairs, these members of the parrot family can be extremely satisfactory pets. Of the nine forms, four are usually available in the United States from dealers: the peach-faced lovebird, the black-masked and blue-masked, and Fischer's lovebird. These breed freely in captivity (and do not require several pairs looking on, like the budgies, though otherwise their care is similar). Only the sexes of the blue-masked species can be differentiated by color; the others can be sexed only through surgery or by observing their behavior. They are all small, short-tailed birds of 6 to 7 inches in length and are mostly green in color, but their markings are varied and quite beautiful.

Cockatiels

These large (12-inch) birds originate in Australia and are particularly noted for their crested heads and their gray-white coloration. Adult males have yellow faces with orange cheeks; females are lighter yellow about the face and dull orange under the tail. They can therefore be sexed easily by color, usually at about six months, although they do not reach full plumage until they are about two years old. These birds are not difficult to breed in captivity, but their space requirements are greater than those for the smaller birds. They need a large breeding box (at least 15 inches high and 9 inches × 9 inches in floor space) with wood chips in the bottom; the box should be hung high in the cage with an entrance about two-thirds of the way to the top and a ladder attached from the door to the floor inside.

Cockatiels are among the most peaceable of the parrots and can even be kept with smaller birds, such as the finches. They can be taught to talk, to do tricks, and are very tame, especially when handled from youth. In fact they often become attached to individual humans, requiring far more attention than most birds. In addition to talking, cockatiels may be taught to whistle or drum rhythmically. Their dietary requirements are the same as for lovebirds and budgies, and they tend to overeat given the chance. They also enjoy chewing things up, so when you release them in a room for exercise, keep a constant eye on your valuables.

Bee Bee Parrots

These charming birds are similar to lovebirds in size and can make delightful pets, singly or in pairs. Individuals vary in aggressiveness to each other (they should be introduced with special care), but most of them are responsive to human attention and enjoy being handled. There are four popular color types—canary-winged, oranged-flanked, white-winged, and orange-chin—but the basic color is green. Like most parrots, these birds can be taught to talk as well as to do simple tricks, such as walking up arms, small ladders, tightropes, and alighting on shoulders and fingers. An Alexandrine

ONE OF THE MOST RESPONSIVE BIRDS IS THE COCKATIEL, WHICH WILL WHISTLE AND TALK AS WELL AS DEMONSTRATE ITS AFFECTION FOR HUMAN FRIENDS.

parrot I once knew learned to turn lights on and off, and was trained to turn on the radio, because she apparently enjoyed dancing to music, so who knows what a bee bee can be encouraged to do. Some parrots display distinct preferences among their human companions. One man had a male parrot which became increasingly aggressive toward men, even the owner, and as it grew older would peck at ears or necks when irritated. Attempts to discipline it (tapping gently on the beak and saying "no" very firmly) were useless, since the bird took the gesture as a threat and didn't understand English (like most parrots). Happily the man found a good home for the bird in a local zoo and found himself a female Cuban parrot which is very affectionate, except that she is aggressive toward *women* and will bite the closest female ear she can find.

Since all parrots, even the smallest ones, use their beaks constantly as a tool for climbing and as an exploratory device, as well as for cracking seeds and in self-defense, most bites are inadvertent and relatively painless, though there are exceptions. The larger the parrot, the more painful such a bite is likely to be. Great care should be taken in handling all parrots, even tame ones, for they are easily frightened or upset by quick movements and loud sounds, which is kind of surprising when you think of the terrific noises they make. Small children should not be allowed to handle them unless carefully supervised.

REPTILES AND AMPHIBIANS

Most people, when you mention the word "pet," will think of something furry or feathered and prefer not to think at all of something scaly or slimy unless it is a tropical fish of an exotic variety. But what do you do if a child is allergic to cat hair, say, or if you cannot tolerate the noise of a bird? What do you do when a child comes home with a tiny inoffensive garter snake—displaying none of the revulsion of his elders toward this charming and docile creature? Actually, for many children—and adults—the study and keeping of reptiles and amphibians can be fascinating and rewarding, and I know many people who would rather have a "cold-blooded" pet than the most appealing puppy, which is, in fact, a far more difficult animal to keep properly. Since I am assuming that my reader is an animal lover, reasonably well read in animal lore, I don't have to go into much detail in explaining that snakes, for instance, are not slimy, or that most species are not poisonous but harmless and extremely gentle (if slow witted and slow moving) when subjected to frequent handling. Though some species are tricky to keep, many reptiles and amphibians require very little care if the appropriate living conditions and food are provided. Unfortunately, most pet shops and veterinarians know little about what these conditions are, and anyone interested in investigating these animals as pets should be sure to inform himself as thoroughly as possible about the various species and their needs. Because most of the animals require special diets—some involving live insects or rodents—they cannot be considered the easiest of pets, but once a source of supply for mealworms, live or frozen mice, brine shrimp, earthworms, crickets, etc., has been located, upkeep and maintenance are minimal. Nevertheless, some species of lizards and snakes, because they are expensive to obtain or relatively difficult to keep, should not be considered easy pets, and they are so listed in the charts at the back of the book, although general information about care will appear in this chapter.

"Cold-blooded" is a misleading term, implying that the animal is unresponsive, or even cruel, but this is most definitely not the case. All reptiles and amphibians have blood, just as birds and mammals do. Because their body heat is dependent primarily on the temperature of their environment and rapid change may cause disease or death, they prefer a limited range of temperature. Too much heat—such as that caused by direct sunlight—will dry them out or "bake" them to death, and too much cold will send them into a torpid state during which they are inactive and do not feed. Any reptile in good condition can survive a fast of days and even weeks, as is often required in the wild, but this situation cannot continue indefinitely and the break-fast meal had better be pretty substantial. The best temperature range for most of the reptiles is between 80° and 85°, and for most amphibians 65° to 72°F., but the charts at the back of the book will give the specific temperature ranges for a few of the species described below, along with particular dietary requirements. See also Chapter 7 for information about caging and food. The following generalizations about living conditions should be mentioned first, since they apply to all of these animals.

Because the environment of any reptile or amphibian kept in captivity must be controlled, enclosures should be equipped with a heat source and constant access to water, even for land species. They should be well ventilated and roomy enough to allow the animal a certain amount of exercise and to allow the owner to open the top and remove feces or uneaten food without disturbing the animal (a screen with a latch makes a good cover). The rewards from these animals are in observing them, so the best enclosure is a glass-sided tank, preferably one fitted with an incandescent bulb (60 watts is sufficient for a 20-gallon tank and an aquarium reflector or a gooseneck lamp makes a good holder), which will act as a source of both light and heat; it should be turned on and off from outside the tank. A thermometer inside the tank is a must. Newspaper makes the best flooring, and natural materials, such as twigs and branches, are good for climbing and resting; plants are tricky though attractive, because they may be eaten by some animals, and most reptile owners I know have either plastic plants or nothing at all. Woodland environments or vivaria are very attractive and make excellent homes for these animals, but it is important to keep the ecological balance working. One special note: be sure the enclosure is completely escape-free; these animals can quickly disappear into obscure parts of the house, and they can also disturb other people who may be less well informed about their good points than you are. It is a good idea to have an extra container on hand to hold the animals while you clean the regular cage or tank. Before you get your pet, you should be sure that you know what kind of enclosure will be most appropriate; some aquatic species will require water that must be aged for a couple of days before it can be made tolerable and plants should be given a chance to settle in before animals join them.

Pet shops carry different kinds of snakes, lizards, toads, and so on (they no longer can sell small turtles, which until mid-1975 were sold in quantities of over thirteen million a year), but you may want to capture your own from a local stream or woodland area. Be sure to take a plastic bag or jug to hold the leaves and water the creature will need to survive until you get it into its new home. Before you go, study the types of animals that live in the area you plan to explore so that you can recognize the species you capture.

Some reptiles are to be avoided—poisonous species, of course, and any species that is protected by state law because of its scarcity in the wild. These laws apply mostly to turtles (the bog, for one) and snakes (our two native boas), and you should check with local authorities before you go out hunting. If you are in any doubt as to an animal's identity, leave it alone. Some foreign species have been favorites as pets for years, but many are no longer readily available here and none of them is cheap to buy. But there are plenty of native reptiles, and these make better pets in any case; most of them don't grow to the tremendous size of the exotic types and are somewhat easier to keep. They can also be released if you find that you no longer want to keep them or have run out of a steady source of food.

All of these reptiles and amphibians can be made accustomed to a certain amount of handling, but this should be done with care and in short, regular periods. Snakes, lizards, toads, and frogs consider any sort of handling a kind of disturbance that they simply tolerate, and "taming" indicates only that the animal has become used to the routine, though some individuals may actually learn to enjoy it to a certain extent. They can never learn to recognize their handler, however, or distinguish him from another person, which means that anyone who handles these animals in the same way as the owner does can do so in perfect safety.

Turtles

It may seem odd to put this animal into the "easy" pet section when it is no longer available in pet shops; that is, no turtles under the size of 4 inches in diameter are sold. Their sale is now outlawed because of the high rate at which humans were picking up salmonellosis, a bacterial infection of the intestinal tract, carried by turtles as well as other animals and transmitted to humans; the disease can be treated and is rarely fatal, but it is dangerous, and so many pet turtle-linked cases were reported (280,000 in 1972 alone) that the FDA decided it was best to play safe and ban them altogether. Salmonella bacteria are rare in wild nontropical species, but dealers would collect young turtles in great quantity, put them in with already infected captive turtles, and the disease would spread quickly. There is no positive cure for the disease in turtles as yet, and carriers should be isolated, but there is a test for it and contamination can be prevented by careful washing after handling the turtle or its enclosure and by disposing of water through sanitary facilities (toilets) rather than sinks.

Actually, this curtailment of the pet-turtle industry is going to do turtles and turtle lovers a lot of good, since many of these pets suffered considerably if they survived very long after leaving the shop. Who among us does not remember the brightly painted circus turtles that came so conveniently equipped with boxes of "turtle food"? These poor animals rarely lasted a month—not only because of the paint on their shells (which prevented them from growing properly) but mainly from an inadequate diet. If they didn't starve, they probably went blind from vitamin deficiency. With good knowledgeable care, however, turtles (or terrapins or tortoises, whichever you prefer, since they're all chelonians under the shell) should not be difficult to keep successfully.

Water turtles (or terrapins) require a largely aquatic environment—a glass tank filled with water (properly aged to get rid of toxic elements and at room temperature) and a few rocks or twigs to provide islands and shelter is probably the easiest to set up, although another easy arrangement is an aquarium tank with a few inches of gravel (not sand or earth which can be swallowed and makes the water muddy) or tanbark and a large container of water (plastic or stainless steel) that can be easily removed for cleaning. Water turtles do nearly everything in the water—eat, eliminate, swim, rest, and so on—and a thorough cleaning should be done regularly unless the water is filtered; food should be placed in the water for these fellows since many species will not eat on land areas.

Land turtles (or tortoises) require far less water than water turtles, but the second arrangement described above will do very well and the water dish need not be so large. The most important element for both types of turtle is temperature (between 75° and 90°F. for terrapins and higher for tortoises); direct sunlight is good for land turtles (shade is also necessary) and also for terrapins. The size of the enclosure will vary according to the size and number of the inhabitants: a 5-gallon tank is fine for any small turtle; a 10-gallon tank can hold a turtle 4 inches long; and a 50-gallon tank will hold two turtles that size or a single turtle 6 inches long.

Most turtles are omnivorous, though some land turtles are exclusively vegetarian and some water turtles eat only meat. Provide both vegetable and meat, however, for "meat" to a carnivorous turtle means a whole animal not just the muscle meat. A well-balanced diet consists of a mixture of greens, carrots, and chopped beef, beef heart, fish, or a good brand of canned dog food, with a daily calcium supplement (a cuttlebone or some bone meal sprinkled over the food). Surprisingly enough, a well-balanced "complete" dog food that contains meat, grains, and vitamins and minerals is probably the best steady diet for carnivorous turtles; vegetables should be offered to all the others. Whenever possible live food should be given—insects such as crickets or earthworms are particular favorites, and mealworms are available at most pet shops—but this is not essential to good health if care is taken to supply all necessary nutrients in the basic diet. Turtles should be fed two or three times a week, although they can go for as long as a few weeks without eating and remain healthy. Because aquatic turtles tend to be messy eaters, you may want to feed them in a different tank filled with water, allowing them sufficient time to eat (a couple of hours). Otherwise, try to remove untouched food from the regular tank (a plastic feeding dish will make life easier for you), and be sure the area is cleaned pretty thoroughly at least once a week.

Turtles native to the southern states include the red-eared turtle, the Mississippi map, and the Florida slider—all of which were once pet-shop favorites. Other types commonly found throughout the rest of the country are the box turtle, the painted turtle, the diamondback terrapin, as well as the spotted, mud, musk, and wood turtles. Many turtles grow to a length of a few inches and live many years (the box turtle can live up to a hundred years or more), so keep this in mind when you pick out a baby. Do avoid keeping any protected species in captivity, as its future is endangered.

When you wish to handle a turtle—either in catching it or moving it from the tank—lift it by the shell, never by the tail. Any turtle not accustomed to being handled is capable of biting or scratching vigorously, so be careful and use gloves for any large individuals. A healthy turtle is one that does not drag itself along the ground but lifts its body off the ground when walking; the shell should be firm without sores or soft areas, and the eyes should be clear. Most of the health problems in turtles are caused by deficient diet and exposure to parasites, so if you are careful to get a turtle in good condition, keep it properly clean, well fed, and far away from any sick turtles. It is not a good idea to keep different species of unequal size together, for large turtles may subject smaller ones to constant stress. Other kinds of animals may also suffer. Two friends of mine (she a turtle keeper and he a collector of tropical fish) put their animals together—for the convenience of the sitter and perhaps out of sentiment—when they went off on their wedding trip. One marriage managed to survive happily, but the aquatic one did not; on their return they found two extremely well (and expensively) fed turtles quite alone awaiting yet another exotic meal.

Male and female turtles of some species may be differentiated by their physical characteristics; males have long fingernails, a rather concave undershell (or plastron), and a protruding vent, while the female has a flat or concave plastron, short nails, and a vent rather well hidden beneath a short tail. All of these differences work very well for mating purposes (something that turtles have been doing successfully for millions of years); once mating has been accomplished, the female may hold the sperm for a while or she may produce fertile eggs rather quickly and bury them in warm sand (about 6 inches deep). Hatchlings may appear in 45 to 300 days (or they may not) if the temperature is kept consistently warm. Some turtle enthusiasts have had success in hatching turtle eggs by removing them from the sand, placing them in a container with air holes, covering them with sphagnum moss, and keeping them under a chicken incubator. After hatching, the little turtles may be put in a glass tank with 1 inch of sand and fed on brine shrimp, chopped smelt and chicken liver, and a mineral supplement, until they are large enough to take an adult diet. At this point they can safely be released into the wild.

Snakes

In spite of the fact that many people take all the legends seriously and think of snakes as evil, dangerous, or just plain revolting, they are among the easiest of animal pets—easy to keep, quiet, odorless, and relatively undemanding. Perhaps if you think of them as lizards without legs (which is not entirely inaccurate since the two are members of the same order), they may seem more appealing; at least you might try this idea on skeptical visitors. Keep in mind, too, that children have no natural fear of snakes but must be carefully taught by adults to find them anything other than interesting animals. There are only a few venomous snakes to fear in this country, and these should, of course, be avoided at all cost, no matter how eccentric you are; there are also a few types that require live food, but most snakes native to the United States can be kept successfully in captivity with little effort or expense.

Boa constrictors and certain types of pythons (reticulated and Burmese, for example) are still available in some pet stores, although import restrictions and costs have made them increasingly expensive. Indigo snakes have been a popular species for pet owners, but the eastern indigo is now endangered in Florida and should be allowed to remain in the wild. Anacondas are sometimes offered for sale, but they are aggressive and grow to a very large size, as do many of the imported snakes which, of course, cannot be released when they become impractical. The best species to start with are the relatively docile snakes native to North America; garter snakes, king snakes (which should be kept alone for they will eat other snakes), corn snakes, and yellow rat snakes are all known to thrive in captivity under proper conditions. Most of them will live eight to ten years, and larger species will live for twelve or fifteen or even longer; some giant constrictors will live thirty years or more. As a snake ages, it continues to grow and the size of the enclosure should be increased accordingly; as they age, however, they tend to eat less often and are not so much trouble to feed and clean.

Most snakes that have not been handled will bite in self-defense, so caution should be taken in capturing one and in picking it up the first few times. Wear heavy gloves and avoid rapid movements until the animal becomes used to your presence; a firm grip with both hands (one just behind the head and the other supporting the rest of the body) should make the snake feel secure; in time, with regular handling, the snake should become quite tame, even responsive, at which point the gloves can be discarded. Some snakes can be carried for hours; the warmth of the human body in warm weather is something even a reptile can learn to love.

Avoid handling a snake with cloudy eyes; this indicates that the animal is about to shed its skin, which occurs periodically when the snake has outgrown its old coat. Because the snake cannot see clearly at this time, it is more likely to bite or behave aggressively. The bites of harmless species less than 5 feet long need not be painful and seldom become infected if the wound is kept clean. Because a snake's teeth slant inward, the snake may be difficult to disengage if you try to jerk away when bitten, and lacerations may result. If you are bitten, seize the head and push it forward, as you put pressure on the sides of its jaws, which will force the mouth open. Clean the wounded area and apply iodine if the skin is broken. Careful handling is the best preventive against snake bite, which is the only damage a snake can do. The tongue, which is used for sensing its environment, cannot sting, nor can the tail, though it may be lashed furiously if the animal is upset. Snakes that kill their prey by constricting usually cause no harm to humans; even children may easily disentangle a snake smaller than 7 feet.

The cage for a snake should be at least as long as its body and half as wide. A glass tank or a wooden cage with a glass front is best; the lid should be of fine screening with a secure latch. If you keep several snakes together in an uncovered enclosure with corners, you may find them piled up some day with one missing or on its way out; round enclosures will prevent escape, but covers that can't be dislodged will be foolproof. Although earth or tanbark makes an attractive floor, it is difficult to keep clean and the snake may burrow out of sight. The most practical flooring is a few layers of newspaper fitted to the bottom which can be changed easily when soiled. Snakes defecate infrequently—sometimes only two or three times a month—and the feces are liquid and smelly at first but will dry out and should be removed. A water dish, large enough for the snake to submerge itself but shallow enough that the snake can get out and sturdy enough that it can't be overturned, is a necessity. A box, a piece of bark or plywood, or an arrangement of stones will afford adequate shelter. Twigs or branches should also be placed in the cage, especially if the snake is a climber. The temperature should be kept between 82° and 85°F. (some desert species may want it even higher) and can be regulated by a lamp placed over the cage. In most kinds of weather, the lamp may have to be kept on all day, but in summer it need only be lighted when room temperature drops below 75°F. Be sure to keep the cage out of direct sunlight unless you have a large enough shelter for the snake to escape the danger of being overheated.

All snakes are carnivorous, and although many species prefer live food, most can be taught to accept dead food sooner or later. Some small snakes will accept earthworms or mealworms once or twice a week. Larger snakes (over a foot in length) will require larger whole animals (three or four times a month)—white mice and rats, baby chickens, or other reptiles, and some amphibians and fish. These may be obtained at pet shops or raised or even trapped at home. Because you may wish to buy food in quantity and freeze it for the sake of convenience (the alternative being to support a living colony of animals or insects or buy them on a daily basis) accustom your snake to taking dead food. You may want to dip the frozen mouse or whatever you have in hot water just before presenting it, and you may have to wiggle it to simulate natural movement and remove a bit of skin to allow odor to escape, thus getting the snake's attention and stimulating it to eat. Odor is what guides most snakes, particularly nocturnal species. Ronald Rood, in his delightful and informative book *May I Keep This Clam, Mother? It Followed Me Home,* tells how a clever youngster, who couldn't bear the idea of feeding toads to his hognosed snake, managed to trick the beast by letting a live toad sit near some sliced meat until its odor had permeated the food. In a similar manner, he supplied "frogs" for his garter snakes and "mice" for his milk snakes without ever subjecting the live creatures to any danger at all.

Garter snakes have been known to survive happily on pieces of fish and raw hamburger supplemented with calcium and vitamins; the beef is first mixed with earthworms and gradually the worms are eliminated until the snakes eat only the meat. You can leave dead food in the cage overnight since many snakes are nocturnal and prefer to eat in the dark. However, if you present live food, do not leave a rat or mouse in the cage for more than an hour or so, because even small mammals can turn on a snake and cause it injury. Be careful not to disturb a snake while it is eating and do not feed a snake food that is much larger than its head (though most snakes can handle surprisingly large pieces). If you have more than one snake in a cage, take care that they do not begin to eat the same object; a larger snake, in fact, will often consume the smaller one, since neither is likely to let go.

Animals in the process of shedding their skins will probably not eat, and a snake in poor condition from disease or feeling stress from being in captivity may refuse food as well. It is possible to force feed a snake by pushing food into its esophagus with dull forceps and massaging it down to the stomach (one-third the length of the snake). It is probably a better idea, however, to release this snake if it is a local species, and avoid the necessity of repeating this difficult and tricky procedure. Do not let it go so long without food that it becomes run down and unable to survive either in the wild or back at the pet shop where you got it originally.

If a snake is infected with external parasites, such as ticks or mites, these may be eliminated by placing the snake in a plastic garbage can with a one-inch piece of No-pest strip attached to the lid for two or three hours. Ticks can then be picked off by hand. The cage should then be cleaned thoroughly to prevent reinfestation. A snake in good health should have no injury or swelling about the mouth and the skin should be free of blisters or blemishes. About a week before shedding (when the eyes become cloudy) the humidity in the cage should be kept relatively high, because the snake loses moisture at this time. When molting is just about to take place, the snake may need something to rub against; twigs or branches may be sufficient, but a stone or a small brick will probably be more effective. If the skin is shed incompletely, you may have to help a little by peeling the remaining sections, removing them with tweezers, or soaking the snake in water. A number of disease conditions may prove fatal to snakes, and these are difficult to diagnose or control without expert advice. Pneumonia, upper-respiratory ailments, and mouth-rot are not uncommon in captive snakes, and the symptoms to watch for are refusal of food, mucus discharge from the nostrils or mouth, and inability to close the mouth completely. Although many veterinarians are unfamiliar with reptile diseases, which can be complex, there are a few specialists that can be consulted and several good texts are available. If a reptile appears to be injured or ill beyond saving, it may be best to destroy it, but this decision should be left to an expert. If you are without an expert and without hope for the animal's recovery, and it appears to be suffering, the most humane form of euthanasia is simply to let it become chilled and then frozen. The animal will become sluggish, then drowsy, and will gradually die.

If you are interested in breeding snakes, try to select only those which bear live young, since the care of reptile eggs is difficult. Snakes born live are completely prepared to fend for themselves and are much easier to care for. Many native snakes are oviparous (egg layers) but three groups are ovoviviparous: garter snakes, water snakes, and pit-vipers (this group includes the poisonous cottonmouth and copperhead, so don't let yourself get carried away). It is difficult to sex snakes, though the tails of females tend to taper more or less abruptly near the vent whereas males have a uniform width for a longer distance behind the vent. Pressure on the tail or injection of sterile saline may bring male hemipenes into view, though this is sometimes a difficult task to accomplish safely. If your snakes are correctly sexed and do breed, gestation will take about three months if the temperature is kept stable, so that mating in the spring will probably result in young during the late summer or early fall if reasonably natural conditions are allowed to prevail.

Lizards

There are over two thousand species of lizards, of which a few are suitable as housepets. They are more active than snakes and to many people more interesting to watch, but their needs are more varied and they require more attention. Like snakes, lizards are clean and carry few diseases that can infect humans; although they do bite with fairly sharp teeth, there are only two poisonous species (the Gila monster and the Mexican beaded lizard) and they can be conditioned to regular handling. Lizards vary greatly in size and exist in all sorts of natural habitats—desert, tropical, and temperate zones. Before you obtain a lizard, either from a shop or from the wild, study the various species and know what you are getting and what its requirements are.

The most popular pet lizard is the misnamed American chameleon sold commonly at circuses and fairs; this is actually a Carolina anole, not a true chameleon, but it can change its color to match its surroundings under the influence of temperature, light, and its own excitement. Anoles are a large group of New World lizards, but only the Carolina anole is native to North America. Green iguanas, also New World lizards, can also be good pets, although they do grow to be quite large (sometimes up to 6 feet in length) and may well be aggressive and difficult to handle. Old World lizards, such as the monitor and the gecko, have also done well in captivity; however, they are becoming increasingly difficult and expensive to obtain.

Monitors also grow to a great size, though species vary. Horned lizards (sometimes called horned toads) do not make good pets because they require an enormous number of live ants daily, and several other kinds of insectivorous lizards may die from nutritional deficiency after a few months in captivity.

Lizards may be kept in many types of cages, as long as they are roomy enough, easily cleaned, and the temperature (72° to 85°F.) is carefully controlled. Tree-climbing species will need branches on which to climb and rest, whereas terrestrial types should have boards or rocks to hide under. Have water accessible at all times; lizards that will not drink from a dish should have it sprinkled on twigs and branches daily. Most lizards thrive in a relatively warm and dry atmosphere; few are semiaquatic and none is truly aquatic. A sandy floor is best, but be sure the sand is clean and only 2 inches or so deep. Some species require special conditions, such as exposure to high temperatures for daily periods; check the charts at the back of the book.

Most lizards are carnivores or omnivores (only two American species, the chuckwalla and crested lizard, will survive on a diet of fruits and vegetables alone) and should be fed three or four times a

THESE TWO IGUANAS LIVE IN AN OLD CHEST FURNISHED WITH LAMPS AND A LINOLEUM FLOOR; THE WOODEN PANELS ON TWO SIDES HAVE BEEN REMOVED IN FAVOR OF A GLASS FRONT FOR VIEWING AND A SCREENED SIDE FOR VENTILATION.

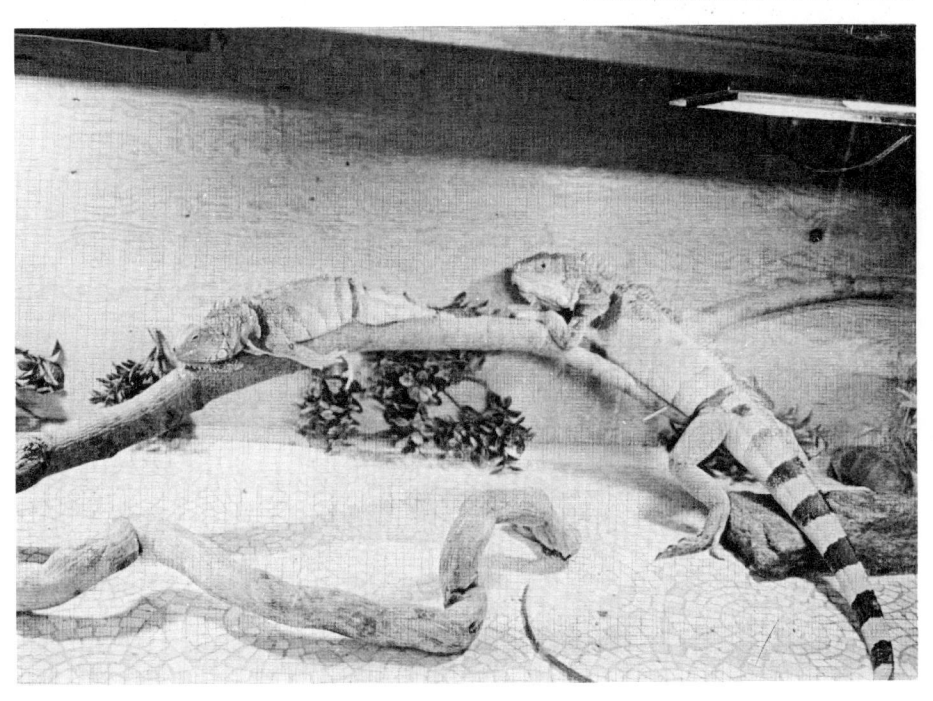

REPTILES AND AMPHIBIANS

week, though they can survive, if healthy, for several days without being fed. Some species, such as the anole, require live insects (flies, crickets, mealworms, etc.) whereas others, such as the basilisk, will eat mice, other lizards, or even canned dog food, with fresh greens and small amounts of raw fruit. All lizards need calcium and bone meal, and small amounts of pediatric vitamin drops should be mixed often with the food. Meals may not always be accepted at once, so give the animal time to react to it; remove all untouched food after a few hours before it begins to spoil.

A healthy lizard will feed regularly and behave in an alert manner. All of them molt occasionally, though the frequency varies considerably. In general, young lizards shed more often than older ones. The molt does not come off in one piece as it will with snakes. Provide something against which the lizard may rub itself, and be sure there is enough water around if the animal feels like taking a dip to speed up the process. Lizards are not so easy to bathe as snakes and using silica-gel mite powder may be the safest way to get rid of pests. Internal parasites and various digestive and respiratory diseases are common in captive lizards, and the treatment for them is similar to that used for snakes. The careful choice of an apparently healthy animal and good care should reduce the possibility of most health problems.

In handling lizards, do not lift them by the tail, since one form of defense for many species is to leave their tails behind. They then can form a new one. Hold the animal by the body as firmly as you can, so that the legs and head are controlled, to avoid bites or scratches. They can move very quickly and are experts in escape tactics, so if carrying a lizard from one place to another, the best method is to use a bag or pillowcase, knotted tightly at the top. Do not try to catch a moving lizard but wait until it becomes motionless; a wire or nylon noose attached to the end of a fishing rod is probably the most effective device for catching the animal.

Lizards can live for several years in captivity, and many will become quite docile and accustomed to handling, even stretching their necks to be scratched and stroked. Their primary interest for owners, however, is their appearance and behavior since they don't always respond well to frequent handling.

Salamanders

Although these long-bodied creatures resemble lizards, they are quite different indeed, because, as amphibians, they require a moist or semiaquatic environment in order to survive. There are many species native to North America, and most of these can be kept with relative ease; examples are the mole salamanders (which include the tiger salamander, the marbled salamander, the Jefferson, and the spotted varieties), woodland salamanders, and newts. Some of these are available in pet shops but many can be captured in the wild, if you know where and when to look (pond areas at night, generally). Adult salamanders live on land, but in the larval state or when they are breeding, salamanders stay in water. An aquarium or a large jar set up as a woodland or semiaquatic environment makes a good home for these amphibians as long as it is kept humid (a piece of plastic should partially cover the tightly latched top of the enclosure). There should be a sufficient supply of water in which the animals may submerge themselves, and some land area with twigs, branches, or rocks to act as shelter. Keep the enclosure fairly warm (65° to 75°F.) and out of direct sunlight.

Most salamanders are insectivorous and many can be taught to eat dog food or pieces of meat, served in a small shallow dish or from small forceps which you can use to dangle the food to make it appear alive. Small slices of beef or chicken liver are also good, as well as earthworms or live insects, such as crickets or flies. Some will eat tubifex worms, available through tropical fish dealers, and some like small fish. Although larger animals will survive on weekly feedings, it is a good idea to feed daily, when you change the water. Cage cleaning should be done thoroughly at least once a week, and more often if the water becomes cloudy. In preparing a semiaquatic environment, be sure to "age" all tap water for at least two days before adding it to the enclosure, to allow for the evaporation of chlorine. Some types of newt will thrive in a completely aquatic setup with some floating plants and a rock or two under which the animal can hide. The enclosure should have a firmly latched roof, since the animals can jump or climb out in a matter of seconds.

Salamanders can be handled, but only with wet hands (moistened with water from the aquarium) and only when necessary. Keep the head between your fingers and cup the body in your hand; don't hold very small animals for longer than a minute or so. A plastic bag or jar containing aquarium (or pond) water or damp leaves or cotton is the best way to transport them; be sure to punch a few holes (small ones) in the bag or the cover of the container to allow for the transfer of oxygen. While cleaning the aquarium, you need another moist enclosure to hold the salamanders. Cleaning can be facilitated if you use a piece of tubing to siphon out soiled water in the tank.

As with lizards, the tail of small woodland salamanders should never be grasped because their natural defense mechanism is to shed a piece of tail to occupy a predator's attention while the rest of the animal escapes.

Frogs and Toads

A young man of my acquaintance, who lives in an apartment in New York City, is considered a frog "nut" by many of his friends; in addition to collecting pictures of frogs and porcelain miniatures, he collects live frogs (usually "rescued" from Chinese markets) which he keeps in an otherwise unused bathroom. A bathtub with about three inches of water and a weekly feeding of crickets, which he orders in quantity from a supplier in the South, seem to be all that the animals need to thrive. He has found that a tiny frog can escape under the door and go to some closet to dry out and die, so he likes to keep large ones. The only precautionary measures he uses are to keep the door and the toilet seat closed at all times and to warn unsuspecting guests of their presence.

The practice of keeping frogs and toads is not at all unusual, though it is far easier to keep them in an aquarium tank where they can be observed. A gallon glass jar with a wide mouth can also be used for small frogs, and a 10-gallon tank can hold up to six or seven medium-size frogs. Many pet stores carry these animals, but they are easy to catch in the wild, particularly during the warm months of the year. About a hundred species live in North America and many of them make good pets: the tree frog (which will bark, no pun intended); the wood frog, or spring peeper as it is often called; the leopard frog (which should not be confused, as it often is, with the pickerel frog that emits a strong secretion which harms other amphibians); the spadefoot toad (not a true toad); and the true or "hop" toad, which feeds on many harmful insects in the wild, is a real boon to farmers, and does not, repeat *not,* produce warts in humans though they may give off substances harmful to other animals.

Aquatic frogs do best in an aquarium filled with several inches of water and an island made of rock; this should be cleaned at least once a week (or less if you have a filter) and should be kept at a reasonably steady temperature of 60° to 70°F. Animals that spend most of their time on land need only a dish of water in which they can soak and a layer of tanbark or soil over an inch or so of clean gravel. Leaves, and twigs—or rock "caves"—afford good hiding places, and some of the tree-climbing frogs and toads will appreciate a carefully arranged series of branches. Since tree frogs spend most of their time in the branches, you needn't put any flooring at all in the cage, but simply clean it from time to time with a cloth and see that the water dish is emptied and refilled once a week or so. Every few months, a thorough cleaning of the tank and the branches should take place, but, otherwise, this is the simplest type of environment to maintain.

Frogs and toads should be fed twice weekly, though like all healthy reptiles and amphibians, they can go for several weeks without eating. With some effort, they can be trained to take bits of meat (ground beef, sliced beef liver or heart, or dog food) from a piece of string or forceps which can be jiggled to make the offering look like live prey. Some may never learn to do this, however, and live insects (crickets, grasshoppers, or houseflies) may have to be provided. Tubifex worms or mealworms (which should be used with caution because of their hard skins) are available at most pet shops, and earthworms and caterpillars will be taken by many species. If you find that you are having trouble in getting the right food, be sure to release the animal before he gets so emaciated that he cannot survive in the wild.

Some toads, it would seem, are not as fussy as others. Jeremy, a toad kept in a New York City classroom, once managed to swallow a penny, and the children were hard put to find a way of getting it out. Finally, they hit upon the idea of lowering Jeremy's temperature, which sent him into a relatively drowsy, semihibernating state, at which point they could open his mouth wide and extract the coin with tweezers. Even without the money, Jeremy was no poorer for the experience.

Amphibians will probably not breed in captivity except under expertly controlled conditions, but the fascinating process of watching tadpoles turn into adults is not difficult to arrange. Pet shops may sell them, but you can catch them yourself in ponds and on lake shores (frog eggs are laid in clumps and toad eggs are in strings) with a small net. Keep the eggs and the tadpoles that hatch from them in water at all times, changing half the water volume no more than once weekly. Some species develop very quickly from the tadpole stage, though some bullfrogs may take a year or more to grow up. The best diet is probably a baby cereal with a high-protein content; however,

DIGNIFIED AND MONUMENTAL, THIS SMALL AMERICAN TOAD CAN MAKE A FINE PET FOR THOSE WHO ADMIRE HIM.

you can also feed them fresh greens and bits of egg yolk. When the legs appear, put in a rock island, and gradually create a woodland environment. A 5-gallon tank is sufficient for half a dozen tadpoles, but don't try to keep them all when they mature; release most of them where you found the eggs so that they can start their own cycle in a more natural environment.

In lifting and carrying a frog or toad, grasp it firmly but gently around the body just behind the front legs. Small animals may be enclosed in the hand but only for a minute or two. Transport them from place to place in a damp bag with air holes.

INSECTS

Most people think of insects as nasty pests to be sprayed, swatted, or otherwise wiped out, and indeed many of those we inadvertently support do cause a tremendous amount of damage to our food, our clothing, and our bodies. But these creatures hold a great deal of fascination for us, particularly the ones that live in complicated societies that we can compare to our own, and many of them do us a great deal of good. In this section, which will include insects that may be kept with a minimum of effort, we will discuss a number of different types: ants, crickets, earthworms, butterflies and moths, praying mantises, and spiders. As with reptiles, a restricted and controlled environment is required to regulate the insects' living conditions and food, and to prevent them from escaping into the "wild," so to speak, which may be simply the rest of the living room where they might not be quite so intriguing. Most of these creatures, however, can be kept quite easily and safely in a simple gallon glass jar with a wide mouth (the kind used for pickles or mayonnaise) or a small glass tank. Nylon or cheesecloth, held fast with a rubber band, is a simple but effective lid that will allow air to circulate but not the insects. A jar is probably the best container for a colony since it lets us watch the insects as they burrow through the earth.

Before you go out hunting for your insects, select and clean a container and prepare the earth and a tiny environment for them. For insects that require earth, be sure the soil you collect is free of parasites before you use it. Avoid sticky clay or heavy loam or pure sand; the best soil is light and sandy, with all lumps, stones, and other objects removed. Sift it with your hands and spread it out a couple of inches deep on a shallow tray and allow it to dry for a few days. When you are ready to use it, remoisten the soil and pack it into your clean jar; keep it moist but never soggy. Commercial potting soil can also be used if you haven't got any dirt at your doorstep. Collect your new pets in a plastic bag or plastic jug together with some leaves, twigs, and other natural objects to keep the new place feeling like

EASY PETS

home. Feeding most of these animals will be a simple procedure because they require very little care once you have got them comfortably settled. They will repay you by providing some fascinating entertainment—as one little girl put it, "This is almost as good as television!"—and in the case of crickets, at least, some pleasant song. Even those keepers who plan to use their pets as food for larger animals that need a steady diet of live insects can get some satisfaction out of creating a livable home for some tiny "wild animals."

Ants

Once upon a time a bored and lonely prisoner befriended a tiny ant that had wandered into his cell, feeding it crumbs of his stale bread and giving it sips of his meager water supply. After a while, the story goes, the prisoner decided that he would try to train the ant and in a couple of years actually managed to teach the insect to turn right on command. Another couple of years passed as he taught it to turn left, and by the time he had trained the ant to walk in a circle, he was released from prison. Cupping the ant in his hand, he walked confidently into the first saloon that he came upon, and putting the ant down on the bar, he called over to the bartender. "See that ant?" he said, pointing to the bar.

"Sorry about that," replied the bartender, crushing the ant under his thumb.

Ant sympathizers (or even those sympathetic with prisoners or bartenders) who have for years felt distress at hearing this old yarn need suffer no longer. An ant couldn't possibly have lived long enough for the story to be true (they live somewhat less than a year), and ants are impossible to train (unlike fleas) unless you're head ant. But they do make for entertaining companions, in spite of their short lives and lack of interest in humans that aren't having picnics.

Ant colonies or farms can be purchased commercially with all the equipment and instructions you'll need, but it is much cheaper and more fun to make your own. When you collect your ants, be sure that you get a queen along with the worker ants; she is larger than the others, and though the ants will survive for a time without her, they will not breed and will eventually die. After you have found an ant nest, dig down to collect the soil containing eggs, cocoons, and larvae as well as the adult ants and the queen. Transfer them to the jar that you have prepared by packing soil around a piece of wood or brick to keep the tunnels out by the edge where you can observe them. You may want to chill the ants for an hour or so in the refrigerator to slow them down a bit for the transferring process. Once they are in place, cover the jar with mesh and attach it tightly. Wrap the jar in construction paper or cloth to keep it dark and leave it alone for a few days to give the ants a chance to start tunneling.

Keep the jar at room temperature, out of the sun, and away from the radiator. Moisten the earth occasionally with water as you would a plant; too much water will make the earth soggy and mold may develop, so be sparing. Feed the ants every other day or so with bits of vegetable, fruit, bread, cereal, bird seed, or some drops of sugar water. You can simply leave the food on the top of the soil, but it is easier to remove untouched food if you use a piece of cardboard as a dish. Judge for yourself the amount and kind of food the ants like and adjust the diet accordingly; try to vary the type of food but take care not to overfeed, and do not let untouched food spoil. Now all you have to do is sit back and watch them tunnel, order each other around, and maybe even have some baby ants to carry on the family traditions.

Crickets

Crickets are as simple to keep as ants and, though their social behavior may not be as interesting (they don't keep slaves or domestic animals—aphids—as ants do), they do make a beautiful sound and of course they bring good luck. They have been kept in captivity by many cultures, particularly in the Orient where they are prized for their fighting prowess as well as their song. Male crickets are the ones that sing—by rubbing their legs together just as Jiminy Cricket did—and these should be kept one to a jar, because of fighting; the sexes are easily distinguished because the female has an ovipositor tube extending from her back and the male does not. Crickets can be kept in a jar with about an inch of sand in the bottom and some twigs and leaves for shelter. They will eat a lot of different things—cereal, starchy vegetables, and fruits (potatoes, apples, etc.), bits of meat, and fresh lettuce, cabbage, or carrot—and they should be fed at least twice a week. Be sure to check the jar daily and remove all untouched food. Crickets need constant access to water which can be provided in a soaked piece of material; a small tube filled with water and left standing on a piece of cotton will save you a daily chore.

Crickets will lay their eggs in the fall; when the weather gets warm in the spring, the eggs should hatch into nymphs that look like tiny adults. As they grow, they will molt their outer skins; this occurs several times before they reach the adult stage.

Crickets tend to sing faster in warm weather than they do in cold temperatures, and their songs have various purposes—to attract females or to threaten other males. Scientists have calculated that the exact temperature can be determined by counting the number of chirps; however, the various species of cricket vary in their song behavior and frequency. The most common types that are collected in this country are the field cricket *(Gryllus assimil)* and the house cricket *(Acheta domesticus)*.

Earthworms

These lowly creatures *(Lumbricus terrestris)* are not difficult to keep and raise, but they are probably not so interesting to watch as the livelier ants and crickets. Nonetheless, it is fun to observe the ways in which they move, work the soil, eat, breed, and react to vibration and noise. And they also provide a source of food for other pets (insectivorous birds, reptiles, and amphibians) as well as a ready supply of bait for the eager fisherman.

To make them a home, pack soil about halfway up a jar and put a layer of leaves on top; start with six or eight worms, which are most easily collected at night when they are active in any area where there is decaying vegetation. Keep the jar in a cool dark place and keep paper around it so that the light does not penetrate except when you are watching them. Feed the worms fresh greens, cut up vegetables, or corn meal but don't overfeed and be sure to remove anything that begins to spoil. Keep the soil moist but not soggy.

The spring and fall are the most active breeding times for worms, but the high temperatures inside a house or apartment may lengthen this period. Each earthworm produces both sperm and egg cells but it still takes two to produce fertilized eggs, which are deposited in the soil in a kind of yellowish cocoon formed by a jelly excreted by the clitellum, a light-colored ring that is located near the front end of the worm. The eggs take one to two weeks to hatch in warm weather and up to a month in the winter (in nature these periods are quite a bit longer). With luck you may be able to see a new generation of tiny worms to keep your colony going.

Butterflies and Moths

These attractive creatures are also easy to keep, and it is fascinating to watch them go through their various stages of maturation. You can collect them during any of the four stages, but perhaps the easiest form to start with is the caterpillar, which can be found in warm weather on certain kinds of leaves. Simply put the caterpillar into your prepared jar and give it some damp leaves to eat—eating is just about all it does. Be sure to provide the kind of leaves that you found it on and to add new ones every few days. If the caterpillar does not eat, try other kinds of leaves until you hit on the one it likes. Put some twigs into the jar, too, so that when the caterpillar is ready to change into a larva, it will have something to attach itself to. At this point the animal does not eat, but the jar should be kept cool and humid with wet paper towels. The larval stage varies in length depending on the species, and it may take as little as a week or as long as several months before a butterfly or moth emerges. In this adult stage, the insect may not eat at all; some butterflies, however, sip nectar from flowers. Dip some flowers in sugar water and see.

Now it is a good idea to release the winged creatures, though you may want to save two or three in the jar to see whether they will lay eggs and start the cycle all over again. If eggs are laid, keep them moist until they hatch; when they do, begin feeding the larva some leaves. If they don't eat, continue to experiment with different kinds. Some larvae like to have a bit of earth to burrow into; if you have collected the insect in the egg or winged stage, and are unsure about the species or the behavior of the caterpillar, it might be a good experiment to keep them in two separate jars, one with soil and leaves and the other with twigs.

Praying Mantises

Although this intriguing insect practices cannibalism, it has very few other nasty habits and can be very beneficial to man—both as an insect eater and as a surprisingly responsive pet. Because of the usefulness of the mantis in helping us keep down insect populations without the use of chemical insecticides, it is possible to obtain them in egg form from certain garden-supply stores; it is, however, not difficult to capture a grown mantis if you look carefully. Don't try to net a flying mantis but wait until it perches on a branch and then cover it with a small net or capture it in your hands. It may attack your fingers with its toothed claws, but this is not painful; be careful not to squash it. Keep the mantis by itself (or it will eat another mantis) in a jar with twigs, and spray the inside of the jar every day with water. It must be fed live insects—ants, mosquitoes, flies, whatever you can find—which must be moving for the mantis to notice it. Mealworms are also good food and are available in most pet shops.

If you begin with mantis eggs, which are laid in a case or oötheca, keep them in a closed jar until they hatch, which is usually in the spring. When they hatch, you will find that they are perfect tiny replicas of the adult mantis, and they will grow rapidly on a diet of tiny insects, molting their skins periodically until they reach full size. Since they will eat each other, be sure to separate them at some point, releasing those you cannot keep.

The praying mantis, the most common variety in this country having been imported from the Far East in the late nineteenth century, is so called because of the way in which it perches with its front legs folded and body bent forward. This is the position it adopts when it is hunting for food, which it catches—often on the wing—with its pincerlike front legs. The mantis can move its head from side to side and is, in fact, amenable to taming. It can be fed water or food from the finger and eventually may even learn to recognize the hand that feeds it. If you handle it every day, it will gradually become accustomed to sitting on your finger as you feed it.

Spiders

The spider, of course, is not an insect at all but an arachnid—like the scorpion and horseshoe crab—and has inhabited the earth for perhaps as long as 300 million years. There are many thousands of varieties of spiders and very few of them are dangerous to man, although the sight or even the thought of a spider can send some people into fits of revulsion whether they are eating curds and whey or not. Spiders have many admirable traits and kept in captivity can provide a good deal of satisfaction for the interested captor. They can be kept in a terrarium or vivarium or simply in a jar, like the mantis, and fed live insects such as mealworms or flying specimens. Larger species, such as the tarantula, may prefer small mice, which they can dispatch with surprising speed and efficiency.

Tarantulas, in spite of their reputation as deadly or dangerous spiders, are no worse than bees or wasps when it comes to biting—toxic to a few but relatively harmless to the rest of us. One New Yorker used to keep a tarantula on a leash made of string attached to a chair leg and managed to rid his entire apartment of cockroaches in a few days. But to avoid the possibility of escape or of frightening an unsuspecting guest, spiders are really better off in a covered enclosure. As with the other insects, there should be constant moisture—though not sogginess—in the enclosure and ready access to water, served in a dish or sprayed on to the sides of the glass cage. Daily attention should be paid to feeding; some spiders will eat enormous numbers of insects, whereas the larger ones may be happy with a large meal once a week.

Not all spiders spin webs—which are used for a large number of purposes: as traps for insects, as incubators and playpens for young, as lifelines—but all of them (the females, that is) lay eggs and incubate them in a silken bundle or egg sac. This sac nurtures the young after the eggs are hatched. After their first molting, they are large enough to break the sac, at which point they are fed by the mother until they are old or clever enough to catch their own food. Some spiders—the wolf spider, for instance—will carry their young on their backs until they can survive on their own.

It is possible to keep many other kinds of insects in captivity, though some of them are somewhat trickier than those we have described. Bees, for instance, which are covered in the next chapter, need to have access to the outdoors but then they will manage to keep themselves. There are more than 850,000 other species from which to choose so there is plenty of opportunity for you to experiment on your own. The best approach is to get to know the area in which you live or plan to look, learn about the species that are abundant, and then collect one or two, using the basic guidelines given above. If you are successful in keeping the conditions controlled and as much like the insect's natural surroundings as possible, you will find yourself with a whole collection of pets that are fascinating to watch, easy and inexpensive to keep, and relatively troublefree; they make little noise, rarely chew up slippers, and never need a veterinarian.

FISH

Because fish keeping has become such a widespread hobby, with pet shops that specialize only in tropical fish, numerous volumes devoted to fish care, fish behavior, fish species, and fish diseases, as well as enthusiastic amateurs who know a great deal about their animals, I will only describe the various kinds of fish and their care in the most elementary way, so that beginners can have some idea of what to expect before they go far enough to buy special equipment or even a book on the subject. Although the aquarium business totaled more than $60 million in sales in 1974, a tank may still be set up and populated for less than $25.

Goldfish are probably still the most popular beginner's fish, having been domesticated since the tenth century in China, but many small fresh-water and even salt-water varieties are suitable for home aquaria; they require relatively little space, are not costly to maintain, and on the whole are odorless, noiseless, and fun to watch. As many doctors with aquaria in their offices will attest, the presence of a well-established fish environment can be more soothing than a soft chair or a reassuring word.

Unlike many amphibians, reptiles, and insects, they are mostly diurnal, and their behavior is easily observed in a glass aquarium tank, where they may thrive and even breed, affording the observer a chance to study the entire life cycle. In addition to goldfish, popular fresh-water species (mostly imported from other parts of the world where they have been domesticated) include guppies (from the Caribbean), medakas (Japan), fighting fishes (Siam), swordtails (Mexico and Central America), etc. Salt-water fish are a bit more difficult to obtain and maintain, but the art of marine aquarium keeping can be managed by a dedicated amateur with the proper equipment and information; species include the neon goby (tropical Atlantic and Caribbean), the damselfish (Caribbean and Pacific), groupers or other sea basses (Indo-Pacific), and many others. Native fish may also be kept, in aquaria of course, as can a host of other animals—insects, snails, and similar scavengers—and plants. The species that are readily available in pet shops can vary enormously in size, living requirements, and price, but the following guidelines should be generally useful to anyone interested in pursuing the hobby further.

The best container for fish is definitely *not* the traditional fishbowl, in which the water surface is too small to take in sufficient oxygen (they also offer poor visibility for the keeper), but a glass tank, with a stainless steel framework made watertight by a thin layer of aquarium cement, which allows for changes in water pressure and temperature. This cement will dry out without water and it will lose elasticity as the tank ages, so unless the tank is purchased new, be sure that the container is still thoroughly sealed before you use it. Any tank should have most of its water removed before being lifted and should be held by the frame rather than by the sides. Cracks or leaks may be sealed temporarily with varnish, silicone cement, or adhesive tape, but the best solution is to get a new tank or decide to set up a vivarium instead. A cover is necessary to keep the fishes in and foreign matter out; screening is probably the best material for this, but whatever you use, make sure the lid can be easily lifted for feeding and cleaning purposes.

The size of the tank will vary according to the species and number of fish it is to hold. A useful though not infallible guide to use is that an inch of fish requires a gallon of water; some experts, particularly marine-aquarium keepers, prefer a ratio of surface area to fish size; they allow about 24 square inches for each inch-long fish. A 20-gallon tank is the minimum for a marine aquarium.

Aquaria, which must be kept out of direct sunlight if algae are to be kept from taking over and covering up the sides, should be artificially lighted, preferably from the top, so that the fish can be given at least twelve hours of light a day; temperature can vary from 75° to 78°F. for fresh-water fish (even higher, some say) and may be cooler (around 60°) for salt-water varieties. A thermometer is an essential piece of equipment, as is an air filter, which will insure that the water is always aerated with oxygen. Contrary to what most people think, fish—like humans—need to breathe oxygen, not oxygen that makes up pure water but oxygen dissolved in water; in fact, fish will drown in pure water as readily as mammals. The water in the tank must be specially conditioned or aged before fish can live in it in order to remove toxic elements. Tap water may be conditioned by standing exposed in shallow nonmetal containers, or by having compressed air forced through it, or by introducing aquatic plants.

In marine aquaria, filtration is especially important to keep harmful substances, such as ammonia and organic matter from uneaten food, feces, or dead fish, from building up. Bacteria on the gravel will perform a natural biological filtration; gravel itself will help sift out certain substances; and activated carbon will get rid of the rest chemically and is recommended for all marine tanks. Plants do not guarantee a perfect ecological cycle or balance, since they produce carbon dioxide at night that may be fatal to fish if overproduced; but plants do provide suitable sites for the attachment of eggs, convenient shelters for less aggressive fish, and they make tanks attractive and more natural looking. Water that has been conditioned should not be discarded but saved and used again. Occasionally, when water is too new or when the fish are overfed, the aquarium will become cloudy or dirty; a siphon made from a glass or plastic tube is particularly useful in clearing up the problem.

Sea water may be collected at the shore or purchased through a shop if you live far from the ocean; because minerals do not evaporate with the water, the addition of fresh aged water will keep the mineral concentration of your water at the appropriate level. Let new sea water stand for about three weeks in a dark room to stabilize its biological and chemical constituents before you use it. Siphon out any silt, and aerate the water for about twelve hours before you add the fish. Synthetic seawater is also available and requires less preparation.

Use only commercial aquarium sand or gravel; this is rather coarse with grains of uniform size. Fresh-water gravel should be rinsed thoroughly until the water runs off clear and allowed to sit for a while in conditioned water before the introduction of plants or animals; under no circumstances use regular earth or sand. Marine gravel is best borrowed from another tank (a successful one), but it may also be obtained commercially; it must contain calcium, and crushed oyster shell (the kind used for birds), coral rock, or dolomite are especially recommended. Gravel should be about 3 inches deep. If it becomes dark or discolored in places where uneaten food or other organic matter has accumulated, siphon it out and wash it thoroughly in fresh water. When it has been dried and purified, the material can be returned to the aquarium. No metal should be allowed to come in contact with aquarium water, for the sake of both metal and fishes; conditioned fresh and salt water will corrode many types of metal which may in turn poison the fish.

In purchasing aquarium plants, ask your dealer for advice. There are many suitable varieties—with and without roots. Too many plants—or too much unused fish food—can create a problem so do not introduce more than necessary. If aquarium water turns green there is too much algae in the water; this condition, which some believe to have a beneficial effect on the fish (protecting them from light) may in fact be dangerous, especially on hot days; the problem can be alleviated by starving the plants (feeding the fish live food or less food), aerating the water, or introducing a few quarts of new water from another aquarium.

Plant your plants at least a couple of days before you introduce any animals into the tank. It is most practical to start with some inexpensive fish, adding only a few at a time until you are sure that the aquarium is functioning properly. Other animals may also be added;

some insects are great fun to watch—leeches, water spiders, and various water bugs—and fresh-water pond snails and tadpoles will help clean up after the fish although they may also clean up fish eggs and grab food away from other inhabitants. A marine aquarium can also support tiny crabs, starfish, sea anemones, and sea lettuce, in the right proportions, of course.

It has been said that overfeeding fish is responsible for more aquarium failures than any other error. All unused food will rot and foul the water, as well as stimulate the growth of plants to a dangerous level. There are many excellent kinds of fish food available commercially—fish, shrimp, and brine shrimp being the most expensive, and dried food (made up of beef liver, cereal, and vegetable matter such as lettuce and spinach) being the most economical. A wet mash can be easily made at home from beef liver, Pablum, and salt, blended together and cooked and then dried. Cooked and carefully drained frozen spinach is also a good food. The fish should be fed once a day, and if any food is left after five minutes, reduce the next feeding accordingly. Live food, such as daphnia, white worms, and tubiform worms may be otained from your dealer and may be offered once or twice a week; the real enthusiast, if he has a large collection of fish, can probably manage to raise these at home or hunt up some live food outside.

A fish collection will become larger if you (or the fish) manage to have success breeding. Fish reproduce in several ways; most are egg layers and will scatter their eggs, in clumps (goldfish) or individually (zebrafish); or carry their eggs (medaka); or build nests (fighting fish and paradise fish); some bear their young live (swordtails, playing fish, guppies, and mollies). Consult your dealer or specialized texts for further information so that you will know what you are watching and can learn to prevent the eggs or tiny fish from being eaten up before your eyes. Other problems, such as fish diseases, will also require expert assistance; if a fish seems ill or injured and you can't get help, you are probably better off removing it from the tank and disposing of it before it can hurt the other inhabitants; dead fish should be removed immediately. Keep a close eye on the fish, and, if you want to be prepared to cope, bone up on fish diseases and home remedies.

Speaking of keeping a close eye, watching is not all you can do with fish, although it is a source of great pleasure and interest. Some fish will learn their feeding routines and may even recognize the presence of a human being (or whatever they think it is) at the edge of the tank, especially if you tap the glass. It is even possible to train fish to move to certain locations or in certain patterns if you are patient and use food as a reward. All in all, a rewarding activity for both student and teacher.

Brine Shrimp

These minuscule animals are probably the cheapest if not the smallest pets you can buy. Pet shops sell brine shrimp (or *Artemia*) as food for tropical fish, but they can be fun to raise at home for their own sake; one company sells them by direct mail as pets under the name Sea Monkeys, though they are in no way related to monkeys, of course. Brine shrimp are tiny crustaceans which inhabit salt lakes throughout the world; collected in egg form, they are dried—a process known as cryptobiosis, which enables them to remain alive in a dehydrated state for an indefinite period of time—and then hatched in water. Because they are salt-water animals, brine shrimp require a saline solution or marine environment in which to live. Ocean water or commercial preparations are good, but it is an easy matter to make your own: to a gallon of "aged" tap water (water left at room temperature for a day or more to eliminate chlorine) add 6 tablespoons noniodized coarse salt, 1 tablespoon Epsom salts, and ½ teaspoon borax. Be sure that the container (a glass jar is best) is very clean and that you replenish the water occasionally to keep the level up (aged tap water will do, because the salt will not evaporate). Add just a pinch of brine-shrimp eggs to the water, which should be kept at a temperature range of 75° to 90°F., and within a day or so you will see that they have hatched into tiny shrimp. In a few weeks they will reach a length of ¼ inch, which is about as big as they get. Young brine shrimp move in groups and will gravitate en masse toward light; older shrimp will pair off and swim in tandem, perhaps producing their own eggs in time. (If the eggs are to hatch, they must be allowed to dry first.)

Brine shrimp must be fed every day, and caution should be taken not to overfeed them. Dissolve a packet of dry yeast in ¼ cup water and add just enough to the salt water to turn it slightly cloudy; any more than that may kill the shrimp. Be sure to feed them every day without fail. If the container is kept in the sunlight, green algae may form on the side of the glass; although this may cut down somewhat on visibility, the shrimp will appreciate the extra food.

As brine shrimp die, they simply seem to disappear. But by this time you should have several new generations thriving and happy, if happiness is a state that brine shrimp enjoy as readily as they do cryptobiosis.

Land Hermit Crabs

Another popular pet-store item these days is the land hermit crab (or tree crab), which is almost as easy to keep as that recent fad the pet rock. Unlike sea crabs, land hermits are not aggressive and can be easily handled, although one must be careful to avoid their large pincer claws, which are used for climbing and for defense. A more effective defense, however, are the borrowed seashells the crabs live in to keep themselves safe from predatory land animals and birds. These shells are what account for the name "hermit," although in fact the crabs travel in groups of a few dozen to over a hundred, and one would do well to keep more than just one in captivity. (If you listen closely, you can even hear them communicating with each other.) As hermit crabs grow, they shed their own shells and their borrowed shells as well, exchanging them for more suitable sizes. They are hatched in the sea (which is why they won't reproduce in captivity), but they spend their lives on land or in trees, often going several miles from the ocean in search of food. In the wild, hermit crabs will eat fruits, vegetables, grain, seeds, meat, leaves, and decaying wood, but they thrive as household pets on tiny quantities of dry dog food, uncooked oatmeal or cornmeal, coconut, lettuce, apples, whole-wheat bread, and vanilla wafers, which are a special favorite.

The living arrangements for a couple of hermit crabs are very simple: a bird cage or covered dry aquarium tank with a flooring material such as sand or wood chips, a piece of wet sponge or cloth for humidity, a container of drinking water, and things to climb on. The temperature should be fairly constant at 70° to 85° Fahrenheit so that they will remain active, and a regular weekly cage clean-up will keep them healthy.

Hermit crabs can live up to fifteen years with good care, reaching a size of an inch or more. They need no leashes or clothing, but they will require a selection of pretty seashells to try on for size as they grow. Never try to pull a hermit from its seashell, since it would probably allow itself to be torn to bits before giving up its home. A warm, damp environment and gentle handling, however, will encourage even the shyest crab to come at least part of the way out, quite of its own accord.

3 DIFFICULT PETS

If you actually managed to read through the entire chapter on easy pets, we'll be modest enough to admit that it was probably not because the style of the writing or the quality of information was irresistible. No, I imagine it was that most readers were looking for the section on dogs. Considering that dogs are probably man's oldest as well as best friend, and considering that there are many millions of dogs in the United States alone, most of them pets, it will undoubtedly strike many people as odd or eccentric of me to think of them as anything but easy pets. But what about raising children? Surely as old a tradition and even more popular, but easy? Hardly. I'm not saying that dog keeping is necessarily as difficult as raising a child (puppyhood is much shorter than childhood, for one thing, and you don't need to train a dog to grow up and become successful enough to support you in your old age), but I do submit that keeping a dog is not something to be undertaken lightly, and it cannot be done properly in many households. A lot of people are attracted every year to wriggling puppies in pet-store windows or at humane societies, and they are persuaded by the low price that no great investment is required. But these people are often sorely distressed when they find that dogs need to be walked regularly (in the rain as well as the sun), that they need to be trained, that they need regular medical attention, that they can't be left alone for very long—regardless of breed.

In the last chapter we discussed animals that in spite of their differences require a minimum of care and can be kept in almost any home. There are exceptional situations, of course: an aviary full of budgies, a collection of valuable tropical fish, a houseful of cats may not be practical for most people. But kept singly, or in small numbers and size, and given the appropriate conditions, these animals should afford the average household far more pleasure than they demand in trouble or expense. This "difficult" category of pets, however, includes species that are not so adaptable to the average household or have certain requirements that may not be easy to meet. Problems may arise because of size, temperament, difficulty and cost of maintenance, special habits, limited availability, and legality (zoning regulations, permits, etc.).

The first group of animals in this chapter are domesticated species which, like the easy pets, have made the adaptation to human civilization with a good deal of success. They breed readily under human supervision, and much information has been acquired through research and experience about their proper care.

The second group of animals is rather more problematical. These are the wild animals, either native or exotic, which have been, are now being, and will be used as pets by a great many people. Not all of them—indeed, not many of them—are suitable as pets, for a great many reasons. In the previous chapter we discussed a number of wild-animal pets—turtles, imported and native species of fish and reptiles, as well as insects. Few of them are in any danger of extinction in the wild and none is particularly difficult to keep in captivity, though one should never approach them with the idea of collecting in large quantities, disturbing natural habitats, or keeping animals under bad conditions. To import or confine the wild animals discussed in this chapter, you may have to get a special permit in some states, and most of these animals would undoubtedly be better off left well enough alone, for the sake of the owner as well as the animal. You won't find ocelots, chimpanzees, brown bears, or alligators in this section—even though people have tried and succeeded (in a few cases) in keeping them; some of these species are endangered or threatened, some are downright dangerous, and others get just too damn big to be practical under any but the most exceptional conditions. But you will find skunks, kinkajous and others of the raccoon family, large parrots, and some other popular pets simply because you can find them in pet shops or in your backyard. I would not recommend most of them for any but the most dedicated amateur or professional, but pets they have been and pets they will continue to be until the law says no or until human impulses are no longer motivated by vanity or by the desire to exploit and become decidedly more humane. Orphaned or injured wild animals fall into a different category—though even temporary keeping may require a permit—for they can and should be released as soon as they can fend for themselves. This subject will be dealt with in Chapters 4 and 9. Undoubtedly the most satisfactory way to keep the native species as pets is to let them remain free roaming; the feeding of birds and mammals will be covered in Chapter 7.

Domestic Animals

The animals in this section are not so exciting as the wild species, perhaps, but they can make excellent pets for those people who are willing to dedicate a goodly portion of themselves (and their property) to keeping them healthy and happy. As with easy pets, I have divided the species according to type—mammals, birds, and insects. There are those (probably apartment dwellers) who would consider every animal in this section—with the exception of the dog and the ferret—impossible rather than simply difficult to keep as a pet; and there are others (probably farmers) who could argue that these aren't really pets at all. But somewhere in between lives the sort of person with a little bit of land, no zoning problems, and a real liking for animals who would find a donkey or a duck an attractive companion, probably easier even than a dog and certainly cheaper to feed. None of these is really a housepet (it's incredible what even a mild-mannered pure white duck can do to a room), but pets they have been and pets they will be nonetheless.

For most people who have them, pleasure horses give pleasure not only by giving rides, and I know many people who keep tiny ponies just for the fun of having them around. Goats can be highly entertaining pets; sheep are somewhat less responsive but they are less demanding in terms of space and food, and they do keep the lawn trimmed. Pigs, believe it or not, are both intelligent and affectionate, and even the gentle cow can provide soothing comfort along with a daily bucketful of milk. Obviously, in this day and age of economic stress and overpopulation, when we are beginning to realize that our food supply is not unlimited, it seems pretty self-indulgent to keep a domestic farm animal just because you like to have it around. And there are other arguments against keeping these pets; neighborhood dogs may learn to love chasing sheep, or neighbors may quickly learn to hate being awakened at midnight by a nervous goose, but my experience has been that families who raise a lamb or a calf with the intention of filling the freezer somehow rarely get around to it and end up with what can only be considered a pet. And resourceful people who keep chickens and ducks for the eggs they produce and goats and cows for their milk can keep their pets and eat them, too. So, for those people and for anyone else who feels that it is no more self-indulgent to keep a donkey than a dog, the first half of this chapter will be useful, even though it may seem more like a tour around the barnyard than the backyard. But first, man's best friend.

MAMMALS

Dogs

Most of the animals domesticated by man have earned this special status because of their usefulness as sources of food or raw materials or their ability to do work, but the dog is an important exception. Regardless of the kind of service a dog may be asked to perform, the primary motive for their relationship of both man and animal has always been one of companionship and working together. The dog may be submissive to his master or mistress just as he would be to a dominant member of his wild pack, but if it weren't for the fact that the two species were able to give as much to each other as they take, the relationship would not have been so successful for so many thousands of years. The dog has probably been domesticated longer than any other species, although no one has been able to determine exactly when or where this first took place or even what kind of wild canine it was that became the ancestor of our modern-day *Canis familiaris.* Some say it was the wolf; others lean toward the jackal or a combination of the two or another wild-dog type altogether, but most likely the forebears of our present breeds were several species of wild dogs first tamed and then domesticated in various areas throughout the world. All members of the genus *Canis,* though they may differ geographically and individually, are closely related, and many can interbreed, so it has been possible for man to produce different breeds suitable for different purposes—hunting, animal herding, sledge-pulling, and protection. Some have even been raised for food (in Central America, for instance) and some for fighting (right here in the good old present-day U.S.A., in fact), but most dogs have been servants and companions.

In spite of the lack of specific evidence relating to the first act of domestication, it would seem apparent that from the very beginning, the relationship between man and dog was symbiotic. It would have been a simple matter for a young wild dog scavenging around a camp for a bit of unused or leftover meat to become tamed by one of the human inhabitants, or for a hunter to find himself tolerated or accepted as a member of a pack of hunting dogs. As a social animal, the dog might even have thought of the human being as a kind of superdog, an effective (if dull-nosed) and intelligent hunter who never ate everything he killed. When you consider our vicious and ignorant treatment of the wolf and the coyote today, it is a miracle that we were ever tolerant enough to allow the dog to become a friend, but in those days we obviously had a kernel of sense, from which we have been benefiting ever since.

Whether the dog has continued to benefit from its devotion to man is another question. Of the more than fifty million dogs in the United States today, only about half are licensed; a large number of the others have reverted to a wild or feral state, or live, usually not for long, in a humane shelter for lack of a good home. There are a number of reasons for this surplus population of dogs, and most of them have to do with the irresponsibility of pet owners. A lot of people select certain breeds of dog without knowing enough about them and end up with unsuitable pets because of an incompatible temperament or because the demands of a particular dog are more than they can satisfy. Many dog owners fail to train their animals properly and find themselves with pets that are difficult or impossible to control. And a great many people do not neuter their dogs for one reason or another and produce quantities of unwanted, unplanned puppies. Even the planned ones are not always carefully bred, unless a professional breeder is at work, and the resulting animals are often inferior types. Most of the dogs in the country are mongrels or crossbreeds, and many of these are superior dogs and much-loved pets, but by far the greatest number of them end up in pounds or worse. A lot of bad things can happen to a pet dog—such as deliberate mistreatment, deprivation, and even overindulgence, but the three major failings mentioned above—poor selection, lack of training, and unplanned breeding, all of which result from ignorance on the part of the pet owner—are perhaps the most widespread and could be easily corrected if only adequate information were somehow made available to every person in the market for a new puppy.

There are lots of things to consider when you are looking for a dog. Lifespan, for instance, varies considerably from breed to breed, and generally the larger the animal, the shorter its expected life, though there are exceptions to the rule. Another question many potential owners have concerns the usefulness of their pets as guard dogs. Some breeds such as Doberman pinschers or German shepherds are well known for their intelligence and ferocity when trained as attack dogs; many of these breeds have been superb family pets, but it is rare to find the two qualities in the same animal. Terriers and miniature poodles may make far more effective guard dogs in any case, by virtue of their alertness and high-pitched barks. Any animal bred and trained for a specific purpose should be considered a specialist first and a pet second—or not at all. There are exceptions, of course: a golden retriever can be both a good hunting companion and a wonderful family dog with the children, but any dog owner who wants a pet that will also have some usefulness should consider the latter a happy dividend rather than something that can be taken for granted.

About one-fourth of the dogs licensed in the United States are pedigreed animals, registered as purebred specimens of a recognized breed with the American Kennel Club (over 115 such breeds are now recognized). This means that a lot of people have spent a lot of money for their dogs and should be in a position to feed and care for the animals properly. Many excellent books are available on the subject of dog breeds, and because the subject is a vast one, I won't even try to summarize or analyze the advantages of one breed over another for people in different situations. There are dogs that can be readily adapted to apartment living, and there are dogs that will be perfectly happy confined to a small run in a suburban backyard; there are other breeds or types that will be miserable without a lot of space and the opportunity for extensive exercise. Some dogs are gentler or more tolerant of handling by children than others, and some are skittish or snappish in active or confusing households. A number of breeds are easy to train or easy to keep groomed and in good condition, whereas others need a patient teacher or a devoted brusher to be at their best. It is surprising, therefore, how often a person will select a breed simply because it is fashionable or unusual.

The poodle is far and away the most popular breed in America and has been so for fifteen years; it has a well-deserved reputation as a friendly, intelligent animal that comes in a number of convenient sizes. As with many other popular breeds, however, some inbred strains have resulted from breeders (or puppy mills, which are simply businesses that supply a lot of pet shops) rushing to fill the demand, and many poodles can be high strung and emotionally demanding of their owners, if not downright obnoxious. It is a good idea, even after you have studied the qualities of a breed and made an informed decision, to be selective in choosing the breeder you buy from and the individual dog you take home. Never pick the cute, retiring little runt of the litter because you feel sorry for him; always go for the biggest and brightest of the bunch and you'll be more likely to end up with a healthy, psychologically sound animal.

This advice also goes for potential dog owners who prefer to shop at the pet store, the pound, or the local humane shelter. Put your sentiment aside, and don't fall for the first wagging tail or pair of mournful eyes you see. Almost all puppies are irresistible, and even a grown dog is hard to turn down when you know that its life will be taken if you don't take him. If you decide that a mixed-breed puppy is the one for you, it is, in the best of all worlds, a good idea to get to know something about at least one of its parents. That way you may have an inkling of what the adult animal is going to be like. Many times, if the puppy is already weaned and at the pound, it seems impossible to tell just what sort of lineage the animal has and what it's going to turn into. Practically speaking, the most important factor is the animal's eventual size, since beauty is only in the mind of the beholder and even the ugliest mutt can be a lovable and attractive pet for the right person.

If you are looking at an adult animal up for adoption, the main consideration is its temperament; some dogs may appear friendly enough when they are encountering human affection for the first time in days, but a history of mistreatment or deprivation may make the dog a bad risk for certain kinds of families, especially those with young children. Keep your sentiment out of the way and be prepared to return the dog if it doesn't work out, or shows the least signs of aggression when you get it home.

Once you have made your choice, treat the first two or three weeks as a trial period, but give the dog every chance to succeed. If the animal shows signs of ill-health, bad temper, or refuses to respond even to the friendliest overtures, you should be able to return it to the original owner and get your money back—if you paid any. Most reputable breeders and shops will not complain, though they will probably encourage you to take another one of their animals in exchange. Enter into some informal but written contract when you purchase the dog, guaranteeing you the right to return it for one of any number of reasons. In New York City, for instance, it is now illegal to sell a dog or cat without a health statement from a licensed veterinarian who has supervised or performed the vaccination of the animal and is willing to claim that the animal is free from all observable illnesses and congenital defects. If within two weeks the owner can present a statement from another veterinarian to the contrary, he is entitled to a full refund or another pet of the same value. (Intestinal parasites or injuries occurring after the purchase are not grounds for returning the animal.) If the seller claims that the animal is pedigreed and eligible for registration with a registry organization, he must also produce the documents necessary for registration or written proof that these documents have been applied for; if the papers are not forthcoming within six months, the owner may claim a refund or keep the animal and get half his money back. These laws are certainly a move in the right direction, and similar legislation should be in force throughout the country wherever pets are sold, regardless of species.

I would go a few steps further if I were writing up this kind of legislation and make it mandatory for every owner of a pet dog to make a few promises as well: to guarantee that the dog be properly licensed, checked by a veterinarian and given the necessary vaccinations within two weeks of purchase, neutered within the first year, and given adequate care, food, training, and medical attention for the rest of its life. (People intending to breed their dogs should be required to obtain special licenses or permits.) A suspicious sort might assume that this would be a move toward increasing the income of veterinarians, but in fact preventive measures are far less costly than treatment procedures.

The care and feeding of dogs may vary from breed to breed or size to size, and are influenced by age and condition. This information is available in summary form in the chart at the back of the book, although I would recommend that the new owner read one or more of the books currently available (some are listed in the bibliography). There are many pamphlets published by pet-food companies and booklets available in pet shops, and while many of them contain accurate and useful information, the responsible dog owner should go somewhat further, say in the direction of the local library, just as anyone who invests money or emotional energy wisely learns as much as possible about the investment before making a commitment. Books can also be obtained on handling, training, and even dog psychology, many of which are extremely valuable and should be considered required reading.

In spite of the fact that there is not space here for a detailed thesis on dog keeping, some useful generalizations can be made, regardless of canine blood lines, size, or personality, and should be made in any book intended for animal lovers looking for a suitable animal companion.

A new puppy is a pretty dependent creature—eager to love and be loved, constantly curious, active, hungry, and not very good at a lot of things. It's hard to know where to begin helping him adjust to living with his new people, but perhaps the best way is to feed him. Dogs are carnivores, zoologically speaking, and to most people that means they eat meat and only meat. This is not true, any more than it is true of cats. Dogs can and will eat almost anything that human beings eat, but since we are talking about practicality in this book and because the cost of food of all kinds has risen dramatically as supplies have become scarce, we should seriously consider what is the most economical, yet most nutritionally satisfactory food for your pet. Happily, the most economical commercial diet for dogs is also the most nutritious—a combination of dry pellets or kibble, water, and table scraps or canned meat products for palatability. The section on feeding in Chapter 7 includes detailed information about the products that are available and their relative advantages, or uses, in an animal's diet.

A puppy needs to eat at least three times a day until he is four to six months old, then twice a day until he is full grown, and only once a day during his adult life, though many dogs may be trained to be self-feeders, with food available constantly through the day. Water should be available all the time, and though vitamin supplements haven't been known to hurt dogs, they aren't really necessary unless a veterinarian prescribes them for one reason or another, usually a deficiency. The diet for large breeds, however, should probably be supplemented with calcium in the form of calcium gluconate, calcium lactate, or ground, steamed bone meal.

Feeding and watering a dog are only the first steps in its care. In addition to a proper diet, a dog needs a place to sleep that is dry, clean, and of at least a moderate temperature. There is no need to spend money on a special dog bed or pillow; a puppy will simply chew it up, and an adult dog will probably not notice whether it is velvet or burlap. It is never too early to start training a dog to stay off the furniture and out of certain rooms (such as the dining room) where its presence would not be appreciated, but the animal should have a place where it can retire in peace and comfort. A hall area is not good because of drafts, but a corner of some room where the animal can remain undisturbed yet keep an ear alert to the goings-on will serve very well. Another kind of training that should begin immediately after the puppy arrives in its new home is housebreaking, a task that many owners find difficult and frustrating. This needn't be a traumatic experience, however, and suggestions are given in Chapter 6 for the owner who doesn't know how to begin.

One aspect of housebreaking has to do more with training the owner than the pet—and this is the decision of where the dog is asked or allowed to eliminate. This may offer no problem for the apartment dweller who decides to leave his pet paper trained inside the apartment or for the country gentleman surrounded with woods and fields. But the people living in crowded areas should think twice before letting the dog defecate or urinate on the sidewalks and streets. In some cities this is illegal, though difficult to enforce; but in New York City where no law exists, the streets are literally foul with dog feces, which are a real assault on the senses and make walking between parked cars a true city hazard. More serious is the fact that these feces are apt to be reservoirs of infectious bacteria and internal parasites that can be picked up and carried by human or animal. People without dogs are usually the ones who complain about the mess, but dog owners have even more reason to wish for legislation. Neighborhood groups have been successful in some areas in setting aside a section of a block as a dog station and seeing that it is cleaned regularly, but these are not free of disease, often, and individual dog owners should be aware of the dangers as well as of the inconvenience they cause others as well as themselves.

THE CLASSIC PET RELATIONSHIP—A BOY AND HIS DOG, IN THIS CASE AN ENGLISH MASTIFF.

Unless you live in the country far from highways and other people's property and animals, it is not a good idea to give a dog complete freedom. Dogs are territorial and will tend to stay on their home turf as soon as they realize what its boundaries are, but any dog can be persuaded to stray—by a rabbit, another dog, or simple curiosity—and I would recommend keeping the animal confined in some way, either by a sturdy lead attached to a post or in a run or fenced-in backyard large enough for him to get exercise. Every dog should also have a leather or fabric collar to hold its license, rabies tag, and identification and a substantial leash. All dogs should be given at least a minimum of training: to come when called, to heel at its master's side, and to obey other simple commands (see Chapter 6).

Even before the housebreaking routines are completed, the dog should be taken to a veterinarian for its first checkup if it is a puppy or for a general examination if it is an adult. This will include a test for worms (take a fecal sample with you), a three-in-one shot for distemper, hepatitis, and leptospirosis, and a general analysis of the animal's condition. Additional vaccines will then be needed at four months of age; a rabies vaccine is given at about six months which is when most local authorities require canine registration. Yearly booster shots for distemper and the others, as well as a yearly examination, including a test for internal parasites, are all that's needed after the first year. A rabies vaccine should be given every one to three years depending on local laws and the type of vaccine used.

The first visit to the veterinarian is a good time to discuss feeding schedules and diet as well as to ask him for any advice that you may need concerning such subjects as neutering, which can be performed at any age but may be done as early as six months. Males and spayed bitches are usually registered for the same fee, and unspayed bitches cost somewhat more, but this higher fee, unfortunately, is very little inducement to owners of female dogs to have them spayed. It cannot be stressed enough that allowing any dog regardless of sex to go unneutered and unconfined is a real irresponsibility. (The law makers, incidentally, don't seem to have heard of sexual equality; unneutered males can cause just as much population increase as unspayed females.) Population control is an important motivation, but there are others as well; neutered male dogs, like male cats, are less likely to stray or get into fights. Female-dog owners will not find themselves collecting large numbers of males when their animal is in heat, which is often inducement enough to have the female spayed or to board her in a kennel until estrus has passed. Unless they are breeders, however, these owners are simply postponing the inevitable or evading the issue. Problems such as uterine infections, ovarian tumors, and mammary tumors are usually not present in spayed females, which many owners do not realize.

Because dogs are both intelligent and responsive, their owners often tend to treat them like real members of the family and to identify with them to some degree. Anthropomorphism is not necessarily harmful, though it can be expensive if one is into buying little Chanel-type collars, and otherwise putting on the dog; but it is unrealistic, and when the question of sterilization arises, the easy excuses are usually just a cover up for the real reason, which may simply be: "I wouldn't do that to myself!" Cost is the most frequent excuse, and it often comes from the same people who will spend up to $10 a day to board their animal during estrus (a three-week period twice a year). Castrating a male dog is a far less serious operation than spaying a bitch, but both types of surgery can be costly; an increasing number of neutering clinics are being established every year, however, and humane societies are helpful in providing owners with information about them or about veterinarians who will perform the surgery at a nominal fee. The ASPCA, incidentally, requires anyone taking one of their animals to guarantee in writing that the animal will be neutered within six months; only about 4 per cent of these agreements are ever honored, however. It is not a simple matter for the society to follow up on the failures, though they often end up with the results. See Chapter 9 for more information about both breeding and not breeding; the possible complications of raising a clutch of puppies may convince you that it's not worth the risk or the trouble, for either the animal or yourself.

Ferrets

I once kept a pet ferret named Stanley who was certainly as warm, intelligent, responsive, and reliable as any dog I have ever had. Yet when I would mention my pet ferret to anyone who had not met Stanley, the reaction was almost universally skeptical. "Isn't that some kind of weasel?" I'd hear, along with all those unspoken assumptions about the creature's ill temper. "What, a nasty polecat?" or "I hear that ferrets smell as bad as skunks!" And I always had to admit that there was some truth in these remarks. Ferrets are mustelids, members of the weasel family that also includes minks, skunks, badgers, otters, and others, and they do have two anal glands which can (in the males especially) emit a rather unpleasant odor. They are also polecats, or, more accurately, descendants of the European polecat (which was neither a cat nor Polish), though there are some distinct differences between the species now. What most people don't realize about ferrets, however, is that they are technically domesticated animals, having been raised since Roman times for the purpose of hunting rats, mice, and rabbits, and that any ferrets sold as pets nowadays are directly related to that species. (I

DIFFICULT PETS

am not talking here about the American black-footed ferret, a wild species native to the Northwest and now endangered.)

When European ferrets were originally imported into the United States, around 1875, their natural aptitude for ratting made them extremely popular. Many people raised ferrets in their backyards and professionals bred them in large numbers (in fact New London, Ohio, used to call itself "Ferretville, U.S.A." because many thousands of these animals were once raised and sold there). But because ferrets are natural hunters and because they are hardy, they soon became a plague for poultry farmers who were appalled at the ease with which a ferret could learn to love chickens and a life in the woods. So regulations were passed in many states, and the widespread popularity of the species became relatively narrow. It is still, in many places, necessary to obtain a permit to keep a ferret, but it is neither impossible nor extraordinarily difficult to keep one as a pet. Ferret breeders still exist (raising them primarily for fur), and most pet dealers can obtain them on request if they do not have one in the shop. Actually, it is probably best to go directly to a breeder for your ferret, in order to be sure that it is young enough and of a strain that has proved to make successful pets. Your most important responsibility—to the poultry farmers this time rather than to the ferret—is to see that it has no chance of escape. Releasing a ferret deliberately would be as irresponsible as abandoning a dog or cat or letting a cow or sheep wander off into the woods to live on its own. Ferrets would undoubtedly pull through, but you would have committed a grave disservice to your fellow man.

Unless one plans to breed ferrets (and this I do not recommend for the average pet owner for reasons that will become clear), it is undoubtedly best to pick a very young female. Young, because ferrets (like any animal) become more attached to their owners if they have been raised from an early age. And female, because they tend to be somewhat smaller, livelier, more responsive if less docile, and they don't have nearly so much odor. (They do display a rather unattractive vulval swelling during estrus, so if your esthetics are centered in your eyes rather than your nose, you might wish to reconsider and pick a male.) Although ferrets do not live very long—four to seven years—they do make ideal pets under good conditions. They can be given the run of the house, for they will quickly learn to use a litter pan, and they are no more dangerous (to humans or their possessions) than the average puppy. Their principal requirements are a good, balanced diet, a clean, very clean, place to eat and sleep and eliminate (all in different areas), and a certain amount of attention. Although ferrets are naturally nocturnal, they will learn to adjust to your schedule if you learn to adjust to theirs; most ferrets will sleep after eating, which can easily be arranged to occur in the evening.

Ferrets can also, of course, be kept in cages when unsupervised, so long as the cages are large enough to afford a certain amount of freedom and those three different areas for a ferret's natural functions. The cage must be kept scrupulously clean, and a nest box of some sort should be available for sleeping purposes. Ferrets have a habit of hiding uneaten food and it is usually in these nesting boxes, so be sure you ferret out the uneaten bits after each meal. These adaptable creatures can also survive in an outdoor cage, even in northern states, provided there is a warm nest box, a very secure latch, and no exposure to other animals, parasites, and nasty weather. Many ferret keepers like to combine all three—an outdoor hutch for good weather, the house when the family is home to enjoy it, and an indoor cage for nighttime.

Because ferrets are relatively intelligent (meaning more than a cat and less than a dog), they can be trained to obey simple commands, to be led by a leash, and to observe certain disciplines. Although they have traditionally been bred to hunt (and have been very useful as exterminators), hunting with ferrets is still illegal in most states, so this kind of obedience training is not recommended.

Otherwise, ferrets are more or less like dogs in terms of care. They will thrive on a balanced dog-food diet, though supplements of mink feed, chicken parts, eggs, milk, vitamin concentrates, and table scraps can be as useful as they will be welcome, provided the balance is kept, the portions are moderate, and new foods are not suddenly introduced. Ferrets are susceptible to distemper—both canine and feline—and inoculations against this disease and rabies are definitely recommended. Ferrets can also catch the common cold—from humans as well as from other ferrets—and because the symptoms and cure (rest and keeping warm and dry) are the same for both species, ferrets have frequently been used for laboratory research on this disease.

As I hinted earlier, breeding ferrets is not really as much fun as it might seem. First of all, keeping two ferrets is twice as difficult as keeping one. Second, the breeding process itself would appall any sensitive, romantic soul (if there are any left). The male ferret employs a form of courtship that only a female ferret could love; he (the "hob") literally beats her (the "jill") into submission, often injuring her, and carries on for several hours at a time. (Male chauvinists of all species, pigs or otherwise, please take note.) After a gestation of up to 45 days, she will produce six or seven kits in a litter, which he is likely to kill if the pair is not separated before the kits are born. Once the babies are born, the female must be left alone for about a month, by you as well as the father, and even then your presence must be unobtrusive or she will become frightened and possibly kill them herself.

Except for these trying times, however, any ferret that has been treated well and handled regularly and gently can be trusted to display only the most amiable of dispositions. As with any animal, even the timid guinea pig, precautions must be taken when children are handling ferrets; quick motions, loud noises, and rough handling may provoke a hiss or a nip, but only out of fear not out of viciousness. (Of course, the word vicious does not rightfully belong in a discussion of animals, since it implies vice and evil motives; it is far more appropriately applied to the bitten than to the biter, if the biter is a wild animal, who has been frightened, inadvertently or not, into using defense mechanisms in a perfectly natural way.) A cousin of the ferret, the wolverine, doesn't need much provocation at all—in fact, catch me in a weak moment after an afternoon of trying to treat a wolverine and you might hear "vicious" in the stream of other adjectives applied to the beast—but the domestic ferret has none of that temperament and responds as affectionately as any "easy" pet to kind treatment. Bites delivered in play are to be taken no more seriously than "love bites" from a cat or nips from a puppy, for the skin is rarely if ever broken, and chances of infection are nil if the wound, assuming there is a wound, is kept clean.

You have probably noticed that I have not talked much about the problem of odor. Right. There is no getting around it, ferrets do stink, and neutering doesn't help, as it does with male cats for instance. The scent glands can be removed, though it is not a pleasant piece of surgery; it must be done relatively early in the ferret's life, as many veterinarians are learning to do with all those poor skunks that pet shops have found such popular (though not recommended by me) items. But many people do not seem to mind the odor so much that they would give up the animal, and some have even turned it into an advantage, a kind of perverse air cover up for other household aromas. It's also a good way of finding out who your real friends are. However you may react to the ferret's own musky perfume, do not connect it in any way with a lack of cleanliness. Ferrets are naturally fastidious animals, requiring no grooming for they clean themselves regularly. No extra amount of cage cleaning, important as it is for the ferret's health and well being, will improve the scent. Keeping in mind, however, that females have far less natural odor than males and that their personalities are so naturally attractive, it is not impossible to live with this relatively minor problem.

Horses, Ponies, and Donkeys

All of these noble beasts of burden are domesticated species of the odd-toed order of perissodactyls (so-called because weight is supported by the third toe of each foot) which also claims the zebra, the tapir, and the rhinoceros; these for obvious reasons will not be mentioned anywhere else in this book. Horse keeping has been dealt with in numerous manuals, and I need not go into detail here about them, but tiny ponies and donkeys are often overlooked in those books. Most people assume that they are simply smaller versions of the horse. Actually they are far easier to care for and require much less food, because they are small and do not usually work as hard as their larger cousins. Although Argentine pygmy horses can run the affluent purchaser a $1000 or more, Sicilian or Sardinian donkeys, even those with pedigrees and elegant names, rarely cost more than half that, and a lot of them cost far less. In fact, their equipment—saddles, bridles, harnesses, etc.—may cost a good deal more than they do.

Horses come in all shapes and sizes—there are well over a hundred breeds. Though ponies are officially horses that are less than 14½ hands at the withers (58 inches) and belong to the same species *(Equus caballus),* they are different in conformation and temperament, as well as in scale, and are now thought to have descended from different prehistoric types. Certainly they are much hardier than horses and, like a humble donkey, require less than a quart of feed (if any), a day, plus hay or grass.

Truthfully speaking, the donkey—or, more accurately, the ass *(Equus asinus)*—is hardly a humble creature at all, and many enthusiasts believe that they are more intelligent, more responsive, and far more successful as pets. Asses were domesticated as beasts of burden long before the horse—over five thousand years ago—and although they thrive in hot dry weather, they are adaptable to temperate climates and exist in probably every country of the world. The name donkey comes from the English word "dun" and means small, dun-colored animal; the Spanish word "burro" is a translation of this nickname. In the United States, the word "burro" refers to the "native" ass, a misnomer because it was brought to America by the Spaniards. It is a combination of many breeds and an animal that, like the mustang, has in many areas reverted to a wild, or feral, state. Jacks and jennets (or jennies) are large asses (male and female, respectively), and the noble mule is an infertile cross between a jack and female horse; the hinny, somewhat less common, is a cross between a stallion and a jennet. The best pets of this group are probably the miniature donkeys imported originally from Sicily and Sardinia, but now bred in this country, and the burro. They are both small (28 to 50 inches high), docile, and easily trained. Unlike most horses and ponies, the donkey is not likely to panic in bad situations; their ancestors, the wild asses, were far more likely to retreat into the rocks than to run, and the first instinct of the domestic ass is to freeze, which has earned it unfairly the reputation of stubbornness. In fact the trait is one of common sense and the animal is being cautious rather than plain ornery. When well-treated, the animal develops a kind of doglike affection for its master, and experts say that it has more affinity for humans than the other equines.

One family that lives on a couple of acres of land recently fenced in a lovely large pasture area for Maggie, their Sicilian donkey, but they quickly discovered that Maggie far preferred to be near the house. Indeed, she would probably just as soon live in the house with the family and the other animals with whom she has developed a strong bond. Once, when Maggie got loose, the neighborhood children headed for the woods to look for her, and it was only after some hours that they realized she had gone to the nearest collection of people, a group of carpenters working on the house next door; they had simply tied her up and continued with their work. Maggie also gets along brilliantly with the local dogs; a husky once became quite infatuated with her charming ways and would stare longingly at her for hours at a time. Finally she got tired of his devotion and sent him on his way with a gentle but well-placed kick, the only one—to my knowledge—that she has ever aimed at a friend.

Maggie, like most donkeys and ponies her size, is perfectly content (except for wanting to live in the house) with a half acre of grassy land, which is carefully enclosed with fencing and furnished with a

MAGGIE, THE SICILIAN DONKEY,
GIVES MUKLUK, THE SIBERIAN HUSKY,
A WITHERING GLANCE
FOR ALL HIS DEVOTED ATTENTION.

small shelter. Her owners were not required to obtain a permit to keep her, but they did have to clear with the local zoning board before they built the shelter, which is no more than 5 feet square. A Shetland pony might need a slightly larger stall (8 feet square), but otherwise both species would find these conditions adequate for exercise and grazing. Water and a salt block should be accessible at all times, and a supplement of grain (Maggie gets Purina Omalene) and some hay given if the grass is not sufficient. The stall and paddock must be free of protrusions and noxious weeds, and all windows covered with screening to prevent accidents. Various kinds of bedding material may be used in the shelter (see Chapter 7); the stall should be cleaned thoroughly once a week and the bedding replaced, but droppings must be removed daily, along with any soaked bedding.

Grooming need be done only once a week or so, but if the animal has become caked with mud or acquired a batch of burrs, an extra brushing is in order. Hooves need to be trimmed when they seem to be getting too long (every five or six weeks if the animal is shod); a veterinarian should be able to handle the job, or a blacksmith if you can get hold of one, but the task is not difficult with the correct tools and the aid of a good text.

Tests for worms should also be done regularly, since parasites can be picked up from grass where their eggs are laid, but these animals are otherwise quite hardy, and disease is rare. The following symptoms, however, should be considered trouble signs and a veterinarian should be consulted if they appear: refusal to eat or drink for twenty-four hours; repeated coughing; high temperature (over 103°F.) and shivering or excessive sweating for no obvious reason; diarrhea for twelve hours or more; severe injury with obvious damage to skin or muscle; frequent lying down and rolling, with or without groaning.

If you are considering a pony or donkey as a pet for children, remember that these animals will far outlive a human childhood—they live twenty or twenty-five years. And remember, too, that ponies are animals and not simply furry bicycles or minature automobiles; they require careful handling if they are to remain good tempered and in fine condition. Feeding and cleaning schedules must be rigorously maintained; occasional treats are nice, particularly if they are used as rewards for good behavior, but too many of them can make an animal nippy when a carrotless hand is proffered. And any frightened or ill-treated pony or donkey is capable of delivering a pretty sharp kick, so one's movements should be steady and kindly.

Sheep and Goats

Tradition would have us try to separate these two species, and they certainly are different in many respects, but in terms of care, feeding, and petability, so to speak, they are similar enough to share a few paragraphs. Goats are smart and rambunctious, whereas sheep are dumb and relatively docile, but both require a good deal of grazing room (at least an acre apiece) and must be tethered or fenced in. Tethering is particularly desirable for goats because they are terribly good at getting out of fenced-in enclosures and because they love to nibble on trees and shrubs and can be moved into woody areas for brief periods. (Be sure you use a chain, though; they will eat organic tethers.) Both species need shelters as well, simple but secure, draft-free, and clean, with water and salt always on hand. Feeding is simple, especially if your grass is good most of the year round, and neither animal is likely to come down with diseases that a veterinarian can't handle. They sound, in fact, like ideal pets, but they aren't, for a number of reasons. Though quiet enough, these two animals can cause a good deal of trouble in suburban neighborhoods, mostly through no fault of their own. Anyone interested in having a woolly lawnmower or a ready supply of goat's milk at bargain prices should probably consider more conventional sources. Many communities, for instance, do not allow farm animals to be kept in the backyard, and zoning regulations must be checked before the animal is purchased. Perhaps more troublesome and less foreseeable is the distinct possibility that neighborhood dogs may respond to an ancestral habit and give them a merry chase, or a not-so-merry run for their lives.

All this aside, sheep and goats can be both attractive and useful to have around, and for the right person with the right place, one or the other (or both) might be just the thing. Although sheep may prove themselves useful by allowing themselves to be shorn for wool once in a while and by clipping the lawn, they are not nearly as responsive to humans as goats are. One friend of mine, who keeps several, doesn't mind at all that his sheep can't tell him from anyone else in the family who feeds them; he finds their presence both comforting and pleasant to contemplate.

Goats, on the other hand, may be less comforting, but they are far more interesting and equally useful. They provide manure for the compost heap; they can be used to carry saddlebags on a hike or to pull a small cart; they will provide wool for clothing; and they give milk that is far cheaper and, some say, better than cow's milk. Milking breeds (Nubians, Toggenburgs, French Alpines, etc.) will give up to three or four quarts a day for ten months of the year for up to ten years. Goat's milk is not acid and is less fatty than cow's milk (though equal otherwise in food value), and it also makes terrific cheese. The wool goats (Angoras and cashmeres) do not make good milkers, but their coats are splendid and shearable (if you can get the goat to cooperate). According to a woman named Oressa Young, who raises goats in Maine and is known locally as the Goat Lady, picking a good goat is a tricky business. While showing off one of her animals, she says: "He may be nice looking but I don't like him and I never did. If you take away his food dish, you wanna watch your hands." They are sensitive animals and sometimes downright ornery. Oressa prefers to tether her goats, not only because she doesn't have a large pasture but also because she believes that pasturing promotes parasites and food poisoning.

Though goats are capable of eating almost anything (except tin cans), they do much better on a regular balanced diet of grass, alfalfa hay, and root vegetables, supplemented with dairy pellets for the milkers. Given the chance, a goat will head for the nearest branch of leaves, much as a deer will, and they also like weeds and shrubs. Some plants do not make good fodder, however; cherry laurel plants, yew, and even buttercups can be toxic, and some firs and pines are too rough for a goat's relatively tender mouth. Goats tend to be hardy, healthy animals as long as they are kept dry and clean and are given sufficient access to fresh air, sunshine, and exercise. The same is true of sheep, which can be maintained on grass when it is available, good hay when it is not, plus root vegetables (carrots, beets, and turnips) every now and then; special concentrates may be fed but are usually reserved for pregnant or lactating females. With both sheep and goats, be careful about introducing large quantities of new food into the diet suddenly; this is often a problem in spring when the animals are let out to graze on the fresh, rich grass for the first time after winter. Whatever you feed, make certain it is clean and fresh; goats, for all their appetites, will usually not touch dirty food and can be quite fussy about the way in which they are served (some dislike eating from the ground, for instance). Like most domestic animals, goats and sheep like routine; if you are going to milk your goats, be sure to do so once or twice every day on a regular basis. Grooming may or may not be necessary, but see that the feet are kept trim and the hooves are not allowed to grow too long.

Before I make these animals, especially the goat, sound too attractive to resist, keep in mind that male goats can get very large, give off a rather bothersome odor, and become quite aggressive if offended. Both male and female goats are difficult to confine. They will jump any fence lower than 5 feet (although they may learn to keep away from an electric fence), and if they do, they'll head right for the flower or vegetable garden or go into any open house. They will also wake you up in the morning with a very noisy "baa," should you be late with the feeding detail, and they can be quite moody just when you don't need it. But if you're willing to accept these minor faults, they will be affectionate, fun to watch, and useful in their own special way.

Llamas

If sheep seem a little too tame for you and goats too bumptious, you might consider the possibility of another domesticated animal having the good qualities of both and some special ones of its own. This is the llama, a relative of the camel and a native of South America, where it has been bred in captivity since the time of the Incas. There are about two thousand llamas in the United States, almost half of them owned by private individuals who find them affectionate as pets when they are young, extremely useful when they mature (both as pack animals and as wool producers—about five pounds' worth a year), and wonderfully exotic as back-yard attractions. The care and feeding of llamas are much the same as for sheep, although they are quite a bit larger, measuring about 45 inches at the shoulder, and they need more room for exercise and grazing. They can (and should) be halter-broken at an early age, and can be convinced to carry packs for hikers or small children. Like the camel, the llama has a temperament to contend with, for it will lie down on the job if the pack is one straw too heavy and it will tend to spit and nip at strangers or even at people it doesn't like. This is especially true of males, which may become aggressive as they reach maturity. But if they are handled frequently and given enough exercise, they should remain docile and even good-natured with people they know. I once raised a baby guanaco (a wild relative of the llama) in my house because its mother was unable to nurse it, and found that within a month the animal had paper-trained itself to a convenient spot in the kitchen and had learned to play a rousing game of tag with my children. Even today, at the age of five, Suzie still remembers me, and, although she is no longer treated like a pet, she will come running across her pasture to greet me, not for a handout of food but simply for a reassuring hug. Guanacos are much more difficult and expensive to obtain than the llama, which is now being raised in this country, principally in California. A baby male can be purchased for a price ranging from $400 to $800 but a female might cost twice as much. Because the llama will live as long as a horse, you can count on having it around for twenty years or more. And if you buy a pair, you can start to grow your own.

Pigs and Cows

Like goats and sheep, these two species are members of the even-toed order of hoofed animals (artiodactyls), but unlike those relatively practical creatures, pigs and cows are difficult to consider as pets because they grow to rather enormous sizes. A full-grown cow can weigh up to 1500 pounds and require over 5 acres of grazing land—more than a horse and you can't even ride her. A young calf can be very entertaining in a small pasture, but a cow is fairly content without human companionship, except at milking time when she requires it. (A cow that has been bred and conditioned for milking can die if she isn't milked regularly.) Steers are raised from calfhood by many people who aren't farmers, and other than providing information about their care in the chart (see page 326), my only advice is not to name it if you plan to slaughter it. It's not easy to eat a steak when you know that it was once part of Junior or Joe.

Pigs are different. They, too, grow to very great size (a 2-pound piglet will at the age of six months weigh in at over 200 pounds if it's fed enough) and they, too, make excellent and economical material for the freezer, but they also make superb pets for those who can keep them. For one thing, pigs are smart, responsive, and easily trained—more so than cats, horses, and almost any mammal you can name. One young girl on Long Island taught the members of her dog-training class a good lesson by entering her pig and showing them how much more quickly it learned to heel and sit than their fancy shepherds and poodles.

Pigs have terrible reputations for being dirty, sloppy, nasty, and for eating like pigs. Consider for a moment, however, the conditions in which pigs are raised—small pens full of mud and garbage and too many pigs. You'd be dirty and sloppy and nasty, too. Given enough space, a pig will defecate in one particular area (unlike the cow), and given leftovers, a pig will naturally root out the best first, pushing the spoiled food aside. Unlike many animals, the pig never overeats to the extent of making itself sick, and that many of them do become obese, no matter how you look at it, is a simple result of breeding. Because pigs are generally more efficient in their conversion of food materials than most mammals, breeders long ago discovered ways of getting more for their money by getting more pig for their garbage. And as for nastiness, this part of the bad reputation comes from the well-publicized habit in sows of killing and even eating their offspring; chickens do this, too, but not for the same very good reasons. Experts believe that the sow behaves this way only if there are more piglets than she can raise or if the nutrients in her food are not sufficient to raise them properly or if she feels distinctly insecure about her surroundings.

Pigs do like to wallow in mud, of course, and this habit hasn't helped endear them to humans; according to Ronald Rood, who has written eloquently on the subject of animals that nobody likes, pigs love to wallow in good, clean straw as well and, furthermore, will stack it up neatly after doing so.

Like the ignoble rat, the pig shares many traits with human beings, which is probably why we distrust them so, yet if we are willing to forget our prejudices and admire the animal for its many good qualities, its appearance and its grunting squeals can be as attractive as anyone's, and not just to another pig.

BIRDS

Chickens and Guinea Fowl

Many an Easter morning has been brightened for a small child by the sight of tiny, fuzzy chicks fresh from the shell, and many a parent has been disappointed to find that these cute little things (if they survive their first few days) grow up very quickly into noisy, messy birds that can't be kept or killed for dinner ("But Mom, that's George! We can't eat *him*!"). Yet with the proper facilities and foreknowledge, chickens (and their gallinaceous cousins the guinea hens) can be perfectly good pets, and at least some of them can provide their owners with regular breakfast eggs. What is needed is space for scratching, a coop for nesting and for protection against the elements, grain, water, and neighbors who don't object to being awakened at dawn if the pet chick turns out to be a rooster. What with the growing costs of food, many people who have the room and no zoning restrictions (apartment dwellers need not apply) are finding a flock of laying hens a comforting hedge against inflation as well as an enjoyable and relatively easy hobby.

There are many different kinds of chickens, each one developed for a specific purpose, mainly food of one sort or another, though several varieties are bred more for show than for eggs or meat. White leghorns are the most popular producers of white eggs, whereas Rhode Island reds and barred or white rocks are good both for meat and for brown eggs. Brahmas and Cochins are usually raised as meat chickens; the elegant and often fascinating ornamental breeds—the white crested Polish, the long-tailed Yokohama, the Araucana (which lay blue and green eggs), and the aptly named Frizzle—are bred mainly for looks. One of the most successful varieties for a beginner with a small amount of space is the bantam which attracts serious fanciers and hobbyists of all kinds. There are a number of bantam breeds, each with different characteristics—mostly of color—but all of them are small and easy to keep in small quantities.

A small flock of six to twenty hens, with one rooster, is a good size for a single family to keep. They may be confined to a henhouse all year or given a small yard in which to scratch and take dust baths and a coop in which to sleep and lay eggs. Confinement of some sort is recommended to prevent wandering and damage at the paws or claws of predators; any shelter must be free of drafts and weather and securely protected against raccoons, dogs, foxes, and whatever else might care to drop in. Allow about 3 or 4 square feet in floor space for each bird, with one nest for every five or six hens and sufficient space at the feeder, water container, and on the roost. Since hens will stop producing eggs during very cold weather, an electric lamp will help keep production up during winter. Molting, which will take place occasionally (and even frequently if the birds suffer from changes in feed, temperature, lack of water, or sometimes for no apparent reason at all), will also stop egg production, but that will revive when the molting period has passed.

Frequent cleaning of the coop will help prevent disease and parasites, and fresh bedding (sawdust, wood shavings, straw, etc.) should be added to absorb moisture. Cleaning can be made simpler if the droppings can be caught in a screened-off area beneath the roost where it is unlikely to contaminate the chickens (droppings are an excellent addition to the compost pile, incidentally). Feed—which can be laying mash or growing mash, depending on the age and function of the birds, and which can be obtained from your local feed store—should be available at all times, as should water; grit is also a good idea because the calcium gives strength to their egg shells and the digestive process will be helped along if there is little opportunity for scratching. Table scraps, lawn clippings, garden weeds, hay, and goat or sheep pellets are excellent supplements. Eggs should be collected twice a day (more during warm weather).

If you should want to expand the flock and are fortunate enough to have a broody hen which seems interested in sitting on eggs all day long (this is a characteristic bred out of most laying breeds, but not bantams), simply collect a batch of eggs from one day's production and let her sit for 21 days when they should hatch. (If you let her simply accumulate eggs, they will hatch at all different times; to avoid confusion, mark the date they were laid on the eggs with a felt-tipped pen.) If you want to take the time and can afford the expense, you can hatch the chickens yourself with an incubator setup.

Chickens may be purchased at various ages—very young, which means that they must be kept warm, isolated from chickens of other ages, and fed chick-starter mash until they are feathered out; young pullets (twenty- to twenty-six-week-old females); or laying hens. Commercial poultry men or mail-order houses are the usual sources, and prices will vary according to breed, age, and quantity. Sometimes it is possible to buy chickens with clipped wings to avoid straying problems and with trimmed beaks to prevent cannibalism. If you are planning to add new birds to an existent flock isolate the newcomers until you are sure that they are healthy and will not contaminate the others. Regular care, good feed, and sufficient room should prevent most chicken diseases; mites should be watched for (they can be controlled by a special powder if necessary), and any sick bird removed immediately. (Have a veterinarian examine any bird that dies suddenly and without apparent reason.) If all is not well with your chickens, they will let you know it quickly enough by giving each other a difficult time; bad conditions can lead to serious henpecking in the hen house as in the human house, and cannibalism is a pretty ugly sight, so keep alert to any signs of aggression in your birds. Healthy chickens are usually very hardy and troublefree and will live as long as six to ten years, though active egg production may continue for only about three years.

If you are one of those people unfortunate enough not to live where chickens can be kept easily and to be the recipient of one of those tiny Easter chicks (the sale of which has been outlawed in many places), you may be able to find a poultry man to take it off your hands sooner or later. In the meantime, it must be kept warm (a box with some sand or litter in the bottom and a lamp to keep the temperature at 85°F. or so will be adequate) and fed. Chick starter or—if you can't get that—infant cereal softened in water will be fine; water, too, is essential and should, like food, be accessible at all times. If you keep providing the right conditions, the bird will grow up eventually into either an alarm clock that will get you up early or an egg layer, but if you are the type that would rather sleep through breakfast, and you enjoy a clean, quiet house, you'd better find the chicken a good home elsewhere as soon as you have a chance.

Unlike chickens, guinea fowl are game birds with rather less domestic history. In the sixteenth century the Portuguese first brought them to Europe from Africa, where they still exist in several wild species. The domestic guinea fowl, though raised commercially for meat, still have some characteristics of their wild forebears—a gamey flavor, an exotic appearance, and an exceptional capacity for making noise. Because they are naturally insect rather than seed eaters, they should be allowed a certain amount of freedom to scratch and wander (they will come home to roost with the other chickens), though a dietary supplement of high-protein grain is usually a good idea. They are more flighty and wild in personality than chickens, which makes it a bit dicey to keep them caged, but which also makes them more fun to watch, if you keep your ears covered against the high piercing chants they tend to emit when disturbed—and they are disturbed a lot of the time. The most common varieties are pearl, lavender, royal purple, and white African, and they are only slightly more costly than well-bred chickens. A guinea hen can produce one or two hatches a year, and given her freedom, she will do so entirely in private out in the meadow or behind a shrub. Sooner or later, however, the whole brood will turn up, extremely fuzzy and very fast moving. They will live from 4 to 5 years, alerting you to any and all intruders and keeping any close neighbors in a constant state of either alarm or irritation.

Ducks

Ducks make nice family retainers, like chickens, though they, too, have certain space requirements that must be taken into considera-

A PEEKING DUCK.

tion. Some friends of mine did keep a duck in their garden apartment for a while, taking it to the country on weekends so that it could swim, but the havoc wreaked on their porch was enough to drive them permanently out of the place. (In fact, they did move to the country, and I have a sneaking suspicion it was because of the duck, with whom they could not bear to part. In any event, they are much happier and so is the duck, which now has its own pond and some mallard companions.) Domestic ducks come in various breeds, and the easiest to keep are those that have been bred not to fly—such as the large white Peking. Unless you plan to trim the wings of the flying breeds, it is probably pointless to stock a pond; content yourself by watching the visiting wild species. A pond is only one requirement for ducks, however; an indoor shelter or coop should be made available in winter months when the pond ices over. Many ducks will find sufficient food material in a natural pond, but most domestic varieties should be fed grain (turkey or duck pellets) daily—about a handful for each. In addition to supplying eggs, ducks also afford a good deal of esthetic pleasure—from the Peking and

Mandarin to the more exotic Australian shell duck and the northern versicolor teal.

Although ducks don't rate very high on the intelligence scale, they do have certain traits that are interesting to watch, such as the imprinting behavior about which Konrad Lorenz has written. Shortly after hatching, a duckling will start looking around for a mother figure, and many amusing stories have been told about ducks that became inordinately attached to boots, dogs, and even grown men. A couple to whom I recently gave two young ducklings put them in with the chickens until the spring thaw opened the pond. But by the time the pond was ready and presumably irresistible to ducks, the now good-size white creatures were convinced they were chickens and refused to leave the coop. Even after they were carried down to the pond and set afloat, they would return to their "non-kind" time and time again.

Geese and Swans

These elegant birds are similar to ducks in many ways, Hans Christian Andersen notwithstanding, but they aren't quite so easy to keep at home. They are considerably more expensive, the rare breeds especially, and males can be quite aggressive and noisy. Both geese and swans are strongly territorial and will probably stay put, but since many of them are good flyers, feather-clipping on one wing is a good idea. Geese don't need a pond; in fact, they are just as happy in a pasture or on a lawn (though you might not be so pleased if you like to walk around barefoot; their droppings are enormous and not particularly pleasant to step into). Nevertheless, they will fertilize pastureland, and they do help keep down the weeds; however, they don't like tall grass. Young goslings grow quickly on a diet of high-protein grain, milk, and cheese, but adults will consume at least 75 per cent of their diet in green plants. In fact, many people have traditionally kept geese for the purpose of weeding gardens and trimming hedgerows. Extra food and shelter are not necessary for grown geese unless the weather gets very bad, but if you want to keep up some kind of relationship with them, a small amount of food every day will help. They do need access to water for drinking and preening, particularly when the pond has frozen over, so be sure to provide it, as well as some shelter for young geese.

Speaking of protection, geese can make excellent night watchbirds, and their tendency to react noisily in fear—often a disadvantage in well-populated neighborhoods—can be a real boon to the country gentleman who does not keep a dog. Their honking and hissing can be heard for some distance.

Geese, like swans, have the reputation for viciousness, and although it is true that a male during breeding season or a bird of either sex confronted with a stranger is capable of biting, they do learn to recognize the people who feed them and can be counted on to behave respectably if treated in like manner.

Swans are probably less useful on the whole than geese, and they certainly can't be considered as palatable, but the rewards of keeping swans are obvious. They do require open water year round, but who would want a swan without a pond anyway? Like geese, grown swans can fend for themselves and survive perfectly well on whatever they can dig up in the pond. But if you want to get on friendly terms with them, they will respond to a certain amount of handling, especially if the hands involved are well filled with grain or some nice green tidbits.

Peacocks and Pheasants

These two comely members of the galliforme order (whence the term gallinaceous, which accurately refers to turkeys as well as to game birds) were probably originally domesticated because of their prime asset: beauty. In this country the pheasant's beauty has been mostly in the mind of the hunter, as he contemplates trophies or dinner, though there are breeds raised by and for fanciers and collectors, who care for nothing more than to look at them. The strutting peacock—held sacred in India and profane in Rome as a symbol of vanity—can make itself useful as a watchbird, but still and all, it is primarily valued for its looks, which for many people is reward enough. Both birds were originally native only in Asia, but they have been commonly bred in captivity all over the world for centuries; in some countries pheasants have become feral by adapting to wild living far away from their natural habitat. In the United States feral pheasants are protected as game birds and cannot be kept in captivity without a permit. Because raising these birds is a fussy business, they are not cheap: an adult Java green peacock can run you over $600 though an egg might set you back only about $10; the more common blue India can be had for less than $50. Exotic breeds of pheasant (not our local ring necks) tend to cost somewhat less: a pair of tiny Mongolian pheasants may be had for less than $50, though a Mikado or Impeyan pair may cost upwards of $200.

Once the hurdle of expense has been crossed, however, and once you have set aside enough space for them to show off their plumage (as well as enough foliage for them to hide it in when alarmed), you will find these are hardy birds that will live to a ripe old age of thirty-five or so, given the absence of disease and predators. Being of the same family as turkeys, they are prone to blackhead, an intestinal disease carried by domestic fowl and nearly always fatal. And being as noisy as they are striking in appearance, they may arouse the predatory instincts of an angry neighbor, who can become as much of an enemy

EVEN IN BLACK AND WHITE, THE PEACOCK'S TAIL
IS AN IMPRESSIVE SIGHT.

as the hunter, the fox, or the local Irish setter. The piercing voice of a peacock, although it may ward off the marauder, is so human when raised in alarm that the disturbance is usually not simply an auditory one.

Most people who have no need to fear predators like to keep these birds free to wander on a lawn or piece of ground at will, as they would geese or swans. But they can also be confined in a wire enclosure (no less than 15 feet square for a pair) with a roost about 3½ feet above the floor and a ceiling at least 2 feet above that. As much space as you can afford is best, though, for they are excellent flyers and need room to fan out without endangering their feathers. Commercial game-bird diets are excellent for both maintaining the birds and breeding them. If no older chicks or adults are around, young chicks must sometimes be stimulated by green objects in the food to initiate pecking behavior.

Pigeons

Like the canary, the pigeon *(Columba livia domesticus)* is a domesticated bird, though it derived long ago from a number of wild species. However, because of its tremendous and varied usefulness to man, it has not generally been considered a pet. Pigeons are bred for racing,

DOMESTIC ANIMALS: BIRDS

for exhibition, for laboratory work, for meat, and, during wartime, pigeons have served many nations as message carriers. There are many breeds, some of them quite recent and some very old, since pigeons have been bred in captivity for centuries—in the Orient, by the Romans, and during the Middle Ages. About five thousand years before the Christians adopted the dove as a symbol of the Holy Spirit, the bird was venerated by worshipers of Astarte, the Sumerian goddess of fertility and sexual love, and it is still revered in Mohammedan countries. The Old and New Testaments are filled with references to the sacrifice of doves and pigeons for religious purposes, and even today the dove is a universal emblem of peace. Dumas, Dickens, and Elizabeth Barrett Browning, who kept doves as pets, were only a few of the writers who have extolled the usefulness, beauty, and virtue of this gentle bird. In the United States alone, there are thousands of pigeon breeders who raise them for fun as well as for commercial reasons and, in large part, for the love that pigeons have inspired in man since the earliest days of human civilization.

City dwellers may find this affection for the pigeon odd or even unbelievable, since the pigeon at liberty (simply a "common" version of the domesticated variety) has a bad reputation as a disease carrier and a general nuisance. Yet this reputation is somewhat overblown, for pigeons are not exactly the pests that wild mice and rats can be. Many so-called wild pigeons do carry ornithosis which they can transmit to other birds and to people, but pigeons well kept in captivity are no more a health hazard than any other animal.

Most pigeon fanciers do not keep a single bird or a pair but large numbers of birds in aviaries or pigeon houses of every variety. Yet it is possible to keep just a few birds, and since they respond well to gentle handling and can be interesting to watch—both for their behavior and their appearance—they can be classified as pets. A great deal has been written on the care and breeding of pigeons for the various purposes to which man has put them, but in a small flock, these birds require no elaborate facilities or attention. Before learning what pigeon care is all about, however, let's try to decide what kind of pigeon you wish to keep. There are flying pigeons, bred for racing or for their elegant types of flight, and there are fancy pigeons bred for their beauty.

Of the racing pigeons, the most popular breeds are probably the American domestic flight pigeon and the racing homer. These birds, whose owners have formed huge national and international associations that sponsor races (and the gambling that results therefrom), are trained to fly long distances and the bird that makes the distance in the shortest time, of course, is winner. Because pigeons have a natural homing instinct, they are simply released at a certain distance from "home" and their return is timed; young birds are begun at about 5 miles and well-trained older birds can do up to 600 miles, even in a single day.

Tumblers, and varieties of tumbler such as the roller and tippler, are bred for their natural ability to make elaborate patterns in the air as they fly. Tumblers are one of the oldest known varieties of pigeon, and their ability to turn themselves over in mid-air like footballs or athletes performing the backspring has been written about for centuries. They are bred in all shapes and colors, and their performances vary as well. The roller pigeon makes its series of revolutions or spins in an unbroken sequence at great speed for a good distance, whereas some tumblers make short rolls of only a few yards, and others "twizzle" (an undesirable trait) by spinning on the same plane rather than heading downward toward earth. Tipplers are known for their ability to sustain long rather than complicated flights, and the champions of this strain can stay aloft for as long as 15 hours.

Nonperforming pigeons are often bred for exhibit where their shapes and colors are the distinguishing features. Some of the best known breeds are the elegant fantail (called a "peacock" in France), the chesty pouter, the dainty nuns and stout priests, and the delicately hooded Jacobin. Many breeding associations in this country specialize in one or another of these types, and a pigeon show can be a most entertaining display of feathers arranged in an infinite variety of ways and colors.

The living arrangements you devise for your pigeons will depend on the type of pigeon you own. Flying or performing pigeons usually prefer to have their nests suspended or attached high up on the wall of the flight cage; other breeds—such as the fantail, parlour tumbler, and runt—are best off with their nests on the floor because of their lack of flying ability. Pigeon houses or lofts can be open to the air (though drafts should be avoided and roofs are essential), since pigeons can adapt to a wide range of temperatures. The height of the roof can vary, but 7 feet should be the maximum so that the enclosure may be easily cleaned and each pigeon easily caught. Floors can be either wooden or concrete, and there are advocates of both; whatever the surface, it should be kept clean and well-drained, and the walls—of wood or hardware cloth—should be firmly attached to prevent intrusion by rodents or other birds.

Nests should afford maximum protection and security and can be made of wood (orange crates are practical and cheap) with solid flooring to hold nesting materials of pine needles, straw, hay, twigs, or burlap. Perches are not necessary, of course, for the nonflying pigeons, but if they are installed, be sure that they are no higher than 4 feet from the floor of the cage. This way, the pigeon can never rest higher than the eye of the owner and will remain more docile.

Feeding troughs or hoppers should be large enough so that all the birds may eat simultaneously; the types manufactured for domestic poultry are perfectly satisfactory and not expensive. Water for drinking should be provided in vessels so constructed that the pigeon can fit only its head inside; since pigeons bathe in water, a separate container about 5 inches deep should also be available at all times. Grit containers can be of any shape, about 3 inches deep, and set, like the food container, as far as possible from the flying area so that it will remain clean.

Individual breeding coops are perfect for the owner with only one or a pair of birds, since they are easy to keep clean and help the birds to become generally more docile and more easily handled. Bathing vessels are not necessary but there should be individual containers for water, food, and grit. Sawdust or wire mesh (through which droppings may fall) are practical kinds of flooring.

INSECTS

Bees

Although MacDonald apparently didn't have them at his farm and one doesn't automatically picture a beehive as part of the farmyard scene, these hardworking fascinating insects have certainly done a good deal for man's stomach and thus can be classified along with the other domesticated animals. They are not generally thought of as pets but as honey makers, yet there have been people who kept them as much for their interest as for their usefulness. There was even a man in New York City who kept a hiveful on his fire escape for the fun of it (he lost them, however, when they swarmed around a lamp post on Broadway and were removed by another beekeeper), but most people would be advised to raise their colonies where there is a bit more room and fewer lamp posts. Observation hives—as opposed to the workmanlike commercial variety—can be kept in city windows if they are open to the outdoors and if that outdoors provides some park land or window boxes nearby. Anyone who has ever watched bees can tell you that there is a lot to observe; Karl von Frisch, who has written the definitive work on honeybees, observed so carefully that he learned to interpret their way of communicating with each other—a kind of dance language with elaborate patterns that can direct receptive bees to specific locations, even to places miles away.

Most bee keeping, however, is a real business, and there are several companies that produce equipment (and bees) for anyone who sends in an order. For the beginning keeper, kits are available for less than $50, including a hive—a wooden box with a metal top and several wooden frames to support the wax that will eventually support the honey—a veil and gloves, a feeder to hold the sugar syrup on which the bees feed at first, a smoker to remove them when it's time for extracting honey, and an instruction booklet. It is best to begin a bee colony in the spring, when the warm weather permits daily flights for the bees who will quickly learn to keep themselves with little assistance from you. You can start a colony from someone else's swarm but to avoid disease it is probably best to buy a package of bees which can be shipped when you want them. What you will get are a collection of worker bees (unreproductive females) and drones (which will breed with the queen and not do a great deal more than that). The queen is shipped in a separate packet; she is head bee, laying eggs and running the whole show.

As soon as all the bees have been transferred to the hive (a delicate business involving cooling, moving, and feeding the bees) you can assume that—with proper management and a lot of local flowers— you will have a flourishing colony by early summer. Bees will need to be fed until nectar is available, but after the first few weeks, they will make their own way around the neighborhood and build up a hefty supply of honey and some more bees. The color of the honey will vary according to the types of nectar that the bees select; clover honey comes early in the season and is light in color, whereas autumn honey comes from flower nectar and tends to be darker. The amount of honey produced in any given season can vary greatly, mostly because of the weather but also because of the number of bees you've got. When you extract honey, be sure to leave some for the bees to eat during the winter months (about a pound for every one thousand bees); otherwise, the only protection they need against the cold is a box placed over the hive, with an exit for warm days.

Because the extraction of honey from a humming hive is a technique that needs some special instruction and I am no expert on the subject, I would refer you to one of the various excellent texts available. Fair warning, however, in an area in which I can claim to be a victim if not an expert: bees do sting when they are alarmed. Nervous jerky movements will be enough to alarm them, as might your simple presence at the hive, no matter how much experience you have had as a beekeeper. Many people can withstand the pain and discomfort of an occasional sting, but many stings at once can be dangerous, and some people are so allergic that a single sting can be fatal if not treated instantly. Although gloves are helpful against stings, they are awkward in handling bees, but a veil is absolutely necessary, no matter how fearless you are.

Except for the stings and the swarming which occurs when a group of bees, centered around the queen, attempts to form a new colony, bees are not all that difficult to keep. They survive in cold weather when they pretty much stay in the hive, nourishing themselves on the honey they have labored to produce all summer (mixed with pollen, it is called bee bread). Their constant movement keeps the temperature in the hive as high as 90°F. regardless of the weather outside; if the temperature gets too high, the drones will make themselves useful by fanning the place, like the well-trained harem attendants they are. It is this hive heat, incidentally, that evaporates the water in nectar and transforms it into honey, which it becomes when the water content is reduced to 18 per cent. A simple process but one that man has never been able to reproduce. Perhaps we should pick up a few steps of that dance language. . . .

Wild Animals

Considering the number of books that have been written on the subject of wild-animal pets, the number of people who have kept them, and the number of wild animals we are still lucky enough to have in our woods and fields, this section of the chapter may seem surprisingly short. But it is clear that most wild animals do not make good pets, no matter how conscientious the keeper and no matter how much fun a living-room zoo might seem to be. No amount of conscientious care will replace the natural habitat for which the animal is adapted, and providing a substitute is not often much fun once the novelty has worn off. The species described in this chapter, however, have won themselves such fine reputations as pets (through no fault of their own) that they are given prominent places in pet shops and good copy whenever they appear in print.

Although some people keep them, endangered and protected species are not included in this chapter; for very good reasons (legal and otherwise) they are impossible as pets and will be treated as such in the next chapter. Also in the impossible category are animals removed from the wild and confined as adults and any animal that even if raised in captivity by a human "mother" may become dangerous when it reaches maturity, if not to "mother" then at least to the neighbors, the children, other animals, and even to itself. There are individuals of each species that will prove an exception to the rule: some tame bobcats may never scratch a living soul, and some chimpanzees may be happy enough learning a language rather than learning to make life miserable for their owners. But these are rare exceptions indeed.

"Difficult" wild-animal pets are neither endangered nor exceptionally dangerous as adults if raised from an early age by humans, even though they may be entirely impractical for other reasons. Some of them must remain confined if they are to be kept at all—safe from other animals, from the risk of infection, and from their own destructive tendencies (if you think that eating a curtain hurts the curtain,

DIFFICULT PETS

112

think of the animal's digestive tract), as well as from escape into an environment they cannot cope with. Most owners will agree that keeping these animals constantly in cages is an unsatisfactory solution, for almost invariably this practice reduces them to captives rather than responsive pets. The most satisfactory way of keeping certain wild animals is to use no confinement at all but to treat them as free-roaming pets—temporary guests who continue to retain their freedom but will allow themselves the indulgence of a relationship with human beings. This can only be accomplished with native wildlings, of course, and only in areas in which they naturally thrive.

Some of the species listed below are exotic animals that are imported from abroad because they are not native and have not been bred in sufficient quantity here to satisfy the pet market. There has been, unfortunately, an increasing traffic in (and increasing prices for) imported animals for this purpose (as well as for furs and scientific research), and the regulations governing this traffic are as inconsistent and inadequate as those controlling automobile traffic in New York City. The Lacey Bill, passed in 1900, was designed to control importation by requiring permits so that animals that could be proven dangerous—either to agriculture or to human beings—could be kept to a minimum.

Aside from that very vaguely defined and ill-enforced law, and the U.S. Department of Agriculture regulations restricting certain birds (primarily because of disease—both psittacosis and Newcastle's disease), there is only the 1973 Endangered Species Act to regulate the often inhumane but always very lucrative business of importation. There are, of course, some interstate regulations federally enforced, many different state laws, and local laws prohibiting traffic in wild or exotic animals or requiring permits to keep them. And there is also considerable pressure on the federal government to strengthen its present laws and cut down on importation almost altogether except for the purposes of zoological study and other significant and valid scientific projects. But the fur trade as well as the pet dealers and too many "researchers" have so far kept the regulations as vague and as open to interpretation as possible. Although it is likely that it will become impossible in another few years to import boa constrictors and tropical fish for private use as pets, most exotic-pet dealers will manage to survive. Some will turn to native species, a few will enter the black market, and—since many of these animals live a very long time with proper care—most will probably become used-pet dealers, if they can turn a profit doing so.

But at least the horrors now committed for the sake of the pet market will then be limited to a large extent. Because only young animals can be marketed as pets, dealers must rely on foreign hunters to find baby animals and to ship them to the United States. Consider the fastest, most convenient way to get a baby kinkajou, for instance, from its habitat to a home in central Ohio. Kill the mother, take the young, and ship them as quickly as possible in as large a quantity as possible to the dealer, who will distribute them to pet shops or directly to purchasers. If the animals don't die en route (and many do for lack of food, water, and even air), they will surely not survive the trip without acquiring permanent scars. Many die soon after arrival from traumas suffered during the shipping process or because the new owners have insufficient knowledge of their care and feeding. No wonder only about one exotic pet in twenty manages to live through its first year in captivity, as the American Humane Association has estimated. Even if it does survive, the exotic pet may soon lose its novelty as the new owner realizes what a bundle of trouble he has bought for himself. Release into the wild is not possible because these exotics are far from their natural habitats (who would go to the expense of returning a coati-mundi to Panama and what good would it do anyway since the animal would undoubtedly now be incapable of surviving on its own?). Most reputable zoos will no longer accept hand-me-downs, knowing that an animal raised as a pet usually makes an unsuitable exhibit or breeding specimen. Humane societies and shelters are usually the only alternative, and recent statistics show that the number of exotic and wild pets ending up in these institutions is increasing every year. Most of them, like the millions of cats and dogs that are deposited there, are destroyed for lack of a willing adopter.

Native wild animals may perhaps not suffer quite so dramatically, but suffer they do nevertheless at the hands of unscrupulous dealers who collect them by the carload in the wild (again after shooting the troublesome mamas if they must) and ship them to areas where they may have difficulty adjusting to a new environment. Many states do have laws protecting certain species, and some cities have ordinances forbidding their being kept in captivity, so that anyone who keeps a wild animal, regardless of how or why it was acquired, must check with the local and state authorities before he is fined or relieved of his pet, probably both. Ignorance of the law, as we all know, is no excuse for not obeying it, so it is essential to take this step, preferably before you take the animal, for its sake and your own. Though some of the laws are there for the sake of the hunter's pleasure, some are for the sake of the unsuspecting animal lover who does not realize that many skunks are rabid or that a grown bobcat can be dangerous.

One of the most important things to remember if you are considering the purchase or adoption of a wild animal rather than one of a domesticated species is that this creature is not in any way prepared by nature for a secure life in human environment with freedom from predators, hunger, and disease, as are the domesticated breeds which man has molded and adapted over generations of breeding to eliminate some of their natural equipment for coping with life in the wild. Fangs, claws, and other physical forms of defense are obvious pieces of this equipment, but so are the less visible psychological attitudes of fear, aggressiveness, and so on that enable an animal to deal with enemies or search for food. No question but that life in captivity frees the animal from the struggle to survive; nevertheless, all wild animals retain their natural inbred fears and aggressions which are far more difficult to remove than claws and scent glands.

Most enthusiasts for wild-animal pets will agree that it is essential to get an animal when it is very young (old enough to survive without its mother but young enough to be conditioned to life in captivity), but even the most devoted and loyal of wild animals will revert at some point to its innate instinctual mechanisms of defense, usually at maturity or later, when alarmed or threatened. On the other hand, having been raised in captivity, the animal has missed the conditioning that it would have received in the wild, so that often a pet has become equally unsuitable for survival there. A raccoon or a deer that has lost its fear of man would last no longer in the woods than would a descented skunk or a declawed mountain lion. There are even examples—usually high-strung animals such as cats and primates—of animals raised in a home environment that become unadaptable to any other; a recent situation involving the confiscation of some pet ocelots, which were removed from a private home and placed in a zoo, brought forth the opinion of experts that the animals would probably not survive in their new surroundings, regardless of the quality of care they received. So if you are planning to adopt a wild animal on a temporary basis, be sure that you don't make it ineligible for release by encouraging it to drop its defenses. In other words, don't make the animal a pet if you can possibly help it. Some animals are more adaptable than others—primitives such as the oppossum and the armadillo are easier to release than raccoons, for instance (see Chapter 7 for more information about feeding free-roaming pets and Chapter 9 for details on hand rearing wild-animal babies).

In other words, before you make your decision about the kind of animal you want, think about what kind of pet you want—one that will thrive in your care and share your home and your life, as it was bred to do, or one that will simply survive there.

MAMMALS

Armadillos

Imagine a mammal that is even-tempered, hardy, silent, cheap to feed, and easy to keep, with no fur to shed or get matted and no front teeth to bite fingers or chew slippers. An animal that will tolerate handling (even as a wild adult), that can be easily trained to a litter box, and is not endangered. Before you run out to buy, borrow, or trap an armadillo, however, consider the fact that although there are few disadvantages in keeping one, there aren't many advantages either. It's probably as difficult to love an armadillo as it is to hate one. It is not particularly responsive to human beings, except when it's hungry and realizes that the human being is a source of food; it is clumsy, has a pungent odor, and sleeps a lot (being crepuscular, it is most active at dawn and dusk); it has a tiny brain and is, as a result, slow-witted, hard of hearing and has poor vision; it cannot climb or swim very well, and its armorlike skin isn't particularly pleasant to pat. Because that skin has only a few hairs, armadillos cannot survive in cold climates and need a relatively constant temperature of 70°F. or more. And because they (like the other edentates, the anteater and the sloth) have no front teeth, their food must be soft and mushy.

Nevertheless, even if the armadillo doesn't make a very appealing pet, it is a remarkable creature, if only because of the way it has evolved with the relatively little equipment it has. Not originally native to the United States, the armadillo has, in a sense, adopted this country as a habitat, moving north from Central America into Texas about a century ago. Since that time it has continued to move north, in spite of predators and increasing cold, and is now common in most southern states and getting more so in Kansas and Missouri. Although the thick layer of calcified skin that covers its body is not as impenetrable as it looks, it does give the animal the ability to crawl into bramble bushes and thorny areas where predators cannot follow, and the smooth surface makes it a difficult animal to hold on to once caught. Actually, because the armadillo tends to be a single-minded eater, it is not difficult to approach one hard at the job of digging insects out of the ground or fallen logs with its long claws and even longer tongue. The armadillo has other defenses as well, which include digging instant burrows, finding existing ones very quickly, and walking through water. Through a curious capacity for self-inflation and an ability to hold its breath for as long as 10 minutes, the armadillo can simply walk along the bottom of a stream, which saves it the trouble of swimming and confuses a good many enemies. Internal enemies—the parasites—are few (perhaps they, like people, find the armadillo relatively uninteresting to live with), and though little is known of its diseases, it seems to be an extremely hardy beast that will live up to seven years if predators can be successfully kept at bay and food remains plentiful.

In captivity, the armadillo's needs are few—warmth, a clean nest for sleeping, water, and a balanced diet (mashed dog food with an occasional cooked egg), and a bit of room for exercise. But somehow there doesn't seem to me to be much point in keeping it safe in a house when it does pretty well by itself in the wild. It's not easy to tell when an armadillo is enjoying itself except at supper time, but I think we should assume that it enjoys itself more when it can forage on its own.

Opossums

Like the armadillo, the opossum is a pretty unappealing pet; it is stupid and slow moving, unresponsive to humans though easy to raise and keep, and increasing in number throughout the eastern United States (the opossum can survive in considerably colder weather than the armadillo). Unlike the armadillo, the opossum is a marsupial (the only native American species of this group), a primitive mammal that raises its young, which are born at a very undeveloped stage, in a pouch. And also unlike the armadillo, an adult opossum tends to be irascible and filled with internal parasites (it is not clear which came first—the parasite or the bad temper—but there may be a connection). In captivity they do little more than sleep and eat, so that a full-grown opossum can end up weighing in at 15 pounds. They are not particularly clean animals, and if not kept clean by someone else, they can look and smell pretty awful. Outdoor cages are recommended (out of direct sunlight), lined with newspaper and furnished with a pan of earth so the animal can get as dirty as it likes; at least it will be your good clean dirt.

Baby opossums when blind and hairless are almost impossible for humans to raise, but when they have open eyes and some hair and their mother has been hit by a car (which is usually what happens), one can rear them on a formula using a tiny dropper every 2 hours or so. They are ready for solid food when they refuse the formula. They will eat almost anything—dog food, cat food, people food, anything—as often as they can get it, though three meals should suffice until they are half grown and ready for release. (One of the best reasons to release an opossum is that it has fifty very sharp teeth and a very bad temper. An angry opossum will attack any comer and hang on for all it's worth until shaken free; gloves are useful.) They can be released without much preparation or difficulty, as they adjust readily to the wild (or not so wild); in fact, after a day or two an opossum probably won't even remember it hasn't always lived there.

The woolly opossum, a native of South America, is quite a different sort of animal, rather more responsive if no more intelligent. Its nocturnal activities if unconfined (not recommended) can include climbing the curtains or getting lost in the house, and it is likely to wake you up pretty early in the morning, just as it is about to go to sleep, for a bedtime banana. They can be convinced to share your afternoon hours when they will crawl all over your shoulders, but most of the time they should be kept in a cage. In spite of the name, the woolly opossum has a naked tail and ears.

Squirrels and Chipmunks

These furry wild rodents can be made so tame with hand feeding that it surprises most people to find them so wild when kept in captivity. Even a tiny chipmunk raised from infancy by humans will always have to remain caged if it is not going to wear out its welcome; like the domesticated mice and rats, chipmunks are high strung, curious, and disappear very quickly from sight given the chance to leap out of human hands. Unlike the domesticated rodents, however, chipmunks and squirrels—even those that are relatively responsive to people—will almost invariably bite if startled or handled roughly, and because many wild strains carry disease organisms (rabies being only one), a bite can be a risky proposition. Also, as anyone who has had an infested attic will readily report, these wild rodents (tame or not) are extremely destructive and can rip a pantry or a living room apart in a matter of minutes.

Nevertheless, lots of people have raised baby squirrels and chipmunks and have found them to be attractive pets, at least until the animals reach maturity and get the idea to strike out on their own. I have raised plenty of them myself and can testify that it is a very rewarding experience to watch a squirrel grow up from a tiny helpless baby to a beautifully furred adult, but I would always recommend their release as soon as they are eating solid food and are nearly full grown. Don't go running out to rob a nest, however; there may be plenty of these small animals around, but there used to be plenty of passenger pigeons, too, and robbing the wild of its wildlife for the sake of human pleasure or curiosity is hardly a justifiable activity. If you live in an area where squirrels or chipmunks abound, sooner or later you will come across a lost baby—one that has been abandoned by its mother for one reason or another. Be sure the baby is abandoned or orphaned; observe it for at least an hour or more before you take the step that will change that animal's life. Many mothers go off hunting for food and leave their young periodically, so don't jump to a quick conclusion. Pet shops sell squirrels occasionally, but because these are older animals, usually weaned, they will probably make unsatisfactory companions, even temporarily. They will have no particular reason to respond to humans except as captors and given the opportunity to join their own kind will definitely prefer to do so, unlike some hand-reared individuals.

Because baby rodents (and baby rabbits, too) have high metabolic rates, they digest the small quantities they can eat very rapidly and need to be fed rather often—every two hours until they are two or three weeks old and every three hours after that until their eyes are open (see Chapter 9 for advice about formulas and feeding methods). Solid food, which can include sunflower seeds, bits of apple, and toast or dog biscuits, should be introduced as soon as their eyes open and they begin to show signs of wanting to nibble. Combinations of vegetables, raw peanuts (or roasted unsalted peanuts but not too many of these), acorns, and other tidbits will satisfy their diet requirements. Water, of course, must be available constantly. Besides dishes to hold food and water, exercise wheels and branches for climbing, pine cones for nibbling (they must keep their teeth trim), and cedar chips for bedding are useful furnishings for the cage which should be large enough to allow considerable movement. Clean the cage regularly and remove any uneaten food that might spoil. You may also find yourself having to clean nearby walls, because these animals have a habit of urinating through the bars of a cage. They will also grab anything (curtains, for instance) they can reach through the cage, so be careful where you put it.

Once the animal is self-feeding, set up an outdoor cage, the larger the better; it should be outfitted like the indoor cage with the addition of a cover and screened sides to keep out direct sun, rain, and predators. When the animal has become acclimated to the weather outside, it is ready for release; leave the door open and let the animal choose its own departure time. They will adapt readily to the wild, particularly if they can count on free handouts from time to time. Don't overfeed them, however; as with all free-roaming pets, too much reliance on their human sponsors will make them less wary of predators and too dependent on a source of supply over which they have no control.

There are several species of native rodents—including the familiar gray squirrel, the rather obstreperous red, various ground squirrels, the eastern chipmunk, the least chipmunk (so called because it's very small, weighing less than 2 ounces at maturity), and the flying squirrels. I've heard many stories about flying squirrels from people who have kept these marvelous creatures in large "flight" cages (they don't actually fly but they do glide from tree to tree with the help of folds of skin between their limbs and flat tails that act as rudders) and who find them to be affectionate individually as well as entertaining to watch collectively. This is true, but rather than put up with the incredible noise and the mess involved in keeping these animals in a cage attached to the house (or in a screened-in porch, as many families have done), why not let them stay in their own trees and visit from time to time? They will certainly stick around long enough to raise their babies, and they will always show up regularly for snacks if you provide them. Bananas, apples, almonds, pecans, and grapes are good supplementary food for this purpose.

Anyone who thinks he might like to keep a tame squirrel in the house yet can't bring himself to keep the lively thing confined to a cage should read Douglas Fairbairn's *A Squirrel Forever*. The author's stories about the difficulties involved in getting the animal to a vet who could hold it, let alone treat it, and of trying to maintain his dominance of the living-room territory (he failed) over his intensely possessive—and very angry—pet should convince even the most ambitious that squirrels belong in the park or the forest and not in the home.

Skunks

Very few people would walk up to an adult skunk in the woods and try to pet it or coax it into becoming a friend, let alone a captive. If the fear of rabies is not enough, the threat of a potential squirt from the skunk's extremely effective defense mechanism certainly is. Yet there are many books and articles written by people extolling the virtues of pet skunks and describing the immense satisfaction involved in keeping them in the house. There are also many pet shops and dealers who are doing a flourishing business selling descented skunks and promoting them as animals that are easier to keep than dogs or even cats. They are praised as neat, affectionate, easily trained to a litter box, and immensely entertaining, provided they have been raised in captivity from a very young age and get sufficient attention on a daily basis. It's curious, then, how many skunks end up at the humane societies for disposal, and curious how many former skunk owners there are who have gone back to dogs and even cats. It is true that there are some dedicated skunk owners who love and are loved back by their pets, but in New York City, for instance (where it is a misdemeanor to keep the animal), a number of these dedicated skunk people found it necessary to form a club for the purpose of dealing with the very large number of problems involved in keeping them. The founder of the club, in fact, says that she spends most of her time trying to place rejected skunks in new homes. Because a descented skunk is relatively defenseless in the wild, one cannot release a pet skunk without ensuring it a quick and probably cruel death. And there are so many formerly pet skunks around, zoos and nature centers have more than they can deal with already. If a new owner for a skunk cannot be found, death at the hands of a humane society is probable as humane an end as can be provided.

The skunk—a relative of the otter, mink, and the other mustelids—is an attractive little animal, though it is probably its reputation as a repellent character that accounts for the novelty of owning one. (There are many cats and dogs that are equally beautiful if you're talking about pure esthetics, but where is there a Llasa Apso that will cause everyone on the street to look back at that furry beast on the end of a leash?) The skunk's reputation is, of course, based on the fact that it possesses two very powerful scent glands that emit an offensive musk when the animal is attacked or threatened with attack. We are all familiar with this odor, though few of us have probably ever had first-hand experience with it; the fresh odor is even stronger than the second-hand aroma we get from a dead skunk on the highway or from poor Rover after an unlucky run-in with the animal. (It is true, by the way, that tomato juice, together with some detergent and much water, will help remove the odor from clothing and Rover.) Most of us are also familiar with the fact that these scent glands may be removed (not simply tied off) from a young skunk, no older than 2 months, by a willing veterinarian. As pet skunks—particularly the striped skunk—become more popular, more and more veterinarians are becoming familiar with this nasty piece of surgery (and perhaps less willing to perform it) and also with the treatment of the animals, though there are still plenty of them who will not do the job themselves or even give a needed rabies shot. Rabies in wild skunks is prevalent in certain areas, and a pet skunk must be inoculated regularly, just like a dog or cat; they also are susceptible to canine distemper and feline infectious enteritis (also known as distemper), and should be inoculated against these as well.

Once the offending part of the skunk and the possibility of disease have been eliminated, however, the skunk is still not a untroublesome animal to have around. It is possessed of a set (four sets actually) of long claws which are as capable of wreaking havoc on flower pots, rugs, wastepaper baskets, and closets as they are on the fallen logs and underbrush for which they were designed. And since any skunk, no matter how tenderly handled, can display aggressive behavior when alarmed, these claws, though dull, can cause considerable damage to human flesh, as can the sharp teeth. Although it is possible to have the claws trimmed (or even removed), again it is a question of finding a willing and knowledgeable veterinarian. Trimming will have to be repeated at intervals. The only way of keeping the teeth harmless (short of defanging which is not all that effective unless you remove all the teeth) is to avoid alarming the skunk.

Surprisingly enough, most of the people I know who have kept skunks—albeit on a temporary basis—have left the animals entirely whole, scent glands and all, with never a mishap. Baby skunks are docile, like many other wild-animal babies, and usually thrive as much on the loving attention they receive as they do on the food they get. Unlike most wild animals which make delightful pets as youngsters—the raccoon for instance—the skunk may, with gentle and frequent handling, remain relatively docile and responsive to its owner. Because skunk owners are likely to be thought of by their pets as large skunks with curiously little hair and because skunks never use their odoriferous defense on other skunks, owners may feel quite safe with an intact pet, though friends, children, and other animals should beware.

But even devoted skunk people admit of occasional moments of aggression and irritable behavior, especially if their pets are confined in a cage. They can be given the run of the house or of at least a room or two, and need only a dark warm place to build a nest and sleep, a couple of dishes for food and water, and a litter box that will not get used. They may be destructive, however, and should either be supervised when loose or have no access to things that mustn't be destroyed or stolen for nest building.

Skunks are nocturnal and will cling to their natural tendencies unless patient training succeeds in "switching" them to a human schedule, but switched skunks, like housebroken skunks, are extremely rare. Another natural habit in which the wild skunk indulges is hibernation in winter, after a busy summer and fall of eating a great deal. A house-bound skunk may not hibernate, but it will sleep more and grow sluggish. One should avoid letting them overeat during the cooler months of autumn (apparently the shorter days act as a kind of signal) to avoid their becoming not only torpid but also obese, which can be unhealthy. A skunk's winter coat will become somewhat coarser and less shiny, but otherwise—except for increased sleeping—a skunk varies little in appearance or behavior.

Even in the best of times, skunks do very little more than sleep and eat, for though they look as sharp as raccoons, they are relatively low-keyed animals and little given to otterlike frivolity or responsiveness. As with any species, individuals can vary considerably—depending not only on their handling but also on their genetic makeup. One family I know has two skunks, one of whom is an affectionate, sweet-tempered creature who obviously likes people and the other of whom is a diffident animal whose biting habits encourage the wearing of heavy leather gloves. Both animals have grown up in the same household, having been captured as babies and have received the same kind of care, but different they are, for no apparent reason. Nevertheless, most skunks tend to be fairly placid animals by nature; with their effective means of defense they have very little need to run fast or think cunningly (their only real enemy, aside from man's bullets and the automobile, is the horned owl). Their ability to fend off potential predators along with the fact that their foraging range in the wild is not large account for the relative success of the species, one that can survive in limited forest areas in spite of civilization's inroads. There are probably more skunks in the United States now than there were in Columbus's time, and the striped skunk is still native to all states except Alaska and Hawaii.

Pet skunks may quickly become upset when they are lonely or ignored, and they can be very demanding of their owners for attention, which is why many owners like to have two skunks or a dog or cat companion for a single skunk. Skunks tend to hold their own with other animals, and if raised with a puppy or kitten, they may even become affectionate as well as tolerant, eating the same food, for skunks are omnivorous and need a balanced diet of meat and vegetable material. In the wild skunks are natural insect eaters—

one of the reasons several states have seen fit to protect them, requiring a permit for keeping them in captivity. They will also thrive on mice, rats, and other small rodents, as well as on snapping turtle eggs, so that most farmers (who will forgive the loss of an occasional chicken) find them far more useful than they are offensive. Far more useful, indeed, than they are in a human home, chewing on cat food and sleeping all day long, if you think about it.

The Raccoon Family

The enchanting group of animals known as procyonids (meaning predog for some reason or other) includes not only the familiar masked-bandit raccoon, but also the exotic kinkajou, the feisty coatimundi, and the greater and lesser panda bears, which aren't bears at all. The first three species are native to the Americas, and though the raccoon is the only one common in North America, the other two do extend their range into the southwestern states from Central and South America. All of them are clever, bright, amusing to watch, and extremely responsive to humans—at least when they are young. And all of them have been touted over and over again as marvelous pets, easy to care for, and easy to love. Let's see about that.

RACCOONS. Sterling North's classic book *Rascal* has delighted the hearts of millions of readers who have undoubtedly yearned for the chance to own a pet raccoon, failing to note that the book ends on a rather disappointing note—disappointing for the raccoon owner, that is. Rascal, when he reached the age of about a year, became far more interested in exploring his sexual prowess and the surrounding wilderness than he was in sticking around the house where he was once so well adjusted. And this is usually the way it is with raccoons. Nothing is more delightful than raising one or two orphaned raccoon babies (be sure they are really orphans, though, and be sure that your capacity for delight also includes a good deal of time and energy), and few wild animals are more rewarding in terms of reciprocated affection, if you can put up with their antics, which can be as destructive as they are amusing. Remember that raccoons are protected in many states and that it may be illegal to keep one confined without a permit (though it may be perfectly legal to shoot it most months of the year).

Baby raccoons should be treated with great care, for they are quite helpless at birth and relatively slow to develop (their eyes open at three weeks), and they need a cosy dry nest with plenty of warmth and no drafts, as well as some gentle handling to overcome their fears. Until they are about eight weeks old, they should be fed warm formula from a dropper or bottle (see Chapter 7 for details), but when they can lap up their food from a saucer, solid food may be introduced into their diet, for this is the time when mother raccoon would begin taking them on foraging trips. By the time they are three months old, they should be entirely converted to an adult diet, which as some garbage-can owners can tell you is anything and everything. Do take care that the diet is balanced; include no greasy or spicy food, and supply plenty of water. See that the water bowl is large and sturdy, and that the water is frequently changed because raccoons will not only drink it but also wash, play, and even urinate in it. While a growing raccoon should be allowed to eat until it is no longer hungry (about three times a day), don't overfeed them because like humans, they will become obese if given the chance. Plumpness in the fall is natural as a preparation for reduced food availability in winter, but too much fat will make them sleep rather than exercise or do anything else. Mother raccoons do not feed their babies but allow them to pick their own berries or find their own garbage cans, so don't attempt to hand feed a raccoon after it has started on solid food; it would not understand the gesture and might even bite for fear of losing the tidbit.

Raccoons are responsive, intelligent animals, but they really shouldn't be allowed an unsupervised run of the house, unless you are willing to bear the considerable consequences. Some friends of mine who raised a pair found that though the raccoons were easy to housebreak in that they would invariably use the same area for defecating, they were not exactly convenient in that they needed an area in each room and that area in the bedroom was the pillow on the bed.

But housebreaking is only a minor problem. Raccoons are insatiably curious and exceptionally deft with their tiny handlike paws, and nothing is safe from them. Perhaps a single room can be made hospitable—free of windows that can be opened (don't underestimate a raccoon), wires, holes in the baseboard, tempting cabinets full of medicine or clean linen, peeling paint or wallpaper, and just about anything else that can be picked up, pried open, or climbed. If that begins to sound like a cage, you've got the idea. Most people do use cages—roomy ones—for periods when the animal must be left alone, but be sure these can be securely fastened. One Connecticut family, trying to catch a raccoon for release somewhere not on their property, found that the animal managed to release itself four times from the Havahart trap before it could be captured. If you do keep a raccoon in a cage for any extended period of time (and I'd hate to see your house if you don't), be sure you give him plenty of indestructible toys to play with. A bored raccoon will soon fascinate himself with the lock on the cage, and you may find yourself having to furnish your living room all over again. If the cage is raised about 2 inches from the floor over a layer of papers or a metal tray, droppings will be easy to remove. Even if you leave the cage in a barn or outdoors, cleaning should be regular and so should playtime, or the animal may become hostile toward humans.

Raccoons are mainly nocturnal, but they can be switched more successfully than most animals, so that cage time can be sleeping time and room time can be supervised. The animal should be protected from other animals—dogs particularly. However, household pets and raccoons generally get along quite well, even if the permanent residents often harbor jealous feelings because raccoon guests can be quite demanding of human attention. (A woman once told me that she could swear she heard her cat breathe an audible sigh when her husband drove away with the raccoon on its way to release.) In the wild, adult raccoons are usually solitary, except at breeding time, but when they are young they are very gregarious, probably because raccoon litters are fairly sizable.

When the raccoon reaches about three months of age, make sure that the veterinarian checks it over for internal parasites and gives it inoculations for rabies and both feline and canine distemper. With proper care, they are hardy and should remain disease free until they are ready to be released. Raccoons as they approach maturity will become increasingly difficult to predict and may get quickly enraged or alarmed. Most raccoons can be released when they reach the age of about eight months, though some may be ready earlier and others may decide they would like to stay around for a bit longer. Sexual maturity may occur at any age after the first ten months, and it is at that time when release becomes almost mandatory.

One cannot simply drive a raccoon to a remote forest area and dump it, however. They must become accustomed to the wild gradually, with continued human support until they are capable of surviving by themselves. A raccoon must learn to forage for food and to adjust to a territory where it will not be attacked by other members of its species. Raccoons differ widely in personality and some take longer than others to adjust. Some people prevail on friends in raccoon country to see that the animal has sufficient food and water and an outdoor cage with the door left open so that the animal can choose its own time to leave. Others may release hand-raised animals in state parks (with the warden's permission) or accustom the animal, by daily trips in the car to the woods, giving the raccoon a chance each time to strike out on its own. The release area shouldn't be too close to densely populated areas, for human-oriented raccoons can quickly make pests of themselves by boldly marching up and demanding handouts from less obliging humans.

Obliging humans, of course, may welcome the chance to give treats to visiting raccoons, which they can consider free-roaming pets that will repay the kindness by showing off their young and allowing them to be played with. Of course raccoons are just clever enough to know that this is the best way to ensure a steady supply of handouts for generations to come.

COATI-MUNDIS. Coatis are like raccoons only more so. Most of the pet coatis that we see today are imported from Central and South America—though some have been found in the southwestern United States—and we must consider them exotic rather than native wild animals. This is too bad, of course, because it isn't easy to release a coati when it reaches adulthood, and most people who own them usually end up wanting to do just that. Although coatis are mostly weaned by the time they reach their human owners, they are not difficult to tame if handling starts at an early age; and they will be responsive, bright, and fun to keep. But they are as destructive as they are curious. They must be given as much freedom as possible because they are natural climbers and love exercise; however, they can't be allowed that freedom unsupervised if you care at all for your possessions. Be sure that the cage, if you use one and you undoubtedly will, is roomy, stoutly constructed, full of things to do and play with, and kept warm, for coatis are tropical animals and do not develop thick raccoonlike coats.

Like raccoons, coatis are omnivorous, and once-a-day feedings of canned dog food, dog biscuits, vegetables, fruit, and occasional eggs will be both balanced and varied enough for their needs and preferences. In addition to a good diet and a clean, warm cage (with a nest box for sleeping), the coati will need injections for both feline and canine distemper, A rabies vaccination is not necessary since it is unlikely to become infected if kept indoors. Internal and external parasites are potential sources of trouble, and the animal should be tested and treated for them as you would a cat or dog.

All of this sounds well and good, and so it is, for a while. As a coati gets older, however, it will almost invariably develop a belligerent attitude toward his former playmates, and play may quickly disintegrate into a startling display of hostility. Coatis are about as unsociable when adult in the wild as they are sociable when young, which is very. And in captivity, that unsociability can be downright dangerous. A coati can deliver a serious bite with very little warning and on very little pretext, so most coati owners, if they can't find a receptive zoo, end up having to confine the animal to its cage and give up all hope of maintaining a warm relationship with their pet. The coati by this time has become simply a tolerated resident that will spend the rest of its life trying to figure out how to get out of its cage.

KINKAJOUS. These charming creatures are as unlike raccoons as coatis are like them. Often called the honey bear, the kinkajou actually resembles a monkey more than anything else; it has a rounded face and prehensile tail, which it uses to grasp branches for support as it travels through the trees in its native habitat (Central and South America). Like the raccoon, the kinkajou is predominantly nocturnal, but it is not amenable to attempts at switching its schedule around and will invariably remain active at night, spending the daylight hours curled up in a round, undisturbable ball. Happily, the kinkajou makes up for this by remaining rather more docile in adulthood than its relatives, and with regular, gentle handling, it can be a reasonably trustworthy pet. They do, however, have the family trait of destructive curiosity and must remain confined when they aren't being supervised. The cage should be large, with branches for climbing and a nest box for sleeping (placed near the top of the cage); it should also be warm and free of drafts, because kinkajous are tropical animals and may not do well at temperatures below 70°F.

Although they are classified as carnivores, kinkajous don't seem to be aware of the fact and prefer an almost strictly vegetarian diet of fruits and vegetables, with dog biscuits and an occasional egg. Some will eat liver, bits of chopped meat, or live insects (mealworms, for instance), however; you can offer these as well, if you like, though many kinkajous may not touch them. Sweet foods appeal to the kinkajou as to other members of the raccoon family, but take care not to feed them too much; bananas, apples, and oranges are far better for them than marshmallows, and small amounts can be used to satisfy the sweet tooth. Water, of course, should be on hand all the time, but do try to keep the liquor out of reach. Kinkajous have a taste for cocktails, it seems, but very little capacity, so keep your drinks covered when your pet is on the prowl.

Once you get a kinkajou, have it checked by a veterinarian for internal parasites and given the feline and canine distemper inoculations. Kinkajous are reasonably hardy, except for a susceptibility to upper respiratory infections and a peculiar sensitivity to insecticides, and with reasonable care can live for as long as fifteen or twenty years. But most of that time the kinkajou will have to be kept in a cage, remember, which is a pretty long sentence for a relatively harmless creature that has been so beautifully designed for traveling long distances through the tops of tall trees.

CACOMISTLES. Imagine a combination of raccoon, cat, squirrel, and kinkajou, and you'll have a cacomistle, which has as many nicknames as its appearance would suggest: ringtail, coon cat, civet cat (not the musk-producing civet cat of Africa), cat squirrel, and *Bassariscus astutus* (meaning smart little fox). It is not cat, fox, or squirrel but a cousin of the raccoon, a very shy animal that inhabits the dry regions of the American southwest and one that has not yet, happily, become as popular in the pet market as its cousins,

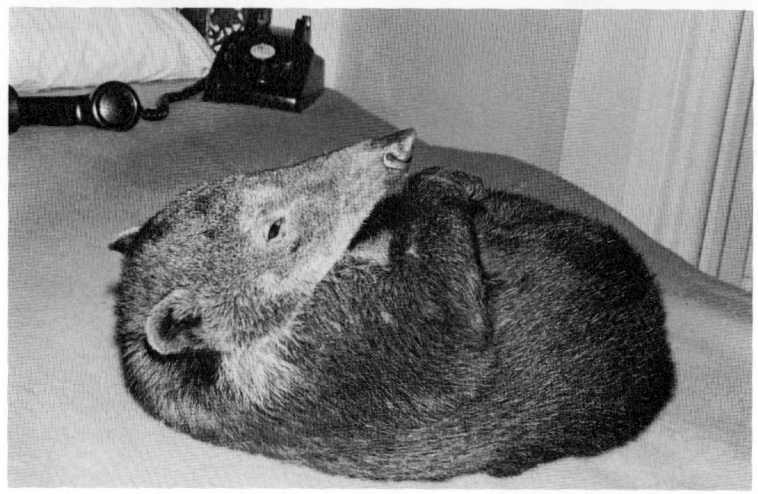

A RELATIVE OF THE MISCHIEVOUS RACCOON, THIS COATI-MUNDI HAS ITS OWN IDEAS ABOUT HOW TO RAISE

HAVOC IN THE HOUSE.

129

although some years ago trappers and hunters nearly wiped it out. These days the animal is protected in most states, so that pet cacomistles must be obtained from a breeder, and even then a permit may be required to keep it. Many people in the southwest prefer to keep them as free-roaming pets, because they are extremely active and difficult to keep indoors. Because of their natural appetite for mice and rats they make excellent pest chasers, and, therefore, are as useful as they are beautiful. They share many characteristics with the raccoon—nocturnal activity, clever hands, curiosity, and the ability to climb and eat almost anything. As pets, they are slow to become tame and trusting, although they will eventually become responsive if patience and gentleness are employed over a long period of time. They will remain shy in the presence of strangers, but unless you have friends who stay all night, this might not be a problem, for cacomistles are extremely reluctant to adjust to a daytime schedule. Since they require regular handling if they are to remain good pets, this nocturnal behavior may prove a problem for most pet owners. The cacomistle will quickly revert to being shy, and even to defensive hostility if the owner does not spend a great deal of time playing with it. The cacomistle should be cared for in the same way that the kinkajou is, with rather more meat in the diet (though overfeeding should be avoided), and rather more attention at playtime.

BIRDS

Parrots

Parrots were once imported in large quantities for the pet market and fancier trade, but restrictions are now nearly prohibitive for amateurs. Nevertheless, many of the larger parrots will live for decades and many will breed readily in captivity, so the possibilities for obtaining a bird of this type—be it an older bird on whom someone has given up or a young fledging—are not so remote that they must be treated as impossible pets. They can, however, be very expensive and this should be kept in mind. Like the small budgerigar, bee bee parrots, and other species discussed in Chapter 2, most parrots are seed eaters and, except for their size, are similar in terms of care. But that difference in size can make a considerable difference in more ways than one. Not only is a larger cage required, but also a stronger one (macaws have been known to demolish anything less than $1/8$-inch-thick steel bars). Handling is rather tricky until the bird has been thoroughly accustomed to it; a great beak and those large talons can cause a great deal of damage to human flesh as well as to steel. Even the noise seems to be bigger, though the vocabulary may be the same—or smaller, especially in some species such as the cockatoo from which talking is difficult to elicit.

AFRICAN GRAY PARROT. This species was once very popular because it is probably the best talker of all the parrots, but it is a poor breeder in captivity and has become extremely expensive to buy and difficult to obtain. Some of these birds will live up to fifty years, and it is sometimes possible to purchase "used" birds with full-fledged vocabularies; even these will not be cheap, however, and they may also bring along a set of bad habits that will prevent them from adjusting readily to a new owner or new surroundings. As with young birds, patient and gentle handling may work wonders but don't expect an ideal pet and do be prepared for a few idiosyncracies, verbal and otherwise. African grays are not unlike budgies in terms of care, except that they will need larger cages, wide enough to allow for short flights between perches, and some large sunflower seeds and unsalted peanuts in addition to canary seed and millet. They will also enjoy having some tree branches for chewing (maple, elm, birch, or any other nontoxic variety). Both sexes are gray with a short red tail.

MACAWS. These are the very large, long-tailed, brilliantly colored birds that are occasionally seen perched on people's shoulders in city parks or chained to huge perches in hallways and drawing rooms. Either way of handling this bird is unsuitable, however, because the macaw is an extremely powerful, potentially dangerous creature that needs a great deal of room to move about. They are hardy and live for many years (up to fifty), and all of the various species are very intelligent and very noisy. They do need a great deal of attention if they are to become and remain docile, but with good, constant handling they can be fine household pets.

The best way to keep a macaw is at liberty or in a large aviary. Like some other parrots they will become very frustrated and noisy if they are confined to a small cage or chained, and the sounds they make can be deafening, though their speaking voices are relatively soft. Because they are powerful enough to give a wire cage (or a finger) some serious trouble with either bill or claw, macaws should be approached with great caution.

There are several species of macaw, all from Central and South America. The most common varieties seen in this country as pets are the scarlet, the blue-and-gold, and the military, which is, as you would imagine, olive-drab in color with a bit of red on its forehead, wings, and tail. The first two species are brightly colored, and all types have bare skin on their faces. One couple I know has a military macaw which blushes quite considerably when he is excited, at which point he also comes forth with an extremely strong collection of obscene expressions that would redden the faces of many civilians. Cappy, as he is called, was given to them by a friend who commuted between New York City and Puerto Rico, carrying Cappy on his shoulder, and when settled giving him the freedom of the house and grounds. Although Cappy could fly into the jungle whenever he chose, he never failed to return at dinner time, and even now with his new owners and a relatively stable life in a New Jersey house, he is as tame as ever.

COCKATOOS. These are beautiful, large white birds from the Pacific Islands with distinctive crests on their heads. Like macaws, they need very strong chainlink cages and enough room to move around without feeling restricted. Although they do not tend to be as talkative as the macaws, they are very striking looking and will make reasonable pets if they are handled and treated properly. Like macaws, they are seed eaters and can be fed like the smaller parrots (the usual supply of seeds, fruits, nuts, water, grit, and vitamin and mineral supplements), with the addition of a little raw meat or mealworms every now and then if they will take it. They also enjoy tree branches (nonporous) to chew on.

AMAZON PARROTS. There are many varieties of these Central and South American parrots and as many colors as there are varieties. All tend to be large (about 15 inches long) and need the extra space and food required by the other big parrots. The yellow-headed

THE MACAW MAKES A MAGNIFICENT BUT NOT TERRIBLY COMFORTABLE SHOULDER ORNAMENT.

Amazon is probably the most common of this group, and there are various subspecies that go by different names; all are primarily green in color with yellow heads and touches of red and blue elsewhere. They can become good talkers if they are obtained at an early age. Because they do not breed well in captivity, they must be imported and are therefore extremely expensive and hard to get, but since they will live for some fifty years, you may be able to find yourself an Amazon that has outworn its welcome elsewhere.

Mynah Birds

Like parrots, mynahs are exotic creatures (though under the skin not much different from their relative the starling), and being foreigners, they must be imported unless they are bred in this country. Either way, prices may be quite high, because mynahs do not breed often in captivity except in large aviary systems offering maximum privacy with nest boxes. For some people the expense is negligible, because the mynah is probably the best talking bird around, repeating not only words as the parrot does but also human tones, as the parrot does not. The species is native to tropical areas of southeast Asia and India, with subspecies that vary greatly in size, though the average is 8 to 12 inches long. These are black birds with yellow bills and feet, and white patches on the wings; both sexes look alike. For best results, the birds should be obtained young and training begun right away; methods of training are the same as those used for parrots. Mynahs are easy to tame but because of their cost and also because they are extremely messy birds to care for, they must be classified as difficult pets, though most mynah owners are happy to accept the difficulty.

The reasons that mynahs are messier than most parrots is that they are fruit eaters rather than seed eaters, and their droppings are frequent and loose, so that the cage must be cleaned once or twice daily. As with all caged birds, enclosures should be adequately large to allow the animals some room to fly from perch to perch—of greater length than height, with large next boxes just in case they get the notion to breed. There are several pellets made for mynah birds and a regular diet of these, supplemented daily with fresh fruit (apples, peaches, bananas, etc.), and water, should be sufficient to keep them in good health.

STARLINGS. These relatives of the mynah bird are one of the few species of North American birds not protected by federal regulations, which means that it is legal to keep them in captivity without a permit. (This is no longer true of crows, however, which are indigenous species, as starlings are not.) But since a tame starling (and taming them is not difficult) will tend to stick around where it is welcome, it will be much better off as a free-roaming pet. When kept indoors, these relatively large birds need large cages which demand frequent cleaning because the droppings are similar to those of the mynah bird and can be quite tiresome to clean. Young birds that are being hand reared should, of course, be kept confined and warm for their own safety, but adults will become frustrated and noisy if they are kept in a small area. Crows, starlings, and ravens can be taught to talk when they are young, which doesn't make farmers or the Army like them any better but it does please a good many people who don't have the wherewithal for a more exotic species.

Infant starlings are not difficult to raise if they are not harmed or chilled when they are rescued. A warm, dry box and a special formula mixed with meat (see chart and Chapter 9) served at frequent intervals are about all they will need until they are full grown, at which time they can be released. As these birds grow older, they can be kept in cages outdoors, as long as they are shielded from direct sun, precipitation, and wind; a large flight cage is necessary, surrounded on three sides with plastic covering or some such protective device. Because these birds can be aggressive, it is best to keep them singly, until they are ready to be released. Starlings are famous for being thieves, but this is just because, like crows, they enjoy bright, shiny objects and don't see any reason why these things shouldn't be hidden in a secret cache for safekeeping. If you have valuable rings, therefore, you had better anticipate the bird's thievery and keep them tucked away in your own secret hiding place.

Toucans

Although these birds are difficult and expensive to obtain and very messy to keep (being fruit eaters like the mynahs), they can be successfully tamed. They are brightly colored, active birds and can be housed in aviaries with other species, after good, careful introductions have been arranged, of course, for the sake of health as well as peace. Even if kept alone, a toucan will need a good-size cage or aviary because it flies in jerky movements, particularly when alarmed, and can damage itself in a small cage. The roof of the cage should be covered with some soft substance so that the animal does not hurt itself.

These birds are native to the American jungle areas but like mynahs they will thrive on a diet of mynah pellets along with fresh fruit and some raw meat. Although they are tropical birds, toucans—and the other members of the ramphastidae family, such as the aracaris—are quite hardy and may withstand temperatures as low as 55°F., though drafts, of course are to be avoided.

4 IMPOSSIBLE PETS

The word "impossible" as used in the context of this chapter reminds me of that old military saying "The difficult we can do immediately; the impossible may take a little longer." In other words, as far as animals and people are concerned, the term is somewhat flexible. There are a number of dedicated people throughout the world who have managed successfully to keep in captivity any number of animals that I have put into the impossible category—even the toughest ones. Zoos do it all the time, and private individuals are doing it even as I write. Nevertheless, the animals that will be discussed here rarely do well in or around the house and owners almost invariably keep them in cages or enclosures that resemble old-time zoo conditions, usually without the professional expertise that any good zoo must provide. Amanda Blake, formerly Miss Kitty of television's *Gunsmoke,* has received a good deal of publicity for her success in breeding cheetahs on her ranch in the southwest, but she makes it very clear that not only does she have the required permits and the assistance of professionals when she needs it, but she also has no intention of treating her animals like pets. In fact, her unusual success with them is probably accounted for in part by that attitude.

Many owners of these impossible pets are the first to say that they would not recommend them to anyone else. These are special people, willing to rearrange their homes and their lives for the animals they live with, even to the point of breaking the law in order to keep them. Many will admit that they wished they had never started in the first place, and they routinely give out advice discouraging people from following their example. They know from bitter experience that it is not easy to dispose of an animal once it has proven itself difficult to keep, and they themselves are dedicated enough to their original commitment to stick with it, sometimes even taking in unwanted animals from less dedicated individuals. Although I have included information about the care of these animals in the charts at the back of the book, I have done so primarily for the sake of those who own them now and have limited means of obtaining adequate up-to-date information. Most veterinarians cannot or will not care for animals with which they are not familiar and many of the books and papers that are currently available are unknown to the general public; I have included some of these in the bibliography. It is my hope that the charts will supplement the brief species descriptions in this chapter and indicate to the curious pet seeker the expense and difficulty involved in keeping these animals alive, let alone healthy.

It is surprising to me, even shocking, that some of these animals continue to receive excellent publicity as potentially good pets. I have seen booklets written for children that make monkeys and alligators look as attractive as rabbits, cats, and dogs. There are pet stores in my neighborhood offering monkeys for sale with few or no warnings about the problems they may cause, and I know several animal dealers who advertise their ability to obtain for anyone (for a price) almost any animal that can be shipped from any place in the world and kept alive at least until the check clears. I have read books by people who have kept badgers, bears, wolves, owls, rattlesnakes, and chimpanzees—all of which exude the joy that these animals have provided. But these authors, even those who include the negative aspects along with the positive, do a disservice to the animals they love; invariably the enthusiasm that prompted them to write the books in the first place only whets the reader's appetite for a similar experience. One must remember that those glamorous advertisements showing beautiful human models sitting at dinner with a leopard or in a Rolls Royce with an ocelot are trying to sell jewelry and cars, not leopards and ocelots; gullible innocents searching for elegant possessions may not realize that these animal models are not pets but trained professionals requiring delicate handling by experienced individuals.

My criteria for including certain species in this "impossible" category are as follows: any animal currently on the endangered or threatened species list or that is generally "protected" by the federal or state governments; any animal that has been taken from the wild as an adult and confined; any animal—exotic or wild or both or neither*—for which being kept as a pet may be a dangerous situation. The word dangerous, like impossible, is a flexible term; some of the animals discussed in the previous chapter—such as the raccoon and the opossum—may become dangerous in a home situation, if not to their owners then almost certainly to strange humans and other animals. But they can be considered "difficult" rather than "impossible" for the simple reason that, although they may be kept satisfactorily in captivity for only a short time, they can be released safely when they no longer require or tolerate human support and be treated as free-roaming pets without threat of harm to human or animal.

*Laboratory-raised primates and ranch-raised minks fall into this category.

It is true that many of the species described in this chapter are readily adaptable to human handling when they are young, becoming impossible only when they reach maturity. Wolves are an excellent example; as cubs they are responsive and irresistibly appealing to people, but when they grow older, they, like any mature wild animal, can be extremely demanding, relatively independent and unresponsive if not actually aggressive. Yet by this time they have probably become unsuitable for a life in the wild, unable to fend for themselves without human help. The kind of expertise and devotion required to release such an animal into an area where it can become accepted by its own kind, knowledgeable about its enemies, and able to protect itself against starvation, exposure, and other threats to life, is far beyond the means of the average animal lover. If you come across a clutch of orphaned wolves—or foxes or any wild animal that you find listed below—don't despair at the thought that you must leave them to perish; "release" them into the hands of an expert who can provide professional care and save yourself—and them—the traumas involved in making them into impossible pets.

Endangered Wildlife

There would not be much point in taking the space here to list all of the species on the current list of endangered fauna; this list is readily available from the United States Department of the Interior (Fish and Wildlife Service, Washington, D.C., 20240). There are actually two categories of endangered animals: species in danger of extinction throughout all or a significant portion of their range; and species likely to become endangered, i.e., threatened species. A list of federal restrictions and regulations may be obtained from the Fish and Wildlife Service, and state and local restrictions—which vary widely—can be obtained from appropriate departments within each state, county, and city. Animals that are not endangered or even threatened may be protected in certain areas (deer, for instance, are "protected" in most states except during hunting season and then they are fair game only to licensed hunters), and permits must be granted if they are to be kept in captivity, even if one simply intends to care for an abandoned or injured animal temporarily. In some areas these permits are difficult to obtain and in others they may be impossible unless you can prove professional status. In New York City, for instance, one of the most restricted of all cities except perhaps for Los Angeles, it is illegal for any private individual to keep in captivity any wild animal considered dangerous to humans by the Board of Health. When I asked a local pet dealer why he was offering skunks for sale in a neighborhood where they they could not be kept, he just shrugged and said, "Well, maybe someone from out of town will buy it. It isn't illegal for me to *sell* it." Of course, he was counting on the fact that many people do own these animals in the city without knowing the law—and without trying to find out whether permits are necessary or even possible to get. Nevertheless, city and state authorities are increasing the number of confiscations each year, forcing people to move, give up their animals, or behave furtively and live in constant fear of being found out.

In spite of the incredible variations in these laws from one place to another and in spite of their occasional stupidities (ferrets, for instance, which can be as easy to keep as dogs and are even technically domesticated, are considered dangerous wild animals in New York City, while legally certain kinds of monkeys and all dogs, no matter how aggressive or untrained, are harmless housepets), the regulations pertaining to endangered species are entirely sound and not enforced nearly as often as they should be. Although I don't like to echo the hysterical tone that animal lovers indulge in from time to time as they protest captivity for all wild animals, I must admit that they often have sound reasoning to back up the moral outrage. There is, to put it simply, no excuse for anyone in this enlightened day and age to buy, steal, or smuggle any endangered or threatened animal for use as a pet. One cannot be an animal lover and restrict one's affection and admiration to a single individual at the expense of the species as a whole. If it is "love" that prompts someone to purchase an ocelot (and it takes a lot of something to want to spend over $1000 for an animal that is likely to overturn your household if it doesn't destroy itself first), then it is simple love of self, not love of animal. I am not denying that those people who already have ocelots feel a genuine love for their pets—they'd have to or they couldn't keep the animals—but one cannot love a pet before one gets it home.

Although most people would probably not be interested in keeping a humpback chub, an unarmored three-spine stickleback, or a sperm whale in the living-room aquarium, there are many species on the endangered list that seem attractive to potential pet owners for any number of reasons. The peregrine falcon, several kinds of Chinese pheasants, Australian parrots, and Caribbean finches would certainly be impressive additions to an aviary if you didn't know they were on the verge of extinction. Brazilian woolly monkeys and Costa Rican spider monkeys are also on the way out (thanks in large part to the demand for them as pets as well as to encroaching human civilization in their native habitats). The eastern timber wolf might make a fine guard dog, and the black-footed ferret of western Canada and the United States could undoubtedly be tamed into pleasing submission with the right handling, if one could find them, that is. And, of course, there are the cats—the beautiful, exotic, and at one time exceedingly popular (popular as coats even more than as pets) ocelot, tiger, leopard, cheetah, and jaguar. All of these, and others, are becoming increasingly rare. Yet there is still a demand for them, and that demand will continue to diminish their numbers. It may look like fun to walk down a busy street with a cheetah or a leopard cub on a leash, but you may be sure it's no fun for the cat and that the environment requiring separation from its own kind will ensure its development as a neurotic animal that may never breed or raise young successfully. Unfortunately wild animals are often unable to adapt to an environment—even a more natural or congenial one—other than the one in which they were reared, which brings us around to the fact that an animal captured in the wild can never become a suitable pet if it is not taken in infancy and reared in captivity by human beings.

Adult Wild Animals

There have been fascinating studies published about the socializing behavior of adult wolves with human beings, indicating that even wolves that were not hand reared from infancy or even confronted by people until adulthood could become responsive in appropriate conditions, displaying friendliness and even affection toward humans. Nevertheless, these wolves required nearly a year of frequent and expert handling before their fears were sufficiently allayed to enable them to approach humans without aggression. And when you consider that wolves are unusually intelligent, curious, and social by nature (like our domestic dog, to which it is so closely related), you can imagine how much longer it might take for another kind of animal—less intelligent, less social—to become adequately accustomed to human handling. In these studies even wolves raised from infancy with humans showed a tendency to revert to a "wild" aggressive state if careful handling were not continued well into adulthood, and under the best of circumstances they proved dangerous with strangers, particularly animals and children, to say nothing of destructive to objects.

T. H. White in his book *The Goshawk* explains in eloquent and painful detail the ordeal involved in taming and eventually winning over his new bird, acquired as an adult. The process of dispelling a wild animal's fear of anything unfamiliar is an exceptionally time-consuming occupation, requiring the utmost dedication and patience on the part of the human involved. Even after a certain amount of trust or understanding has been achieved, the animal never becomes so "trustworthy" that it can be treated as an equal or as a member of the family, so to speak. The least hint of something unfamiliar—be it a place, an object, or a strange person or even a strange gesture—will set off the natural fear processes in the animal and it will respond by trying to escape or to attack the offending party.

Although one may be successful in controlling the behavior of his captive, by use of restraining devices or expert handling, a wild animal will never become a pet in the true sense of the word, because one can never let down one's guard, even if the feeling of companionship seems to be mutual and communication is two way. A wild animal (and even many domestic ones) can't be entirely trusted to behave predictably unless the human also behaves predictably in the eyes of the animal. The animal may become accustomed to a person's presence and willing to tolerate that presence so long as conditions are acceptable. But only those people who have an enormous amount of experience in handling wild animals are likely to know enough about what those conditions are to make certain that they are maintained.

Dangerous Animals

Roger Caras once wrote a long book devoted to animals that have proven dangerous to man; I do not need to list them all here, since he included many species that not even the most eccentric animal lover would care to consider a pet. He also left out a number of animals that many people consider dangerous in the extreme (such as human beings). Most pet owners can tolerate a few bites or scratches—assuming, correctly enough, that an animal's instinctive reaction when frightened or threatened is to use the equipment it has to defend itself. Most wild animals will flee rather than attack an enemy, but in a captive situation an animal often has no opportunity to flee and must use whatever means it has (even if those means were designed for hunting food) in a desperate attempt to survive what it senses is a threat to its life. But although these tolerant people may be willing to risk their own safety for the thrill of handling a so-called dangerous animal, no one who lives in a social situation—be it a household or a neighborhood where other people or animals are living—can afford to put others into jeopardy. Recently, a young boy lost his pet Egyptian cobra in Illinois and became distressed by the furor raised by neighbors and the police. "Seymour isn't dangerous," he said, "but I'm worried that somebody is going to get hurt because of all the hysterics." When you realize that the venom of an Egyptian cobra is powerful enough to kill a human being within a matter of hours, however, there would seem to be plenty of reason for hysterics.

Not only wild animals may be dangerous; a perfectly well-bred dog can also "turn" and become a biter, and if it is a large mastiff or a Saint Bernard, the damage done may be considerable. But these so-called vicious dogs are the exception rather than the rule, and their behavior may be caused by anything from bad treatment to physiological disturbance. Animals carrying lethal disease organisms—such as rabies, which can infect any mammal that has not been inoculated against it, or the plague bacillus, once commonly carried by fleas that were carried by rats—will, of course be dangerous to man as well as to other animals. However, animals that are dangerous because they have been mistreated or because they are diseased do not come into the range of this chapter (see Chapter 6 for the former and Chapter 8 for the latter). One should, however, be extremely cautious in handling any domestic animal that is unusually aggressive or any wild animal that is unusually tame. Infected wild animals may often fail to show normal signs of fear and should be avoided like, well, like the plague.

Some species I consider impossible as pets because their size is as dangerous as their temperament. A hug delivered by a chimpanzee or a bear even as an expression of affection (unlikely in any event) can be a pretty bad experience for a human being; a timid deer if cornered can do a great deal of damage with one well-placed kick. But size is not always the most important consideration; a tiny field mouse—even one that is not dangerously infected—can be a harmful animal to keep as a pet for it can never be as successfully tamed as its domestic counterpart and will always be more likely to bite the hand that feeds it than to tolerate a caress.

Another element of danger in pet keeping all too few people tend to consider: danger to the animal. We have spoken of the danger involved in raising wild wolves in captivity—not only the danger they themselves may cause as aggressive animals but also the danger to the animal caused by rearing them away from their own kind. Captivity poses a particular threat to highly social animals, as monkeys, causing such great psychological damage that physical health may be affected. Because amateur pet owners may not be expected to have the facilities or expertise to provide the conditions required by particularly demanding animals, certain creatures must be considered impossible as pets. I would discourage anyone from keeping an animal without sufficient knowledge of that animal's needs which must determine diet, housing, social life, and so on; but when it is unlikely that even the most dedicated owner can satisfy these requirements—as in the case of monkeys about which too little is known even by experts—that animal should not be kept in the home, for its survival will be severely threatened.

You will find in the following pages many animals to which more than one of my criteria will apply. Some endangered species and most adult wild animals are dangerous to man or excessively demanding in their requirements for survival, so that they may be impossible to keep alive for long in a captive situation. Many people will argue that zoos, circuses, research laboratories, and the like should also be discouraged (if not officially prevented) from keeping these species in captivity and, in some cases, they may be right, especially when they refer to situations in which the animals are exploited and mistreated. This, however, is not the place to enter into argument; we are talking here about pets and private individuals not about institutions whose purpose is to use animals for one reason or another, whether it be for display or scientific experimentation and observation. Nor is this the place for me to make moral judgments about other people's behavior; if one can get hold of an animal legally and chooses to do so, being fully aware of the complications in store, one is, of course, free to do so. I can't help pointing out, however, that the freedom of choice he exercises is a completely one-sided arrangement requiring the sacrifice of the animal's right to function under the same principle.

MAMMALS

The Rodent Family

WILD RATS AND MICE. Hardly anyone needs to be told that the wild rat is to be avoided (except for purposes of extermination); no animal has received so much bad press as that wily adaptable creature which has infiltrated, infested, and infected our cities, our buildings, and our backyards, to say nothing of our ships and even our buses (as was reported not long ago in New York City). But a lot of people find it difficult to resist a cute little field mouse or house mouse; even the stereotypical housewife, screaming from the top of the kitchen table, has to admit that the wild mouse is not an unattractive creature. Indeed, if Walt Disney had not tolerated the presence of a house mouse in his St. Louis studio many years ago, there never would have been a Mickey Mouse. Nevertheless, the wild relatives of the domesticated mice and rats rarely make good pets and should not be kept in confinement. Their temperaments are never as even as those of the domesticated strains, and they may harbor a number of infectious diseases that can cause a good deal of harm to their captors. An animal dealer who specializes in reptiles once told me that he would never feed a wild rodent to his animals for fear of contamination, though they are certainly cheaper than the domestic varieties. Many people inadvertently keep these pests as free-roaming pets by leaving food around for the taking, but doing so on purpose—because they are cute or seem tame—is only asking for trouble.

PORCUPINES. I don't really know why anyone would want to consider a porcupine as a pet, for not only are they dangerous but they are also relatively slow moving and not particularly alert or interesting to watch. If you think about it, of course, there's not much reason a porcupine should do much of anything beyond growing quills, foraging for food, and finding a mate to perpetuate the species, because its ability to use quills against predators is far more effective—as any hunting dog would testify if it could—than any kind of interesting behavior pattern. Although porcupines can be persuaded to tolerate the presence of people for the sake of a few handouts (salt and hemlock shoots seem to be their favorites), caging one would be both cruel and pointless. What there is of special physical interest about the animal would have to be removed (can you imagine what would be involved in dequilling a porcupine?) to make it a fit companion for anything but another porcupine. One way in which people occasionally deal with porcupines—or parts of them at any rate—is by engaging in the unpleasant chore of removing quills from a dog that has been unfortunate enough to alarm a porky into using its excellent defense mechanism. The quills are released by a swinging motion of the tail—not shot, as is commonly assumed—and because of their barbs can be difficult to remove. If allowed to remain imbedded in a dog's face or coat, the quills may cause infection or abscess, and quick removal—unpleasant as it may be—is necessary. Do not simply pull the quills out but cut the tips to release the air pressure and work the ends out slowly so that the entire quill is removed; if necessary, restrain the dog by tying its legs or muzzling its jaws to prevent injury to the quill remover. The job is best performed by a veterinarian, but if you can manage to do it yourself, fine; be sure that the dog gets some medical attention soon, however, just to be sure that no fragments remain.

BEAVERS. Beavers, perhaps the most intelligent of the rodents, will tend to become tame as free-roaming pets through the use of food, and they are very attractive animals to watch. But in a cage they suffer considerably and for no real purpose. One of the real dangers involved in taming beavers is that you will reduce their fear of man, making it likely that they will become more convenient for trappers to catch. Besides being such clever animals—their engineering skill in constructing dams (and destroying forests) is well known—beavers are remarkably adaptable, becoming nocturnal when their predators are daytime stalkers and vice versa, and being able to survive in an extremely wide geographic and climatic range (though their numbers and their range have been severely reduced by trapping). It is an interesting, though rather appalling, fact that beavers were actually domesticated during the Middle Ages in Europe by monks who raised them for food, having convinced themselves that the aquatic life of a beaver enabled it (the rear end in any case) to qualify as a fish, and it could therefore be considered edible on fast days.

PRAIRIE DOGS. These burrowing creatures are not dogs, of course, but rodents that have become adapted to life on the flat plains, escaping their many predators (hawks, coyotes, and ferrets*) by means of elaborate tunnel systems, which, when the prairie dog was a common species, were large enough in size to be called towns. By an act of Congress in 1914, farmers and ranchers were given the go-ahead to "control" (meaning exterminate) predators, including wolves, prairie dogs, and others. Prairie dogs are no sort of predator, of course, but their burrows and their taste for grass "endangered" the cattle industry so that they were poisoned in great numbers, an easy task because of their tunnel towns. Two species, the black-tailed and the white-tailed, are now endangered and protected for that reason. Although it is possible to keep prairie dogs in captivity, where they may be given conditions under which they will burrow and breed, they cannot be recommended as pets because of their scarcity.

WOODCHUCKS (Groundhogs). The only animal to have an American holiday named in its honor is considered by most people to be a great pest. Chuck holes in fields have broken many an equine and bovine leg, and the appetite these animals have for chucking vegetables along with wood has made them very unwelcome to farmers. Although some people like to keep them around as free-roaming pets, retaining them even in this manner can't really be recommended for not only will an owner infuriate every gardening neighbor he has, but he may also inadvertently incur the wrath of the woodchuck, which in maturity can be an exceptionally cranky animal, happy to bite all comers.

The Weasel Family

Not many people would care to keep a mink, a weasel, or a wolverine as a pet, for their fierce reputations are too well known and attractive books about the joys of keeping them at home simply do not exist. But some members of this mustelid family have been singled out as candidates for captivity—among them the skunk and the ferret, which have been discussed elsewhere in this book.

*One of the explanations for the endangered status of the black-footed ferret in the western United States is the reduced number of prairie dogs, its natural prey.

Although the native black-footed ferret is the only endangered species of this group in America, the enormous amount of trapping has seriously reduced the populations of several mustelids, including the otter, so that they are rigidly protected in most states. Nevertheless, the badger, the otter, and the marten have received so much publicity as affectionate, entertaining pets that they should receive some individual attention here, though they are impossible pets, for reasons that will become obvious.

BADGERS.   The badger is one of the few animals for which man has been able to find little or no commercial value except in its natural role as a rodent hunter. Its fur has never been particularly attractive to coat buyers; though fierce enough when cornered, it has never been accused of killing humans or livestock; its shyness tends to keep it from becoming a pest worthy of extermination; its carnivorous nature has never made it a threat to the cabbage patch. For all these reasons, and more, the badger should be left alone, though people have enjoyed taming and keeping them as free-roaming pets. Even as temporary guests, however, badgers don't have much to recommend them; they are exceptionally strong, and their claws are more powerful than any other North American mammal with the exception of the bear and the wolverine. To this combination add a vast array of very sharp teeth and a grouchy disposition and you have a pretty formidable visitor on your hands.

OTTERS.   Nothing is more attractive than an animal that seems to be having fun, which is probably the primary reason why we find puppies, kittens, and young animals of almost any species irresistible. It certainly is one of the few reasons why otters hold such a dramatic appeal for us; these "clowns of nature," as they are so often called, simply love to play and they do so throughout their lives (up to twenty years), sliding down banks into the water, splashing around in ponds, and otherwise raising merry hell. Unfortunately, the otter has been the source of a considerable number of coats as well as amusement for humans, and its numbers have become drastically reduced, so much so that a pair of breeding otters can cost upwards of $10,000. The animal is now protected in most states. Nevertheless, the appeal of the otter as a pet still remains, though they are extremely expensive to acquire and almost impossible to find. Ernest Thompson Seton called otters "the most beautiful and engaging of all elegant pets," failing to mention—as Gavin Maxwell makes so clear in his book *Ring of Bright Water*—that the otter can also be one of the most difficult to keep. They are affectionate and only occasionally aggressive if hand reared and given constant, gentle handling. But they are very demanding indeed; they have special requirements as to housing

THE IRRESISTIBLE OTTER
IN HIS PROPER PLACE—HIS OWN HOME.

and diet, difficult for the average householder to provide, and they are very destructive of property. They can be trained to a leash and learn any number of tricks, and they afford a great deal of entertainment in the bathtub, but handling an otter is a full-time job (that "constant, gentle handling" mentioned above is not to be taken lightly). They are simply too active to be happy confined in a cage, and if happiness is one of their principal attractions, then why confine them anyway?

MARTENS. These beautiful animals were apparently common pets in the Middle Ages when farmers—who did not in those days keep chickens—found them to be tamable and very useful in keeping down the rodent population. Their attraction today is, unfortunately, for their thick, brown coats, and trappers annually kill many thousands for the fur industry. Like ferrets, they are also raised in captivity for their fur, and what is not made into coats is made into the sable-hair brushes used by artists. Though the tractable disposition of the marten might make the animal an affectionate, responsive pet, the expense involved in purchasing them (a color-matched

IMPOSSIBLE PETS

breeding pair will, like the otter, cost several thousand dollars), and the serious diminishing of their number in the wild has put them into the impossible category.

The Cat Family

Although many beautiful stories and photographs have been published to show us how affectionate and docile a big cat may behave as the member of a human family—be it in Africa as in Joy Adamson's *Born Free* or in Westchester County as in Jack Paar's home movies—tigers, jaguars, leopards, and lions are simply beyond the pale for any pet owner. Not only are the first three species endangered and illegal to keep without extremely hard-to-get permits (granted only to professionals), but all of these become so large and so dangerous that only a professional would want to take the responsibility of keeping them beyond cubhood. Other species of wild cats are also endangered, but because they are still popular in the public mind as pets and because so many amateurs have kept them and still do, it's worth taking a little time to describe each one individually.

OCELOTS. These beautiful, relatively small cats are native to Central and South America, although their range has extended into North America as well. Because of the heavy demands of the fur and pet industries, ocelots—and their look-alike cousins the margays—are now endangered, and it is not possible for individuals to obtain them legally. It is even impossible in some states and communities to obtain permits to keep ocelots that were imported before the Endangered Species Act was passed in 1973. There are, however, still plenty of pet ocelots around the country, many of them kept by serious animal lovers who work at trying to breed the species (a very difficult business), though a lot of them are kept simply as pets for the private pleasure of their owners. That there is pleasure involved is not surprising, for these animals can be very affectionate and are unquestionably beautiful creatures to handle and to watch, but the pleasure that any ocelot owner receives is well paid for in answering the demands that the animal makes in captivity.

Although a well-mannered ocelot may be allowed the run of the house without biting the people in it (these are few enough, for ocelots demand constant handling to remain good-natured and even then cannot be trusted with small children or strangers), the house must be reasonably free of any object that could cause the animal damage. And that is just about everything one normally has in a house. These extremely active, agile cats can and will climb on curtains, furniture, lamps, bathroom and kitchen fixtures. They will eat (not just chew, *eat*) anything they can get into their mouths from electric wires to towels, soap, and rubber balls, causing themselves severe digestive problems. They will scratch their way into whatever they can reach—cracks or holes in the wall, medicine cabinets, oven doors, television cabinets, bookshelves, you name it. In other words, if you are planning to live with an ocelot, plan to live without any furnishings or give the animal a separate room where it can survive. These cats can be trained to a leash, but this only works as a restraint when an owner holds the other end of it; when left alone, the ocelot simply must have some area that is as unadorned as a cage, which is where many an ocelot ends up anyway, becoming less of a pet and more of a prisoner.

In addition, ocelots are expensive to feed (an average ocelot will need over 10 pounds of meat a week as well as regular supplements to balance its diet) and impossible to travel with or board or leave with friends for the weekend. They can also help you incur high veterinary bills (if you can find a vet to treat them), and they need that constant attention if they are to remain fit for human company. All of this means that if an ocelot owner suddenly finds he can't take it any more, he has no choice but to give it away to another ocelot owner (one who knows what is involved and doesn't mind that the animal will never really take to him) or to a zoo, which is not always

THE ELEGANT (AND ENDANGERED) OCELOT LOOKS DISTINCTLY OUT OF PLACE IN A LIVING ROOM ON A LEASH.

possible. Most home-raised ocelots are incapable of making the necessary adjustments to a life entirely behind bars with a minimum of human attention. Even if they could survive, they would probably not be inclined to breed which would be any good zoo's reason for accepting the animal in the first place. Defanged and declawed ocelots would not be taken in any event.

CHEETAHS. These are also endangered and for that reason impossible, though many people believe that, unlike most big cats, the cheetah can make a fine pet for a human being. Cheetahs were kept commonly in ancient Egypt and, more recently, throughout North Africa, not only for their exotic appearance and docile manners but also as hunting companions. Although sleek and extremely fast running for short distances (over 50 miles an hour), the cheetah is in some respects more like a dog than a cat, remaining responsive to people even in maturity. Yet, even so, cheetahs do need constant handling from babyhood if they are going to stay friendly, and they are so large that even the most dedicated amateur would have difficulty coping with a cheetah at home, that is, if the local authorities would let him do so.

MOUNTAIN LION. This largest of the purring cats is also called cougar and puma (pronounced pee-yu-ma), but by any name it is a considerable beast with an undeserved reputation that has earned it considerable trouble at the hands of man. Once roaming over the whole of North America, the cougar has been persecuted like the wolf by those who believe all the legends about the damage it has caused man and domestic animals alike. Actually, almost no incidents involving cougar attacks upon humans are known, and the animal is so shy that it has rarely caused enough violence on livestock to make it a real threat. Thanks to our ability to find fault where none is due and thanks to the attraction of bounties offered for dead cougars, the species is now endangered in the eastern United States and becoming increasingly rare in the west. In spite of its size and alleged ferocity, cougars have also attracted the affection of many people, some of whom have boasted of their great success in keeping them as pets. I can attest myself to the fact that baby cougars do make endearing pets, because I had one in my own house—along with two small children and a number of house cats—for a matter of weeks. Carlos was certainly loving and adorable once he had settled in and grown accustomed to my strange household, but soon he felt so much at home that he began to ruin the furniture and attack anyone in sight in mock battle. Since he packed a mighty wallop even as a cub and did a good deal of damage with his claws and teeth, his career as a pet was short lived.

COUGARS ARE TOO DIGNIFIED
TO BE COOPED UP.

A writer friend of mine has managed to keep a full-grown cougar on his property for several years, in spite of constant battles with the zoning board (most localities will not give permits because cougars are considered dangerous, often with good reason as panic creators if not as predators), but then he has a wolf, too, and obviously enjoys making as many problems for himself as he can. The cougar is no longer welcome in the house because of its size and is confined to a cage in the backyard, which his owner admits isn't much of a life. Once the animal managed to escape and ended up in a nearby town innocently following a man who was on his way home from a party. When the two of them arrived in the kitchen, the man's wife dissolved in a state of hysteria, though whether she was more upset with her inebriated husband or with the sight of a cougar lapping up the dog's food was never determined. In any event, the confusion and widespread public furor that was raised nearly brought about the animal's death, which isn't much of a life either.

BOBCATS. Trapped by fur hunters, shot or poisoned by farmers who believe the animal poses a threat to livestock, and feared by anyone who has ever seen the beast snarling ferociously from a tree or cage, the bobcat has somehow managed to survive over a wide range as successfully as the equally detested coyote. Like the coyote, the bobcat is clever, prolific, and thrives on a rodent diet, though it is capable of killing larger animals if necessary. It is an extremely active, agile animal, quite powerful for its relatively small size, and as exotic in appearance as its cousin the lynx. These last few attributes are probably what lead many animal lovers to believe that the bobcat can become a satisfactory pet, but happy bobcat owners are few and far between. All of the problems that I outlined earlier in the section on ocelots are true of the bobcat as well, except bobcats aren't endangered; however, these animals—even if hand reared from a very early age—are likely to become exceptionally dangerous as adults. Although individuals can vary considerably, most become sullen and hostile after they become a year old, erupting into fits of anger and aggression that seem unprovoked but are probably caused by fear. For this reason most bobcat owners declaw and defang their pets, making them ineligible for release and, in fact, for much of anything, because a frightened, hissing pet, even if it can inflict no injury, is simply not much fun to have around.

THE BOBCAT CAN'T HELP LOOKING RESENTFUL IN CAPTIVITY.

Wild Dogs

Although it is true that the domestic dog is closely related to the wild dogs we know today—the wolf, the coyote, the fox, the hyena, and the dingo, among others—and that all of them sprang from common ancestors, the many thousands of years of breeding that have gone into producing the modern-day dog have made it a very different animal from its wild cousins. Not only has man been able to develop different shapes and sizes and types of dogs for various purposes, but he has also been able to eliminate numerous behavioral characteristics of wild dogs to make the domestic version a suitable companion rather than simply a tamed captive. And a tamed captive is all that a wild dog will ever be, no matter how carefully or devotedly a human may rear a wild-dog pup. Like all puppies, wolf cubs and baby foxes are very appealing animals; they romp and tumble with their brothers and sisters, and they chew on things with their sharp little teeth as they explore the world around them. If treated gently and fed regularly by one or two humans, the wild pups will demonstrate genuine affection and even remain responsive into adulthood. But unlike dogs, these wild creatures will always remain wild at heart; even as puppies they will display fits of temper if they are frustrated, and this willfulness can never be eradicated even by the most patient handling. It may be possible to maintain a relationship with a grown wild dog through an understanding of its gestures and of its natural social behavior, but there is no way of making the animal dependent on your moods or whims or anything except your food and physical care. If you are to get along with a wolf or a fox, you must be willing to adapt yourself to its moods and needs—no question about it.

Because wolves and coyotes and other members of the dog family have for so long been considered dangerous predators and even evil creatures whose howls cause chills to run up the average human spine, they have for many years been a target for persecutors of all descriptions. The wolf and the fox have suffered the most—to the point where several species are endangered or threatened with extinction.

The coyote, however, a resourceful, prolific animal with a preference for rodents, has managed to outwit man and adapt to a wide range; this animal is so successful, in fact, that bounties are still offered for their pelts, thanks primarily to the complaints of sheepherders and the growing market for coyote fur (to replace the wolf fur that is becoming so rare). Anyone who has read Farley Mowat's *Never Cry Wolf* or the many other books and articles defending the wolf needs no further convincing that this particular beast is a noble one deserving of all the protection it can be given; Hope Ryden in her book *God's Dog* has, along with other people, made a heartfelt and moving plea for the protection of the coyote as well. These arguments are well taken and should be noted by anyone who still remembers the wolf as the one who ate Red Riding Hood's grandmother or the fox as the sneaky devil who shows up in so many of Aesop's Fables. But too many people seem to have overreacted to the point where they think of these animals as worthy of our personal love, as dogs in wolves' clothing, so to speak, which need only tender loving care to become as faithful as Fido. Not so. These are wild animals just as the cougar, the bear, and the badger are wild, and though they may be held in captivity—and even breed and thrive there—they will never be good pets, in any sense of that word.

FOXES. If the word fox doesn't conjure up the sight of a bushy red tail leading a pack of hounds in turn leading a herd of horses carrying an assortment of red-coated riders, then it probably makes you think of elegant fur coats or frightened chickens or sour grapes. Foxes have been the focus of human wile and wit for as long as there have been foxes, and because they are small and pretty wily themselves, they have managed to hold on to their territory in many areas and continue to thrive. The kit and desert kit foxes have no done so well as some of their cousins and are now seriously endangered, but the woodland and arctic foxes have managed to flourish.

The intelligence that foxes have shown in their successful avoidance of extermination is what makes many people think that they might make good pets. Certainly they are mischievous and clever and fun to watch, and certainly they are difficult to watch in the wild, for they are notoriously shy of humans. But as captives they are about as much fun as a full-grown raccoon and probably twice as hard to keep. Their curiosity and cleverness make them very destructive, and their wild temperaments make them difficult to control or even to understand much of the time. They can be trained to a leash when young and taught to do various tricks, but they are also very demanding of attention and need constant supervision if they are allowed to run free through the house, where they may be difficult to keep an eye on because of their natural shyness. Often, owners who have not the time or energy to spend on their pet foxes (fifteen years of constant supervision is a pretty long stretch of supervision) may feel the need to cage the animal, but like any intelligent creature, a fox will soon become bored and frustrated and probably aggressive as a result. The only alternative, of course, is release into the wild, and that is like giving a death sentence, since the animal will probably not be prepared to fend for itself or to establish relationships with other members of its species.

COYOTES. Most of the predators that Americans once persecuted with vehemence have been reduced in number so that the only threat they offer is that of becoming extinct. But man's war against the coyote continues unabated, partly because the coyote has been very successful in its fight for survival, and partly because the animal is the victim of many false accusations about its feeding habits. Most people are willing to admit that they might have been wrong about the wolf, but they still cling to the age-old notion that the coyote is the primary killer of sheep, chickens, and whatever else they can get their teeth on. Actually the coyote is by nature a rodent eater and makes up for whatever few lambs and chickens he eats by ridding farmers of rats, mice, and other pests. But we always seem to need some devil to shoot, poison, or trap, just for the hell of it, and the coyote is still a prime target.

As people who know them well will tell you, coyotes are, in fact, rather engaging animals. As pups they are very much like domestic dogs, far more affectionate and playful than wolves, and very good-looking indeed with extraordinary voices that can carry for miles. Some of them grow up into tractable doglike adults, which can be trusted even with children and other animals around the house. But coyotes vary considerably from one to the next, and in general I'd be inclined to believe that these docile members of the species are more the exceptions than the rule. Coyotes are naturally high-strung and athletic creatures, accustomed to covering many miles a day in search of food, and though they are social animals, they do not stay in one place except for the time it takes to raise a litter. Therefore, if one were to keep a coyote as a pet, one would have to allow the animal its freedom to come and go, and nine times out of ten, the animal would go. Caging a coyote or confining it to the house would be a surefire way to make it so nervous that it would quickly lose all the attributes that made it a good companion to begin with; it would simply roam up and down the cage or room, bored and frustrated and probably hostile to the extent that one would hestitate to let it out even for play. Coyotes are by nature boisterous, curious animals so that when they are given the run of the house and yard, no object is safe. Furniture, rugs, curtains, slippers, toys, whatever you leave within reach will be chewed, tossed around, pulled down, and probably destroyed. Discipline is possible, coyote owners say, but it takes a good deal of patience and a real understanding of the animal's temperament and moods, which may not always be easy to read. Like any high-strung wild animal, coyotes may well interpret attempts at training as attacks and react accordingly.

Giving a coyote room to wander is a risky business, not just for the owner; one man in California reports that when his pet coyote was napping on the front porch of his house, a car drove up and its driver pulled out a rifle and shot the animal, presumably intending to do a favor for the household. Furthermore, the communities where one could get a permit to keep a coyote on the premises are few and far between—yet another reason why one should consider them impossible as pets.

WOLVES. This beautiful animal is becoming quite rare and some races are endangered, so wolves are not as easy to come by as they once were. Most people who have kept wolves have raised orphaned cubs and then released them, though a few individuals are willing to undergo the tremendous sacrifices involved in maintaining an adult wolf. Not only are these animals large and potentially dangerous (zoning restrictions are very tough in most states), but they are also destructive—even as cubs—difficult to handle, and expensive to feed and keep. It is possible to socialize adult wolves—or to maintain socialization in wolves raised from infancy—as I pointed out earlier, but the amount of time involved in just the preliminary steps of taming the animal and reducing its fear should be enough to restrict the activity to experts or profes-

THE TIMBER WOLF MAY LOOK LIKE AN OVERGROWN DOG,
BUT THAT CAGE WALL IS, UNFORTUNATELY,
A NECESSARY PART OF HIS RELATIONSHIP WITH HUMANS.

sionals equipped to handle the job. Once the animal has become tame, the handling must continue on a regular basis. The friend I mentioned with a cougar and a wolf penned in his backyard was sick for a period of time and could not visit his animals on a regular basis; after just a few weeks, both animals became unruly enough so that he had to start almost from the beginning to regain their trust, and even now he is hesitant about entering the wolf's enclosure. A man who lived in the Bronx in a relatively small apartment once kept a full-grown wolf for a short time, but he was obliged to lock the wolf up every time the family sat down to dinner or the animal would become extremely aggressive as well as possessive about the main course.

Ungulates

In addition to the domestic species, a number of ungulates may legally be kept: bison, for instance, are now being raised in captivity, not only because man is trying to repopulate the country with the animal that was once so bountiful, but also because a bison can provide meat for a potential commercial market. Because elk, moose, and caribou are simply too large to be considered as pets, though they have been kept successfully in deer parks or reserves, they do not merit consideration in this chapter.

The most common wild ungulate—the deer—is protected in every state and cannot be kept without a special permit (one that is usually not granted), though it is the most likely candidate for pethood because of its abundance in areas near human dwellings and because raising an orphaned fawn can be a very rewarding experience. Protection is granted the deer because it is a game animal, so that while it may be illegal to keep a deer alive in a corral, it is perfectly all right to shoot it—in season, of course. Since hunters are prevented from shooting female deer and are encouraged to aim only at the largest bucks after the breeding season, a large number of targets is always guaranteed. Because the deer are therefore allowed to breed as much as they want, and because civilization is constantly encroaching on deer habitats, overpopulation in some areas has caused deer to overrun gardens and highways and to starve for lack of food—a situation caused by the curious hunting laws yet used by hunters as the justification for their sport. If culling deer were the real reason for hunting, females and males alike—before breeding—would be selected for shooting, but this, of course, would mean that the deer population would stabilize and hunting would have to be limited.

This does not seem to be the right place for an argument against sport hunting, even though it is the hunting activity that has made deer illegal to keep, and impossible even as free-roaming pets. But deer themselves, though they will thrive in captivity with proper food and enough room to exercise, do not make good pets under any circumstances. Baby fawns can be gentle and even affectionate—rather like baby calves—and raising one for release (with proper permits, of course) can be fun. But a full-grown deer is not at all like a cow; it is nervous and shy like any wild animal in the presence of man and capable of delivering a very harmful kick—with the front legs—if it feels cornered and unable to run. Though deer may be tamed so that they will eat from your backyard and even from your hand, it is a bad idea to encourage this activity, not only because of the danger involved but also because it would be inhumane to allow the animal to become too accustomed to humans. Farmers and neighbors with gardens will not thank you, although the next hunter who comes along may be very grateful indeed for your services in giving him such a cooperative target. Male deer, particularly in the breeding season, are dangerous and will use their large antlers and powerful legs to inflict severe injury even on humans with whom they are otherwise friendly.

Bears

Just about the only kind of bear that makes a good pet is a teddy bear—cuddly, mild mannered, and definitely not real. One hears engaging stories about bringing up bear cubs in the woods, and I know it has been done, but no one who lives anywhere near other people or in a house where the furniture is supposed to last through a season should even try. Baby bears are cuddly but they are definitely real and not at all mild mannered. The various species of North American bears do vary considerably in aggressiveness (the Kodiak and the polar bears are the most, and the black bears are the least), but all of them are large, dangerous, and increasingly rare. Impossible pets. Enough said.

Primates

Probably the first animal that comes to mind when you think of an exotic pet is the monkey. These small members of the primate family have been kept in menageries and attached to organ grinders for centuries, mostly because of their curiosity value. Many people find it amusing to watch these bright, disturbingly humanlike creatures perform tricks or wear clothes, like little replicas of themselves, but because monkeys are very difficult to keep in captivity—at least in a household situation—they can be very disappointing pets indeed. The survival rate of pet monkeys is low, many with potential natural lifespans of twenty years or more lasting less than one or two. The reasons for such high mortality are varied: poor and unbalanced diets; loneliness or lack of contact with their own kind (most monkeys in the wild are highly social animals); disease; bad housing; or nasty temperaments that cause owners to dispose of them. Any or all

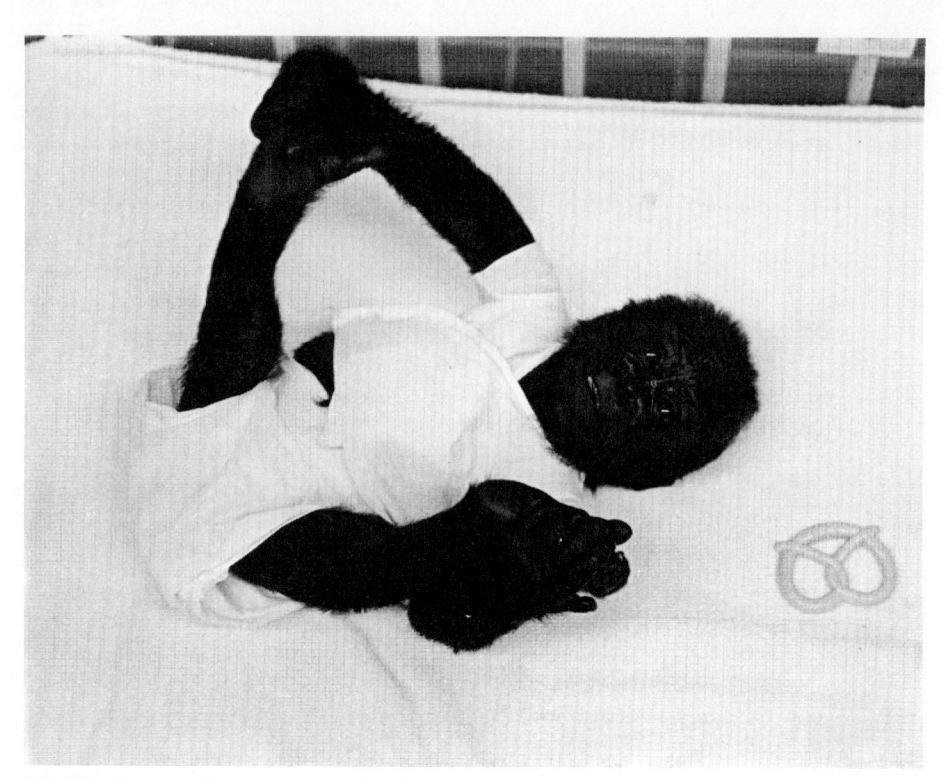

THIS BABY GORILLA'S RESEMBLANCE TO A HUMAN INFANT IS NOT ACCIDENTAL; YOUNG PRIMATES ARE FAR MORE TROUBLE TO RAISE AND FAR LESS ENJOYABLE IN THE LONG RUN.

of these may contribute to the short life of the average pet monkey. Happily, the United States government has recently seen fit to prohibit the wholesale importation of monkeys and other primates—for reasons of human health—for any but the most serious teaching and scientific purposes, so the pet-shop trade in monkeys has come to an abrupt halt for imported animals. But, as with many other difficult-to-get animals, monkeys have not lost their appeal for those who can afford the price, much to the distress of the animals involved—and of the owners, too, for that matter.

Both New World and Old World monkeys have been popular as pets, though members of the former group are probably far more common in this country. Such species as the spider monkey, the marmoset, the squirrel and woolly monkeys, and the capuchin were once captured by the carload in their native South and Central America jungle habitats and unceremoniously hauled onto ships and airplanes for distribution to pet shops and homes throughout the United States. Some Old World monkeys and apes are as well known here as they are in the Old World. Rhesus monkeys and chimpanzees are raised in large numbers here for laboratory work, and some of them are occasionally available through dealers for use as house pets. But regardless of source, and even if the animals do survive the adjustment to their new homes, they invariably suffer traumas that may later manifest themselves either psychologically or physiologically or both. Most owners are not aware of the potential disease hazards involved in keeping primates. Monkeys caught in the wild are usually shipped in groups, without any examination or quarantine, and may harbor any of a number of disease organisms, such as rabies, tuberculosis, hepatitis, and yellow fever, all of which can be transmitted to humans. Even monkeys that are healthy on arrival can pick up viral infections and other diseases from humans, and most people know so little about proper diet and housing requirements that these fragile creatures will often succumb to illness before they have been "home" for more than a few months.

In any event, if the monkey survives its first year in captivity, owners generally find that they have more on their hands than they can manage. Monkeys, being curious and clever animals, are usually fairly destructive, and as they approach maturity, they become stronger and more aggressive, so that few can be handled in safety. Rather than risk nasty bites, most owners simply confine their pets to cages, where they become little more than prisoners. Even the relatively equable woolly monkey will become aggressive after five or six years—contrary to popular opinion—although few manage to survive that long in captivity because of their particularly fragile physical make-up and great emotional needs.

Although as a monkey grows older, it may become possible to train it to do a number of tricks, training is a difficult business. Often the animal will react to discipline as if it had been attacked or threatened, which is almost sure to mean a counterattack of some sort. And there is no point at all in trying to housebreak a monkey; as clever as they are, they are never as submissive as dogs or as dainty as cats, and simply cannot get it into their messy heads that their droppings should not simply fall where they may. Diapers are necessary if a monkey is to be allowed the run of a house, and constant cage cleaning is essential, for the smell can become quite unbearable even after a few hours. Monkeys are also messy eaters and must often be given more than they will actually eat; if you were accustomed to eating at the top of a tree, you'd probably refuse to go pick up the lost banana yourself.

Nevertheless, the traffic in pet monkeys will undoubtedly continue, in spite of importation laws. Below are brief descriptions of the most common pet monkeys, just for the information of those who need further convincing that these primate babies are even more troublesome and far less rewarding than human ones.

CAPUCHIN MONKEYS.   Also known as sapajous, these small New World monkeys are called capuchins because they have monklike hoods (actually crests of stiff hair) on their heads; in temperament they bear no resemblance at all to Capuchin monks, being very temperamental and aggressive, mischievous, and extremely messy eaters. Though some people say that if they are raised in captivity from a very early age, they will be gentle and loving, they can never be trusted to behave well with anyone other than their owner. Also, because they are naturally lively and curious, they will quickly overturn the average household and must be restricted to a cage much of the time. Furthermore they cannot be housebroken, although they can be taught any number of tricks, as the organ grinders used to do with them. Hardier than most monkeys, capuchins still require a balanced diet of vegetables, some meat, monkey pellets, and seeds and nuts, as well as supplements of calcium and codliver oil, much of which they will waste by spillage and throwing around at mealtime.

MARMOSETS.   These are not monkeys exactly but they are in the primate family and can be treated as such for the purposes of this chapter. Actually, they resemble squirrels somewhat, because of their tiny size, because their long tails are not prehensile, and they do not have grasping hands like those of monkeys. Each of the twelve species of marmoset varies considerably in coloration and habits, but all are social animals, highly active and noisy, and become eventually ill-tempered in captivity. Because they are small, owners often make the mistake of keeping them in small cages, but these do not permit the animals sufficient room for the exercise they need, and many suffer as a result. Rickets and cage paralysis are common with marmosets, whether because of incorrect caging or inadequate amount or type of vitamin D. Because they are social animals, traveling like other primates in groups, they require a great deal of attention from their owners if they are kept singly. They generally do better in pairs and may even breed in captivity, though they will tend to be rather less responsive to their owners (except at feeding time) as a result of having a member of their own species around, a situation they obviously prefer.

SPIDER MONKEYS.   These monkeys are almost as popular as marmosets and equally unsatisfying as pets, for they too are extremely active. (The very long limbs they use for swinging through the jungle are the reason they are called "spiders.") They require a good deal of space, much more than the marmosets because they are larger in size, and, like the other monkeys, they become aggressive as they grow older. A spider monkey can be a formidable character, for it will use those long limbs to grasp a victim (i.e.,

BECAUSE MONKEYS CANNOT BE TOILET TRAINED
OR TRUSTED AS PETS, THEY MUST BE KEPT IN CAGES.

beloved owner) and can inflict an incredible number of bites before it can be disentangled.

SQUIRREL MONKEYS. These, too, are common New World monkeys and are popularly sold as pets, though they are very high strung even as youngsters and few live out their natural lifespans in captivity (fifteen or more years), the average pet living no longer than three years. However, they vary considerably from one individual to another in terms of hardiness. They have large heads and small bodies, proportionately speaking, with nonprehensile tails.

WOOLLY MONKEYS. Woollies are the monkeys with the best reputation as pets, though even they may become ill tempered as they mature. They look more like people than most monkeys; they usually have dark, hairless faces, hands, and feet, but their coats may vary in color depending on where they were found. They are larger than most other New World monkeys, weighing as much as 20 or more pounds when full grown, and have very long tails. Like other monkeys, they are clever and gregarious, though somewhat less active because of their stockier physique, but they make up for their lack of agility by a remarkable range of facial expressions and a relatively placid temperament. They are not as mischievous as the other primates, but they will eat almost anything they can find and are prone to potbelliedness and, paradoxically, deficiencies of various kinds, since most owners assume they will thrive on what they like to eat. Actually, they are very susceptible to sickness when they are under- or malnourished, and this is not a simple matter to remedy, since they are intermittent eaters. Respiratory ailments are common, and usually fatal, because they are very vulnerable to chills from drafts, exposure to respiratory infections carried by humans, and they do not do well in dry atmospheres. Ideally, a woolly monkey should be kept in conditions resembling those of the jungle to which it is native—high humidity and warmth; however, such an environment is very difficult for the average householder to simulate without giving the rest of the family a pretty uncomfortable home.

CHIMPANZEES. Because of the expense involved in obtaining a chimp and the well-known problems involved in raising them to adulthood, very few people actually keep a chimpanzee around the house for the fun of it. If they start out with that intention, they soon find that they have more than they can cope with, for raising a large primate is undoubtedly more trouble than raising a human baby, and they are faced with the almost inevitable prospect of ending up with a hostile, unloving, and certainly ungrateful child. Not many people would go into child rearing if they knew that a monster would be the result, and yet that is almost invariably the case with chimps raised in a family environment. The well-publicized stories about homegrown chimpanzees are usually written by or about scientists of various disciplines—psychologists, generally—who are interested in observing the humanlike characteristics of the most humanlike of primates and in testing their potential for language, personal relationships, learning behavior, etc. Because teaching chimpanzees is an extremely time-consuming business (one fourteen-month old chimp in New York City learned to express fourteen word signs and how to dress itself at the expense of some 10,000 man-hours of work), the animals must be in a situation where they can virtually live with their human teachers, and the home is often the best place—if it can be adapted for the purpose. As a chimp matures, which is at a slightly faster rate than a human child, it will become progressively more curious, more knowledgeable about dealing with its humans, and stronger, meaning that a temper tantrum can be a pretty hair-raising business for anyone trying to control the animal. Like monkeys, and infant humans, for that matter, chimps cannot be housebroken (diapers are a must), and feeding must be handled with great care and knowledge about the animal's requirements.

Zoo chimpanzees have often been hand reared by humans, if only because zoo conditions are not always conducive to bringing out the maternal instincts of adult females. Yet, even the hand-reared animals, once confined to a cage, fail to respond as affectionately as one might hope to their human "mothers" for more than a short time, unless they are constantly handled by that same person. Chimpanzees are highly developed socially, as we know from reading Jane Goodall's *Under the Shadow of Man,* and they prefer their own species to humans given the opportunity to remain with their own kind. And, of course, any zoo worth its salt will give the chimp that opportunity, because the curators and keepers know that they can never develop a highly successful breeding colony unless the animals are allowed to develop their natural social behavioral characteristics.

Circus chimps, which we see all dressed up and doing tricks with what seems to us to be the greatest of good nature, are, like all circus animals, performers and not pets. They are handled by professionals who use love only as a reward for a certain kind of behavior, and the chimps are never expected for a moment to behave in such agreeable ways without supervision. Some people I know who have a small zoo—one of the few small zoos where the quality of care and housing is excellent—have had a performing chimpanzee for some ten years. Although the animal was once an outgoing member of their family, he is now relegated to being breadwinner rather than pet, for his aggressive tendencies are increasing, as he has reached sexual maturity, and he cannot be trusted to behave like the child he was in his earlier years.

REPTILES

All endangered or protected species of reptiles must, of course, be eliminated from consideration as potential pets, and there are a surprising number of these species, including the American alligator and the bog turtle. In addition, any poisonous reptile should be considered an impossible pet; the danger is obvious though curiously attractive to those few eccentrics who feel that nothing is more amusing than entertaining friends with a caged rattlesnake. A few reptiles may be obtained legally but should be considered, for all intents and purposes, impossible for anyone but the most expert and professional. The caiman is often promoted as a good pet, however, and that notion needs some revision.

CAIMAN. This smaller relative of the alligator is not difficult to obtain, but it should be. Although they look like harmless lizards when they are young, they very quickly grow—within three years or so—to a length of seven feet and acquire just as quickly a very nasty temper, even nastier than the average alligator. When you consider that you must provide this unpleasant beast with warm sun (or a lamp) most of the time and change its water frequently to

ALTHOUGH THIS LOOKS LIKE A JUNGLE, IT IS REALLY
A SMALL BACK-YARD AREA SET UP FOR A GROUP OF ALLIGATORS
THAT QUICKLY GREW TOO LARGE FOR THE LIVING ROOM.

avoid smelling up the house, the idea of keeping one in captivity becomes even less attractive. On top of that, most caimans prefer a regular diet of live minnows, frogs, worms, live insects, and small mice, though some can be tricked into attacking raw meat dangled on a string, if you have the patience. And if you are not entirely convinced, remember that, except at feeding time, the creature just lies there basking in the sun doing not much of anything that is very interesting to watch.

BIRDS

The Migratory Bird Treaty Act protects nearly all native American song birds, with the exception of the English sparrow and the starling, which are not indigenous in any case, and prohibits the hunting and confinement of all insectivorous birds. Migratory waterfowl, such as ducks, geese, and cranes, may be killed only during specific seasons with a license, and birds considered injurious to agriculture, such as the monk parakeet and others, may only be killed with a permit. As of 1972, crows, eagles, hawks, and owls achieved a protected status, and anyone wishing to keep any of these species in captivity must obtain a permit. The ancient sport of falconry—hunting with birds of prey that are trained to attack and retrieve birds in flight for their handlers—has become increasingly popular over the last few years, and there are now a few thousand birds of prey in use in the United States, most of them short-winged hawks and falcons. Because this is a difficult sport and one that arouses a good deal of controversy, owing to the scarcity of certain birds of prey, only experts or those willing to devote a good deal of time to apprenticeship should be encouraged to pursue the activity. The North American Falconers Association and the North American Peregrine Falcon Foundation are good sources for information on the care, keeping, and training of these birds.

Injured Birds

Although it is illegal to keep native birds in confinement, many people cannot help responding to the sight of an orphaned or abandoned baby bird or an injured adult, knowing that leaving it alone will bring about certain death. Suggestions for the care of baby birds are given in Chapter 9, and though success rates are low, it is often worth trying to raise the bird to the age at which it can be safely released. Injured adults are also difficult to save, because when they are found, they are often diseased or in a state of shock and their body temperatures and fluids balance cannot be restored. However, sometimes only a few hours of confinement in a warm quiet spot and a bit of nourishment are enough to enable the bird to regain health, and even certain injuries may heal quite quickly with the proper care.

Do not chase a bird that seems injured or stunned but approach slowly and handle it with great care. The bird will probably be weak from lack of water and food; pick it up gently in your hand, enveloping the whole body and closing your fingers around its head to prevent excited movements without putting pressure on the bird's chest. Identify the bird and find out what its natural food requirements are (suggestions for feeding captive wild birds are given in Chapter 7). Set up a lined cardboard box with a cover that is easily removed and furnish it with an untippable water dish and some soft food. If left alone for a few hours, a bird that is simply stunned or in shock may recover and be ready for release.

If the bird appears to have a broken leg or wing, take it to a veterinarian or wildlife clinic as soon as possible; bones will set quickly which can be dangerous if they are not set properly. If professional assistance is unavailable, you can try to immobilize the fractured limb yourself, but be sure to use extreme caution and get a helper to keep the bird calm. Using tape or a clean bandage, bind an injured wing to the bird's body in a normal position, letting the uninjured wing remain free. Broken legs will mend quickly with a splint made from a small flat piece of wood a bit longer than the bird's leg; straighten the leg until the broken bones meet and, using gauze, wrap the leg and the split together as smoothly as possible and bind them with tape. The splint should extend slightly beyond the toes so that no weight can be put on the leg, and the bandage should be wrapped so that the bird cannot pick at it. Three weeks of relative quiet in a box, with the proper food and water, should see the bone nicely healed and the bird ready for release.

Trembling, excited behavior and screaming are signs that the bird may have been poisoned, in which event a clinic or a veterinarian should be consulted. Other symptoms that may indicate disease are lethargy, paralysis, clouded eyes, diarrhea, and hemorrhaging. If you notice that large numbers of birds seem to be affected with these symptoms, report the situation right away to your state's fish and game department as an epidemic or poisoning may be responsible. There is not much that an amateur can do for a diseased or poisoned bird beyond keeping it warm and comfortable and quiet in a lined box until it can be taken to a nature center or veterinarian. Be sure that all infected birds are isolated from other birds. If you feel you have to keep a bird for more than a few days, you must obtain a permit, and applications often take quite a while to process, so your best bet is to turn the bird over to an appropriate wildlife agency or bird-rescue center. Although the permit requirement may seem inhumane, it has as its objective the prevention of illegal capture and restraint of wild birds for commercial purposes.

Oil-damaged birds are among the most unfortunate results of the oil spills that have been occurring along our coastlines in recent years, for the oil will cause almost certain death unless steps are quickly taken. The weight of the oil makes flight difficult, but it also affects the structure of the feathers by disrupting their natural oils; and when a bird can no longer shed water, the feathers are no longer effective insulators, so that the birds die from chilling, if exhaustion and starvation do not kill them first. The ingestion of oil can also cause death (whether it is taken in by drinking oily water or preening feathers), and certain toxic substances in the oil can cause irritation to the skin. The immediate attention of a veterinarian is necessary, but the first step should be to see that the bird gets warmth. Keep it in an environment of at least 80°F. and put a rubber band around its beak to prevent ingestion of more oil. Wrap the bird loosely in a towel to conserve heat and prevent struggling, and place the bird in a lined box by itself.

If expert help is not imminent, you may try to clean the bird yourself, but make sure that its temperature is normal (temperatures range from 108°F. for a small bird of less than 100 grams to 103°F. for birds over 2000 grams) before you cause it further stress. Use mineral oil or a mild warm solution of Ivory Liquid in water, immersing the bird in the bath up to its neck and allowing the solution to prenetrate the feathers. Do not rub the feathers but gently agitate them in the water, and use a series of baths until no more oil remains. Rinse the bird with warm water until the liquid begins to bead up on the feathers, which should appear dry and shiny. Be sure the bird is kept warm until it is completely dry. Give the bird sugared water (¼ cup of sugar to 2 quarts of water), using a dropper if the bird will not sip from a dish; do not feed it milk or bread. As soon as possible, see that the natural diet is provided for the bird. When it is eating properly, it will probably be ready for release, although the feathers should be completely restored before it is let go. An isolated area with sufficient natural food and cover is the ideal spot for release; some birds, however, may require a little food supplied by you for a day or two before they become entirely self-sufficient.

Free-Roaming Pet Birds

Wild birds that are completely healthy should never be kept for any reason, of course, but there are ways to keep them around your house so that you can enjoy their colors and their behavior patterns. The most common method to keep these as free-roaming pets is to have a bird bath regularly filled with clean water, a feeder full of seeds, and a yard free of predators and supplied with adequate cover. Feeding birds can be an absorbing activity, even in crowded cities or suburban neighborhoods, where there are always a few species that can be persuaded to drop their natural shyness and accept a palatable handout. But a responsibility is involved in keeping these creatures even partially dependent on you, although most people don't realize it. Some unfortunate birds become so dependent on a regular source of supply that they cannot support themselves when that supply is suddenly discontinued. What happens when you go off on a winter vacation and leave your feathered friends behind with an empty feeder, thick snow which covers up natural forage, and no close neighbors with feeders to which they can go? The most humane solution is probably to cancel your vacation, but that is usually not the most desirable alternative; the most practical method is to have someone else feed them while you are away, or to avoid making the birds so dependent on you in the first place and not to feed them at all during the autumn and early winter months. Summer feeding will attract many beautiful birds, but your food will probably not quite match up to the natural food that abounds on the berry bushes, fruit and nut trees you have been thoughtful enough to plant for them. Winter feeding in the northern states will attract only a few species that remain: woodpeckers, cardinals, and chickadees, among others. As in summer, food can consist of wild-bird seed mixtures, extra sunflower seeds, beef suet, peanut butter, cracked corn, and pieces

THIS BEAUTIFUL SAWHET OWL CANNOT BE KEPT WITHOUT A PERMIT, BUT WHO WOULD WANT TO RISK ENDANGERING ITS LIFE ANYHOW?

of fruit for variety. You can also save the most palatable leftovers from dinner and find a few comers; some insect-eating birds I know absolutely love spaghetti, though I can't imagine what sort of strange worms they think they have found. See Chapter 7 for more detailed information about appropriate foods.

In addition to attractive food, birds also need a sense of security if they are to come around in any number. Predators—such as hawks, shrikes, cats, and some rodents—will not be so much of a threat if a bird has good visibility at the feeder and can remain alert to enemies. Heavy cover near the feeder is likely to keep them away, for fear of the evil that may lurk within. Food thieves are also a problem, and you should keep the feeder protected against them. Be sure that it is located far above the ground (even ground eaters, like the junco and goldfinch will fly up to a feeder if they have to) with protective shields against climbing animals—above the feeder if it is suspended and below if it is raised on a pole. You can also keep your supply of food from being gobbled up by big birds by creating a shield of wire mesh that has openings large enough for the smaller birds to get through. Remember, too, that your own presence, even at the window, may be disconcerting to birds; keep your movements to a slow-paced minimum until they become accustomed to your presence. Although open space around a feeder is a good idea, birds do need some cover themselves and some woods nearby; a shrubbed lawn with berry bushes and flowers will be most inviting.

Various books and booklets are available on gardening with wildlife in mind, and the thoughtful and enthusiastic birder can do a great deal to improve his property for everyone involved, not just the humans in the neighborhood. Especially thoughtful hosts will supply nesting boxes or birdhouses to attract visitors, if no suitable hollow trees or nesting places are around. The pattern given in Chapter 7 for a nesting box will do very well. It should be painted if it is to withstand the elements; natural brown stain is also attractive, but white will deflect sunlight and make for a cooler interior. A southern exposure for the front door and a perch outside are traditional but not always necessary. You will, however, need to clean out the box after it has been used, unless you feel like giving houseroom to a family—more likely a horde—of insects or other small creatures during the winter months. Flying squirrels may quickly settle into a birdhouse that is large enough, but don't be alarmed if you find these squatters have moved in for they are delightful creatures and fascinating to watch if you are fortunate enough to see them. Be sure that the house, like the feeder, is well protected against less welcome guests—marauding cats and rodents, for instance. And keep your nose out while the place is occupied, just as you would with a natural nest, or you'll wreak utter havoc with those tiny creatures. Better to sit back and let your free-roaming pets choose their own time to entertain you, which they will undoubtedly do if you have the patience to sit still long enough.

PART TWO
Keeping a Pet

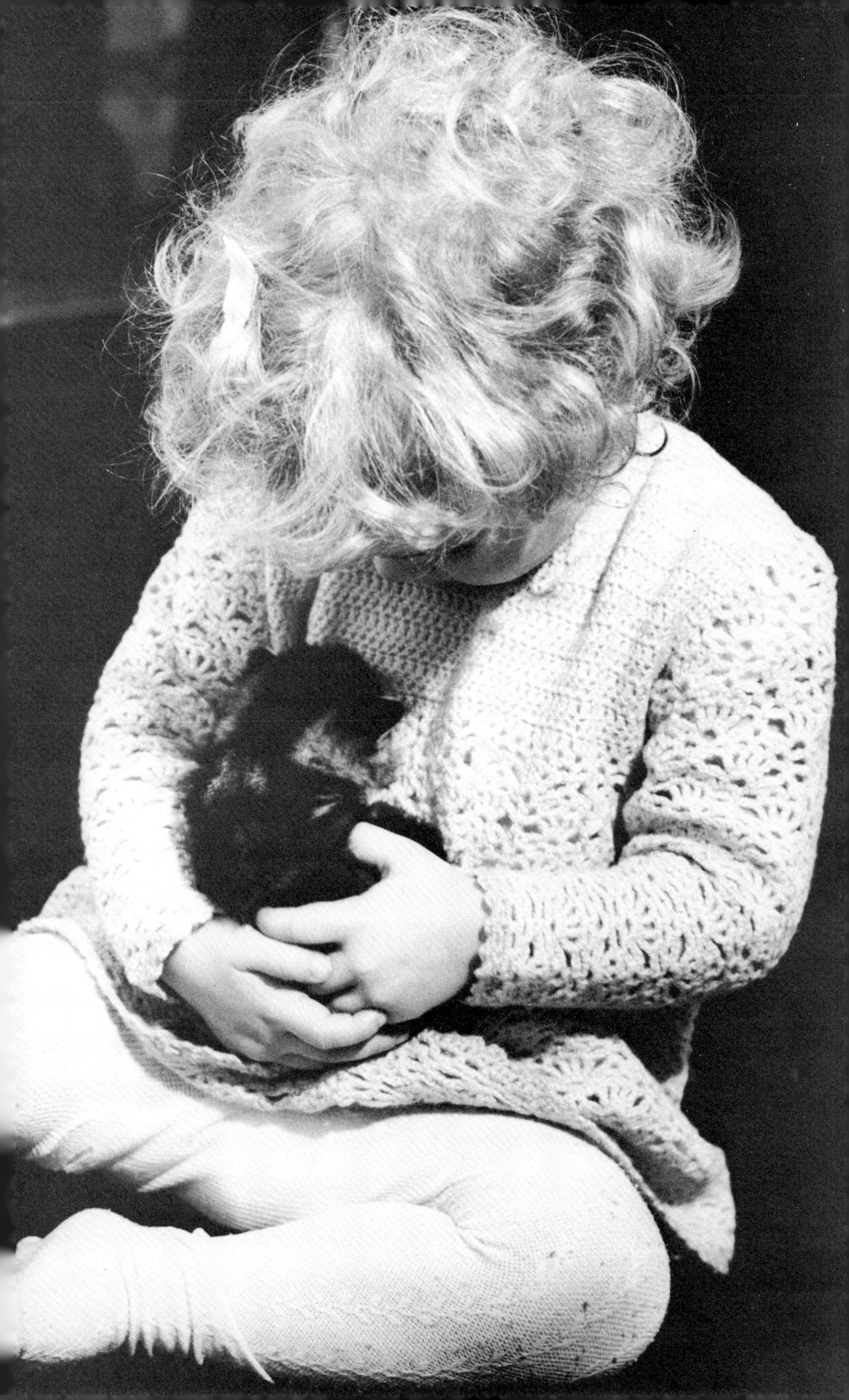

5 HOW TO GET A PET—AND HOW NOT TO

How many of us can walk by a pet-shop window without stopping to admire the puppies and kittens and to consider, even for just a moment, the possibility of taking one of them home? How many of us could enjoy a visit to the local humane society, knowing as we do that the animals in those cages are doomed to die shortly if they are not rescued? And how many of us walk away coolly from an abandoned baby bird without a twinge of conscience? Not many, I'd say, and for good reason. Nothing is more appealing than an animal that desperately needs the attention and care of someone who will keep it for better or worse, especially if the initial investment doesn't seem very extravagant. But we all know that much more has to be considered than just the purchase price, and so we are usually able to keep our heads long enough to add up the rest: the considerable costs of maintaining that animal for the rest of its natural life, not only in terms of food, housing, and veterinary care, but also in terms of emotional and physical energy. Even if we are simply "taking in" a stray or an injured wild animal or a pet that someone no longer wants—and we are determined to make the relationship a temporary one—we must realize we are taking on a responsibility that cannot be treated lightly.

Assuming that one has taken all these matters into consideration and that one has decided, after much thought and research, what kind of animal is best suited to become one's pet, the first step is to get the animal. This may be accomplished in a number of ways, and even when the choice may seem to have been the animal's rather than your own, various alternatives should always be considered—most of them requiring at least a modicum of knowledge and common sense. Whether you are buying or accepting an animal, a great deal of trouble can be avoided by taking some precautions before you take the animal. Learn what an animal of the species you are interested in looks like in good condition; look at as many examples of the type, or breed, as you can before you go out looking for your own. One must look not only for clear, alert eyes, unblemished coats or skins, a generally lively manner and other signs of good health; one should also be aware of what would be considered by an expert a "fault" in a particular species or breed. Dogs with tails between their legs and an excessively submissive manner may not be the gentle, retiring souls they appear to be; kittens with runny eyes and pitiful meows may not be simply starved for affection but for some medical attention as well. While deciding on a pet, sentiment must be replaced by practicality; the runt of the litter needs you more than you need it, and misplaced kindness can often result in suffering for everyone concerned. Do not necessarily assume that you can "save" an animal in bad condition; some have done so with great success but too many well-meaning people either end up with more animals than they can handle—sometimes infecting the ones they already have—or find themselves facing huge veterinary bills and prolonged suffering of an animal that can't survive anyway.

Always be willing to consult an expert for advice and be sure to follow it—if the expert is a disinterested party, that is. Many new owners rely heavily on dealers or breeders for a good deal more than the animal itself. It is probably unrealistic to assume that pet-shop owners and breeders, who are after all businessmen and not zoologists or veterinarians, know all there is to know about the animals they sell. In reality, because they are businessmen, they are not likely to divulge to potential customers the impracticalities involved in keeping certain kinds of animals. Yet the new owner will often look to the seller as the source of whatever information he will ever need to have. Although many excellent books are available on many species commonly kept as pets, the pamphlets sold in pet shops and the information casually but authoritatively handed out by dealers and their assistants are usually all that buyers are encouraged or willing to absorb. Some of these pamphlets are good enough for uncomplicated animals and useful as far as they go, but many of them are produced by food or drug companies and are simply promotional material for their own products and should be read as such. Many noncommercial pamphlets are outdated and written by enthusiasts rather than by professional experts. Anyone willing to make a commitment to keeping an animal should be interested enough to take a quick trip to the library to obtain sound information—not just after the fact but before the animal is obtained—if for nothing else than to know what the extent of that commitment is to be.

There are various specialists, of course, who can be good sources of information—animal trainers and keepers, veterinarians, laboratory handlers, zoologists—but as specialists they have limited time and particular interests that may not always be useful for the new owner. Many amateur enthusiasts are often as knowledgeable as the experts, and they have formed associations and produced newsletters that can be of great value to other enthusiasts in the same field. A list of these organizations and periodicals is given at the back of this book, and any serious inquiry will be greeted with a genuinely interested response. Many of these groups are not only concerned with sharing information and anecdotes about their animals but also with improving the conditions of pet shops and introducing legislation to protect animals of all sorts.

Once you have decided on a particular kind of animal and selected the best of that kind you could find—not the first or the cheapest (or most expensive) but the best—be sure to have it checked out by a veterinarian, unless you can be absolutely sure of its health and good condition from birth. Many animals will require inoculations very early on, particularly dogs and cats. A veterinarian can not only determine the animals's health and suggest preventive treatment for disease but will also give recommendations as to diet, housing, and even training procedures. If you are farsighted enough and able to do so, have the veterinarian check the animal before it actually comes into your possession and before you have begun to make your emotional as well as financial investment in its well-being.

EVEN THE MOST ORDINARY CAT LOOKS APPEALING IN A SHOP WINDOW.

HOW TO GET A PET—AND HOW NOT TO

Pet Shops

Dealers who handle a large number and variety of animals—from tropical fish to exotic wild animals and everything in-between—are usually well meaning, but all too often they can be the source of as much trouble as pleasure for both their animals and their customers. Because there is a good deal of money to be made in the pet trade these days, pet-shop owners are often more eager than they are able to please. Beyond the purchase of a license, there are few qualifications required to open a pet shop, and most experienced dealers have received what knowledge they have on the job rather than by any special training.

The department of Agriculture enforces the Laboratory Welfare Act which licenses and inspects animal dealers and breeders who sell to pet stores and research facilities, and inspections are carried out through the Veterinary Services Division. Nevertheless, the animals sold in pet shops can be in poor condition—not because of deliberate mistreatment but because of ignorance; a friend of mine recently purchased a relatively expensive Peruvian guinea pig from a reputable shop and found it suffering with scurvy—a condition common in these animals because few people realize they must have extra supplements of vitamin C. Often shops cannot afford the space to isolate all incoming animals, and many pets are exposed to diseases and parasites, the symptoms of which do not become visible until the animals have found a new home, since the turnover in these shops is usually quite rapid.

Because there is a steady demand for certain breeds of dogs, for instance, pet dealers must rely on steady sources of supply, which means quantity not quality. Stories abound about midwestern "puppy mills" which breed dogs in great numbers, taking little care about bloodlines as long as the parents are of the same breed. Puppies are frequently removed from their mothers before the age of eight weeks, crated and shipped in small, roughly handled cases, and sold before the signs of stress, trauma, or disease become apparent (usually about one to two weeks afterwards).

Many cities have begun to initiate legislation protecting the buyers of pet-shop dogs and cats: dealers are required to produce veterinary certificates guaranteeing the health of the animal and allowing for refund or credit if the animal can be proven in poor condition by another veterinarian within a certain time after the date of purchase. Many humane groups have also made progress in improving pet-shop conditions—for the sake of animals as well as customers. And an individual—or group of individuals—can do much to avoid problems for both animals and humans. If you find a pet shop where conditions are bad, report it to your local humane society or ASPCA. Try to convince local pet dealers to improve conditions on their own by suggesting that they display their "wares" in attractive settings and encourage browsers, much as a zoo or nature center would do, offering educational as well as commercial come-ons.

If you are purchasing an animal, demand a written bill of sale guaranteeing the health of the animal and enabling you to return the animal should it be proven within a month of purchase that a disease condition came with the animal, or entitling you to some kind of compensation or credit should the animal die within a short period of time of ill health. Internal parasites—to which most animals are subject—should not be considered a disease condition, nor can psychological damage to the animal because of its handling before it was sold; without knowing the parents of the animal, even an expert could not possibly determine the temperament of the animal or congenital defects the pet dealer may himself have inherited, so to speak. But ill health because of neglect or disease should not be tolerated. All too often, unfortunately, new owners become attached to their sickly pets and fail to return them, piling up huge veterinary bills rather than giving up on their commitments, feeling that they would be sentencing the animal to almost certain death. The cost, in these cases, to both animals and owners can be very great indeed.

One kind of animal dealer that does not really fall into the pet-shop owner category is the one who specializes in importing vast numbers of animals from abroad—now primarily mammals and reptiles, since in recent years the importation of birds has become severely restricted. Large numbers of animals—destined for scientific laboratories as well as for the pet trade—are collected from their native habitats, crated, and flown quickly to this country, many of them dying in the process or soon after arrival and almost all of them suffering considerably in the process. Bird collectors have told me of the bad old days when they would go to huge bird "worlds" to select a new animal and find hundreds of birds caged together in crowded aviaries where disease, fighting, and neglected birds were the rule rather than the exception. Since the turnover was so enormous and the original prices so low, the dealers didn't have to worry about those who were injured or sick and would sell anything that could still move to the first bidder. Importers still exist for all animals, but because prices are considerably higher and turnover therefore somewhat less, conditions have improved. Many humane groups look forward to the day when this wholesale marketing of exotics will be stopped, and thanks to legislation now in the works—amendments to the 1900 Lacey Act and various other federal restrictions—that day may not be far off.

The tone of my descriptions of pet shops and pet dealers has been rather more negative than positive, I will admit, and this is not fair to the individuals who are in the business for more than simply the money. Many dealers are reputable, and many shops are clean and manage and care for their stock very well. Some pet shops specialize in only a few types of animals—tropical fish, for instance, or reptiles—and because they want to encourage steady clientele rather than rapid turnover, they can usually be trusted to know what they are about. Many dealers have launched young enthusiasts on a lifelong commitment to animals, and will trade them back and forth as a customer's experience and interest increase. Urban pet shops often provide the only opportunity for youngsters to see animals up close or to handle them, and they perform a great service in educating people to an awareness of and respect for animals in general. A number of good-hearted dealers will even provide space for the adoption rather than the sale of young kittens, ensuring that the animals find good homes. These shops and dealers are not as yet commonplace, but they do exist, and it would be in everyone's interest to see that they are encouraged and praised for their good work.

Breeders

Most dog and cat owners, whether they have obtained their pets from a pet shop or the pound, are aware of the considerable activity and money spent on raising special breeds—sometimes creating them, often improving them, and, with the most popular breeds at least, occasionally making them worse. Unless specifically interested in breeding or showing (both highly professional businesses these days), the average pet owner has little reason to spend the kind of money involved in purchasing a purebred animal with the very finest lineage. There is, however, a good deal of usefulness in knowing about an animal's forebears in terms of temperament and behavioral and physical characteristics, although the number of people who have had success with pedigreeless mongrels would seem to make this a minor point.

An animal's papers proving that it has champion parents are no guarantee that it will be a good pet, but if you want to be relatively sure about what your youngster will become when it matures, the best approach is to take a good look at a breeder's stock and judge for yourself, or have a veterinarian or other expert check out the young animal before you invest any considerable sum. Many breeds of dog have suffered greatly from eager breeders who have irresponsibly allowed certain congenital faults to continue in their breeding stock, both physical and temperamental. Nevertheless, most breeders are careful about their breeding techniques and will do their best to see that poor animals are either destroyed or neutered to prevent the propagation of bad traits. And breeders like these are not hard to find; the national breeding organizations for different species can

BECAUSE IMPORT RESTRICTIONS ON BIRDS ARE SO STRICT, BREEDERS ARE OFTEN THE BEST SOURCE OF SUPPLY FOR PETS.

give you lists of local breeders, and your veterinarian is probably in the best position to give the good ones a recommendation.

One good way of obtaining a purebred animal with papers and without paying a lot of money is to look for a grown animal rather than a young one that has breeding or showing potential; caution is advised in this search, however, because animals that have been raised in a kennel or cage, without much personal attention, may not be suitable as pets right away and require a good deal of patience on the part of the owner. Be sure in any event, no matter what breed, age, or sex you buy, and even if no money changes hands, to make some kind of written agreement with the breeder in which he guarantees the animal's health, papers, and returnability if the arrangement does not work out.

Dogs and cats are not the only animals on whose breeding time and money are spent. There are pigeon fanciers, rabbit breeders, and many other specialists who raise animals for show, racing, meat, fur, or as pets. Laboratories involved in extensive research projects in genetics and other areas also raise strains of small rodents, rabbits, puppies, and other animals—some of which may occasionally be available for public sale or adoption. Not all of these animals make suitable pets, or course—even those advertised or sold as such—because they are raised for purposes that may have nothing to do with good temperament and that may have involved very little human contact. But if you have done some research on the species involved and on the breeder as well, you may end up with just what you are looking for, paying no more than you can afford.

Humane Societies

The old cartoon of the dog catcher hunting for local strays is not as outdated as you might think, nor is it very funny any more. The number of dogs and cats rounded up and destroyed each year by humane societies and municipal shelters has reached enormous proportions and shows no sign of abating. The disturbingly high statistics are caused primarily by irresponsible pet owners who have let their animals run free, who have abandoned them for any number of inexcusable reasons, or who have failed to neuter them and cannot deal with the unwanted offspring. Privately and publicly funded organizations are filled to overflowing with unclaimed animals yet even now most of them can do only a fraction of what would be required to gather up all the ownerless animals that are running free. Many of those which are not caught become feral and, like wild rats, can become real nuisances—genuinely dangerous as disease carriers and harmful to people, property, and other animals. Some people who find that they can no longer keep an animal (often the situation with wild or exotic species that prove very difficult after the charm has worn off) will turn them in to humane societies, which generally charge a fee of some kind and eventually destroy the animal. Most of the animals that find their way to these shelters have the same fate in store, although some of them are given a few days' chance to be reclaimed by the original owner or adopted by a new owner. Except for the fact that visits to inspect these doomed creatures can be heartbreaking, this is often an excellent way to obtain a pet for very little cost. Usually a large number of purebred animals as well as mongrels can be found, and those that have been well treated in the past may become ideal pets. Don't let sentiment sway your decision, however; pick only the liveliest, friendliest, healthiest looking animal and have it examined immediately by a veterinarian. And always keep in mind the fact that the animal's adjustment to you and to its new home may take some time, particularly if the animal is full grown or has suffered from some mistreatment in the past.

Many societies now charge a nominal fee as a down payment toward a neutering operation when an animal is taken and demand a written assurance from the new owner that surgery will take place within a specified time. Only about 4 per cent of these agreements are honored, which is a disgrace if not a crime, but at least some progress is being made in the direction of keeping shelters in the future somewhat less crowded.

Gifts from Friends

This is potentially one of the most uncomfortable ways of getting a pet (particularly if the benefactor is unhappy with the animal), but often it is a successful arrangement, since most friends will tend to put friendship first, no matter how eager they are to dispose of their animals. Nevertheless, it pays for everyone concerned to take the gift animal just as seriously as a purchased one. Be sure you get satisfactory answers if you have questions about an animal's history—medical, temperamental, and so on. Why does the friend want to get rid of the animal in the first place? If it is a simple matter of too many puppies, kittens, or white mice, or if the friend is moving to new quarters, the answer is obvious, but other questions should be asked, not always of the friend doing the giving. Find out as much as you can from reliable sources about the best kind of care and feeding you can provide, and understand that once you have had the animal for a month or so, it is yours for keeps and can't simply be returned because you find the new routines too troublesome. And do, for the sake of the animal as well as yourself, look that gift horse (or whatever) in the mouth. Have a veterinarian examine the animal and give it whatever inoculations are necessary. Many amateur breeders (or professional ones for that matter) do not take this step with new puppies or kittens but assume this is the responsibility of the new owner. If possible, use the same veterinarian your friend did; he will have accurate records and probably more knowledge of the animal than you do.

Strays and Beggars

Since many a pet was once a foundling, a word on the adoption of a stray or abandoned animal, whether full grown or immature, belongs in this chapter. The adopter does have some choice in the matter, though the animal may appear to be the chooser. When a domestic or wild animal comes calling—or is found—in a state of apparent homelessness, there are various ways of handling the situation. Obviously, if the animal has any identifying tags or marks, every effort should be made to locate the owner and return the animal as soon as possible. If you feel reasonably sure that you can trace the owner, no harm and a great deal of good can be done by feeding and otherwise caring for the lost animal, particularly if it seems in poor condition. One couple I know started a long-lasting friendship with the mayor of a large city just by taking the time and trouble to find the owner of a rather scruffy looking dog and to give it a temporary dose of food and kindness. Even if the animal has no identification card, with name, address, or telephone number, and no license that can be used to trace an owner through city or county authorities, a rabies tag will sometimes give the name of a veterinarian, through whom the owner may be found.

An animal without a collar but well behaved or well fed is probably someone's lost pet, and, again, efforts should be made to find out whose. You may turn the animal over to the local humane shelter; though little active effort will be made to trace the owner, the shelter will be required to hold the animal for a while in the hope that the owner will turn up. Anyone not wishing to sentence an animal to almost certain death, however, can make local inquiry or run advertisements in lost-and-found sections of newspapers or over the radio, a service that may be performed at no charge to the finder. You should also keep an ear and an eye alert for the loser's plea. Often the inconvenience is well worth the trouble, for many owners will show gratitude in a generous way, making the finder's pleasure even more pleasurable. Do not, however, ask for a reward; you will only arouse the owner's suspicion that you actually took the animal they have been looking for, rather than taking it in.

Many people react in a less welcoming way to strays or beggars and refuse to offer food or other creature comfort. This is not entirely a heartless reaction and in some situations may even be a sensible one, especially if the family has children or other animals. Many times a stray animal is only exploring and is perfectly capable of finding its way home. Many times an animal may be bad tempered or diseased and should not be handled at all. It is often difficult to tell exactly what led the animal to your door, though a careful examination from afar, if the animal has hung around for more than a day or so, should allow for some kind of sensible conclusion. Most animals that are ignored for any period of time will look elsewhere for food, but don't forget that an open garbage can or a half-full dish of your own pet's food is the same as a deliberate handout to a hungry stray. If you are determined to be inhospitable, be sure that your children, your pets, and your own humane instincts don't betray you.

If you finally break down and take pity on the creature, remember that you may have yourself a friend for life, *its* life, anyway. Do just as you would do with an animal purchased or obtained in any other way; have it examined by a vet as soon as you are reasonably convinced that it has no legitimate owner, and if it is a dog, have it licensed. If it is a wild animal—tamed through hunger, or too young to know any better—check with the local authorities to see whether it is legal to keep it at home and, if so, determine as soon as you can what kind of food and handling it requires. Because any animal taken from the wild can never be a completely trustworthy or satisfactory pet, try not to make a pet of it and prepare it and yourself for release when whatever crisis brought it to your door has passed. If necessary, release the animal far enough from your home so that it cannot find its way back but close enough to an area with which it is familiar so that it can make itself a new home. With young animals, this may take some time and a good deal of patience—as well as some unhappiness on your part if you have grown fond of the temporary resident—but this is part of the responsibility you incurred in the first place. If you truly want to help the creature, do the whole job.

Most official organizations and government agencies discourage people from taking in even wounded animals, in spite of the fact that the injury or illness will lead to almost certain death in the wild; they must take this position because they realize that an animal that builds up a dependency on humans is often particularly vulnerable and they know too well how often good-hearted souls are unable to be of real help. They also realize that once a wild animal has become tamed, the tamer is usually reluctant to let it go and will be tempted to disregard the illegalities and impracticalities of keeping a protected animal in captivity. It may be inhumane to allow an animal to die in a helpless, defenseless state in the wild, but it is, after all, entirely natural and has been going on for millions of years. An animal suffering because of human interference (inadvertent or not) is, I believe, deserving of help from humans, but only if that help is sensible and knowledgeably given.

But back to the new pet. If you have selected well and found just what you want (or, as should perhaps be the case, the animal has found just what *it* wants), the time has come for you to figure out the best way to keep the happy situation happy. Living arrangements, feeding, care, handling, medical attention, and breeding (for those of you who are certain you want more of the same) are the subjects covered in the next few chapters. Some of this material has been given in the sections (and charts at the end of the book) devoted to the individual species, but the following chapters provide more detailed information and advice about these particular aspects of pet keeping. First, however, a few words on the general subject of learning to live with a pet, a process requiring patience and perseverance of both human and animal but one that can promise even more rewards than problems.

6 LEARNING TO LIVE WITH A PET

Considering the amount of suffering that human beings cause each other every day in ways great and small, obvious and subtle, it is surprising that we are able to get along at all with any other species. Furthermore even those of us who have trouble being mates, parents, children, colleagues, friends, or even decent strangers can have excellent relationships with the so-called "lower" animals. Psychiatrists have discovered that schizophrenic children who have difficulty relating to other humans can sometimes be reached through animals; lonely people, who have very little contact with others because of age, illness, or whatever, may enjoy a more fulfilling emotional life thanks to a pet; and advisers to the lovelorn often recommend owning (and walking) a puppy as a way of getting to meet other puppy owners (and walkers). Perhaps it is simply that we are as capable as we ever were of making honest, simple connections with other living creatures but that the increased complexity of modern life has made this more difficult to accomplish except in an atmosphere of complete trust. We are finally beginning to realize that the faithfulness we have always expected from Fido (which, spelled Phydeaux or not, is still derived from the Latin word for faith) no longer deserves to be taken for granted. The steadily growing number of pets and of recent books on the subject of man's relationship to animals—not only those detailing our use and abuse of other species but also those analyzing the ways in which their behavior patterns may resemble our own—seems to indicate that through the animal world we can learn more about ourselves, not just in a general scientific way but on an individual, personal level as well. We may eventually see a day when the epithets "dog," "snake," "rat," "skunk," and even "son of a bitch" will be taken as compliments rather than insults.

Writers have spilled gallons of ink telling us how to get along with other people—even with ourselves—and the basic requirements, however variously they may be disguised, are pretty much the same: honesty, trust, self-confidence, common sense, a willingness to give, and the ability to receive. But these, of course, are attitudes, and without knowing the appropriate ways in which to communicate them, getting along with anyone—of whatever species—is likely to fail in one way or another. Even though we may *know* what is involved in "proper" behavior, we must learn to *act* accordingly if we are to have any hope of success. We must learn to read the attitudes of others through their behavior patterns, their gestures and language, in order to adjust our own behavior so that ours, in turn, may be read correctly by others. It takes time, patience, practice, and consistency to develop the ability to observe, draw conclusions, and respond appropriately, and these are the most important qualities in learning to get along with animals, especially those that share our bed and board. Putting bed and board aside for the moment, let's consider what else is involved in living with a pet. It may not be so difficult as living with a person (animals, after all, can't leave the cap off the toothpaste) but it does entail a certain amount of adjustment on both sides. Before dealing with the details of adjustment, however, we should look at a fascinating new field—animal communication—in which discoveries are being made every day, for this is an area in which even the most inexperienced pet owner may be able to make exciting new discoveries for himself.

Communicating with Your Pet— and Vice Versa

You probably know that if a cat wags its tail, it is expressing displeasure of some sort, but that a wagging tail on a dog indicates the opposite: friendliness, even happiness. You probably also know that you have nothing to fear from a dog whose ears are laid back but that you'd better watch out for a horse doing the same thing. Observations of animals in the wild or in the presence of members of their own species have taught us how to interpret these gestures more meaningfully: the dog's wagging tail and lowered ears are signs of submissiveness and are the same gestures that a wild dog will use to announce its inferiority to a dominant member of the pack. The cat's tail indicates simply that the animal is being watchful, perhaps suspicious but not aggressive or fearful, whereas the horse is displaying aggression, making a threatening gesture with its flattened ears to warn all comers. None of this is new information, but a great deal more can be learned from watching animals.

People who work with animals, in addition to making simple observations and drawing conclusions, have learned to make gestures that the animal itself will understand and to which it will respond. We have read about experiments that have been made with adult wolves, and we know that much is being done in the field of animal language with whales and dolphins, which resemble humans in that they use a vocal system, and with chimpanzees, which can learn human words and concepts, although they cannot speak the language. Even among less exotic animals (and plants, too, for that matter), marvelous experiences await the amateur. Did you know that if you blow gently in a horse's nostrils and then place your arm across its neck, you'll be well on the way to reassuring it that you are friend and not foe? Did you know that if you behave submissively to your German shepherd by showing fear, crouching, and avoiding eye contact (and wagging your tail if you have one), you may be well on your way to arousing its sense of dominance and allowing it to get the upper hand, possibly with unhappy results? Did you know that if you walk erectly, sneer, and stare directly into the eyes of your cat, you may send it cringing into a corner in confusion and even a state of alarm?

Animals are quite as quick to pick up human signals as the signals of their own species, or as we are to pick up theirs. Experimenting with animal language may not always be successful, nor is it always necessary even for advanced forms of training, but it is one of the most interesting aspect of pet keeping, and it affords a unique opportunity for amateurs to explore a world that may have seemed the exclusive bailiwick of scientists. Much of the work in the field of animal behavior has taken place in a laboratory situation—with rats running through Skinnerian mazes, pigeons pressing buttons for food pellets, chimpanzees learning to imitate forms of human behavior. At the other extreme, research is being done in the wild by zoologists who observe animals in their natural habitats, often at great risk to their own safety yet invariably with fascinating results. Somewhere between these settings comes the domain of the pet owner and his beloved animal; this is surely not a cold laboratory setup where records are carefully kept and life is all work and no play, and surely not a natural environment where the animals interact only with other animals. Nevertheless, as we have hinted, there is a great deal to observe in housebound creatures, and the activity of observation can be one of the most rewarding that we know. Even a tiny white mouse or a lowly earthworm can be a source of pleasure, particularly if we take the animal on its own terms and drop all of our anthropomorphic tendencies to grant it human motivations and human reactions.

Taking an animal on its own terms, of course, means that we must learn to use a certain amount of discretion in our observing as well as in our interpretations. Ants, for example, will probably not tunnel very energetically if you watch them for long periods of time, letting in the light and distracting them with noises that may send them into periods of inactivity. Hamster mothers may gobble up their new offspring if they are disturbed in the nest; this is not a natural act except in times of extreme distress, which might simply be caused by someone innocently wanting to take a peek just when the hamstress needs assurance that she and her babies are perfectly safe.

Observing need not always cause trouble, of course; it might even make you aware of gestures that you make without thinking but which your own animal knows how to interpret, often to your amazement. Say, for instance, that you inadvertently but invariably comb your hair before leaving the house. It doesn't take the average cat or dog long to realize that when you pick up a comb, you can be expected to disappear for a while, or perhaps take them for a walk. The presence of suitcases on my bed always sends my cats into a nervous pacing routine (usually into a suitcase), and though that particular act on my part may be obvious enough, another less obvious gesture may be just as clear a tip-off to the animal that watches you more carefully than you watch yourself. Because we may not always see these gestures as the animal does, we may assume that the animal is behaving unpredictably if clairvoyantly; but in fact animals are rarely unpredictable, for unlike adult humans, they do not lie. What is written in their eyes, in their gestures, in their behavior patterns is almost always a pretty accurate indication of what they are feeling or thinking. It is not difficult, once you know the vocabulary, to figure out just what to expect of the animal. It is not always so easy to read us humans clearly, because we can be inconsistent and even deceptive in our behavior, and so it is with animals that they, too, can become easily confused by us.

Gestures are not the only way of communicating with animals; anyone who has ever tried to work with animals (or even just play with them) can tell you that tone of voice is very important, far more significant than the actual words you use. "No!" delivered in a soft, friendly voice is not likely to have the effect of a disciplinary command, whereas "Good dog!" spoken gruffly is probably going to be taken as a reprimand rather than as a compliment.

Members of the same species usually share the same or a similar vocabulary, whether because of heredity or social interaction, yet individual characteristics can also be picked up through experience with humans—both good and bad. A horse that has never been mistreated is not likely to bite or kick a human who gives it no cause for fear, just as a deer lovingly raised by a human family is likely to be fearless standing ten feet away from a rifle-toting hunter. In nature, however, both species are naturally shy and fearful, running away from the slightest hint of an unfamiliar being. Animals that spend much or all of their time in the presence of humans, without their own species around, especially when they are young, may in fact cause some peculiar problems that responsible humans simply have to learn to cope with. Baby pheasants, for instance, without the example of an adult pheasant, may have to be taught by people how to eat if they are to survive. Wild animals that give birth in captivity will often fail to rear their young properly, not always because conditions are bad but often because they simply don't know how to do it. Gorilla babies born in zoos must frequently be raised by human mothers; experts believe that as social animals in the wild gorillas learn maternal behavior from other gorillas, an educational opportunity that most zoos cannot provide.

Konrad Lorenz has written extensively on animal behavior, and one of his most fascinating theories—with which he experimented at home as well as elsewhere—is that of "imprinting," by which he means the tendency of young animals to attach themselves to a mother figure, whether or not "she" is of the same species, and to identify with that figure. He tells a charming story on himself about an episode that took place while he was playing mother to a flock of mallard ducklings, which responded to his sound rather than his appearance, though he had to crouch fairly low to make his "quack" heard. One day when he was waddling around the backyard, making his intermittent quacks, with his brood of ducklings in tow, he noticed several neighbors looking over the fence with a collective expression of astonishment and even horror. Looking back to his ducklings and gesturing to indicate the row of little reasons for his odd behavior, Lorenz realized that all of them had disappeared into the tall grass, leaving him to waddle and quack quite alone, suddenly bereft of an easy explanation.

Hans Christian Andersen, a century earlier, gave us a story of imprinting when he told of the ugly duckling who believed he was simply a malformed duck until he grew up into a swan and saw that he wasn't a duck at all. Unlike the ugly duckling's "step-mother," however, Lorenz went out of his way to teach his charges behavior appropriate to their own species, but most people do not take the same kind of care. By treating a puppy, for instance, as a member of the household, they may in fact help exaggerate certain infantile canine mannerisms at some psychological expense to the animal; a dog that constantly plays the submissive game by lowering its head, rolling over, even urinating (another way of putting out the white flag), may be repressing aggressive tendencies that will suddenly appear in the adult dog when it is placed in a dominant role, a position for which it is relatively unprepared.

Perhaps a more common problem in dogs is their tendency to become "one-man" animals, so attached to single individuals that they cannot get along with other people or dogs. Although some dog owners take pride in telling their friends how their pet responds to no one else, many people are unhappy to find that their good-natured pet behaves jealously, even to the point of aggression, with a new friend, lover, or strangers. There are many reasons why a normally well-behaved dog may suddenly bite, but the increasing rate of dog bites—many of them involving children—may be caused by animals that people encourage to be wary and aggressive as guards and protectors of the home. (The increased number of dogs, of course, also contributes to the higher statistics.) Defense of territory plays a large part in this behavior, for it is well known that dogs—like the wild canines—are highly territorial by nature.

Theories about this instinct, like those about imprinting, give us another form of behavior to observe in our pets; birds in an aviary, rats in a cage, uncaged animals in a household, fish in an aquarium may all display territorial behavior—marking in various ways what area is theirs and drawing invisible lines for other animals that cannot be crossed without a threat or a fight. It is fascinating to watch this kind of behavior, as it is to observe pecking orders among animals, relative dominance in a group, and the rules that the dominant animal imposes on the others. Many times this dominance has nothing to do with size; remember that tiny cat who ran a houseful of birds, iguanas, others cats, a German shepherd, and even a baby gorilla.

It is fun to watch animals surprise us by getting along together in a household although in the wild they would be natural enemies. Dogs and cats that grow up together or live in the same house long enough will usually call a truce, if they don't actually end up sleeping in each other's paws. I even know of a barn owl and a brood of chickens that got along so well they believed themselves to be members of the same family. The barn owl whose eggs were unfertilized was encouraged by her keepers (at a small city zoo in New England) to incubate the eggs of a Bantam hen that had died just after laying them. When the eggs hatched, the barn owl carefully raised the chickens—her natural prey—in the nest, which was placed near the top of her cage; even after the chickens decided they preferred the floor to the nest (since they couldn't fly), the owl, in true maternal fashion, continued to try rounding them up and getting them to fly back to the nest.

Although the barn-owl incident may not have been a problem for anyone but the barn owl (and an annoyance to the chickens), there are—as I have indicated—some problems to be observed in animal compatibility as well as some situations that are just plain interesting to watch. The more closely we observe, and the more accurately we can determine the nature of an animal's behavior, its motivations and its meaning, the more likely we will be to achieve success in solving the problems that living with animals may incur. Many of these never need arise in the home, however, if we have managed to adjust ourselves and our animals to the basic conditions of living together.

If you have some idea of what to expect from the animal you own or are about to own, both in terms of temperament and physical requirements, you'll be well on the way to success in developing an excellent relationship.

Adjusting Your Household to the Animal

Assuming that you have selected a kind of animal about which you know something, you will probably be prepared to make certain changes in your own living arrangements to accommodate the animal's specific needs. If you are getting a parakeet, you'll probably set up a cage and buy some seed and grit before the bird moves in; if you are about to adopt a kitten, you'll have been told that a litter pan, some food and water dishes, and the contents for each of them will be part of the equipment. If you are about to become the owner of a large animal, you will be prepared to provide suitable living space and to fulfill its food requirements. But if you've never had an animal before—or are getting one of a type you've never had before—you may not realize that these are not the only items you must supply.

Even before you decide to get a pet, you will have to consider the readjustment of your own schedule, of revising your routines to see that the animal gets regular care and attention. This rescheduling doesn't involve simply feeding and cleaning times but also periods for playing with the animal, exercising it, grooming it, seeing that it remains in good health. Even if most of these chores (if you consider them chores) will become the responsibility of the children, you will still have to supervise the care of the animal to make sure that it doesn't get forgotten when the Little League beckons. Animals quickly become accustomed to a routine of feeding, exercising, sleeping, and so on, and they may suffer if that routine is interrupted. You should make a formal or informal schedule or agenda for attending to the needs of your pet on a daily and weekly basis, and then stick to it. It's very easy with a new animal, particularly a quiet one, like a fish or an ant, to forget to adjust the heat and light, or to remove uneaten food, or whatever has to be done. But remembering to do so, by whatever means it takes to remember, can obviously be a life-saving matter, particularly for a fragile creature that could not survive a day's neglect.

Young animals need far more care than most adults, which means that during the early days and weeks of its life with you, your pet will require the utmost attention. It is difficult to resist paying a lot of attention to a cute puppy or kitten, but it should be kept in mind that once the routines have been established—and the animal's dependence on you has become complete—your responsibility for good management has only begun. Once the novelty of owning an animal has worn off and the cute little baby has become a larger and possibly less interesting adult, you cannot assume that the animal is any less dependent on you than it was at the start. In some cases, the animal may seem more demanding by requiring more food, more discipline, and more space, yet if the early days of its life in the household are properly handled, these demands may not seem too arduous, for the animal will by then have become a member of the household where its role is important and even necessary to the other members.

Aside from the matter of incorporating the animal's routines into those of the household, there is also the matter of space. A mouse in a cage may not take up much room, but the mouse does need a place which belongs to it alone. One cannot move a cage around the house without causing the animal distress and disorientation; birds are particularly sensitive to this but even the tiny rodents may go off their feed or react badly to a sudden change of environment, and consistency of heat, humidity, and noise level must be maintained. Cats seem to fit almost imperceptibly into human spaces, adjusting their sleeping locations to the nearest available warm body and their

EVERYONE IN THE HOUSEHOLD MUST MAKE SOME ADJUSTMENT WHEN A NEW PET ARRIVES ON THE SCENE.

ADJUSTING YOUR HOUSEHOLD TO THE ANIMAL

play areas to whichever chair they hit first. It is important, however, even to the most adaptable cat that it knows where it can always find its food, its litter box, and a place for curling up in privacy. And, of course, more active, destructive or larger animals will need well-defined areas in which they can live, exercise, eat, and sleep without requiring constant supervision to prevent their escaping or damaging property or themselves.

If any animal is to become part of a human household, the owner must take into consideration not only himself as owner and the animal as pet. Remember that other people may be involved: children, other adults, neighbors, visitors; and other animals: your other pets, neighborhood pets, and visiting wild animals (squirrels, birds, raccoons, etc., that frequent populated areas). Humans can, of course, be prepared for the new arrival in advance, but other animals may at first cause a certain amount of discord, if not total confusion. Small, vulnerable baby animals will be at the mercy of a resident cat or a neighborhood dog that may resent the intruder for disrupting the established pecking order. Until a new pecking order is set up, the period of adjustment may not be an easy one, but it can be made somewhat less troublesome if the owner takes some care in introducing the new pet. For reasons of health, it is often a good idea to isolate the newcomer, not only to avoid possible infection from parasites or diseases that it (or the residents) may carry, but also to avoid fighting or simply a disagreeable atmosphere. Even if you eventually plan to put two birds together in the same cage—say, for breeding purposes—they can't simply be thrown together without some preparation. Placed in separate but adjacent cages, the birds may become acquainted and learn to accept each other's presence, and then later be placed without incident in a cage new to them both. Species differ in temperament, of course, some being more aggressive than others even toward their own kind, but the tamest, most agreeable birds need a period of adjustment before they can be expected to get along.

With uncaged animals, the introduction may be far more sudden and involve a certain risk, but careful handling by the owner—involving careful supervision for the first day or two—will probably keep trouble to a minimum. Often, though not always, the prior resident will take the upper hand, establishing dominance over the newcomer, who must accept a low place on the totem pole or risk insult and even injury if it tries to argue. A family I know owns a tiny Pomeranian dog which even manages to keep their full-grown wolf in line; the wolf came as a cub into the household when the Pom was already grown, and even though there is now an enormous difference in size, the dog is quite unafraid of the wolf and is quick to make its prior claim very clear. One day, when the Pomeranian got into the wolf's cage, the owners were astounded to find it entirely unharmed and the wolf suffering from a bloody nose where the little dog had delivered a disciplinary nip when the playing had got too rough. Yet I also know a big red cat that recently moved in with a family that already included two adult cats and during the first day established himself as head cat by reclining imperiously on the living-room rug and allowing the others to pay their respects. Stories abound of cats and dogs that eat, sleep, and play together; this is not at all unusual but simply the result of a well-established household hierarchy. Cats and dogs can even learn to adjust to the presence of a caged bird and be trained with some discipline on the part of the owner to leave the creature alone.

Adjusting the Animal to Your Household

No matter how much one may wish to turn one's life upside down in order to make an animal comfortable and happy, there will always be times when it is necessary for the animal to make some adjustments if it is to become an acceptable member of the household, which is, after all, designed primarily for human comfort and happiness. The relatively unassuming mouse or garter snake must—if it is to be a real pet—learn to tolerate a certain amount of handling, and even the most aloof cat must adapt its habits to those of its owners. More demanding animals will undoubtedly have to undergo a certain amount of training if their presence in or around the house is to be accepted, let along enjoyed. Taming and training are only two of the ways in which an animal's behavior may be modified; some owners use restraining equipment of some sort, and others even choose the alternative of surgery to change their pet's behavior or its effects.

TAMING

This is a relatively simple process, though it can consume a great deal of time and patience. Taming can have very rewarding results, however, for it means that an animal has lost its natural fear and has learned to accept human handling. Deliberate taming is not generally necessary in dealing with young animals, even wild ones, or with domestic animals that are handled from birth as a matter of course. But with reptiles, birds, and adult wild animals, taming—which is about all one can hope to accomplish—must be undertaken with care. Even though these animals may spend most of their lives in a

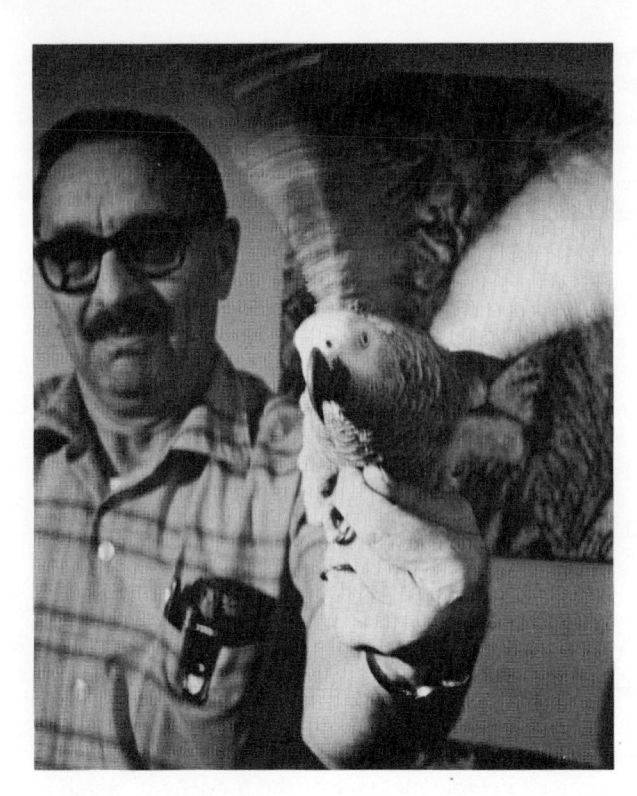

TEACHING A BIRD TO LAND ON YOUR HAND WHEN YOU CALL IT WILL ENABLE YOU TO ALLOW IT TO FLY OUTSIDE ITS CAGE.

cage, they will be little more than captive prisoners unless an effort is made on the part of the captor to gain their trust, even in a small way. The response on the part of the animal may not be much more than a passive one, but life will be far easier for the owner who can clean the cage, feed the animal, and deal with its ailments without frightening the animal or allowing it inadvertently to escape.

The first step in taming a caged animal is to make the animal aware of your presence and accustomed to you without showing signs of fear. Once a bird, for instance, has learned to accept your hand on its cage, it is only a matter of time before it will allow you to put your hand in the cage without reacting either fearfully or aggressively. Short but regular periods of this kind of attention should bring about gradual acceptance of your hand, and before long you'll find that the bird can be encouraged to move on to your finger when you press your hand against its breast. Once this step has been accomplished, you can begin to let the bird out of its cage (after closing all doors and windows, of course, and removing all other living beings from the room). After the first flurry, the bird will gradually calm down and may be persuaded to alight on your finger or back on its cage. These brief flights should be made a regular part of the bird's routine (at least twice a week), affording it some chance for necessary exercise and you some time to clean the cage without disturbing the bird. Birds do not like to be fondled or patted, but they will learn to enjoy the opportunity to sit on their owner's shoulder, nibble at his ear, or otherwise show affection. (Speaking of nibbles, it is good to remember that a bird's beak is one tool it has for exploring the world; even if it hurts, a nip or peck may not indicate aggression but simply curiosity or, occasionally, insecurity.)

Snakes and lizards may never show genuine affection, though I have seen many a lizard close its eyes in utter content while being rubbed along its back. Snakes will soon learn to submit without protest to being removed from their cages, carried about, and petted by human hands, and even a praying mantis can be made to perch on a finger while munching happily on a nice, damp leaf. For many animals, wild ones especially, food is one of the best ways to attract their attention and to earn their trust (however, with animals that are not fed so often, such as snakes, this method will not work at all).

It may take a good long time for the back-yard songbirds to tolerate your presence, but it can be done, sometimes so successfully that the birds will eat from your hand. One family managed to tame their wild-bird visitors by using a scarecrow figure and keeping its out-

SNAKES, WITH PROPER HANDLING ON A REGULAR BASIS, CAN BE EASILY TAMED; THIS BURMESE PYTHON EVEN SEEMS TO ENJOY THE ATTENTION.

stretched hand filled with seeds; when the birds had become accustomed to the generous, if inert, figure, members of the family managed to elicit the same response by dressing in the scarecrow's clothes and standing for many minutes in the same pose. Most people don't have this kind of patience, but some animals—raccoons, squirrels, chipmunks, ducks, crows, and pigeons, for instance—don't require it and will become tame very quickly for the sake of a regular handout.

A lot of people who deal with birds, reptiles, and wild animals use gloves or other protective devices to avoid injury should the animal become alarmed and aggressive, but I don't myself recommend their use in most circumstances. If you are trying to gain an animal's trust, you should have a little trust yourself and count on quiet, deliberate gestures to win the animal over. The use of gloves can, in fact, be a real deterrent, for they can make the hands clumsy and less sensitive to the animal being handled. A couple of small parrots I know get terribly excited and upset when they see their owner's gloves, which they associate with rough handling. If handling does arouse fear in an animal, one should go back to square one and begin again with patience and gentle movements to regain the animal's confidence and dispel its fear. Falconers and beekeepers will be glad to disagree with me on these grounds, because the animals they deal with can cause injury without intending any, but by doing what comes naturally. These, however, are exceptions to the rule, and dealing successfully with these creatures—as with poisonous reptiles or other kinds of dangerous animals—requires some professional expertise along with the protective coverings.

Rats are intelligent and may be trained—an important step beyond taming—but most small caged rodents cannot learn to do much more than tolerate handling. Although they are entertaining to watch in their cages, much of the fun of owning hamsters or gerbils is in picking them up and patting their furry little bodies. But even this cannot be done without some gradual conditioning. Because these small creatures rarely connect the hand that feeds it with their ever-full dishes of food and automatic watering devices, they are far more likely to bite that hand when it is unceremoniously thrust in the cage than they are to welcome it. Nevertheless, high strung as they are, even these active little animals will become used to their people, though certain precautions must be taken if they are to be given even a brief period of freedom. Rather than reaching in to pick up the animal, try coaxing it out of the cage with a piece of food and some softly spoken sweet nothings; once out, the animal should be gently but firmly grasped and held, and returned in a relatively short time to the cage. If you have a room without hiding places (hamsters and gerbils will find some even if you think you haven't any), you can let it run around loose, but be prepared for some difficulty in getting it back to the cage. Whatever you do to recapture the animal, try not to frighten it, for you'll only make the next free run longer and more frustrating for yourself. Larger caged animals, such as guinea pigs, rats, and rabbits, because they are not so easily lost, can be allowed a good deal of freedom, though they must always be supervised. All of these larger, more intelligent animals will probably return eventually on their own to the cages where they know their food and other living facilities await, and some may even become accustomed to using a litter box and other niceties of pet life.

TRAINING

To many people the training of animals is what goes on in the circus or in certain work situations. Tigers that jump through hoops, dogs that fetch or attack, chimpanzees and bears that ride bicycles have, of course, undergone training to achieve these feats, but that kind of training does not concern us here. For many pets, however, a kind of basic training *is* necessary if they are to be good pets, and not just for the owner's pleasure. It's nice to have a turtle eat out of your hand and it's fun to have a dog roll over and play dead or to have a cat that will come when it's called, but the training to which I refer is not simply a matter of fun. Teaching a reptile to eat dog food rather than live animals may be a necessity for someone who does not have a regular steady supply of white mice. And teaching a dog that you are the boss and that it must come on command can be a lifesaver, not only for the dog that is about to cross the road in front of a car but also for the neighbor's cat or child who manages to revive—for an instant—the dog's long-repressed desire for *la chasse.*

It is, in fact, irresponsible of any dog owner whose animal has the freedom of the house to allow the animal to go untrained. Even if you are willing to overlook the bad habits of an animal that urinates where it pleases or jumps all over you when it's happy, undoubtedly someone (or a collection of someones) will suffer from them. And the dog will benefit in the long run as well. As I have said, dogs are naturally submissive to a dominant individual, and an owner who does not establish his dominance is likely to end up being owned. Cats need very little discipline to learn to use a litter box or behave themselves in an acceptable manner befitting a good house pet. But dogs, and the larger domestic animals, are far more demanding and less adaptable, and require a good deal of attention and discipline if they are to become good pets.

The most effective method of training animals is the reward-and-punishment system. The use of a reward—be it a piece of food, a pat on the head, a word of praise, or the relief of discomfort (as when one relieves pressure on a horse's rein if it stops on cue)—is the most likely way there is to ensure that an animal will repeat the desired behavior. The choice of reward will, naturally, depend on the animal. It's not much good to use food as a reward when the animal isn't hungry or when it has a full food dish all the time, as the small rodents do. And it's no good patting a snake on the head when it doesn't realize that a pat is a sign of affection it doesn't crave anyway. But a sensible use of deprivation (not to the extent that the animal will suffer, of course) and reward will do wonders in teaching an animal to do what we want it to do.

Let's say that you want to teach a dog to sit on command. At some point shortly before you are to give it a meal, put the animal on a leash and remove yourself to a quiet undisturbed room. Ask the animal to "Sit" using a firm tone of voice and at the same time placing your hand on its hindquarters forcing it to take a sitting position. Praise the dog with a bit of food, and repeat the procedure. Most responsive dogs should get the idea pretty quickly and sit when you give the verbal command without any physical encouragement. When the dog has performed two or three times correctly, stop the training session, before the animal gets bored, and bring on dinner. Repeat the same lesson for a few days in a row—at the same time of day—and you'll be ready to progress to another command, such as staying in place, coming when called, or standing at your side (heeling). Bits of food are not always necessary, and most dogs will perform just as willingly for praise or a friendly pat on the head.

Housebreaking a puppy is usually an ordeal for new dog owners, but it needn't be if the owner is willing to add a little common sense to his supply of patience—and newspaper. Again, the principle is one of rewarding the animal for doing the right thing, which in this case is a natural behavior but one to be performed in a place and at a time according to the owner's convenience. In an apartment or house where the pup might be left alone without supervision or easy access to the outdoors, paper training is the best way to begin. (For small dogs in city apartments, this is often the best way to continue.) For the first few weeks, confine the puppy to a single room, if possible, or fenced-off area preferably near an outside door, and cover the area with newspaper, so that the pup cannot avoid eliminating on the paper. After a few days you will find that the animal tends to use a single area of the room, usually the part farthest from its feed dish. Praise him when he goes to that spot and uses it, gradually removing the papers from other sections of the room. Before the week is out, the puppy should be using only the papered area, and you should have some idea of his schedule. When you are ready to train him to go outside, interrupt him just as he is heading for the paper, leash him quickly, and take him outdoors. When he eliminates, praise him heartily. Repeat the procedure (returning to the same spot each time so that he will be sure to get the idea) whenever the puppy needs to eliminate, and remove the paper.

Before long and before too many mistakes are made, the animal should have the right idea and will learn to display signs of wanting to go out whenever his needs arise. If you catch the puppy in the act of making a mistake, firmly remove him to the outside rather than punishing him. I've never known a dog to feel anything but confusion when his nose is rubbed in his own excrement; this act is far more repellent to the human being involved than to the dog anyway and is just another form of anthropomorphism. Another tip: when a mistake is made, clean and deodorize the area thoroughly so that the puppy won't associate the right smell with the wrong place.

Many of us inadvertently teach our animals certain kinds of behavior without deliberately setting out to train them. I once had a guinea pig that would whistle enthusiastically every time I went near the refrigerator door because it would expect a tidbit and had connected its own whistle with the appearance of food. Of course, the guinea pig was also training me to produce the tidbit, and it is true that the reward system works two ways. I once had a large mastiff that had been trained by a previous owner to stay in the car for some reason; I never knew what the cue was for the animal to leave, and nothing I tried would work until I discovered accidently that singing to the dog turned the trick. (It may simply have been that my singing so appalled the poor creature that it jumped out of the car to escape the sound, forgetting all earlier training.) Needless to say, whenever I had the dog in the car and was headed home, I would invariably break into "Home on the Range" as we entered the driveway, just like the well-trained owner I was.

The speed with which an animal learns to perform the way we want it to will vary considerably from one individual to another, yet in all training the basic approach is the same—patience, a calm and consistent manner, an immediate reward, and repetition of the lesson (in small but regular doses) until the animal responds properly. Punishment is in general a less effective way of teaching but in some situations the use of a reprimand is the only way to break a bad habit or to prevent certain kinds of undesirable behavior. Behavioral scientists have proven in experiments that whereas the reward system tends to strengthen behavior patterns, punishment does not necessarily weaken them but simply represses them or leads to the substitution of alternative behavior, producing at the same time some unfortunate by-products such as anger, fear, guilt, frustration, etc. Nevertheless, punishment, used consistently and immediately after the wrongdoing (or beforehand if one is alert enough), can be useful in establishing discipline with some animals.

By punishment, of course, I don't mean inflicting pain but only the threat of pain, which for responsive animals that have learned your gestures may be merely a frown or a harsh word. There is no excuse for beating an animal (the whips used by successful horse trainers do not inflict pain so much as they cause fear by the noise they produce and the pressure they incur), especially since the animal may not always connect the punishment with the crime. Furthermore, the "crime" may be a piece of perfectly normal animal behavior. Most wild animals (and some domestic ones, such as the cat) may resent discipline, and a threat will evoke only an aggressive response in return. Most domestic animals, unless they have been "taught" to fear humans, will generally learn what is desired of them with proper training and will act accordingly. Dogs are easier than most to train, not because they are necessarily more intelligent but because they learn to consider their owner as the master. Nevertheless, it is possible to train many animals—cats, horses, pigs, rats, and even fleas—if the methods used are sensible and correctly applied.

Although most forms of training should probably wait until the animal is nearly full grown and physically developed, some early steps—such as housebreaking—can be undertaken soon after an animal is weaned. And a number of bad habits can be prevented right from the start. Many dog owners complain that their pets jump up on them and on visitors; they don't realize that the animals do so because they were probably rewarded for this behavior when they were cute puppies. And cute they may have been until they got too big—and muddy maybe—for the owners to accept the behavior happily. By ignoring a jumping puppy or teaching it another way to show its excitement and pleasure at greeting us (sitting down, for instance), we can avoid the necessity of punishment later on. Other bad habits—such as chewing on rugs and slippers, mauling the furniture, and so on—can also be avoided if one begins early enough; providing an alternative activity is one solution—toys for the puppy, scratching posts for the kitten—and discipline is another. A firm "No" and a word of praise when the animal moves away from the area where he has been misbehaving, if applied consistently and regularly, are usually sufficient. The reasons for failure are many: inconsistency (one can't be on hand all the time to see the wrongdoing and one can't discipline long after the deed) and the fact that the animals are doing something quite natural to them are the most common. But if one is determined enough, an intensive period of time devoted to training and an understanding of what the animal is capable of doing should win out in the end.

If the animal reaches maturity with bad habits well engrained, the same methods should be employed—with even more intensity, patience, and understanding—though many people find that it is worth the money to pay a professional to do the job. Some trainers prefer to train the owner rather than the animal—assuming, and I think correctly, that a well-trained, well-meaning owner is a far better trainer than a stranger the dog may never see again. But many specialized trainers work directly with the animal, often charging high fees for their services. Regardless of what they claim, no "magic" formulas or secrets are used, only common sense and the time and effort the owner is apparently unwilling to spend.

A client once called me about her dog, which regularly attacked strangers who came onto her property. She had apparently wished the animal to act as a guard dog, but failed to recognize early enough the aggressive signs in the dog that would make it a biter rather than a barker. Eventually she realized that a biting dog was a far greater hindrance than a help, but she found that punishing the dog had no effect. She knew that the animal's behavior was caused by her own failure to control it when she had encouraged it to guard the house, and she felt guilty about using punishment which in any case seemed to be making matters worse. Every time the dog saw a stranger and made a move toward the invader of its territory, it would be slapped or locked up and soon learned to associate the presence of strangers with unpleasant treatment. My advice to her was to set up a situation in which the dog's behavior could be altered by rewarding it for a different kind of response. I suggested that she ignore the dog completely for a couple of days, feeding it without a word and withholding all affectionate gestures. Then she arranged for someone the dog didn't know to come to the house, at which time she would immediately give the dog friendly pats and kind words. When the stranger left, the dog would again be sent to the doghouse and be studiously ignored. Two or three strangers later, the dog was so pleased to see a new face—which would mean some affection from its owner—that it would greet anyone coming to the house with a round of joyful barking, an alert system that not only worked for the owner but also saved the leg of the visitor.

This woman's problem raises a question that is causing many people (owners and visitors) a good deal of distress nowadays. As the crime rate increases, we want our dogs (or our geese, or whatever) to protect us by raising an alarm when strangers approach. However, we want to avoid the injuries and lawsuits involved in dog bites. It is very important for a dog owner to decide which is more important —the pet status of his animal or its function as a guard. The two roles can rarely be successfully played by the same animal, and far too many newspaper headlines are created by attack dogs that were unable to distinguish between a friendly visitor and a prowling sneak thief. Although aggressiveness may vary from breed to breed, some making better guard dogs than others, it is not difficult to teach any dog, which is by nature a territorial animal, to protect the property it considers its own. And it is possible to control the way in which the animal does its protecting, by disciplining it at the first signs of aggression—*not* barking but snarling or raising its hair along the back. If those gestures are discouraged and barking encouraged, accidents are less likely to occur. The best kind of prevention, however, is to see that the dog is confined in some way; no burglar will stick around a house with a barking dog in it long enough to see whether it is tied or locked up.

Entire books have been written on the subject of training dogs, because they are undoubtedly one of the most responsive as well as most popular of pets, and horse training has been written about ever since the days of Xenophon. But other animals can be trained, and some of them—even the most modest species—can learn to do quite extraordinary things. One cat I know even learned to flush the toilet (after using it, what's more) because it was praised so heartily the first time the owner managed to make it do so. This was an unusual triumph, because cats are rather more difficult to train than dogs are; but I gather that the cat was rather unusual to begin with and even learned how to turn lights on and off.

Equally amazing to some cat owners with badly damaged upholstery is the notion that a cat may be taught not to scratch the furniture. Some training methods rely on the use of a scratching post or log which the cat may be encouraged (with catnip rewards) to use. At the same time, reprimands must be made whenever the cat begins to scratch at the sofa or rug. Constant supervision is necessary, of course, at least until the training is complete, because scratching is a perfectly natural activity for a cat (for exercise, claw sharpening, and the loosening of old claw tissue). Repellent sprays and lotions are rarely effective—even in keeping dogs from chewing on objects—because they tend to repel people first, although Bitter Apple (manufactured by Irving Grannick of Greenwich, Connecticut) is widely used by people who claim considerable success. I use it myself to keep animals from chewing bandages or licking off dressings, but it must be applied every twelve hours and may harm certain fabrics. Some owners have their cats declawed, but that is a subject discussed later in this chapter. The point here is that it is possible to train cats if enough effort is put to the task.

One writer tells about how a cat was trained to alert its deaf owner to the ringing of the doorbell and telephone simply by feeding it special tidbits at the same time as a bell was rung; like Pavlov's dog, the cat soon learned to run to its owner every time a bell rang. The same procedure has been used to teach cats to jump in and out of their carriers, to come when called, and so on. As with training the dog to obey on command, one simply uses a means of reinforcing or rewarding the animal's response to a given stimulus. No gimmicks or magic are involved, just a knowledge of the animal's capacity and of the basic methods of conditioning, as well as a good deal of time and patience. Horses and dogs that count or do simple arithmetic may seem extraordinary but have simply been trained to paw or bark on command and to stop at a signal from their trainer. Chimpanzees that develop enormous vocabularies in the sign language of the deaf are even more amazing to the uninitiated who do not comprehend the hours of painstaking work that have gone into training. But marvelous these examples are, nonetheless, and an encouragement to any pet owner to try his hand with his own animal.

It is odd when you think that other primates, so close to humans in many ways, cannot talk, whereas several species of birds can learn to imitate human words, and some types, such as the mynah, can even imitate tones of the human voice. The methods used in training birds to talk are quite simple, though they too require a lot of patience. A quiet room, far from the distraction of other sounds, and a bird that has already learned to respond to you and to tolerate your presence without fuss are the first important requirements. Training, then, is a simple matter of repeating a word—a relatively simple one at first— over and over until the animal imitates you. Short training sessions are best, for the bird will tire of the exercise even more quickly than you do, but if the conditions are right and the bird is apt, you should soon have it repeating your words and a whole vocabulary can be built up. Many bird owners tell me that their birds do understand what they are saying, though it is not reasonable to grant the bird as much intelligence as this claim would imply. Some birds will learn to associate certain words with objects or people, but communication will never be as sophisticated as the bird's vocabulary might indicate.

Even songbirds must be taught to sing, as zoologists are beginning to find out from experiments with young birds that are taken before they learn to sing and are raised apart from other of their species; and most canary fanciers find that they, too, must train their birds to get a satisfactory sound. The use of another trained bird or a record player is the usual method, though here too patience and the lack of other distractions (mirrors and other birds included) are necessary for success.

EQUIPMENT

Part and parcel of the training process for many animals—though by no means for all—is the use of certain kinds of equipment. Most horse owners will probably spend more on equipment than they will on the horse itself, what with halters, saddles, bridles, harnesses, and the like, whereas the average hamster owner would be hard put to know exactly what to do with a collar, no matter how small. For dogs and cats, however, as well as for most larger animals, the equipment is relatively simple and inexpensive, though it is possible to spend whatever amount you like, thanks to an energetic pet-supply industry.

We have already made a plea for the use of a collar on every dog and any cat that is not entirely restricted to the house; this item is essential for attaching identification and other tags to the animal but it also comes in handy as a means of controlling the animal, usually attaching a leash or lead rope. Several kinds of collars are available, but the two most popular are the plain leather belt-type collar and the choke collar that works like a noose. Because I have seen owners and animals do damage to dogs wearing choke collars, I do not recommend their use, even for the strongest, worst-mannered beast; if a dog is so large and so untrained that it cannot be made to obey without pulling the handler headlong down the street attached to the other end of a leash, the pair is ill suited and the owner should make all haste to get the animal to behave properly or find a new owner for it. The strong leather collar is perfectly serviceable and holds far fewer dangers for both human and canine. A general rule of thumb for selecting the proper size is to be sure that at least two fingers can fit between the animal's neck and the collar. Because cats like to walk into or through narrow passages, special collars that will release automatically if caught are definitely recommended.

Leashes also come in all shapes and sizes, and as long as the material is not so heavy that its weight alone is burdensome to the animal, any kind will do. For dogs, I like the heavy-canvas type of lead used by dog-show exhibitors rather than the chain type, but this is a matter of personal choice. Cats can be trained to follow a leash as well as a dog can, and I would certainly recommend training a cat to a leash if you plan to do any amount of traveling with your pet. Hanging on to a scratching cat which is frightened of the outdoors or of traffic or of whatever other horrors lie beyond the front door can be a painful experience, and a slip may even result in the loss of the cat. I do know people who have trained their cats to stay on their shoulders as they walk from the car to the front door, but they would be the first to admit to many hours of calling and chasing when something interesting happened to cross their path.

An alternative to the usual collar-and-leash outfit is the use of a harness, especially convenient for small dogs for whom the pulling pressure of a leash would be better absorbed by the full body than by the tiny neck. (This is true also for ferrets, otters, and some cats.) This contraption is also useful for animals who enjoy devising ingenious ways of slipping a collar, no matter how snug.

There are certainly hundreds of other things that dog and cat owners can buy for their pets—from cosy little coats and jackets to umbrellas that attach to collars—but most of these are for the pleasure of the owner (and the amusement of passers-by) rather than for any particular usefulness they might have. (Small, short-haired breeds in cold climates, however, will benefit from the insulation of a man-made coat.) Another no-nonsense piece of equipment is a muzzle, which is probably used as much for its scare value as for its actual effectiveness. A muzzle *is* effective, of course, in preventing dog bites, but it shouldn't be necessary standard equipment for the pet owner; any animal that bites so harmfully and regularly that a muzzle is required should probably not be kept as a housepet in the first place. Nevertheless, a muzzle may come in handy when an animal is injured or sick and cannot be handled safely.

SURGERY

An animal's behavior—or the negative effects of it—can be altered in a number of ways without employing the method of training, and these involve surgery of one sort or another. This is a controversial area in many respects, since surgical alteration for any but medical reasons is considered a radical and even unnatural way of forcing an animal to conform to living peacefully with human beings. Few people believe that neutering a dog or cat is to be avoided for the reason that it is "unnatural," yet they will become speechless with fury at the idea of declawing or defanging an animal whose scratching or biting habits cause the owner damage, either to person or to property. Actually, each case must be considered on its individual merits (or demerits) before any general moral position can be taken. It can be quite sensible for a cat who lives its entire life in an apartment and never needs its claws for self-defense or tree climbing to have them removed; the operation is not a difficult one if the animal is young, and the recovery period is short, the psychological scars nonexistent. The scratching behavior will continue as usual, but no damage will be done to upholstery or children. In an older cat, this kind of surgery may be painful and the recovery time longer, but it won't cause the kind of distress that would result if the owner felt compelled to find the cat a new home. (Remember, also, that a cat may be disciplined and the furniture recovered.)

As for the owners of exotic or wild animals—and these are usually the ones who oppose the declawing operation most vehemently for its unnaturalness—I can only say that forcing such an animal to live in a human environment is unnatural in the first place, and life would be easier for all concerned if the animal were never made a pet at all. Zoos will not accept animals that have been declawed or defanged (or neutered, for that matter, since their breeding potential would be nil) and since most people who own exotics decide soon after they obtain them that life is just too difficult and that a zoo is the only logical place for the animals, care should be taken in making the decision. If one is motivated to declaw or defang a pet by the fear of being injured, one had better get another sort of pet or learn to handle an animal properly. Surely no one would remove the beak and talons from a parrot or deprive the fragile hamster of its only means of self-defense just for the sake of the owner's convenience (and fingers).

Whatever the situation and whatever the animal, any decision about declawing or defanging should—after all the pros and cons of the matter have been given serious consideration—be made as early in the animal's life as possible. An apartment dweller may one day move to the country and an indoor cat given the run of the yard; a declawed cat can still climb pretty well and of course its teeth and ability to retreat from enemies remain unimpaired, but the decision is never one to be taken lightly and deserves the utmost thoughtfulness.

The pet skunk is one animal to which both defanging and declawing are done with some regularity, as well as the more common surgery involving the removal of scent glands. If a skunk is to be kept as a pet for its full lifespan, this is probably a sensible method of avoiding a most disagreeable accident. The owner who has this done, however, must realize that the animal can never be allowed to return to the wild. I have known several people who have kept skunks on a temporary basis, scent glands and all, without ever having trouble; once a skunk has been tamed and accustomed to handling by humans, its defensive scent is not likely to come into use, though any frightening or threatening situation might provoke that familiar sideways stance and arched tail to warn the offender.

Various kinds of surgery can be employed to alter an animal so that it cannot do what it would normally be able to do in nature, but undoubtedly the most common operation performed on pets is that of neutering. This subject and some of my arguments in favor of neutering which have to do mostly with considerations of population control and medical problems, have been discussed elsewhere in the book (Chapters 2, 3, and 9). Yet other arguments concern important behavioral improvements that will take place as well and make an animal easier to live with. The owners of horses take a very reasonable position on the subject of castrating stallions, for instance: not only does castration make the control of bloodlines possible but it always makes the animal easier to handle. This is true of most neutered males; dogs and cats are less likely to roam and run the risk of getting lost or injured through fighting. Females that do not go into heat are also easier to live with, since they don't collect masses of suitors, nor do they display the usual signs of estrus such as crying (particularly objectionable in the Siamese cat) or rolling about on the floor in what appears to be frustration, even pain. The noise and disturbance caused by hordes of males hanging around a female in season need not be elaborated here, nor the rather nasty scent of tomcat urine (very noticeable in housecats, less so in outdoor cats). Neutered animals do not invariably become characterless or obese, as many people believe, although they do tend to become more docile and less erratic. Obesity is caused in most animals—just as in most people—by overeating and underexercising. Certainly a tomcat or a wandering dog may burn up energy by running through the woods or the neighborhood and by scrapping with others of its kind, but that is hardly a humane way of ensuring that an animal will keep its weight down.

Cosmetic surgery, such as tail docking and ear trimming, are difficult to defend on any grounds other than esthetics. Many owners continue the practice for the sake of show, because the judges tend to prefer "looks" that Mother Nature never intended. Hunting dogs, it is true, may have less trouble with bramble bushes if their ears, long tails, and dewclaws are trimmed, but all too often the practice of tail and ear docking is carried out simply because it is traditional. In sheep, tail docking is necessary to prevent soiling and infection of the rear quarters, because the animal has little muscular control over the tail, but doing the same in horses (or breaking the tail to make it "set" in a flashy stylish manner) has no such humane justification.

Although most pet birds are caged, some owners of ducks and geese prefer to keep their birds loose, pinioning their wings so that the animals cannot fly away. The most humane method is to clip the primary flight feathers on one wing so that the bird is made incapable of flying, but surgery is also performed in a number of ways to keep birds grounded for good. This practice should never be performed on native wild birds, nor is it really necessary for most pet owners, who have the option of selecting flightless birds to begin with or of caring for their flighted birds well enough that the desire to leave home never becomes apparent.

Adjusting to Special Occasions

When routine must be broken for reasons beyond the owner's control—or within it, for that matter, such as vacations or some other perfectly acceptable cause of absence—adjustments must be made for the sake of the animal. My cats are perfectly accustomed to my habit of going off somewhere else all day and returning in the evening, but when I leave for a longer period of time, I must make some provision for their care and feeding. Since most animals dislike being moved—unless they have been conditioned to it—it is usually best to have someone come in and look after them if you are to be away. I know parrots that get absolutely apoplectic if you so much as move their cages into an adjoining room, so their owner makes such moves as infrequently as possible just to keep the peace. And some animals will refuse to eat if anyone other than the usual feeder is on hand. This, again, is where training may be effective in altering behavior patterns, but the question of what to do when you go away still remains.

There is a book available devoted entirely to the subject of traveling with pets—by air, car, train, etc.—with all of the regulations involved in international and interstate travel included. An actor I know who owns two exotic cats for which he could find no suitable sitter had to go to the expense of renting and outfitting a camper when he went on a national tour; even then, the cats could not enter all the states because of laws having to do with exotics, and he had to hire a driver to take the camper around those states while he made some of the trip alone.

Most animals do not present this problem to owners who wish to travel with their pets, but there are many potential difficulties in such travel that can be avoided with some forethought. Whether the trip involves a week's trip in the car or a few days of switching planes and boats, be sure that the animal is in good health and has been thoroughly checked by a veterinarian. Ask the doctor for his advice about tranquilizers, since many animals suffer from disorientation in traveling and may become highly nervous or upset. If you are planning to cross any borders, check with immigration or customs officials about any special vaccinations or health certifications that may be required and ask your veterinarian to provide them when he examines the animal. Be sure that hotels and motels you plan to visit will welcome your pet; many do not and have been known to evict pet smugglers in the middle of cold nights when a telltale bark or aroma alerts the management to the extra nonpaying guest.* It is a good idea to trim a cat's claws before travel and to have a good strong leash for the dog and a muzzle if the animal is high strung.

In shipping an animal, do be sure you have a sturdy cage or carrier of your own rather than relying on the cardboard cartons that some companies provide; these can easily be broken open or crushed by other baggage. And see that the carrier is large enough for the animal to stand and turn around in and that it is carefully marked with your name, address, destination, flight number, and any special instructions for feeding or handling. ("Animal Enclosed—Handle with Care" is essential.) You should also make yourself aware of the weather forecast; many pets suffer from exposure—whether the animal is in an unheated baggage area or allowed to sit outside on a platform during the shipping process. (The 747 airplanes are the only ones currently equipped with air-conditioned baggage compartments.) Restrict the animal's food and water before and during travel to avoid digestive upset caused by the stress of travel and of unfamil-

---

*The Gaines Dog Research Center (250 North St., White Plains, N.Y. 10625) publishes an annual listing of American hotels and motels that accommodate guests with pets.

iar people and places. Take some of the animal's regular food with you to avoid the risk of sudden diet changes. When you and the animal arrive at your destination, feed and water lightly at first, giving the pet plenty of affection and reassurance to speed up its adjustment to the new situation.

If you decide to leave the animal behind, you can use one of the thousands of boarding kennels—or even elaborate "resorts"—for cats, dogs, and other species. These tend to be expensive, though the good ones, which may provide a certain amount of handling along with the bare essentials, can be worth every penny. The bad ones are not worth anything at all, however. A strict warning to all potential boarders: personally check the facilities of any kennel you plan to use. One highly attractive-sounding animal home, which advertised unbelievable creature comforts in the country for all their visitors, was found recently to offer minimal care; dogs were chained to trees, and it was only the complaints of neighbors hearing the howling animals that brought the owners of the place into court. It turned out that no owner had ever taken the time to inspect the place to which they were paying well over $10 a day for just about nothing.

Regardless of the quality of the kennels no animal can become quickly adjusted to a home-away-from-home, and owners should take this into account when they make the decision to board. Sitters and dog walkers are usually available to tend the animal in its own home for less money, and sometimes friends with animals of their own can be encouraged to take on the responsibility for the return of the favor at some future time. Be sure, however, to leave specific instructions and try to remember to include any peculiarities of the animal that might have become almost unnoticeable to you but may be downright disturbing to a substitute owner. One couple I know went away on vacation leaving their two cats in the care of a friend who had no idea that one of the cats was in the habit of taking trips of its own, always returning invisibly at night to eat and sleep. The sitter was convinced that she had simply lost the cat, and frantic telephone calls were only barely sufficient to convince her of the contrary.

Leaving an animal to the temporary—sometimes very brief—attention of another person brings up the subject of animal loneliness, one that raises many questions that are not easy to answer. Any creature dependent on humans can suffer from the lack of food, water, or warmth, but how much importance does one place on the absence of regular affection—or even on the presence of a particular individual? It is difficult to generalize, because animals of different species are not equally responsive and individual animals have been conditioned in different ways. A snake, for instance, couldn't care less about being left alone for even a few weeks, since it can survive perfectly well, if it's in good health, for quite a while without eating—though it must have water—and handling is something which it tolerates rather than actively enjoys. But a dog or cat, accustomed to affection on a daily basis, may suffer considerably from its withdrawal, even for a weekend. And wild animals will quickly go "wild" if not handled on a regular basis.

Because I was certain that my cat never quite became adjusted to my being at work during the day, I got another one to keep it company, and the two of them seem to thrive on the arrangement—both in their very different relationships with me and with each other. Animals confined in small, empty cages can manifest boredom or lack of sensual stimulus in various ways: by cribbing (chewing distractedly on their enclosures), stereotyped behavior patterns (swaying back and forth repeatedly, or, as zoo animals do, pacing over the same ground again and again without any particular purpose), or self-mutilation (pulling out feathers, chewing on toes, tails, etc.). Needless to say, all of these forms of behavior are to be quickly corrected if noticed and prevented if possible. It is not easy to know what an animal does when you're not around, unless something, or the animal itself, has been damaged or somehow altered in your absence. But a certain amount of sensitivity (to the animal's response on your return, for instance) and common sense should give you a pretty good idea about how much you were missed. When I return home after a weekend away (during which time my superintendent provides food and water), my cats generally behave in an aloof manner for a few minutes (punishing me?), then come over for a tentative sniff (expecting the worst—adultery with another cat), and eventually climb all over me with the delight they have obviously repressed for my benefit. Of course I am indulging here in pure anthropomorphism, and their responses undoubtedly have some entirely feline explanation, but I always take their cool behavior as a well-deserved rebuff for leaving them alone.

Learning to Love Your Pet

One important aspect of pet keeping—to some people (and pets) the most important—is that of affection, to which I have referred so far simply as a form of reward for good behavior. But the intangible bond that holds animal and man together in an intimate relationship—mutual love, respect, or mere acceptance, however it may be manifested—can be far more significant than many people realize. We may chuckle at the well-dressed woman who pampers her lap dog or feel pity for the elderly or disturbed person whose entire world seems to revolve around a parakeet or an unremarkable tabby, but if we do so we are making a great mistake. These individuals

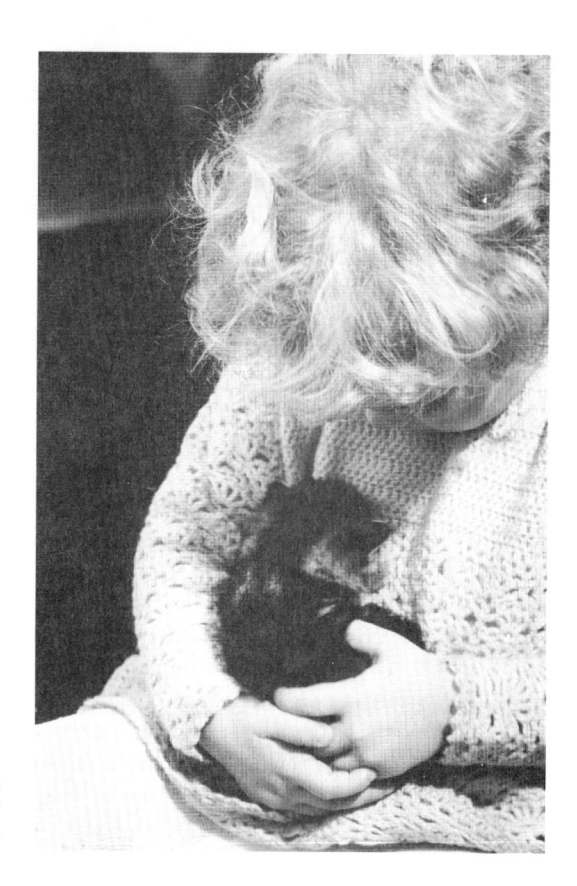

A GOOD RELATIONSHIP
WITH A PET
CAN'T START TOO EARLY.

have a special and rewarding relationship with another living being, and that is never an excuse for a sneer or a sense of superiority. Most people who understand and accept the responsibility of owning a pet would not begrudge the animal its share of attention, and most would be willing to admit that there is some reason beyond that of simply having a sense of responsibility for their taking the time and trouble.

More often than not, the dependency that the animal has on the owner is reciprocated to some extent by the owner. Too much attention or affection delivered at the wrong time and in the wrong way can, of course, be as cruel as deliberately withholding attention; overfeeding a dog and causing obesity because it enjoys treats can be more harmful than withholding food periodically, no matter how much pleasure we ourselves may get from watching the animal eat or do tricks to get the treat. Putting one's hand into a cage to fondle the hamster within may be a well-meant gesture, yet it is likely to be taken by the animal as a threat to its privacy (or territory) and a firm bite rather than a furry body may be the unpleasant reward (or punishment).

Just as people fall in and out of love with each other, so a relationship with an animal may change—sometimes for reasons not immediately clear to the owner. A young wild animal will, in its dependency on humans, behave affectionately to anyone who gives it food or warmth or attention; but the mature animal, which is more self-sufficient, may show little or none of the same feeling, especially when it is frightened. We have spoken of dogs that seem to turn on humans suddenly and aggressively without apparent warning (unapparent because we may not know how to interpret their threatening gestures), and we all know of cats that pick and choose their own time (and lap) for curling up and purring. Much of this behavior may be elicited by humans and some of it may be explained by causes (physiological as well as psychological) quite out of human control. If one has learned to observe the animal and to interpret its behavior with some degree of accuracy, however, problems may be prevented or solved by one means or another. The most effective approach as I have tried to point out, is one that the animal employs itself—to be consistent and honest. If our physical gestures, words, and behavior reflect our true feelings of love and respect, we'll be far more likely to stimulate the same response in return. Although this may not work with a leopard, which would undoubtedly rather have you show your affection by leaving it well alone, it is a significant first step in dealing with an animal whose respect and affection for its owner deserves to be returned in the same measure.

7 CARING FOR A PET

Living Arrangements

Considering the amount of money that people will spend to feather their own nests, it is surprising how little attention and money even sensible animal owners will provide for the sake of their pets. There are always a few people who enjoy buying decorative silken pillows or fancy cages with all the trimmings for their animals, but they give me the feeling that the animal's point of view has been entirely neglected for the owner's sense of esthetics. Even the most delicate pooch couldn't care less whether his bed is silk or burlap so long as it is familiar, and most birds will suffer rather than thrive in a too-small cage whether it is gilded or not. Most people, however, give the subject very little thought at all, assuming that the dog or cat, given its freedom of the house and grounds, will find its own place to sleep, and that the cages sold through pet shops are perfectly adequate for the animals that are sold there. Actually the arrangement of appropriate living conditions doesn't require much thought, only a little sense, some information, and a certain amount of effort.

No animal should be kept without any restrictions at all, with the possible exception of the farm dog or cat, and even these animals should be made to wear a collar with identification tags. Apartment animals are confined by their owners' living quarters, and most city dwellers use leashes for walking or exercising, though I have seen many exceptions and have treated many unhappy results of such carelessness. I assume that owners who let their dogs off the leash are pleased to have everyone observe how well trained Fido is and how obediently he heels and comes when called. But most people are not at all pleased to see how a nicely mannered dog will suddenly pick on a smaller dog, usually one that is restrained by a leash and thus cannot escape, and start a fight or bite savagely. Not only small dogs are the victims—children or unsuspecting adults who might unwittingly (and unwisely) pat the strange animal can end up with a painful bite as a reward. There is no excuse for a city dweller to take a dog off its leash; if one is not willing to run alongside a large animal who needs exercise or if one's apartment is not large enough to enable the animal to stretch its legs, then the two should part company. Some city parks offer dog runs for the purpose of exercising city animals, but these are not fool- or fight-proof, and an owner should use them with caution.

We have already spoken of the unattractive and unhealthy habit of dog owners who allow their animals to urinate and defecate wherever they get the urge, but until well-enforced restrictions are put into effect by city governments, any plea from people who do not own dogs will go unheard. Yet dog owners themselves are as likely to suffer as anyone else and they should realize how vulnerable a position their own animals are in every time they set a paw on a city sidewalk. A curious state of affairs, when you consider that any dog could be easily trained to use a litter pan or a papered area.

Although dog owners in the city seem unwilling to change their ways, nearly everyone else is aware of these problems and would like to see something done. Yet it is probably the suburban dweller who is the greater offender, perhaps only because the problems are less visible. Most dog fights, incidents of theft, running away, and car accidents take place outside the city—usually because owners with a back yard allow their animals to run free. Anyone who cares for a dog, however, is simply asking for trouble by not restraining the animal in some way. It is not practical to ask someone living in the country to keep a dog penned up in the house all day (though this is certainly what happens to the millions of dogs that live in the city and in humane shelters that pick up strays) nor to use a leash every time the dog steps outside the door. But a large run (with a small shelter in case of rain) is a workable solution as is a fenced-in back yard. Expensive storm fencing is not necessary; only some kind of fence that the dog cannot jump over or dig under is needed. A running chain attached to a swivel sunk into the ground is better than a simple chain tied to a tree, and most dogs will become accustomed to this arrangement after a few days, especially if the animal is relatively young. All those people who claim that chaining or penning is cruel should think only of the cruelty that lack of restraint can cause, not only to the animal that is hit by a car, lost in the woods, exposed to infection or injury in a fight, but also to neighbors whose pets, children, and property may be threatened and to the owners themselves who may be subject to lawsuits because of dogbites or the other kinds of damage that a wandering dog may inflict. Owners can also be made to suffer from high veterinary bills, or, worst of all, from the loss of the pet.

ENCLOSURES FOR LARGE MAMMALS

People with larger animals do not seem to have such an antipathy to fences or lead ropes or tethers as dog owners have, which is curious considering that most horses, goats, and cows need far more exercising room than a dog. These sensible people even tend to go too far, selecting enclosures that are too small, unless they are in the business of raising these animals for sale, in which case they want to keep them as fit and healthy as possible. (Farmers who raise animals for meat, however, keep the enclosures as small as they can manage, so that the animals will become fat from overeating and lack of exercise; unfortunately, meat is sold by the pound and fat is a sign of high quality, though exercise will make meat more flavorful if tougher to chew.)

People with only one or two animals, however, should give them as much room as they can afford. It is a sad sight to see a horse trying to graze on a bit of muddy soil or chewing on a piece of fence—not from a desire to escape but out of simple boredom. Feed bills will be higher, for the owner will have to supply both hay and grain, since poor or too small pastureland can supply next to nothing by way of nourishment. A full-size horse needs at least an acre of land (and access to a shelter or an indoor stall measuring at least 12 feet by 12 feet) with good grass as free as possible of parasites and foreign objects that may cause injury and with constant access to water. A small pony, donkey, or sheep does not need so much space but half an acre is the barest minimum. The best way to keep grass in good grazing condition is to divide the pasture area in half, allowing the animal to graze in one half while the other regenerates.

Stall areas for hoofed mammals should be generous in size—a square box stall is best, measuring at least half again the length of the animal (i.e., 8 feet by 8 feet is sufficient for a pony 5 feet long). Wood floors can soak up urine so bedding must be thick and frequently changed; cement floors are easier to keep clean but require heavy bedding to relieve pressure on the animal's feet. Earth floors are likely to become soggy or dug up by a bored animal, though they afford a comfortable floor for standing. Many types of bedding material are available: straw (which may, however, be eaten by a hungry or bored animal), wood chips (large pieces are best; sawdust can be bad for an animal's lungs and eyes), peat moss, or commercial brands of dried sugar cane. Whatever bedding is used, droppings and wet areas must be removed daily and the bedding completely changed at least once a week. The stall area should be free of protrusions, and any windows or lightbulbs should be covered by screening to prevent injury. The stalls need not be heated, but should be well ventilated (without drafts) and light. Unleaded

MAGGIE'S SURROUNDINGS ARE NOT ELABORATE, BUT SHE LOOKS VERY HAPPY THERE.

white paint or whitewash on the walls will help keep flies under control.

Fencing should be sturdy; split-rail fences are expensive although attractive and strong. There are other suitable kinds: post and rail, strong wire (not barbed wire, please), and an electric fence, which is not harmful and which animals quickly learn to avoid. (Deer, wild or confined, may have trouble seeing single-wire fences when running and can do themselves and the fence considerable damage; brightly colored ribbons tied here and there may help.) Gates should also be sturdy and easily opened and closed by humans only. Goats are particularly clever at opening gates and getting out of enclosures, so great care should be taken in planning living spaces for them. Many owners prefer to tether them like dogs with a chain attached to a grounded swivel. This can be moved from place to place as the land is grazed. It is also useful for sheep, which make excellent lawn mowers since they crop grass very slowly.

If your land is not naturally equipped with a source of water, you can use a tub (old bathtubs are commonly used for this purpose) or install self-watering devices in the pasture. Watering buckets should also be kept in the stalls but removed if a horse or pony comes in just after heavy exercise. Feeding may also be done in buckets, kept on the ground or suspended in the stall; it is usually best to serve hay from the ground not just because it is more natural but also because it prevents dust particles from irritating an animal's eyes.

CAGES

Commercially available metal cages designed for small mammals are often quite satisfactory, since they have been developed primarily for use in laboratories where animals are kept in large quantity and must be maintained in healthy condition. Yet pet shops often carry the smallest possible types (probably because of the space they take up in storage), and most people end up with cages that are far less roomy than they should be. Since animals were not designed for cage living, there is probably no such thing as a cage that is too large, but there definitely is such a thing as a cage that is too small for the animal it holds. Minimum space requirements are given in the charts, but a good general rule of thumb is to make a cage twice as long, wide, and deep as the animal itself, when it is stretched out full length. Because all cages will need a thorough cleaning from time to time, be sure that you have an extra enclosure on hand to which the animal may be moved; a carrying case may be used for this, but not for long periods of time.

Commercial cages can be expensive, though they are easy to keep clean, and most animals will do equally well in home-made enclosures of wood with wire screening. Note that cages intended for rodents or rabbits require metal coverings for all exposed wooden areas which might otherwise be gnawed through and provide escape holes. Be sure that cage doors can be securely latched; some animals are geniuses at opening even complicated fasteners. Wire cage floors are the easiest to keep clean because droppings can fall into removable trays or cardboard layers below; also, wire floors will allow rabbits to enjoy being set out on nice green lawns where they can nibble the grass that pokes through the bottom of the cage. Some animals would undoubtedly prefer to rest their feet on a more solid surface, however, such as wood or metal, but the floor should be covered with some kind of material; kitty litter, which absorbs odor and has a scratchy texture that is good for foot development in young animals, is one of the best materials, but wood chips, sawdust, straw, or pine needles are also good. Perches made from nontoxic branches, exercise wheels, shelves, ladders, rocks, and other natural (and unnatural) objects will be welcome to most inhabitants—in fact necessary for exercise—though guinea pigs and rabbits may get their exercise simply by looking at them.

Cages for mammals should also have some kind of box or enclosure where the animal can get some privacy and escape from light or heat for a bit of comfortable rest. Any container will do, as long as it is just large enough for the animal and some bedding material. Wooden boxes may be chewed, metal ones may rust, and glass jars have too much visibility for comfort, but tobacco tins or well-tended metal and wooden boxes may serve temporarily. Cotton, torn paper, wood chips, straw, or cloth will do fine as bedding or nesting material and will give the animal security and warmth as well as something to burrow in or fuss with. Food and water dishes should be sturdy enough to withstand gnawing and not to tip; heavy glass, stainless steel, or ceramic dishes are better than plastic, and all are easily cleaned. Self-watering devices may be purchased but they are simple to make: run a short piece of glass or stainless-steel tubing through a rubber cork that has been inserted in a glass bottle. Keeping your finger over the end of the tube, turn the bottle upside down and attach it to the side of the cage. Amazingly enough, the water won't rush out from any bottle of less than a pint capacity, and the animal can take it drop by drop whenever it likes.

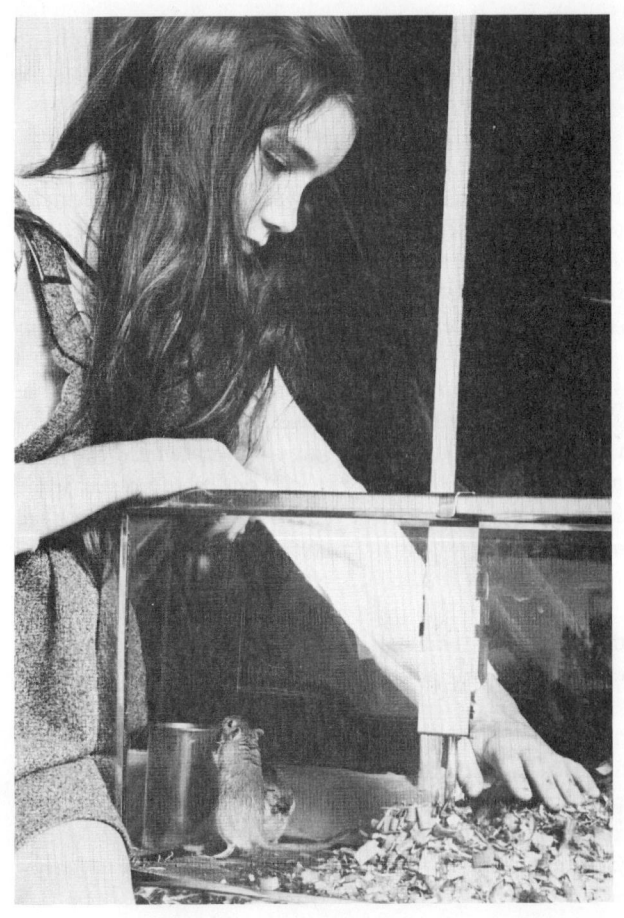

WOOD CHIPS MAKE GOOD BEDDING FOR A GERBIL OR ANY OF THE OTHER SMALL RODENTS THAT LIKE TO BURROW.

Very young animals can be kept in boxes—shoe, carton, or hat—until they are old enough to begin eating on their own and doing some exploring or exercising. A soft fabric, such as flannel or toweling, is probably the most important furnishing for the box, because it will enable the animal to keep warm and feel secure even without its mother or litter mates. Heating pads, lamps, or other devices to keep the temperature level in the box relatively high may also be necessary; be sure that the animal can escape the heat, however, if it wishes.

Bird cages are also easy to obtain through pet or hobby shops, but many bird fanciers find them unsuitable, because the openings are too small, the sizes are not really adequate to allow for exercise, and the decoration is unnecessary. Also, commercial fixtures are usually made of the wrong materials (plastic, for instance, can be chewed to shreds and ingested by some birds). Metal cages can be easily made at home with a little ingenuity and a soldering iron. One couple I know makes nice big cages from bakery trays which are cut up and fashioned into the right shape within a frame made of copper-pipe fittings. Refrigerator or oven racks or sheets of hardware cloth (½ inch square) fastened to a metal or wooden frame are also suitable. Wooden cages are easier to make, but some of the psittacine birds may gnaw on them; the wood may be painted a light color, but only nontoxic paints should be used. Wire-mesh cages are relatively indestructible and provide good visibility, but they do not afford the bird a sense of security nor allow for escape from disturbances and occasional drafts. All cages of any sort should be kept away from open windows and direct sunlight.

Many birds will do well with a wooden breeding box (whether or not you or they plan to have any baby birds) which will afford some privacy for sleeping or whatever it is birds do when they are not being watched. These boxes can be made of wood (with edges lined in metal to prevent chewing) and should have openings just large enough for the bird to pass through and be otherwise entirely enclosed. The floor should be concave so that the eggs, if any, will not roll; birds will use their own feathers for nesting, but frayed rope or string or grass or whatever the birds like may be provided as nesting material.

The floors of the cages may be wire mesh with a removable tray below to catch droppings; some birds that stand on the floor of the cage may not do well on wire unless it is covered in peat moss or some soft substance. Minimum cage sizes are given in the charts; 24 inches high by 24 inches long by 18 inches deep is adequate for most small birds in breeding pairs or for single medium-size birds. Large birds, of course, will need larger cages; each bird should be able to fly between perches for at least a short distance and spread its wings. Perches are best made of natural branches which are not absolutely

BIRD CAGES COME IN ALL SHAPES AND SIZES, BUT THE BEST ONES ARE USUALLY THOSE YOU MAKE YOURSELF—LIKE THE ONES AT THE LEFT, WHICH ARE LARGE AND UNADORNED WITH FRAGILE TOYS AND FURNISHINGS; NOTE THE AVIARY AT THE BACK OF THE ROOM.

round and are of different sizes, but broomsticks, boards, or coat hangers may be used. Ladders, mirrors, other exercise and play equipment, food and water containers, should—as for other animals—be sturdily made; stainless steel, heavy glass or ceramic dishes are good, easy to clean, and can be easily removed. Ice-cube trays are good for a collection of small birds. Cuttlebones and grit containers are other necessary pieces of furniture for the cage, for without them the birds may suffer from digestive problems (without teeth they need grit to digest their food), calcium deficiency or beaks that grow too long.

Indoor or outdoor aviaries to hold a number of birds can also be made of hardware cloth attached to a metal or wooden frame. Outdoor aviaries should have a solid roof to keep out rain and the droppings of other birds, and all aviaries should have a soft roof covering of some sort so that flying or nervous birds do not damage themselves. All aviaries should include a large flight space and a box or boxes large enough to shelter the birds comfortably. The length of an aviary is more important than its height, but the birds should be catchable by anyone entering the area, so the ceiling ought to be no more than 7 feet high and the entrance door about 4 feet. The floor can be made of concrete, wood, or metal and should be lined with some flooring material to absorb droppings and odor (processed sugar cane is effective); aviary floors should be cleaned and flooring material replaced at least once a week. Outdoor aviaries with earth floors and birds that scratch on them need not be covered, but attention should be paid to the feet of these birds because balls of earth may accumulate and will have to be carefully soaked off.

A double layer of screening on the sides of outdoor cages is a good way of preventing predators from getting at the birds inside. One clever pair of raccoons dreamed up an effective system of catching birds inside a single layer; one would rattle the wire on one side of the cage and make all sorts of fierce noises, sending the birds to the other side where the partner raccoon would be waiting with open paws. The enclosure should also be protected against burrowing pests and against parasites. Cleaning will help keep parasites to a minimum; No-pest strips are useful (especially when used in a confined area for six to twelve hours) but they should be hung away from the birds for they may be toxic. Camphor devices, sold as bird protectors, may also be attached to the side of the cage.

Temperature control is important in all cages designed for birds, and care should be taken to see that the cage stands out of direct sunlight and is entirely free of drafts, since birds are very susceptible to respiratory infections. If the room in which the cage is placed cannot be kept at a steady temperature of at least 70°F., special heaters must be provided to keep the cages warm, although some birds may become acclimated (gradually) to a lower temperature, so long as sudden changes and extremes are avoided. Humidity is also a factor, but a moderate range of 30 per cent to 50 per cent is usually acceptable. Any sick bird should be kept particularly warm, either in a hospital cage (available through animal dealers) or in a cage isolated from the other birds and heated with a lamp or other source of warmth.

Speaking of sickness and isolation, do be sure that any new object or animal placed in a cage or enclosure—even if it is only a plaything or piece of decoration, an item of food or a companion—is not contaminated or infected; examine everything thoroughly before you introduce it to a healthy animal. Objects should be nontoxic and clean; newcoming animals should be free of disease and quarantined for at least two weeks even if no disease condition is suspected. All too often a pet owner will find himself with a sick or dead animal and can find no obvious cause, only to discover too late that the branch he used for making a perch or a climbing post was made out of a kind of wood toxic to the animal (pine, maple, elm, fir, oak, and cypress are safe varieties). Sand or gravel gathered from the backyard may contain parasites or disease organisms, and anything that has been exposed to insecticides may cause serious damage to sensitive animals of any species.

VIVARIA AND AQUARIA

Reptiles, amphibians, and fish, whose body temperatures are entirely controlled by their surrounding environment, have more specialized requirements than mammals and birds so far as living arrangements are concerned. Glass aquarium tanks are probably the most efficient containers, since they are strong and water-tight. The glass is set into a steel frame (which is not exposed to the inside area of the enclosure) and the seams are sealed with a special aquarium cement that expands and contracts to allow for changes in temperature and pressure. This cement becomes rigid with time, so old cages must be carefully inspected for leaks if they are going to hold water; if they are to be used as terraria, however, and water will be kept in plastic or glass containers within, an old aquarium is an excellent piece of equipment. Most aquaria are fitted with lights (incandescent bulbs) which are useful in providing daylight hours and warmth, and some have thermostats or thermometers attached. If none of this equipment comes with the tank, a gooseneck lamp arranged so that the

SO LONG AS A SNAKE'S CAGE HAS A LOG FOR CLIMBING,
A SHELTER, WATER, AND WARMTH, THE SNAKE WILL BE PERFECTLY CONTENT;
SOME OWNERS LIKE TO ADD DECORATIONS FOR THEIR OWN
VISUAL PLEASURE (THESE PLANTS ARE PLASTIC).

light shines down on the enclosure and a thermometer affixed to the inside edge of the tank are all that are needed to keep a reptile or amphibian.

Although aquaria for fish or aquatic animals should be covered with glass or plastic sheeting to prevent dust or other foreign material from falling into the water, dry habitats can be covered with a piece of screen. All lids, however, should allow for some circulation of air and all must be securely latched.

The size of the enclosure should vary with the size and number of the animals to be kept. Snakes should have cages that are at least as long and half as wide as the animals are stretched out to full length; lizards need somewhat more room, as do turtles and amphibians, because they are more active. (See the sections on these animals and the charts at the back of the book for minimum space requirements.) Food and water containers should be sturdy enough so that they cannot be overturned, yet shallow enough so that the small animals can get at the contents, whether to drink or to immerse themselves. All containers should be easy to remove and clean.

Large, wide-mouth gallon glass jars (the kind that restaurants buy mayonnaise and pickles in) are excellent for small amphibians and insects; they should have covers of cheesecloth or nylon stocking material that can be tightly fastened with a rubber band to prevent escape.

There are four basic kinds of enclosures that can be devised to simulate natural habitats for reptiles and amphibians: desert, woodland, semi-aquatic or marshland, and aquatic. A desert terrarium is probably the easiest to construct and maintain: cover the floor of a simple wooden cage or glass aquarium with about an inch of well-washed gravel or coarse pebbles, and layer this with a couple of inches of sand. (More flooring than that is difficult to clean and burrowing lizards can spend most of their time entirely out of view.) Rocks and twigs will serve as resting places for the animals and water can be provided in a shallow dish, partially buried in the sand to camouflage its "unnatural" appearance. A less natural looking enclosure, but one that is perfectly satisfactory for most snakes and some lizards, such as iguanas, is a simple flooring of linoleum or wood covered with newspaper. Nondesert snakes do best on a plain flooring since they may otherwise ingest sand along with their food. Although natural rocks and twigs should be available for resting and scratching purposes, plastic plants will add some color (natural plants will probably be eaten).

Although woodland terraria are supposed to resemble the floor of the forest, elaborate constructions are difficult to clean and the simpler the arrangement the better. Proceed as with the desert habitat but instead of sand, use soil taken from the woods (after you have dried it for a couple of days to eliminate parasites) or purchase tanbark from a garden shop. Add some pieces of bark, twigs, and a rock or two to give the animal some shelter. A pool of water can be made with a plastic dish or tub sunk into the soil or simply placed on top. Plants may be added, but some animals will eat or destroy them.

A semi-aquatic environment is similar, but the pool of water should be large enough for the animal to submerge itself. A plastic container will be easy to remove and clean. Another solution is to make an entirely aquatic arrangement with two or three rocks, large enough to allow the animal to get completely out of the water. Be sure that the rocks do not have a high copper content, which can be toxic to animals. Igneus rocks, such as granite, are usually safe.

An aquatic environment is similar to that used for fish (and described in Chapter 2) and can be maintained in a large jar, a glass fish bowl, or, best, a rectangular aquarium with a stainless-steel frame. Clean the tank with tap water (do not use soap or detergent) and cover the bottom with a couple of inches of aquarium gravel. Fill the tank halfway with tap water and let it sit for at least two days before you put animals into it; this will eliminate most of the chlorine

THIS AQUARIUM TANK CONVERTS EASILY
TO A WOODLAND ENVIRONMENT FOR A TOAD.

and other halogen elements that may be toxic. And remember, when animals are settled, to "age" all water you add to the aquarium later on or use distilled water. Tropical fish stores are a good source for plants, such as vallisneria and elodea, that you can root in the gravel. Many excellent books on fishes and fish care are readily available.

Enclosures for insects may be much smaller than those for reptiles and amphibians, and their furnishings should be as simple as possible. All natural materials, such as earth and twigs, should be "cleaned" before the insects are put into the environment; allowing them to sit in the sun for a day or two should remove most parasites or harmful elements. Wide-mouth gallon jars are probably the simplest and most effective containers for insects, though large rectangular covered trays for "cultures" have been developed for laboratory use and are useful for anyone raising insects in quantity. Since no animal can survive without water, moisture is very important; however, too much wetness may cause mold or rot and should be avoided. An occasional spray of water is usually all that is necessary to maintain the correct level of humidity.

Anyone who has an old hurricane lamp will find it an excellent container for insects; clean the glass section of the lantern thoroughly, place it in a flower pot filled with earth, and cover it with cheesecloth or nylon mesh. The water level in the enclosure can be regulated by watering the earth in the pot, and one needn't ever disturb the occupants for this purpose, though food, of course, must be put in by hand. Insects feeding on leaves or live food do not need special food dishes, of course, but to avoid any unnecessary mess in feeding bits of vegetable or fruit, a piece of cardboard is a useful "dish" that can be easily removed and eliminates the necessity of cleaning the interior of the enclosure.

Feeding

Pet food costs Americans several billions of dollars a year and outsells baby food by something like four to one. In an era when food for human beings is becoming increasingly expensive and, in some areas, difficult or impossible to produce in sufficient quantity, these pet-food statistics arouse in many people a justifiable feeling of anger. No one would argue that animals dependent on man for food (or animals upon which we depend for food) should be starved, but it is true that the amount of money spent on developing products and selling them to the owners of pets could undoubtedly be better used in some other way. Packaging dog food to look like hamburger and advertising it on television are probably the most blatant waste of time and money; dogs really couldn't care less what their food looks like so long as it tastes good (they can't tell red from gray in any case), and many of these expensive, attractive-only-to-people foods aren't all that good for them in the first place.

There are many similar misconceptions about pet food, not all of them so obvious. Many people are surprised to learn that a steady diet of carrots and lettuce leaves will give a rabbit—even Bugs Bunny—a chronic case of diarrhea, and that a mouse would much rather have a nice handful of oats than a slice of cheese any day. Hay is still for horses, or course, and dogs do like meat, but several vitamins and minerals essential to these animals aren't available in those basic foods. Many adult cats will turn up their fastidious noses at milk, and one of my own cats definitely prefers corn on the cob to most canned cat foods. But even this famous fussiness of cats is highly overrated and overindulged. Most cat owners will tell you, usually with pride, how discriminating their animals are, and some will go to absurd and expensive extremes to satisfy a feline craving for delicately sauced gourmet goodies, claiming that the dear thing just won't eat anything else. I have never, however, known a cat to be so lacking in sense that it would die of starvation facing a full supper dish, even if it is full of the plainest commercial cat food, and I dare say that all of us could use similar common sense when it comes to feeding our pets.

Most animals, of course, have specific food requirements—just as we do—and it is our responsibility as pet owners to see that those requirements are met as accurately as we know how, in terms of variety, quality, quantity, and regularity. Those who cannot afford to give an animal what it needs should not keep that animal; however, a number of pets can be kept comfortable and healthy for very little money, especially when that money is wisely spent. People who can afford to give their pets more than they need (or food they *don't* need) would be better off indulging themselves directly rather than doing so by indulging their pets and causing them to suffer. Although the amount of food needed will vary according to the animal's age, weight, type, and relative activity, each species has its own requirements, and these are listed in the charts at the back of the book. A miniature poodle will need far less than a Saint Bernard, and a small pony will not consume nearly as much as a working hunter, but the types of food and nutritional needs are pretty much the same for different breeds within the same species. Allowing for some differences from species to species, even groups of animals (rodents, hoofed animals, canines, etc.) may be similar in their requirements.

Contrary to public opinion, carnivores cannot survive on meat exclusively; no matter how much a dog loves the "pure red meat" from its dog-food can, it cannot remain healthy on that diet for long

FOOD FOR ANIMALS SHOULD BE AS FRESH AND CLEAN AS FOOD FOR HUMANS.

without supplements of minerals, vitamins, fat, and vegetable matter. Carnivores in the wild eat the whole carcass of their herbivorous prey, not just the muscle meat, so that they manage to get all the "meat by-products" as well as the stomach contents, which include vegetables and vitamins, the fat, and the minerals available in the bony tissue. And because these wild animals are forced to chew their food rather than gulp it down out of a dish where it has been moistened in "rich gravy," their teeth and their digestive processes are less likely to deteriorate as quickly as they do in domestic species that are not given enough roughage or enough opportunities for chewing.

There are a few strict vegetarians among the herbivorous animals, but most of them are omnivorous, just as humans are. Even some of the seed-eating birds will be delighted by occasional treats of scrambled eggs or buttered toast, and all of them need mineral supplements and grit, as well as straight vegetable matter. Because few of us can reproduce diets that wild animals feed on naturally, we must rely on the data that scientists and domestic-animal breeders have discovered through trial and error as well as in their observations of species in the wild. Happily, a great deal of research has been done in the area of animal nutrition; for domestic animals at least, the food requirements are well known, and special foods have been developed to fill those requirements satisfactorily.

Much commercial food has been developed to ensure maximum size and quick turnover, and these are not a concern of pet owners who simply want to keep their animals in good health for as long as possible. Practically everything we know about bird nutrition, for instance, comes from studies of domestic poultry, and this is useful in terms of general body chemistry though not always sufficiently detailed for application to other species. Birds with specific structural requirements—eagles with beaks designed for tearing, parrots that must crack seeds if their beaks are not to grow too long—need more from their food than a particular balance of nutrients.

In spite of my ill-tempered remarks about the pet-food industry for their attempts to mislead the public in order to sell more—and more expensive—pet foods, it is to the major companies in the industry that we owe our gratitude for having done so much of the research and for providing many of the food products that are available commercially to the public as well as to those who raise animals for food and for other human uses. Although the industry is self-regulating rather than under the control of the Food and Drug Administration, it maintains a pretty high standard for itself, both in supplying nutritionally balanced and palatable foods—using food-processing methods similar to those used for human foods—and in marking their labels with a detailed list of the ingredients of their products. But because these companies produce a wide variety of foods even for the same kinds of animals and because the advertisements are as confusing as they are ubiquitous, it is up to the individual pet owner to sort out exactly which foods are best for his animal.

All one has to do is to learn what the animal's nutritional requirements are, find a food or combination of foods that fills those needs, and then get the animal to eat it. This is, of course, not nearly so easy as it sounds. Most rabbits and rodents will readily eat the pellets especially designed for their consumption and need only an occasional lettuce leaf and some other supplements to do well; but many a dog or cat simply won't eat dry food when there is a dish of moist meaty canned food nearby, even though most experts agree that the dry food is more nutritious and far cheaper. In such a situation, the owner must condition the animal to the most appropriate diet even if he has to make it more palatable by adding a bit of meat or a well-chosen leftover. A nutritionally sound diet isn't much good if the animal won't touch it, just as it is true that the food an animal likes isn't necessarily good for it.

Palatability in bird foods is not so much a matter of odor, as it is with mammals, but of visual appearance, so that the size, color, and location of food are often determining factors in whether a bird will eat or not. Ducks, geese, and gallinaceous birds, among others, seem to be attracted by green foods (dogs are not attracted by red or green or any other color). Some birds will not eat readily when they are isolated, in the dark, in a small space, or when food is placed at an unfamiliar level (too high in a cage or too low). The conditions may vary from one species to the next, but the main point is to avoid causing the animal stress by making abrupt changes in a routine with which it is familiar. If you are not at all familiar with the routine yourself, it is your responsibility to become so as quickly as possible. Birds cannot survive long without food, and force-feeding cannot be maintained over a long period because of the stress it causes.

Some birds—and reptiles and amphibians as well—cannot be made to eat unless the food is living and in the form of insects, small rodents, or whatever the natural prey may be. Although some can be trained or tricked into eating dead food, which is most practical for owners who plan to keep the animals for any length of time, one should not attempt to alter the habits of wild animals that are to be released at some point.

A number of general eaters, such as raccoons and other omnivores that naturally eat a varied diet, will prefer different kinds of foods rather than a steady diet, although the introduction of new foods suddenly may cause some problems for certain species. Even if they will accept the new tidbit, feed it only in small quantities at first if you wish to avoid digestive upset. A cat may be delighted at a dishful of fresh liver and a rabbit will undoubtedly nibble happily at a nice large lettuce leaf, but all too often the result is likely to be diarrhea rather than a contented animal. Wild animals should be fed a variety of foods, simulating their natural diet as much as possible, rather than becoming accustomed to a steady supply of commercial food (peanut-butter and chocolate cookies are special favorites of skunks and raccoons but relatively difficult to find in the woods). Some wild species, of course, are highly specialized in their food habits; koala bears eat nothing but eucalyptus leaves and many birds are similarly unable to adapt to substitute diets. On the other hand a robin will be perfectly happy with earthworms in the spring, cherries in the summer, and palmetto buds in the winter. The less adaptable dog, however, will probably turn up its nose at a change in diet, especially a sudden one, which is something to consider when one is trying to sneak some medication into the bowl. Dietary changes are often necessary, of course, and for any number of reasons, the animal's age and its general condition being the most important. Ailing, obese, breeding, pregnant, lactating, hibernating animals all have different food requirements from animals of the same species in normal condition, and diets must be adjusted accordingly.

Once the questions of what kinds of food in what sort of balance are nutritionally sufficient and palatable have been solved, other factors should be considered. Feeding times are important for some animals; certain species, such as birds or rodents with high metabolic rates naturally should have food available constantly, whereas intermittent occasional eaters, such as the carnivorous dogs and cats, are usually fed at regular intervals, adults once a day. Snakes may require food only once or twice a week, or less. Nocturnal animals may not eat until dark, and diurnal animals may eat only during daylight hours. It is possible to readjust feeding schedules to suit your own; dogs can be conditioned to self-feeding and allowed to eat whenever they please, so long as the routine is not suddenly imposed and the quantity eaten is carefully controlled. Dry foods that will not spoil can be used and this method has some advantages for the owner, who may be happy to do without a once-a-day feeding time, both for the sake of convenience and to avoid the overexcitement that often accompanies the supper bell. Feeding times can also be adjusted to exercise periods, as with horses, which cannot be expected to do well if fed just before or just after a strenuous ride. And since elimination occurs shortly after eating in many animals, this, too, must be taken into account if you plan to show off the rabbit or the guinea pig to a visitor.

One should always keep careful track of the amount an animal has or has not eaten. Refusal to eat for a day or more may in some species indicate a disease condition requiring prompt medical attention; other animals may fast without doing themselves any harm (hibernating animals can go as long as several months without food or water). Overeating, too, is more serious in animals than most people realize and should be carefully avoided. A fat animal is not only unattractive and relatively uninteresting in its sluggish way, it is also more susceptible to viral and bacterial diseases and other physical ailments. Older animals tend to have fewer caloric requirements than young ones, and smaller animals with a higher proportion of body surface area than larger animals of the same species tend to need more energy intake if they are to remain in good health. Active animals with high body temperature levels (birds, small rodents, and others) will also require large amounts of food. (A friend of mine kept a shrew for two days, during which time the greedy little beast ate over half a pound of good hamburger, many times its own body weight!)

Routine is an important consideration in feeding animals, not just in determining time and amount, but also place. Just as many animals

KINKAJOUS ALWAYS
LIKE A SWEET TREAT,
BUT A BANANA IS
NO SUBSTITUTE FOR
A PROPER DIET.

will eliminate in certain areas of their living spaces, so they prefer to eat in a familiar location. Although few animals would turn down a treat served in the living room rather than the dining room, some do suffer from disorientation and stress in unfamiliar places and may refuse to eat altogether. Birds that naturally eat from the ground would be unlikely to enjoy eating on a perch (even if it could), whereas monkeys, which normally eat on the branches of trees, would probably not touch anything left on the floor of a cage (which is the place for droppings and garbage).

As I have tried to indicate, therefore, a knowledge of the behavior as well as the nutritional requirements of each species is important if the animal is to be fed properly. The charts will give basic information about what foods may be taken and proportions in which they should be offered, but every pet owner should be prepared to adapt himself to the individual animal's tastes and habits. Below are brief discussions of the various kinds of food available, their uses, and their importance in nutrition. Please keep in mind that this chapter is focused on the diets of adult animals. The feeding of baby animals that must be hand reared because their parents cannot do the job is quite a different matter and will be dealt with separately in Chapter 9.

COMMERCIAL FOODS

Rodent pellets are available to laboratories and to pet stores in large bags containing 50 pounds or more, but most individuals can buy them only in much smaller quantities, paying a higher price per pellet. Actually, this is not a bad way to purchase, for pellets will get stale or infested if not properly stored and few people have enough pet rodents to make buying in large quantities a safe economical measure. Even in buying these products from pet stores, be sure that you are getting good-quality pellets; sometimes the shops don't have a great deal of turnover and their supplies have been allowed to sit on the shelf for some time. The same is true in buying seeds for birds, whether they are caged or wild; grain prices have risen, making quantity purchases more attractive, but seeds, too, can get stale and infested. Seeds and grains may also be purchased at health-food shops (where prices tend to be high), garden shops, and even in supermarkets, as well as from dealers who supply farmers and breeders. Grains may be purchased separately or in mixes; it is usually cheaper, if you can afford the time and can use up your supply quickly enough, to buy individual grains and do your own mixing at home. All grains and seeds should be stored in tightly lidded containers to prevent pests and unwanted diners from contaminating or stealing the goods inside.

Special pellets are available for mice, rats, hamsters, guinea pigs, monkeys, horses, cattle, pigs, minks, turkeys, and other animals that are commonly kept by humans. These dry foods, or chows, should be kept in cool dry areas, safely protected from vermin and other animals. Many stories have been told of horses that gorged themselves literally to death (because of colic) from an open container of grain, and I know of at least one case in which a supposedly tame wolf held an entire household at bay while it consumed about twenty pounds of Puppy Chow left in an open bag in the kitchen. By the time the wolf finished eating, it was so bloated by the gradually expanding material in its stomach that there was little danger involved in reclaiming the kitchen as human territory. The wolf, in fact, was the one in danger—as any dog or cat would be—from a potential case of gastric torsion.

The dry foods available for cats and dogs, as I pointed out earlier, are nutritionally complete for the most part, though most animals—cats especially—will not find them satisfying as a regular diet and need supplements of meat and fat, the former for the sake of palatability (the dry foods do contain meat products) and the latter for the sake of nutrition. Because these products are dry, the animals must have ready access to water. If you mix kibble with water, as many animals like it, you will see (if you let it sit long enough) that the material expands quite a bit in the dish; this is, of course, what happens in the animal's digestive tract, and you should expect bulky stools as a result. This may not cause a problem for some people, but it will entail more by way of cleaning (and odor tolerance) for people with small apartments and enclosed dog runs. But before you get turned off by that side of the story, remember that the very dryness of these baked foods are what make them particularly good for your animal's jaws and teeth; they provide chewing exercise and help keep tartar from accumulating. The dry foods that are available in flakes or in pellet form contain a combination of cereal products, meat and fish meals, dry-milk solids, and vitamin and mineral supplements, with only about 10 per cent water content. The biscuits and kibble foods are baked products made from a dough of wheat and soy flour, meat by-products, milk or milk products, yeast, vitamins, minerals, and, again, about 10 per cent water.

Semi-moist or soft-moist foods contain about 25 per cent water and are rather more expensive than the dry foods; some of them have preservatives added and other ingredients to "improve" color and taste. Yet they are as nutritionally complete as the dry foods and far more convenient to use. They contain meat and meat by-products with fat, carbohydrates, vitamins, and minerals, as well as soy, meat, and milk proteins for protein balance. Many animals find them more palatable than dry foods, probably because of their odor, and they are clean, easy to handle, and require no refrigeration. A steady diet of these foods is not recommended, however, as a large percentage of the caloric content is sugar, which accounts for high palatability and low perishability but which can lead to obesity and may not be tolerated by some animals susceptible to diabetes.

Canned dog and cat foods are undoubtedly the most popular pet foods and probably the most expensive when you consider that most of the weight is made up of water and that only a few of the brands available are nutritionally complete. As I indicated earlier, those made up almost entirely of meat are not satisfactory from a nutritional standpoint, though they may be very palatable, and they should not be made a mainstay of an animal's diet. Most of the canned foods are not primarily or predominantly meat, however; any can that is marked "beef" or "fish" or whatever must contain at least 95 per cent by weight of that "preferred ingredient," but most of the canned foods have much less, and in this case, at least, "less is more." As meat prices increase, the cans that contain meat by-products and additives, such as soy derivatives, cereals, and other essential nutrients, are becoming far more popular and are, in fact, better for the animals. A can that reads "beef dinner" or "meat balls" or "chicken stew" may contain as little as 25 per cent of the named ingredient, and any can marked "meat-flavored" or "fish-flavored" or just "dog food" or "cat food" contains less than 25 per cent of the highlighted ingredient. The rest is made up of crude protein (which refers to the amount of nitrogen in the food and can come from eggs, soybeans, or other foods), several minerals and vitamins provided by supplements and vegetable matter, and a good deal of water, as much as 80 per cent.

Before you begin to think that this stuff sounds pretty well balanced for people, however, remember that although these foods may be safe enough, they are definitely not fit for human consumption on any esthetic or cultural level. Meat and meat by-products are usually made up from human-food rejects: lungs, spleens, intestines, gristle, and "unwholesome" or damaged muscle tissue which has been "denatured" chemically or "decharacterized" with charcoal before being turned into bone meal or meat meal. No wonder pet-food companies feel that they need to play up the palatability of their products! But of course cats and dogs can't understand the advertisements any more than they can read the ingredient labels, so I don't suppose it really matters.

Because there is such a tremendous variety in quality and type in these pet foods, I am often asked which my favorite brand is, and though I do have favorites, I have them for specific reasons. Some foods that are high in sodium are particularly good for animals that require more salt; animals with diabetic or other disease conditions do best on other kinds of food. There are a number of prescription diets sold through veterinarians because they are designed to fill special dietary requirements, but some of the foods available to the public are better than others for certain needs. I will go so far as to mention a couple of brands that are excellent all-purpose, complete foods: P/D brand prescription diet manufactured for dogs by the Hills Packing Company, which also makes C/D for cats; Ken-L Ration Blue Label Dog Food and M Diet, manufactured by The Quaker Oats Company and Cadillac Pet Foods, Inc., respectively.

Interestingly enough—though not surprising when you consider the research and the different ingredients that have gone into them—these dog and cat foods will often make good supplements to the diets of various other species. Squirrels and other rodents will often eat dog kibble, and some of the canned foods make excellent foods for reptiles—turtles, lizards, and some snakes—as well as for a number of wild mammals and birds. There are specialized foods designed for zoo animals, such as the various Zu/Preem and Science diets for felines, omnivores, and primates, among others. These can be obtained through local distributors or directly from the manufacturer (Hills Packing Company Division of Riviana Foods).

FRESH FOOD AND TABLE SCRAPS

People who believe that only fresh food is worth eating, because of the additives, preservatives, and chemical processes applied to commercial food, may transmit their own requirements to those of their animals and decide that only fresh fish or meat or vegetables will do. Others, who fear the rising prices and increasing scarcity of meat, may even try to turn their naturally carnivorous pets into vegetarians, making their own meatless "mutt loaves" and "mock liver" dishes, using only the best, organically sound foods they can buy. These people all have their reasons, and I imagine that at least some of them have proven successful in keeping their animals alive and healthy, but because it is more expensive and not nearly so well researched, I would say that a fresh-food diet for animals should be approached with the greatest caution. I have nothing against those who want to try making their own pet foods at home, but I must warn them to be sure they have their nutritional facts straight and enough time and money to spend on purchasing the food and preparing the diets. As I said earlier, those with wild-animal pets kept on a temporary basis should take the time and make the effort involved in providing as natural a diet as they can.

In giving an animal fruits and vegetables, one must take care to see that the produce is clean, fresh, and of generally good quality, to guard against overfeeding, which may result in digestive upset, and to avoid introducing these foods suddenly into the diet. Hay, for instance, may vary considerably in quality depending on when, where, and how it was grown and gathered; it is often difficult for inexperienced eyes to detect signs of good or bad quality without the guidance of an expert or trusted supplier. Types of hay matter as much as quality; timothy grass, for instance, is fed to horses instead of alfalfa, which is a legume and too high in protein for equines, though it is excellent food for other animals.

Many birds, as well as rodents and other mammals, even the so-called carnivores, all like a treat once in a while of a piece of fresh fruit or vegetable, and in some cases these are desirable supplements, although most fruits have little nutritional value. Other treats can be fresh meat and fish, as well as table scraps, some of which may be perfectly palatable and good for the animal in small quantity. Some of these can be bad, however; anything greasy or spicy should not be fed, and small bones, as most people know, are to be avoided as dangerous little weapons. Some large bones, particularly joints and leg bones, can be fed safely to dogs and even to cats, preferably with bits of meat still attached; these provide good chewing exercise and some minerals, and they often become well-loved (or well-buried) play toys as well.

Since the dog was first domesticated as a scavenger at man's table, it doesn't seem logical to make table scraps taboo for the animal at this point (though early man undoubtedly knew little of pizza or ice cream), but don't assume you are saving money on pet food by feeding your dog what you don't eat. You are probably spending more money buying just a little more than you need for yourself in order to have enough leftovers for the dog, which would probably be better off with dog food anyway. Raccoons are one of the most prevalent modern-day scavengers, and in or out of captivity seem to thrive on people food, but I have seen plenty of them get sick on overfatty, overseasoned food and would not recommend using this kind of leftover as a handout. Even some birds have taken to garbage as a steady diet, especially those in urban areas—starlings, pigeons, and sparrows—so there is yet another way in which you may recycle your uneaten dinner if you so desire.

Another type of fresh food is that required by many reptiles, amphibians, and wild-animal residents—live insects or rodents. Most pet shops will carry mealworms, crickets, brine shrimp, white mice or rats, and other delicacies, all of which can be raised in the home at less expense. In warm climates or weather, live insects, frogs, and other creatures may be caught outside for inside pets, but this is, naturally, a time-consuming business that only small boys seem to take any pleasure in performing. During cold weather, live food may be more difficult to come by and a regular supply of live mice or rats may not always be available; some animals may be trained to take dead food, i.e., meat or dog food dangled appetizingly from a string or fresh-frozen (and thawed) mice, which are certainly easier to store than live food (though packages must be carefully marked in the freezer if you want to keep peace in the family). Wild animals in captivity, even for a short time, should not be trained to accept anything but their natural food; young animals may, however, need some help in learning to catch and eat their dinner, in gaining the kind of information that their parents would normally have supplied. Cracking nuts for a squirrel is necessary so that it will learn what that tidy package contains; even clever raccoons will have to be taught how to find ripe berries and insects. Birds of prey and larger mammals may need to be handed a live mouse before they will know what rodents are all about and then trained to catch them if they have had no previous experience. And speaking of catching mice, many cats indulge in this activity, and often include small birds as their prey, to the dismay of their owners. This is perfectly natural behavior and can be a great service to the rodent-infested household; the mouse (or mole or whatever) as a food staple, however, is somewhat inadequate unless the cat is able to catch as many as five or six a day, and one should take care to have the cat examined for internal parasites regularly. As a dietary supplement, however, the mouse can be a fine item if it is not infected or otherwise unwholesome.

FOOD SUPPLEMENTS

There are a number of vitamin, mineral, and oil supplements currently available, and although many of them are useful as additions to diets that are deficient in certain nutrients or as aids in rehabilitating an animal that has suffered from a deficiency, they are not designed or needed for use on a regular basis, if the normal diet is nutritionally complete and the animal is in good health. In feeding baby birds, however, certain vitamin and mineral supplements are necessary: Vet-Nutri (made by Squibb), Vionate (also made by Squibb), and Theralin (Lambert-Kay) are all useful powders that may be sprinkled on food. For baby mammals, injured adult wild animals, and ailing dogs and cats, Pet-Tabs are useful (Massengill Company, Ste-Med Pharmaceuticals Division), as are Zymadrops (Upjohn), a liquid supplement often used for human babies. All of these may be obtained through a veterinarian, a pet shop, or in certain drugstores.

Some kinds of foods—eggs, wheat-germ oil, etc.—may be helpful supplements to animal diets for the improvement of a coat or a set of feathers, and should probably be fed on a regular basis—rather than only occasionally—as part of a diet routine. In addition to a basic diet of seeds, insects, or whatever a specific bird requires, grit—made of gravel mixed with ground oyster shell and necessary for digestion—and cuttlebone to provide calcium should also be made available on a regular basis.

THE IMPORTANCE OF WATER

I have already spoken about the necessity for constantly accessible water when dry foods are fed to dogs and cats, and it shouldn't be necessary to point out that all animals require water—fresh, clean, and frequently changed—if they are to remain healthy. The physiological importance of water cannot be overemphasized; no living cell exists without it, and each cell requires a steady supply if it is to function. Water is distributed throughout the body, making up as much as 80 percent of the adult animal, a level that must be constantly maintained if body mechanisms are to function normally. Water is taken in food, liquids, and through the oxidation of hydrogen during the metabolic process; water is lost primarily through the urine and feces, the skin, and the lungs, or in a lactating female, through the milk. Water gain and loss must be balanced, and any disruption in the system—the unavailability of water or the inability of the animal to eliminate properly—will quickly cause problems for the animal; such a situation should be remedied as quickly as possible, either by supplying water or medical attention, whichever is called for.

Animals that are adapted for desert living—the cat and the gerbil are two such species—are able to survive without drinking much water; they obtain most of their fluid from the food they consume and can concentrate their urine, thereby retaining water to maintain fluid balance. Nevertheless, if dry food is fed on a regular basis, water should be made available even to these specialized creatures.

Some animals take in water through their skin rather than orally; amphibians, for example, will dry out and die if kept away from water for too long, as will fish (which take in oxygen through water but will suffocate from too much oxygen if allowed to remain in the air) and other aquatic species. Semi-aquatic animals also need water in which they may soak or in which they will eat, eliminate, and do just about everything else except sleep. Do not use tap water for these animals, because the presence of chlorine and other elements may be toxic; always age the water by letting it rest in a container for a couple of days before adding it to a tank with animals in it. Used aquarium water should be disposed of in the toilet rather than the sink, where it may cause problems for human members of the family.

Up to this point we have been concerned primarily with the feeding habits of common or domestic pet animals. Because many animal lovers like to know what wild animals eat, whether for general information, for feeding free-roaming pets, or for the care of injured individuals, I have added two special sections on the subject: the first devoted to the feeding of wild birds and the second to wild-mammal feeding. Some of the species mentioned will appear in the charts, but many will not, and I hope that the following guidelines will be of help to the interested reader who suddenly finds a helpless or hungry creature on his hands.

FEEDING WILD BIRDS

Whether you are feeding healthy birds in your backyard or sick ones in your kitchen, the question of what types of food a specific adult bird will take is a complicated one. Your first chore is to identify the species you wish to feed and try to determine its natural diet. Most birds can be put into several major categories according to their eating habits, but many of these overlap since many birds are adaptable and will eat what is available to them. Nevertheless, the major categories are: seed and fruit eaters; insect eaters; flesh eaters; fish eaters; nectar eaters; and omnivorous species that will eat almost anything or a combination of seeds, fruit, insects, and sap. Beak shape can be a good indicator of a bird's natural diet; strong conical beaks usually belong to seed eaters, long thin pointed beaks to insect eaters, and strong, straight bills to general eaters; hooked beaks, of course, indicate a flesh-eating bird.

In devising substitute foods for adult birds, the simplest method is to consider two basic diets—meat and grain, the former made up of canned dog food (a good brand, such as P/D), puppy kibbles, live mealworms, strained-beef baby food, hard-boiled egg yolk, and bits of beef or chicken, and the latter made up of high-protein baby cereal, wheat germ, powdered cornmeal or oatmeal. A combination of these two diets, together with special supplements for various types of birds, such as fresh fruit, wild-bird seed, chick starter, and fish, plus a vitamin-mineral supplement, will suffice for most birds you are likely to come across. Hawks and other birds of prey will require whole rodents, though they may also be content for a while with fresh beef heart or dog food or dead roadside specimens.

For seed-eating birds (pigeons, doves, larks, grosbeaks, finches, sparrows, towhees, juncos, etc.), use one-part meat diet to five parts of the grain diet and supplement this with bits of fresh noncitrus fruit and berries and a selection of seeds, such as sunflower seeds (crushed for small birds), wild-bird seed, chick starter, or whatever they seem to like.

Insect-eating birds (swifts, swallows, flycatchers, titmice, chickadees, nuthatches, wrens, warblers, creepers, vireos, among others) will take the meat diet, mixed five to one with the grain diet, and supplemented with bits of noncitrus fruit and berries.

Fish eaters will prefer whole small fish, shrimp, clams, or live insects, but they may also take raw beef, dog food, and beef heart. This category includes large and small shore birds such as diving ducks, pelicans, gulls, and terns. Many aquatic birds will also welcome chicken feed, grain, and game-bird mixtures, available from some pet stores or feed supply houses.

Nectar eaters (hummingbirds, and some parrots) should be fed sugared water (five parts boiled water to one part sugar) plus Esbilac formula (substitute bitches' milk available from pet stores or veterinarians), mealworm innards, and mockingbird feed (found in pet stores).

Birds with more general eating habits should be fed like insect-eating birds with more plentiful servings of fruit supplements, extra mealworms, some peanuts and seeds, and an occasional bit of raw meat or chopped mouse. These adaptable species are the jays, crows, starlings, and magpies, among others.

Any bird that is being held in captivity because of an injury should also receive regular doses of vitamins and minerals and should be fed often, except at night. Anything the bird will eat is probably a good thing, but keep in mind that birds require a good deal of protein and that some need roughage as well if their beaks are to be kept in condition. Although a bird may be perfectly content with a diet of dog food and grains, remember that it will have to be released as soon as it has recovered and try to simulate its natural diet as closely as you can.

FEEDING WILD MAMMALS

All feeding of wild mammals should be confined to raising babies (a subject that is covered in Chapter 9) or to offering handouts. It is usually wise to leave an injured or diseased wild animal alone, unless you can be sure of obtaining veterinary assistance and are certain that the animal will be of no danger to you. Most animals in pain, even docile ones, are difficult to handle, if not downright dangerous, and your best move is to move away in another direction. Nevertheless, many animal lovers take a great deal of pleasure in feeding denizens of the local woods or fields, and though a raccoon might be happy with almost anything, one should take some precautions in feeding visitors. The first is to be sure that you want the animals to be in your backyard at all; if you have animals already in your family, you may cause wild animals some distress or even injury (if they come round at all, that is). You should consider that you will probably not see much of them, since most wildlings stick to heavy cover until nightfall when the going gets safer. You can improve your chances of seeing wildlife, however, by providing some natural as well as man-made shelter in your own yard—hollow logs, leafy shrubs, old woodchuck holes, as well as piles of lumber or brush will all provide good cover for small shy creatures.

The kinds of wild animals that you may attract will depend, naturally, on the area in which you live. Farms or houses in the country far from other dwellings may be surrounded with far more, and larger or shyer, animals than those in the suburbs or the city, but as human civilization has moved in on nature to a great extent, many animals have learned to adapt to residential areas, even cities. A raccoon family was raised not long ago on the median strip of the Merritt Parkway in Connecticut, entirely without human interference except for gas fumes and some awful noise; and squirrels, sparrows, pigeons, and starlings seem to prefer city buildings to trees, nesting on ledges, awnings, and airconditioners, and feeding on handouts, garbage, and whatever else they can pick up.

In more wooded areas, there has been a definite increase in the number of raccoons, gray foxes, coyotes, opossums, rabbits, and many species of birds, some of them not native to those habitats. A study made at Michigan State University showed that more raccoons lived in urban areas than in their natural surroundings with no significant differences seen in their weight, size, or reproduction rate. Other studies indicate that the quality of human habitats improves in direct proportion to the amount of wildlife they can support. Besides offering garbage, settled areas are warmer and have shelters (even if they are only sewers, attics, garages, or abandoned cars), though many animals find that they prefer parks or cemeteries which are wooded and offer peace and privacy without cars and children. Unless you are observant and know just when and where to look, you may not even know what animals live right around you; Ronald Rood, in his book on feeding wild animals, suggests the ingenious idea of making a track record—smoothing a muddy area and preserving tracks with plaster of Paris for later identification or decorative purposes.

Natural foods, such as berry bushes, apple trees, and nut trees, will attract mammals as well as birds, though you can also tempt them with offerings of your own. Garbage, if it is kept in uncovered cans or barrels, will certainly bring out whatever raccoons and skunks live in the neighborhood; even covers can be pried off, however, by clever little paws, so if you don't want visitors, be sure the lids are fool-proof. Good garbage, of course, is perfectly fine food for these omnivores and leaving it in a place where the animal doesn't have to struggle to get it will probably keep your backyard somewhat neater. Your own pet dishes will probably be scavenged if they are not brought indoors, for dog and cat food is also to the liking of many wild creatures. More appropriate food, however, would include pine cones, some ears of dried corn, pieces of fruit, or just plain salt, if you want to use the hunter's old trick of attracting animals. Many species will eat peanut-butter sandwiches and cookies as though they had been raised on such delicacies. And chicken necks will please the carnivores in the crowd.

One family in upper New York State inadvertently happened to supply just the right thing for a particularly savvy female raccoon by leaving a tub full of apples near their barn; the apples had been intended for applejack, but when the cold weather came, the applejack project never got off the ground, and the raccoon started on an ambitious project of her own. One morning in winter, the family was amazed—and delighted—to find the interior of their barn completely festooned with apples, which had been carefully separated and lined up on beams, stall doors, and every available horizontal space. How the raccoon knew the proper way to store apples without having them rot was beyond them, but they were terribly pleased to see that their neglected crop had by spring been completely consumed.

Grooming

This is one aspect of pet care that varies considerably from one animal to the next, but it is a subject that should be given careful consideration at the time (or before) the animal is acquired. Some species need very little and some need a lot; most people with horses, for instance, understand that regular grooming is important not only for appearance but also for the animal's health, and they work out a daily schedule for regular grooming. People with long-haired dogs and cats find out quickly enough, if they haven't already anticipated the fact, that their pets need a good deal more attention than the shorter-haired breeds. What many people don't realize, however, is that all animals (except maybe some insects) should get regular attention paid to their physical condition, whether or not actual grooming is required. Symptoms of disease, internal or external parasites, and injury become obvious sooner or later, but a conscious effort to look for trouble even where none seems to exist is often the only way to catch it in time to do anything about it. Chapter 8 contains a section on first aid and a list of symptoms to watch for, and this should be consulted if anything looks out of the ordinary, but rather than making the trouble shooting a once-in-a-while chore make it a regular habit—performed on a weekly basis or whenever normal cleaning chores are undertaken.

The most effective way to make grooming and symptom searching easier is to employ preventive measures, such as making sure that the animal's space is clean and otherwise suitable for the species you are keeping. Regular cleaning—daily removal of feces and any uneaten food and weekly scrubbings of cages, stalls, enclosures, and replacement of bedding and nesting materials—is the first order of business. Then you can see to the animal itself, making sure that it is clean and free of apparent physical ailments. One important aspect of grooming care is the owner's ability to handle the animal without causing it distress. Even some perfectly docile and lovable animals can be a real pain in the neck to groom if they can't be managed at the same time as you are trying to manage a brush or a comb. Although wild or difficult animals may be anesthetized by a veterinarian so that treatment may be given (which can be anything from surgery to scaling tartar from teeth), this is not a step that the average pet owner can make on his own, once a week or so, whenever nails need clipping or when burrs or mats must be removed from fur or feathers. Your best bet is to get the animal accustomed to regular handling (which is more fun than work in any case) so that you can groom or examine it calmly and thoroughly without bringing on a struggle. If the animal gets used to the procedure and has a sense of confidence, or security, in its owner's hands, troubles may be kept to a minimum, at least under normal circumstances. Pain or real discomfort can make even the most submissive animal behave erratically, and a veterinarian should probably be consulted or called in to help if the situation is more than you care to handle yourself.

It is difficult to generalize about grooming procedures, because animals vary so widely even within the same species, but the following hints should give the beginning pet owner an idea of what is in store and what measures can be taken.

MAMMALS

Nearly all mammals (even the chihuahua and the armadillo) have hair, but some have more than others, and the general rule is that the more there is, the more you should pay attention to it. Dirty, matted fur is not only unsightly; it is also unhealthy, for it may harbor parasites or cover up injuries, and if an animal tries to clean itself, anything from skin disease to intestinal blockage (furballs in cats) may result. Most people will find it most effective—if not always most convenient—to perform regular grooming chores before coat conditions reach a trouble point—once or twice a week under normal circumstances and more often during those periods when the animal is shedding or when it has access to the outdoors with all of the mud, parasites, and burrs it can pick up. Long-haired animals may need daily attention.

If the animal is small enough, have it stand on a table (preferably one with a slick surface) for grooming. Not only does this tend to make it easier for the groom to get at every bit that needs cleaning, it also conditions the animal to being on a table, which will help when you take it to the veterinarian. And get it used to the idea that this is not playtime. Praise the animal for allowing you to groom it, but do not encourage it to leap around excitedly. Normal grooming doesn't

GROOMING IS AN EXCELLENT WAY OF MAKING FRIENDS WITH AN ANIMAL AS WELL AS OF GIVING IT GOOD CARE.

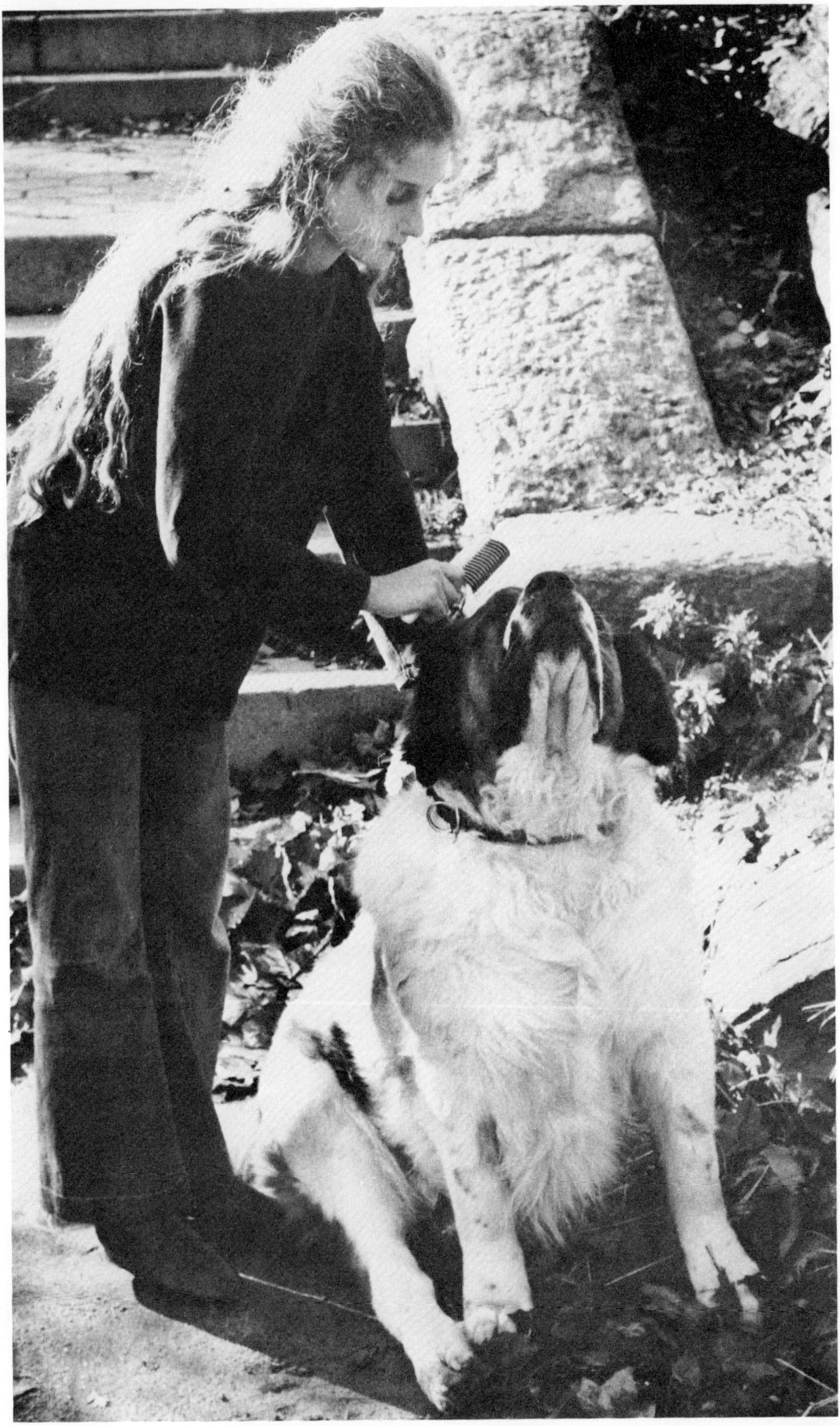

LONG-HAIRED DOGS REQUIRE AS MUCH
BRUSHING AS DO LONG-HAIRED HUMANS AND LONG-HAIRED CATS.

have to take longer than a few minutes, if it is done regularly; however, if you let too much time go by between sessions, the grooming period is likely to be a real trial for both owner and pet.

The kind of comb or brush you use will depend on the species (some will need both); in general, the grooming equipment should be as stiff as the animal's skin can tolerate without becoming abraded or reddened, because the purpose of grooming is not just to achieve a silky coat but also to get out the loose underhairs and to stimulate circulation beneath the hair; for this a soft brush is almost useless no matter how hard you bear down. Combs will remove dirt particles and even bring out fleas; they will also help prevent matting and distribute hair oil evenly over the skin area. Brushing will help finish the job. Always brush with the grain of the coat, paying special attention to the long hairs on the ears, chest, legs, and stomach of the longer-haired animals (dogs and cats can be trained to lie on their sides for this part of the ritual).

Don't count on either a brush or a comb to eliminate shedding problems. Shedding occurs twice a year under natural temperate-zone climatic conditions—once in the spring and once in the fall—and it is the lengthening of days in the spring and the shortening of days in the fall that seem to stimulate the shedding process. If an animal is exposed only to natural light, shedding will take place at those times, but under artificial light, shedding may occur more often during the year. If shedding seems excessive to you, the problem may be caused by diet or parasites, and the veterinarian should be consulted. One of the best ways to remove dead hair from an animal's coat is to massage the coat and skin vigorously with your hands and then stroke the animal with your palms from head to foot to remove the loosened hair. If you do this once or twice a day during the shedding season, your furniture and your fur-allergic friends should be grateful indeed.

Mats and burrs—or any foreign matter that is impossible to remove by brushing or combing—should be cut out with scissors or a plucking razor, though you may be able to loosen the substance with a little oil or petroleum jelly. Use extreme caution with cutting instruments if you have an animal that is the least likely to wriggle. Paint that has not yet dried can be removed with turpentine, but wash the area immediately after cleaning with mild soap and water, for turpentine may provoke a toxic reaction. Dried paint may have to be cut out. Road tar will drop off if the affected area is dipped in or swabbed with mineral oil, but again use caution so that the animal cannot lick the area and ingest any of the material.

Although most commercial powders and dressings for the purpose of producing shiny coats are harmless and may do some good, diet and regular grooming are usually all that is necessary. Many people feel that wheat-germ oil or an occasional egg yolk will encourage a good coat, and this is true to a certain extent, but if an animal is generally shabby—with a lusterless, rough coat—supplements will not cure the problem, which may be a disease condition, and coat "conditioners" may simply cover them up or not work at all.

Flea and tick powders should not be applied on a regular basis, but only when the problem is present, because many of the preparations commercially available can have toxic properties. Flea collars, also, are not to be worn regularly, but only when there is evidence of fleas, in which case more extreme measures will be necessary to exterminate them in the animal's living quarters. Fleas and ticks and other external parasites can simply leap to a new host and return when they have a chance, so the best policy is to remove them from every possible site. Free-roaming dogs and cats will, of course, be a constant site for new parasites (another reason to keep their wandering under control) so more attention should be paid to the coats of these animals. No-pest strips or similar preventives will be effective for a certain length of time, but because these can be harmful to the pet as well as to the parasite, be sure they are hung well out of reach.

As you comb and brush, be sure to check the animal's ears, eyes, feet, and less accessible areas very carefully, not only for dirt and other matter, but also for cuts, bumps, and anything else that doesn't look normal. Trim away excess hair that might interfere with the passage of air into the ears (not too much, though, or you will destroy the animal's natural ability to filter out dirt) and check carefully for ear mites, which can be identified by the black specks or scaley exudate they leave around attached to the hair on the inside of the ears. Every month or so, remove excess ear wax with a cotton swab or Q-tip, applied as gently as you would to a child's ear and only to the visible areas. Do *not* probe or dig around in the ear and do not deal with ear mites or apply medication without a veterinarian's advice. If the ear appears inflamed or hot and has any kind of odor, have the veterinarian check for infection; don't try to diagnose the problem yourself. Unfortunately, I have seen too many cases where home remedies have caused more injuries than cures. Eyes that run constantly or that accumulate mucus in the corners may indicate illness, especially if other symptoms are present, and a veterinarian should be consulted. Occasionally runniness may be caused by anything from dust to foreign bodies that will wash out with tears; mucus that dries in the corner of eyes can be removed by hand or washed out with plain water or a mild solution of boric acid in water.

Check feet for any irregularities and see whether the toenails need trimming. Animals with claws that do not have access to the outdoors or that don't have an object on which they can scratch periodically to keep their claws from growing too long will need regular clipping, and any ragged edges should also be trimmed. Nail clipping is a relatively simple procedure that can be done at home, though many animals resist unless they have become accustomed to having their feet handled. The nails or hooves of large animals may be filed, though trimming with special clippers (such as those that blacksmiths use on horses) is probably the most effective method. Blood veins in nails may be visible in some animals and not in others; proceed with caution rather than run the risk of cutting them too. If you do draw blood, a styptic, such as alum, should stop the bleeding promptly. Trimming should not be necessary more than once a month; if you let the claws go too long, veterinary assistance may be necessary, for the job will become increasingly difficult as the nails get firmer. Don't overlook the dewclaws which, in dogs and cats, grow on the inner leg above the paws. Horses and donkeys should get regular attention from a blacksmith.

In nature, animals tend to keep their teeth clean and trimmed by chewing or gnawing on bones, wood, or other rough objects, but in captivity they often don't have access to this kind of material, so dentistry is occasionally necessary. Rodents are particularly prone to tooth trouble, because their teeth grow continuously during their lives, and regular trimming may have to be done unless the animal is given a small block of hardwood for gnawing purposes. But even cats and dogs will accumulate tartar on their teeth, which can only be removed with special utensils, unless an owner serves a sufficient quantity of hard biscuit or bone. There are tooth powders available for regular brushing, if you feel like purchasing them, though a brush moistened and dipped in baking soda or salt can also be used. If there is any particular odor coming from the animal's mouth, ask the veterinarian about the cause during your next visit. Most of the hoofed animals are ruminants in captivity as well as in the wild and tooth problems are rare, though horses may need their teeth trimmed (or floated) occasionally because rough edges or overgrown molars may cut the inside of their cheeks. But that is a job for a professional and the owner can't do much beyond noticing that the job needs doing.

Effective as combing and brushing may be, occasional bathing may be necessary if the animal is visibly dirty or requires a special parasite bath. Do not bathe too often, for the process is one that tends to remove natural oils and may make an animal susceptible to disease, either by chilling or by removing essential bacteria. When you do bathe an animal, be sure that the water is warm (100°F. or so) and that the soap you use is very mild. Although special shampoos are available for dogs and cats, any nondetergent type of soap will do. If the animal is small enough, fill a basin or tub with water and lift the animal (gently, please) into the water, holding it while you pour handfuls of water over its back. Steady gestures are important here, for an alarmed dog or cat can end up soaking owner and room as well as itself, and the bad experience of being inadvertently dunked may cause panic and will certainly make the next bath more difficult. Once the animal is thoroughly soaked (though not the ears or eyes), rub in a small amount of soap and work it quickly into a lather, rubbing the animal all over. A thorough rinsing with clean water (a second basin or a spray nozzle in the tub is good for this if you have one) and a thorough drying with a towel and the job is done. The drying is especially important, and many people like to use hairdryers for this part, though the animal should never be left unattended if you use one, nor should the temperature be left on "hot" without frequent checking. (Special dog dryers are available—in fact, one of my assistants uses this for *her* hair—but they are expensive and economical only for professional establishments.) Even if you are reasonably sure that the animal is dry, take the precaution of keeping it indoors for a while after the bath.

Take special care that the ears and eyes are not harmed during the bathing process. Two little pieces of cotton in the ears will keep them dry (be sure to remove them), and a drop of mineral oil in each eye will prevent irritation if soap should happen to get into the eyes. During the drying, swab out ears and eyes with cotton to remove excess moisture.

Although many people find it convenient to bathe an animal outdoors, this really should be considered carefully because escape is all too probable, immediate redirtying likely, and chills possible. Other don'ts: Avoid wet bathing very young puppies, pregnant females near delivery, or sick animals. Don't try to comb out snarls when an animal is wet; either do this before the bath or wait until the coat has dried, for wet hair can be torn if you try to force a comb through it.

Dry shampoos are less effective than wet baths, but in some rare situations they may be preferable. There are special shampoos available, although cornstarch is perfectly adequate because it will do the job of absorbing the excess oil from the fur. After sprinkling the powder over the coat, comb it through so that it gets everywhere it should, and let it stand until it has done its absorbing. Then brush the powder out.

Certain breeds of dogs and sheep and goats may all need special attention, because of the nature of their coats, and will probably require the services of a professional. Although a professional sheep shearer may charge as little as $2 an animal in sheep country, a dog groomer may run $20 to $50 for his attentions to a poodle, say, or a badly matted old English sheepdog. Certain terriers also need to have their undercoats plucked periodically so that the short, straight hairs of the topcoat will remain tight and trim looking. Stripping combs are available for this purpose, but the time-honored method of plucking by hand (thumb and forefinger, actually), which takes a good deal of practice and patience, is quite effective. Frequent trimming of the wiry coats is necessary if the quality of the color and texture are to be maintained.

There are innumerable ways in which pet owners can spend money on the physical well-being of their animals; in fact, pet accessories constitute more than $5 million in sales these days. Coats, snowsuits, pajamas, and other items of dress are sold along with leashes, collars, and harnesses, and most of them are more esthetic than practical (depending on your esthetic tastes, of course). However, certain light-coated breeds of dog will be warmed with a coat, especially when it is raining or snowing, even if most of us think they look pretty odd or too cute—which may be true if there is an umbrella attached. There are nail polishes and perfumes sold for use on pets, along with seat belts, hearing aids, tartar remover (called "Happy Breath"), and even veterinary insurance, and although most

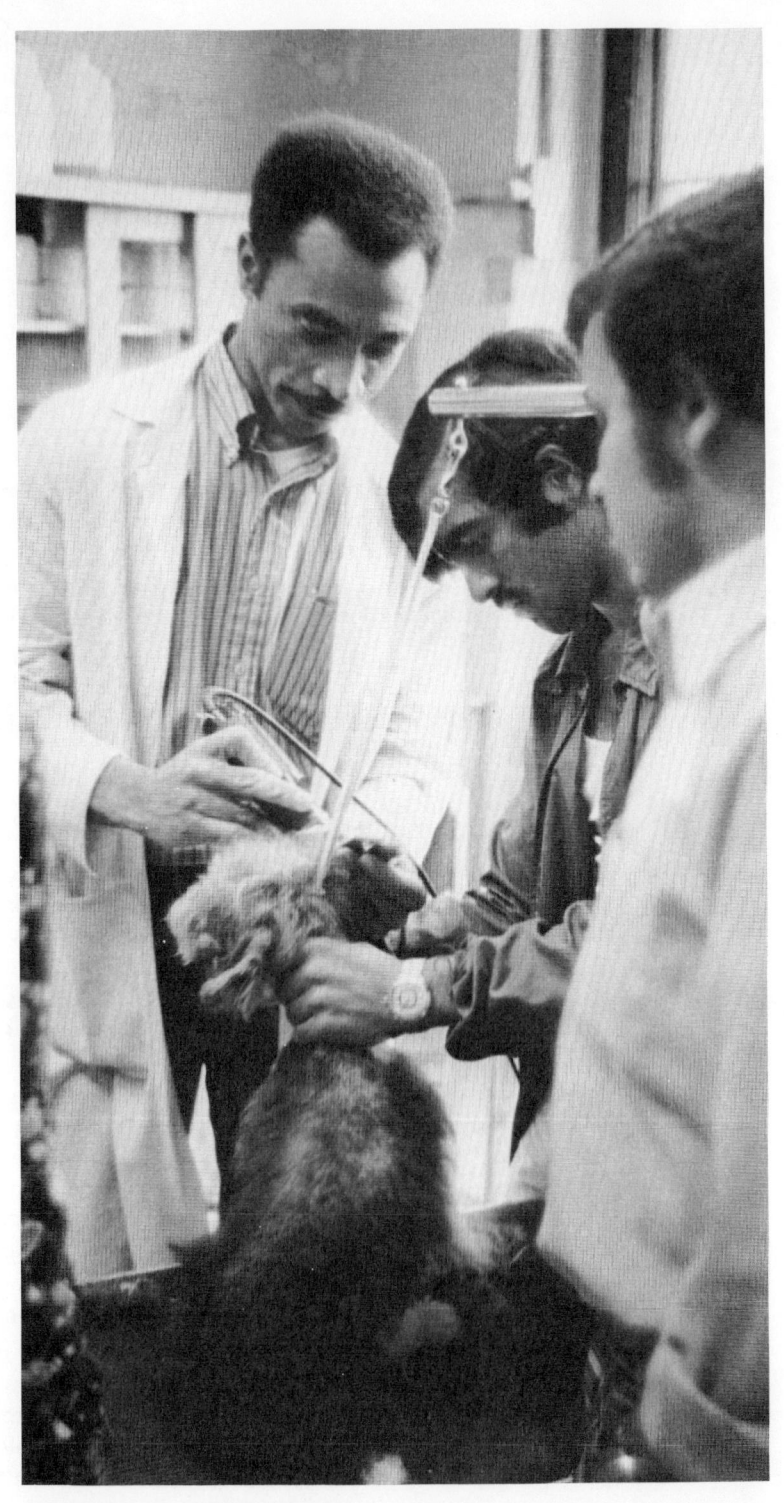

MANY PEOPLE RELY ON PROFESSIONAL
DOG GROOMERS TO KEEP THEIR PETS TRIM.

CARING FOR A PET

250

pet owners won't need much or any of this, a lot of people like to buy it and a lot of pets are tolerant enough to wear, use, or take advantage of it.

BIRDS

Birds make up, in some degree, for their noise by being relatively easy to care for in terms of grooming, which means that they need very little of it. Given appropriate living conditions, they will take care of their own feathers, although extensive plucking can be a problem and should be dealt with by a veterinarian. This condition may be caused by anything from insufficient diet or parasites to excessive boredom, but a bird that is being fed and housed properly and is kept occupied with toys or a companion and occasional handling should not molt beyond the amount that is normal for the species. Most birds molt regularly twice a year or less, depending on their native habitat, and even under artificial light they will molt from time to time. Owners need not be concerned about loss of feathers, unless it persists for a long period, resulting in bare patches. In general the owner need not take any particular measures to keep the bird's feathers groomed, although some people find that in warm weather their birds enjoy being sprayed with a light shower of water on their backs and wings. Some birds even like more regular baths, provided by dripping faucets or a shallow water dish in the cage.

Birds in nature keep their beaks and claws trimmed by using them on nuts, seeds, and branches, so captive birds should be given access to materials for chewing and scratching. In addition to the regular diet of unshelled seeds and nuts and grit, parrot-type birds will need a block of hardwood for gnawing and perches made of rough rather than smooth wood so that their claws can be kept from growing too long. Periodic trimming by a veterinarian may still be necessary, especially for the larger parrots that may be difficult for an owner to handle, although an amateur may learn to do the job for himself after watching a professional do it once or twice,

Occasionally, birds that live in cages or aviaries with a dirt bottom may pick up enough soil in their feet so that balls are formed. Because bird feet are so delicate, removing the balls of dirt is a touchy business and should be done with great care. I find that soaking the feet in warm water and then gradually rubbing the dirt away is the best procedure. Fecal matter that may collect around the bird's vent should also be removed, either by clipping away the feathers or swabbing the area with a Q-tip dipped in mineral oil.

REPTILES

Like birds, reptiles do not need much grooming, although they should be looked at regularly to see that external parasites do not exist and that skin shedding takes place routinely and without incident. When a snake or lizard has outgrown its old skin and is ready to shed it, be sure that you place a container (a flat dish is best) full of water in the cage, so that the animal may soak itself to help the shedding process along. A brick, concrete block, or rock should also be made available, because the animal will want to rub itself until the old skin has been removed. Snake skins are usually removed in a single piece, but because lizards are rather more complicated anatomically, their skins may come off in pieces over a period of time. Any pieces that do not come off after a few days, however, may be a source of trouble, and you might want to help nature along by removing these bits with tweezers. Be careful in handling any reptile during the shedding process, no matter how tolerant they are usually, because many animals display aggressiveness or hostility during this time. When you see that the animal's eyes are clouded, you will know that shedding is imminent; the old skin has begun to loosen itself around the animal's eyes, and this makes it difficult for the reptile to see properly, which may account for the bad temper and defensiveness they display.

As with birds and most other animals, reptiles are susceptible to external parasites, and a periodic check should be made of the animal itself and of the cage to be sure that none are present (see Chapter 8 for the treatment involved in removing these pests). Preventive measures are the usual: regular cleaning and avoiding the introduction of possibly contaminated objects or animals.

Exercise

Although the subject of exercise is covered in other chapters of this book, it deserves a small section of its own, for like clean, well-designed living quarters, a well-balanced diet, and regular grooming and medical attention, it is one of the essential components of good pet keeping. All animals need exercise, some more than others depending on species, condition, and age. For some animals and owners, exercising is a pleasurable activity—dog walking, horseback riding, hamster watching can all be great fun—at least most of the time. But during those other times, when it is raining or when the hamster decides to get his exercise while you are trying to read or sleep, the exercise period might not be such a treat. Nevertheless, it is still important to the animal.

It is difficult to say without knowing the individual animal exactly how much exercise is enough, but the owner can determine this for himself if he takes the time and the trouble to observe his pet. How does the animal's condition match up to others of the same type? Is it

BIRDS ARE VERY DELICATE AND NEED GENTLE HANDLING;
THIS COTURNIX QUAIL'S FEET HAVE BECOME IMPACTED WITH DIRT
AND MUST BE SOAKED IN WARM WATER AND CAREFULLY CLEANED.

healthy looking with clear eyes, good muscle tone, and no extra fatty tissue that might indicate lack of exercise? Does it appear alert and responsive, or sluggish and droopy? Does the animal seem bored—to the point where it spends much of its time walking back and forth in the cage as if it were in a trance? Or does it chew its bedding, parts of its enclosure, or even itself? Many birds will pick at their feathers for lack of physical exercise or stimuli, and some mammals will even chew their tails or pull off fur out of frustration and boredom.

The charts will indicate sizes for cages or enclosures, but please understand, as mentioned earlier, that these are only minimum dimensions and that for most animals, the more space the better. It should be possible for every caged bird to fly at least a bit inside its cage, as well as outside its cage daily if practical, and all snakes should be able to extend to their full length if they feel like it.

But sometimes space is not enough. Some snakes and lizards will

EXERCISE

YOU CAN SIT WHILE EXERCISING SOME PETS . . .

. . . BUT NOT OTHERS.

require branches to climb; some turtles will need water to swim in and rocks to scale; active small rodents will find small wheels and ladders useful substitutes for large spaces and lengthy burrows; some dogs will require miles of running room, others only a small area, and so on and so on. The amount and kind of exercise your animal requires will depend on the animal itself, what age it is, and, for some species, on what time of day or night and what time of year it may be. Some animals are strictly nocturnal and get their exercise at night, sleeping most of the day; some normally hibernating species will become sluggish during the winter months even in captivity. Patience and reconditioning may change the natural cycles of many of these animals, so that nocturnal species may become "switched" (usually by changing the feeding time if the animal will accept food during the morning), and hibernating species can be discouraged from sleeping through the winter season if they are not overfed in the fall months and kept warm during the cool weather.

One important aspect of exercise is that of handling or playing with the animal; I mentioned dog walking and horseback riding earlier, and these are comparable, in fact, to the periods of activity that animal lovers enjoy most with their pets. Not only does this promote a good relationship between man and animal; it also gives both of them the chance to get some exercise. Any animal that is kept in a cage or enclosure all of the time is no more than a prisoner, and I would recommend that almost every pet be allowed at least a few minutes each day outside its home enjoying some supervised freedom. Supervised freedom should, of course, involve much more than that. Some responsive animals will certainly demand much more than that, whereas others—e.g., snakes and other reptiles—will simply tolerate handling, if even that. Iguanas and some other lizards should not be released, because they can be fierce biters and difficult to encourage back into their cages; and, of course, fish would suffer rather remarkably if allowed to "swim" around the living room. But birds, rabbits, small rodents (if they can be prevented from disappearing into corners or into rodent holes not meant for them), and larger mammals can all benefit from a romp. A friend of mine used to own a painted turtle which managed to get some exercise quite on its own; during the day it would sleep most of the time, but every night it would crawl out of its basin and take a walk around the woodwork. Morning would find it back in the basin, happily drowsing.

8 IN SICKNESS AND IN HEALTH

Many people think of the veterinarian as the person to call in an emergency—when an animal has been injured in an accident or a fight or when certain symptoms seem to indicate illness—but, as most animal professionals can tell you, regular medical attention is as important (if less frequent) a part of routine health care as feeding or grooming. For not only will a veterinarian help prevent trouble by inoculating an animal against disease, but he will also assist the owner in providing the best possible care for the maintenance of that animal. Though some animals discussed in this book (fish and insects, for instance) may not require a veterinarian's care on a regular or emergency basis, nearly everyone who keeps mammals, birds, or reptiles should also keep a veterinarian. By this I don't mean that at any time of night or day one should call the vet whenever the cat vomits or when the bird loses a few of its feathers; like human doctors, veterinarians look upon hypochondria with impatience, which isn't surprising when you consider that there are fewer than thirty thousand veterinarians in the United States for all the billions of animals. But I do believe that every pet owner should know a veterinarian and know when to call one, what to say, and how to follow his advice. In this chapter, I will try to summarize briefly what it is that a veterinarian does and how one may go about selecting and dealing with him, as well as provide information that one should have about the care and handling of injured or sick animals.

Selecting a Veterinarian

A veterinarian is a licensed medical professional with an extensive background in his field, including two to four years of undergraduate training in biology, chemistry, physics, etc., and four years of graduate study at an accredited veterinary school. Following the completion of a state veterinary examination, a veterinarian may choose to work in one or more areas: large-animal practice (concentrating on domestic farm animals), small-animal practice (usually restricted to dogs and cats), laboratory animal care, zoo practice, research, and teaching. Most veterinarians who treat pet animals are in small-animal practices, either singly or in groups, although some are in large clinics, such as those connected with humane societies. In these hospitals or clinics, one may often find veterinarians that specialize in different areas of medicine; e.g., neurology, ophthamology, pathology. Some veterinarians also specialize in different kinds of animals—birds, reptiles, exotic and native wild species—and people owning unusual pets should take particular care in selecting a veterinarian, since one with adequate knowledge or experience may not be easy to locate in an emergency.

One should go about finding a veterinarian as soon as one comes into possession of an animal that is likely to require medical care at some point in its life or when one moves with an animal into a new community. If friends or neighbors are unable to provide suitable recommendations, you may consult your local zoo or write to the Zoo Wildlife Division of the Morris Animal Foundation (531 Guaranty Bank Building, Denver, Colorado 80202) for the names of reputable veterinarians in your area. The reasons for selecting one veterinarian over another are generally as personal as they are professional; for the ability of a client to relate to a veterinarian and of the vet to relate to both client and animal may vary considerably from case to case. A good veterinarian is responsive to both the pet and its owner and should be capable of providing consistently good service at a reasonable cost, but these are matters that the client must judge for himself. The question of cost is an individual matter, just as it is with human medicine; some animals require a greater amount of care than others for the same kinds of problems and the cost for services may vary accordingly. Keep in mind the fact that a veterinarian will invariably charge less than a human doctor for similar kinds of treatment, even though he has a far greater overhead cost to bear, since his office must include hospital facilities (surgery, recovery, and radiation areas) along with examination rooms. In any event, the best way to approach the question of cost is directly: simply ask the veterinarian ahead of time what he charges for certain types of treatment or what he estimates the cost will be if surgery is indicated.

Another question often raised by pet owners in the process of selecting a veterinarian is: "Do you make house calls?" Like the human doctor, the veterinarian generally does not perform this service and requests that appointments be made in advance and held during regular office hours (nonoffice hours are usually reserved for surgery or special treatment for in-hospital animals). But veterinarians should certainly be called in genuine emergencies and appointments made at the earliest possible time. Veterinarians in large-animal practices usually spend most of their time making house (or rather barn) calls, since carting Bossy into a clinic would probably cause more problems than it would cure.

A very hazy area in veterinarian-selecting—and one that is strictly a matter of judgment for the client himself—is that of rapport between the doctor and his patient. Regardless of the amount of confidence one may have in a veterinarian's medical qualifications or ability, the way in which the animal is handled will always affect a client's reaction in one way or another. Like children, animals are inarticulate about what is hurting them, and pet owners, like parents, are often protective to the point of confusing the issue. This is not an area in which advice can be given; if the client has reason to believe that his animal is being given unnecessarily rough handling or inappropriate care, it is his prerogative to go to another doctor. One should understand, however, that the veterinarian is an expert in handling as well as in treating animals and that picking up a cat, say, by the scruff of the neck may not be as gentle as cradling it but is probably more natural and may be more efficient in certain situations.

Care and Handling of a Veterinarian

Before we go further in describing what one may expect from one's veterinarian, let's consider some of the owner's responsibilities *to* the veterinarian—or, more accurately, to the proper care of the animal. The first responsibility is to give the vet the opportunity to know the animal as early as possible, before any trouble has a chance to arise. This first meeting would involve an examination of the animal for illness, nutritional deficiency, and external parasites; a fecal examination for internal parasites (the owner should bring a stool sample along with the animal); a discussion of appropriate housing and diet for the animal, as well as of a routine for regular preventive care, such as vaccinations, booster shots, etc. This will give the owner valuable information and the animal an excellent start; it will also give the veterinarian a basic record of the animal, so that he will be prepared to give the best possible care in case of emergency. For owners of unusual animals, this first step is particularly important, for many veterinarians may not be able to help in emergencies and zoo veterinarians can rarely if ever afford the time to be of assistance.

Once a schedule has been worked out as to vaccinations, worming routines, and so on, an annual check-up is usually all that is necessary, unless something goes wrong or complications in breeding arise. Although no particular preparation need be made for a routine office visit, I would generally recommend that an owner keep the animal from eating for a few hours before the visit and, if possible, obtain a stool sample for the veterinarian to examine during or after the visit. If the animal is trained to a leash, be sure to use it, and, if not, see that the animal is brought in an enclosed carrier of some sturdy sort, with newspaper or cloth bedding. Many animals become nervous in veterinary offices (whether because of the presence of other animals, strange odors, or previous experience), and though the owner is often able to have a calming effect, it is all too common for the owner to be the one communicating the uneasiness in the first place. I remember one woman who used to bring her poodle to me, clutching it nervously and telling me how veterinarians frightened the animal. As soon as I could manage to get the dog onto the examination table and out of its owner's shaking arms, the animal would invariably relax and behave like an ideal patient.

Although all veterinarians keep treatment records for the animals they have seen, the owner should be able to provide accurate information about an animal's medical history, and I would recommend that every owner adopt the habit of keeping a separate medical chart for each pet (see sample). This is useful not only for medical reasons—particularly in an emergency when one is away from home with the animal or when one's regular veterinarian is away—but also as a guide for anyone who is "pet sitting." I would also recommend that any new owner take some time to observe the healthy animal's regular habits—such as the way it moves, the condition of its coat, skin, or feathers, the normal type and regularity of its stool, its normal rectal temperature,* and general behavioral patterns when active and asleep. After the first veterinary check-up, periodic checks should be made by the owner of the animal's well-being and all deviations from normal appearance or behavior noted. The best time for such check-ups would be during regular grooming or exercising periods. Some early symptoms of serious illness are very subtle and changes in normal behavior very slight, but often the early recognition of trouble and prompt treatment will make the difference between life and death.

In noting symptoms for the veterinarian's information, a precise description is not always enough; often it is necessary for him to know the exact order in which certain events occurred, such as when the animal stopped eating or drinking, when it began to have diarrhea or began vomiting, and how long these episodes continued.

---

*To take an animal's rectal temperature, shake the mercury down to below 95°F. and coat the thermometer with petroleum jelly. Make the animal stand; hold its tail and insert the thermometer about halfway. Hold it for one minute or two and then read.

Although it is usually not difficult to tell when an animal has been injured seriously enough to require medical attention, even though the cause of the injury is not known, it is not always so easy to determine when certain symptoms should be taken seriously. Illness is not always easy even for experts to diagnose, but I would say, in general, that the following symptoms should be considered cause for concern and sufficient reason for a call to the doctor:

1. *Any major change in behavior,* such as crying, refusal to eat or drink, constant scratching, inability to climb stairs or to walk any distance without losing balance, increased lethargy, unusually bad temperament, fur or feather pulling, labored respiration wheezing, or coughing, repeated vomiting, difficulty in urination or defecation.

2. *Abnormal physical conditions,* such as runny eyes and nose, pronounced change in body temperature, dehydration, loss of color in ears or mucous membranes (if gums or inside of ears become light pink or white), excessive diarrhea, bloody urine, any unusual odors.

None of these signs should be difficult to observe, especially if the animal's owner has an accurate picture of what the animal looks and behaves like in the best of health. Any or all of them may indicate

SAMPLE HEALTH CHART
(RECOMMENDED FOR EVERY PET OWNER)

NAME _____

SPECIES, BREED, TYPE _____

SIRE _____ DAM _____

DATE OF BIRTH (or date hatched) _____ SEX _____

BRED BY _____ Telephone _____
Address _____

VACCINATION RECORD

Vaccine	Date	Booster shot or Revaccination	Date
_____	____	_____	____
_____	____	_____	____

DAILY DIET _____

DIETARY SUPPLEMENTS
Product   Treatment
_____   _____
_____   _____

FECAL ANALYSIS
Date   Findings
_____   _____
_____   _____

VETERINARIAN _____ Telephone _____
Address _____

that a disease process is present, and the earlier the diagnosis, the better the animal's chances are for being successfully treated. If an animal dies suddenly before medical attention can be provided, it may be a good idea for the owner to get in touch with the veterinarian in any case; a necropsy, or post-mortem examination, which will reveal the cause of the animal's death, can be very useful for the owner, especially if he owns other animals of the same species.

Handling an Animal in Trouble

Once the veterinarian has been called and an appointment made for an office visit, it is up to the owner to transport the animal as safely and carefully as possible, and even to employ some first-aid procedures. Animals in pain may be difficult to approach, and all precaution should be taken to avoid further injury—to the owner as well as to the animal. Ask the veterinarian for advice, and above all use common sense. An animal that is unconscious can be moved on a board or in a blanket; fractures should be well padded and immobilized before the animal is moved. Uncontrolled bleeding should be bandaged directly over the wound with pressure applied to stop the

A TOWEL CAN BE AN EFFECTIVE STRETCHER . . .

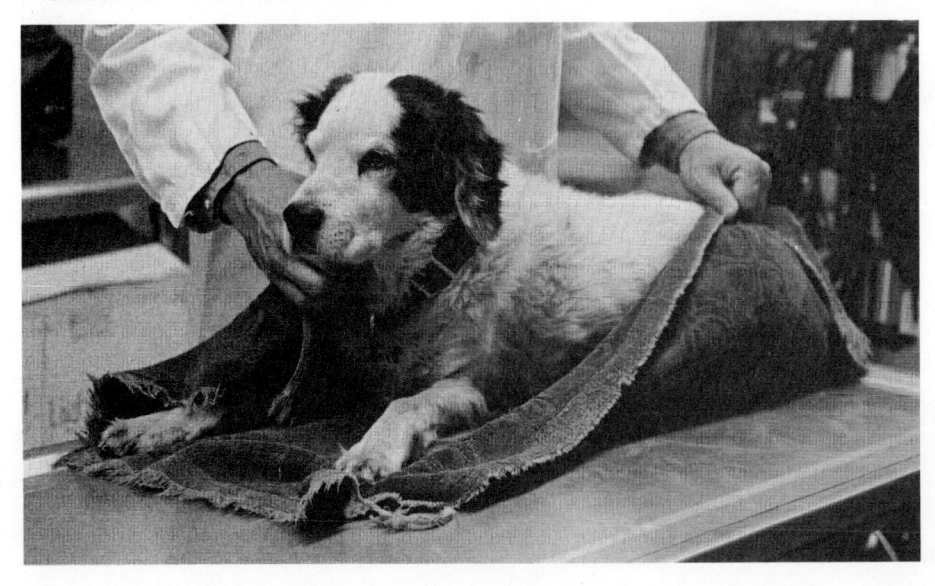

flow of blood. More radical procedures, however, such as heart massage or artificial respiration should not be attempted by untrained amateurs, since they may do more harm than good. Special attention should be paid to the animal's natural defense mechanisms before any steps are taken; excitable dogs should probably be muzzled, and cats or other small animals with powerful claws should be carried in a towel with their paws held so that painful scratches can't be inflicted on the handler. Birds and small mammals that are normally caged do not present as many problems in carrying, but care should be taken to keep the animals from being chilled. With any animal suffering from suspected disease or injury, the maintenance of body temperature is probably the most important first-aid treatment that the owner can provide, since loss of body heat can make almost any condition worse and the animal more difficult to treat. A blanket or towel may be sufficient, but if the animal seems to be losing heat rapidly, you may wish to apply a heating pad or introduce an incandescent lamp into the cage or near the animal.

Once the veterinarian has had a chance to examine the animal and has arrived at a diagnosis, ask him to give you a technical and nontechnical description of the animal's condition, as well as detailed descriptions of the treatments he has made. The owner should clearly understand the regimen of treatment, such as what medication to give, when and how to give it, and when it should be discontinued. Side effects of medication should be discussed, and the owner should feel free to consult the veterinarian at any time he

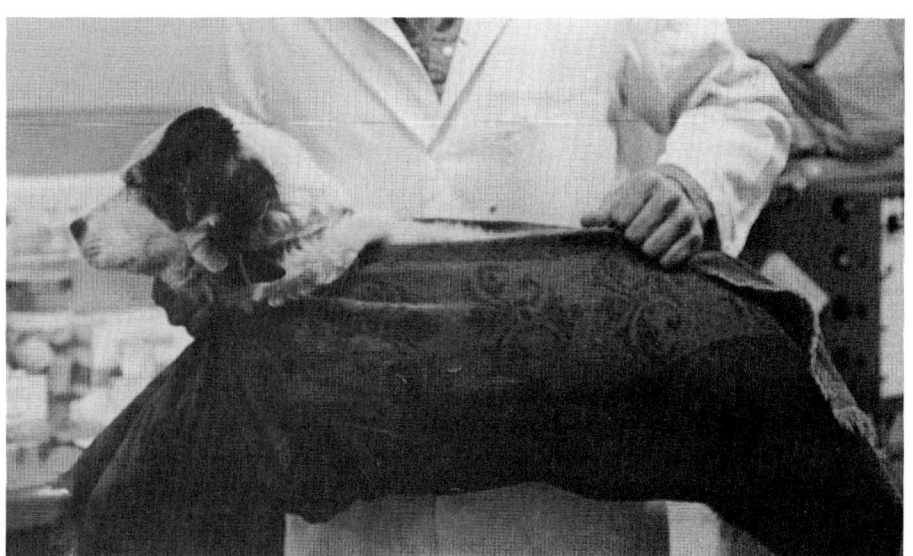

... FOR CARRYING AN INJURED ANIMAL.

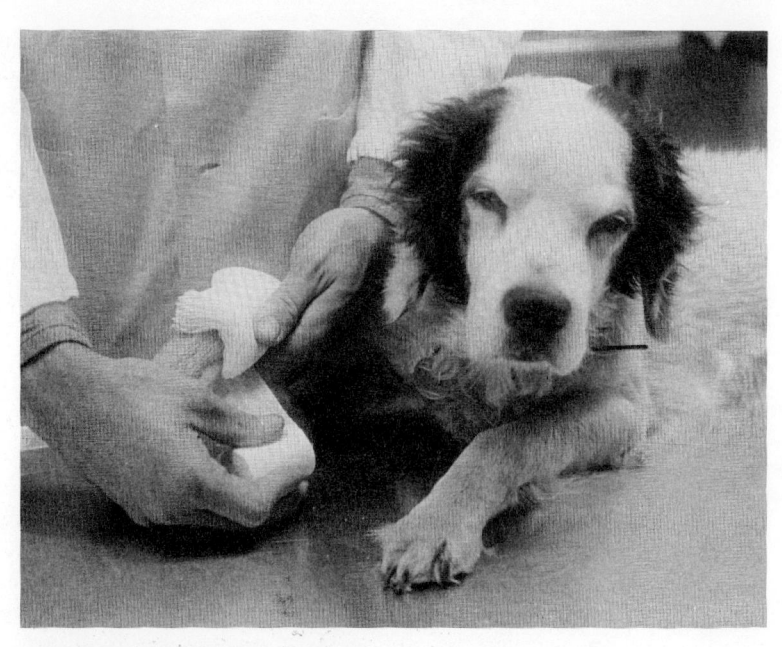

A PRESSURE BANDAGE APPLIED DIRECTLY TO A WOUND MAY HELP STOP THE BLEEDING.

believes the medication should be discontinued or changed. The methods of giving medication should be worked out in the office, with a trial run on the animal if necessary, so that the owner can see exactly what procedures are to be used. Be sure to ask about dietary and exercise changes that may be necessary following any serious forms of treatment or surgery that have required hospitalization. Since an animal returning home may become overexcited by the sight of its owner, the car ride, the stimulation of sights and smells of home, take care to see that a certain amount of peace and quiet are maintained for the sake of the animal's nervous system. Don't let the animal run and jump around but restrain its movements by using a leash or a carrier on the way home, and then restrict its outdoor exercise for at least a week, taking it out if necessary only on a leash. Limit the amounts of food and water so that excessive gulping won't cause stomach upset. Be sure to follow your veterinarian's orders— and if he hasn't given any, ask him whether there are any special precautions you should be taking until the animal has regained its normal condition. If the veterinarian asks you to bring the animal in at a later time for a follow-up examination, be sure to do so, and feel free to call him in the interim if you think that all is not well. If he asks you to give the animal medication, ask him for suggestions

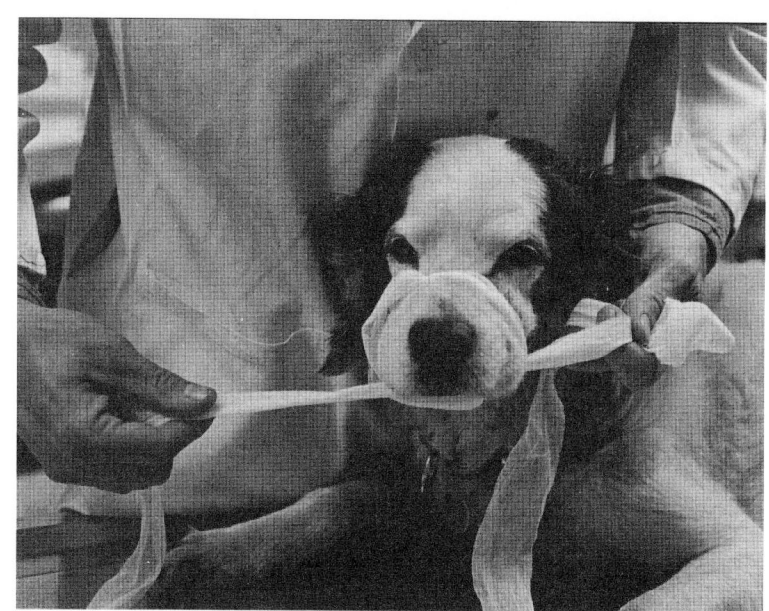

SOME INJURED ANIMALS REACT BADLY IN PAIN,
AND AN EMERGENCY MUZZLE
MAY BE A SENSIBLE PRECAUTION

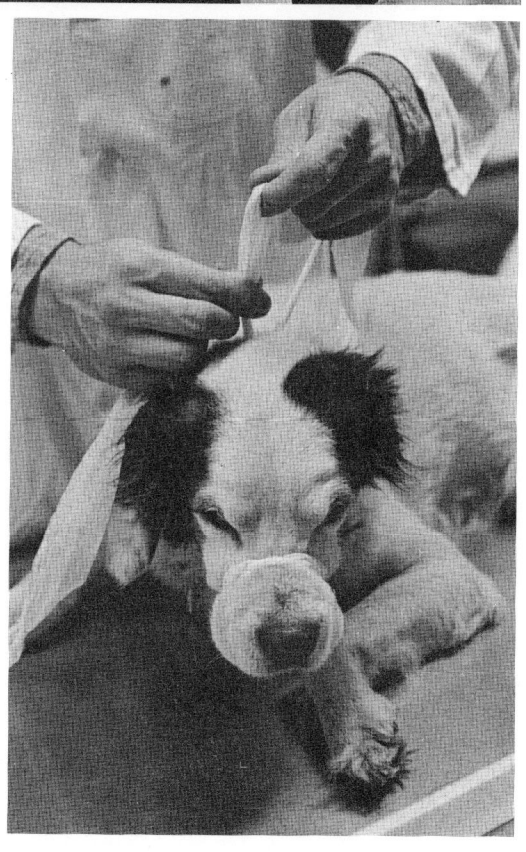

HANDLING AN ANIMAL IN TROUBLE

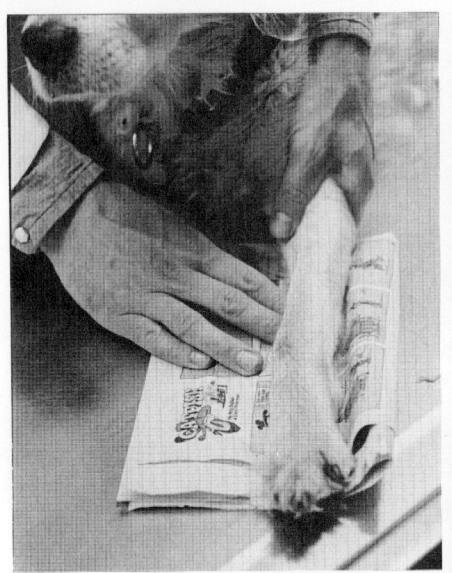

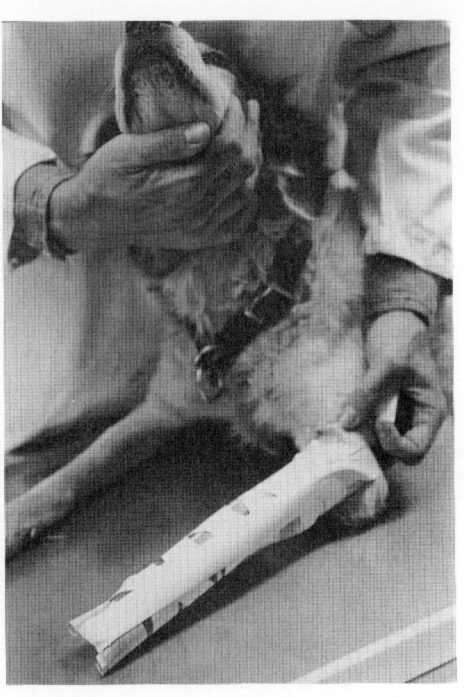

NEWSPAPER AND TAPE CAN BE USED
AS A TEMPORARY SPLINT TO
STABILIZE A FRACTURED LIMB.

A FIRM PAIR OF HANDS AND A POSITIVE ATTITUDE
ARE ALL ONE NEEDS TO GIVE A PILL TO A DOG.

about how to do so effectively. Dogs will usually take pills or capsules readily enough in their food, but cats seem to present problems to most pet-owners since they are more finicky about what they eat and not too easy to convince when it comes to taking pills. The veterinarian will show you how to give the cat (or dog) a pill if you ask, but the process is a simple one if your attitude is positive and your hands are somewhat dexterous. Grasp the cat's head firmly but gently in one hand and tilt it back so that there is a clear passage to the throat. Hold the pill with your thumb and index finger, keeping the lower jaw open and steady with another available finger on the same hand. Let the pill fall into the throat and lift the lower jaw so that the mouth is closed while the head remains in the vertical position. Hold it for a second or two until the cat swallows the pill, and then release. If, for some reason, the cat manages not to swallow the pill and spits it out, try again, using all the patience you can muster. Don't give up. Once the cat gets the idea that you mean business, it will figure out that fighting won't do any good and it should be more cooperative the next time around.

Preventive Medicine

Many small animals—the domesticated rodents, rabbits, and birds—may never need a veterinarian's care, but the larger animals—dogs, cats, farm animals, and some of the common wild animals—will require certain inoculations if they are to be protected against some of the serious diseases that are prevalent in this country. The following is a brief listing of the vaccinations and preventive treatments that are now available.

RABIES: Undoubtedly the most publicized of diseases, rabies is worldwide and can affect all warm-blooded animals, including humans. It is caused by a virus and is spread primarily by infected animals—dogs, cats, wild animals—usually by biting though not always requiring direct contact. The virus is present in the saliva of the infected animal, and when skin is broken by a bite, the virus travels up the nerve trunks toward the spinal cord and then to the brain; once the symptoms develop—after a period ranging from two weeks to a few months—the disease is invariably fatal (although there is one known survivor now). The most obvious symptom is a change in normal behavior, friendly animals becoming aggressive and timid animals becoming bold. Shortly before death the animal may go into a "furious" form of behavior, then into a paralytic or dumb attitude. Only a laboratory analysis of the brain tissue of an infected animal can give an accurate diagnosis of rabies, so if you are in any doubt about an animal that has bitten you (especially if it is wild), consult a physician immediately and hold the animal in confinement

GIVING A PILL TO A CAT
MAY REQUIRE A BIT OF DEFTNESS AS WELL.

if possible so that an examination can be made. Bitten humans may obtain a series of injections to prevent the disease, but the best safeguard is to see that your dogs and cats, or wild animals kept in captivity for any period of time, are given vaccinations against rabies. There are several kinds of vaccine, none of them costly; the vaccination routine will vary depending on the kind of vaccine used, and some communities and states require rabies shots for all dogs on an annual or biannual basis. Because less is known about the tolerance level of wild animals than about dogs and cats, killed-virus vaccine is generally recommended rather than live-virus vaccines.

CANINE DISTEMPER: This is a widespread disease that takes many different forms in dogs, skunks, ferrets, foxes, and the raccoon family, and few unvaccinated animals escape exposure; the death rate is high, and surviving animals may be afflicted for life. The first vaccine should be given as early as six weeks after the birth of an animal, with periodic booster shots given yearly, or as your veterinarian recommends.

FELINE INFECTIOUS ENTERITIS: Also known as feline distemper or panleucopenia, this disease is often fatal to cats. The symptoms are listlessness, vomiting, and refusal to eat, and veterinary attention should be given if these continue for more than twenty-four hours. Cats (and also skunks, ferrets, raccoons, etc.) may be inoculated against the disease as early as six weeks, with annual booster shots to insure immunity.

INFECTIOUS HEPATITIS: This is a disease of the liver that affects canines, with fatal results for about 25 percent of the affected animals, and very slow recovery for those that survive. Even after recovery dogs may spread the virus through their urine for some months. The vaccine for hepatitis is now available in a three-in-one inoculation with distemper and leptospirosis and is recommended for all canines.

LEPTOSPIROSIS: This disease is an increasing problem in some areas. It affects the kidneys and can be transmitted to man through the urine of dogs, cattle, and rodents. Vaccinations may be given along with the distemper vaccine, and because the disease can be fatal to the animal or may inflict permanent kidney damage, inoculation is recommended.

TETANUS: This disease is called "lockjaw" in man and is produced by the toxin of a bacteria that affects the brain and spinal cord. Horses and cattle are probably most seriously affected by this disease, dying usually in convulsive seizures, but dogs, cats, and other animals may also develop tetanus, generally through puncture wounds. Vaccinations are given yearly to insure immunity.

EQUINE ENCEPHALITIS: There are three forms of "sleeping sickness"— Eastern, Western, and Venezuelan, and they are all becoming scattered throughout the United States. Vaccinations should be given to all horses on a regular basis for the disease is invariably fatal.

EQUINE INFECTIOUS ANEMIA: Although there is no real preventive vaccine for "swamp fever," it is a good idea for all horse owners to have their animals tested (through a Coggins test) at least once a year to determine whether the disease is present. It is spread by mosquito bites and is fatal; any infected horse, which may or may not show symptoms (weakness, weight loss, continued lethargy), can transmit the disease via mosquitoes and should be destroyed. In some states, a Coggins test is required before any horse is shipped.

BRUCELLOSIS: This is a bacterial infection found in dogs, cattle, pigs, sheep, and goats, but the only vaccine available is designed for use in cattle, which may abort their fetuses if infected.

HEARTWORM: Most internal parasites cannot be treated preventively, but this particular infestation, which can be fatal to dogs and is increasing, particularly in the eastern United States, can be prevented by the daily use of capsules or liquid (and a prescription food is available from Hills Packing Company). Since the parasites are spread by mosquitoes, the warm-weather months are the period when medication should be given; do not medicate, however, before testing the dog for heartworms that may be present.

FELINE PNEUMONITIS: This is a highly infectious respiratory disease in cats and may be prevented by the use of a vaccine, although booster shots must be given often and regularly. Symptoms are sneezing, refusal to eat or difficulty in eating, and dehydration. The only first-aid treatment is to keep the cat warm and isolated from other animals; call the veterinarian. There are many other kinds of feline respiratory diseases, such as rhinotracheitis and influenza, but only the veterinarian can make the appropriate diagnosis and prescribe the correct treatment.

RHINOTRACHEITIS: In horses and cattle this disease is not generally serious except in pregnant females, which may abort if they become infected. Vaccines are available for horses, cattle, and cats.

TRACHEOBRONCHITIS: This is a respiratory disease infecting domestic dogs and commonly known as "kennel cough" because it is highly infectious and often found in dogs that have recently been kenneled. If you plan to take your dog to a boarding kennel, you may want to take advantage of available vaccines ahead of time.

First-Aid Treatment

For many conditions and diseases no preventive medication is available at this time, but frequently successful treatment can be given if the ailment is diagnosed early enough. Below are brief descriptions of common animal problems; some can be prevented by good management, others may be treated at home, but most will require a veterinarian's care. When in doubt, consult the vet, and if none is available, or if the one you reach can't help your particular animal, try the ASPCA or your local humane society. Because many symptoms are common to more than one disease or condition, do not attempt a diagnosis on your own without the help of an expert, but simply apply some common sense and the following bits of advice until you can get professional assistance.

SHOCK: This is a failure of the circulatory system resulting from injury or illness, a serious condition from which the animal cannot recover on its own. Symptoms are weakness, loss of body temperature, and respiratory difficulty or failure. Keep the animal warm and comfortable and call the veterinarian immediately.

FRACTURE: Simple fractures involve a broken bone or bones; compound fractures involve the broken bone protruding through the skin with external bleeding. If a limb is affected, symptoms are the inability to support weight and swelling and flopping of the limb; broken ribs may be indicated by difficult breathing and painful movements; skull fractures may result in disorientation, stumbling, swelling of eyes with unequal pupil size, painful eating or drinking, and a slack jaw. Fractures of the vertebrae may cause paralysis, pain, and incoordination. The first-aid treatments involve keeping the animal calm and warm, immobilizing the affected area with pads of newspapers or rigid materials. If the fracture is compound cover the area with sterile bandage or at least a clean piece of material and immobilize. If the skull or vertebrae are affected, move the animal gently onto a blanket or board and call the veterinarian.

POISONING: First figure out the source; bring a sample to the veterinarian with the animal if possible. The symptoms will be vomiting, diarrhea, weakness, abdominal pain, loss of appetite, trembling, dizziness, salivation, excitability, or convulsions, depending on the poison. Induce vomiting by using an emetic such as mustard, salt, soap in water or strong tea, or by inserting a finger or blade of grass down the throat; if acid is the source of poisoning, give milk of magnesia in water. Try to prevent the animal from injuring itself if it is staggering or having convulsions, and give it as much fresh air as possible. Training an animal to eat only what you offer it would be the best form of prevention but not always possible; keep all garbage cans covered and all insecticides and other toxic substances out of reach.

WORMS: Internal parasites may cause weight loss, dull-hair coat, loss of appetite (or increase), lethargy, rubbing of the anal area, and the actual appearance of worms in the stool or vomit. Except for heartworm, it is difficult to prevent the occurrence of worms which are usually transmitted through feces; make sure the animal is examined regularly (fecal analyses should be made on each regular veterinary visit) and try to keep the animal from known infested areas. Do not attempt to treat worms without a veterinarian's advice.

FLEAS, MITES, AND TICKS: Intense scratching and chewing can result from these external parasites; close examination of the skin will reveal them or their debris, especially during warm-weather months. Increase your examinations during the summer to once weekly and ask your veterinarian for a dip or bath treatment. Destroy all bedding or material in the area where the animal normally sleeps.

EAR PROBLEMS: If the ear canal is red or inflamed, if the animal shakes its head or paws at its ear, if a bad-smelling liquid oozes from the ear, have the veterinarian examine it for infection, ear mites, or whatever. Check the animal yourself on a regular basis for ticks and burrs, and do not allow water to get into the ears during cleaning. Do not attempt any deep cleaning but consult a veterinarian.

EYE PROBLEMS: Redness, watering, discharge, rubbing or pawing at eyes may indicate anything from a foreign object to an infection. If you cannot see the cause of the irritation, consult a veterinarian.

TOOTH PROBLEMS: If an animal's breath is foul, if teeth are loose or missing, if tartar or debris has accumulated on or between the teeth, if the gums are red or inflamed or bleeding, have your veterinarian scale the teeth of all deposits. This condition may be prevented by feeding bones, dog biscuits, or any rough material; do not feed only soft foods. Brushing the teeth with salt or baking soda may also improve the situation.

SKIN PROBLEMS: If, in spite of good grooming, examination for parasites, and removal of burrs and mats, the animal is scratching, losing hair or feathers, showing draining sores, crusty patches, or reddened blemishes on the skin, the affected area may be bathed with a mild solution of soap (*not* detergent) and kept dry with baby powder. If the condition persists, see the veterinarian. Feather loss in birds may be caused by excessive plucking due to boredom or lack of stimulus; give the animal a toy or something to chew.

FOOT PROBLEMS: Limping, swelling or redness, and raw spots about the feet may indicate the presence of a foreign object or bacterial disease. Clean the area in warm water, remove any objects, and if possible bandage raw feet. If cuts are present or if limping persists, see the veterinarian.

ANIMAL BITES: If a puncture wound is evident, clean the wound and determine the extent of the bite; sometimes the bite may not be evident beyond a tender spot and a slight drainage on the hair; remove hair if necessary, and if the wound needs suturing or appears to be deep or developing an abscess, consult the veterinarian. Do not bandage but allow to drain.

HEAT STROKE: This condition, marked by sudden collapse, a blank expression, deep heavy panting, can be fatal if the animal is not cooled immediately with cold water. This is very common with dogs and cats that are left in hot cars with the windows closed or even slightly open and can easily be prevented. Call the veterinarian immediately.

CHOKING: If an animal gags or coughs, a foreign object may be lodged in its throat. If the coughing does not dislodge the object, call the veterinarian; you may try to dislodge it yourself by holding the animal upside down or slapping it on the back with the head lowered. If the animal seems to have stopped breathing, try to get the object with your fingers or long tweezers, using a gag on the teeth to prevent bites.

INTESTINAL BLOCKAGE: This may be caused by an object in the intestinal tract, by stomach or intestinal torsion, or by telescoping of the intestines into itself. The symptoms are vomiting, constipation, dehydration, lethargy, and loss of appetite, and a veterinarian should be consulted immediately. In cats, particularly long-haired cats, a similar condition may be caused by the development of fur balls in the stomach, but it can be prevented by regular grooming. A first-aid treatment may be given by mixing one or two teaspoons of mineral oil with the food, but if in doubt about the cause, consult the veterinarian. In domestic cats if straining is accompanied by dark bloody urine the cause may be cystitis, which is the inflammation and infection of the bladder, perhaps the result of bladder stones. Collect the urine in a container and take it with the animal to the veterinarian.

This listing by no means covers all the potential problems that may arise with your pet. Fish and reptile diseases are far too numerous even to list here, and I have put certain excellent texts in the bibliography for those who are interested in obtaining detailed information about prevention and care. See also the sections earlier in the book devoted to individual species and the charts at the back for more information about ailments common to particular animals.

Animal Diseases That Man Can Catch

One question that I am often asked by people who are shopping for a new pet is: Am I (or are my children) likely to catch anything from this or that animal? This isn't an easy question to answer in a general way, for over a hundred different diseases can be transmitted from animals to human beings—some of them rare, some rather common. All of the animals we have discussed in this book are subject to infectious diseases, and some can be caught by man; as the pet and human populations grow, the incidence of the transmittance of infectious diseases increases also. Some of the diseases are not serious enough to warrant medical attention, although others may be troublesome and even dangerous.

Perhaps the most common way in which diseases are transmitted to humans is through an animal bite. The mouths of animals can contain any number of organisms that have been picked up from other animals, from themselves (through licking wounds, orifices, etc.), or from contaminated objects or areas with which the animals have been in contact. Aside from the lacerations that a bite may cause, the most feared result of a bite is rabies, a disease that is carried by all mammals. Although the incidence of rabies was once common enough to cause state and local governments to keep strict controls over the inoculation of dogs against the disease and to impound biting animals that might be carriers, rabies is now relatively rare. There hasn't been a case of human rabies from dogs in New York City for over thirty years, for instance, and dogs are no longer held for testing when there has been a biting incident. Nevertheless, caution about rabies should never be relaxed, for several species of wild animals still carry the disease and may infect domestic animals as well as humans. Because inoculating wild animals against rabies is impossible, one should take all of the precautions recommended to avoid what will almost surely be a fatal illness if one is bitten and the disease not identified very soon. If the animal is available for examination, a veterinarian can ascertain its health status within a matter of hours; if the animal is not available and if rabies is known to be present in the region, the bitten person must be treated with antirabies vaccine. For those people who are in constant contact with wild animals, immunizing treatment to prevent infection may be given.

Various other diseases may be transmitted by animal bites—tetanus (which is very rare), rat-bite fever (also rare in this country), monkey-bite encephalitis (unusual and reported only by laboratory workers and scientists), cat-scratch fever (not just from scratches or from cats), as well as a number of bacterial infections that will be discussed later. Cat-scratch fever, which is symptomized by swelling, tenderness of the lymph nodes near the bite wound, and eventual ulceration, is more common in children than in adults, more common in the fall than at any other time of year. It is not dangerous, but a doctor should be given a chance to examine the infected area.

Leptospirosis is probably the most increasingly serious of the bacterial diseases that man may catch from animals, and it is one against which dogs and other animals are inoculated regularly in endemic areas. The most dangerous type is transmitted by rats, but pigs, cattle, and wild animals may also carry it and cause various diseases in man. Another bacterial disease, which is probably the most widespread of diseases carried by animals (transmitted usually by contaminated water), is salmonellosis; it may have various reactions in man, affecting the brain, the heart, lungs, joints, bones, or gall bladder. Salmonellosis can be carried by almost any species, including birds, domestic farm animals, rodents, wild mammals, and some reptiles, especially turtles. Gastrointestinal problems, fever, septicemia, and chronic infections can all be caused by salmonellosis, which can be readily diagnosed and successfully treated if the disease has not progressed too far.

In 1972, an estimated 280,000 cases of salmonellosis were attributed to turtles, and as many as 25 per cent of human cases were turtle associated in some areas. Because about 15 million small turtles were sold in the United States that year, many of them to pet shops, the federal government passed regulations requiring that all small turtles (under 4 inches in diameter) be tested for salmonellae by an approved health official before shipping. Although there is an effective antibacterial therapy that will prevent or suppress organism shedding, its use is not practical for the average pet owner; the best procedure is for all newly acquired turtles to be tested twice, at thirty-day intervals, by a veterinarian or other expert and destroyed if the tests are positive. To prevent the spreading of the disease, all new turtles should be isolated from others, raw meat should be avoided, and water or bedding changed frequently and disposed of through sanitary facilities rather than sinks or garbage pails. All turtle owners should wash their hands thoroughly after handling the pet or the container. Turtles found in the wild are rarely infected, but because the disease spreads so rapidly, captive turtles kept together and exposed to the disease will quickly become carriers.

Tuberculosis can affect many animals in many different forms, including man, of course; however, there is not much evidence that animals infect man directly. Nevertheless, it is not a good idea to keep a pet in which the disease has been diagnosed.

Anthrax was once a frightening disease, particularly to farmers; vaccines have done much to eliminate the possibility of man's picking up the disease in its various forms.

Brucellosis, which usually produces a chronic influenza type of illness in man, was once very common but is rare now, except among those who regularly handle animal products. Pet dogs have been found to be the source of some recent cases, but the disease can be easily controlled with antibiotics.

Most animal viral infections are carried by insects, such as fleas, mosquitoes, ticks, and others. Tick fever is relatively rare now, though in the western states it may be found in some rodents; psittacosis, which can be controlled with antibiotics, is now rare, although it was once a serious problem for pet birds and food birds. It is possible for humans to pick up equine encephalitis (carried by mosquitoes) although this is not as common as it once was; other forms of encephalitis have been found in rodents and other small wild animals in the western states and in some birds in the Midwest. A recent virus that has been found in man caused by pet hamsters, although other rodents—mice and guinea pigs—can also be a source (either from direct contact with feces or from airborne particles), is lymphocytic choriomeningitis. The disease in man—causing headaches, coughs, and fever—is not serious but it can be uncomfortable. In 1974 there was an outbreak of LCM in the southern United States when a hamster breeding colony became infected, probably from wild mice.

External parasites, such as lice, fleas, and ticks, can of course be transferred to man from animals, and children are particularly susceptible to the organism that causes ringworm in dogs and cats, though there are other types of ringworm found in other species that may infect the people who handle them. Internal parasites can also be transmitted to man: tapeworms (usually caused by eating animal flesh but also caused by fleas and direct contact with the feces of an infected animal); roundworms and hookworms carried by dogs and cats (the former causing dermatitis and skin lesions in man, the latter entering the bloodstream through the intestines but quite rare); strongyloids (passed from dog to man through soil contaminated with feces). Other parasites—species of whipworms, pinworms, etc.—which are found in animals are not found in man, and trichinosis, once common in the United States (transmitted by eating raw pork and even bears) is now quite rare. Histoplasmosis has been of recent interest because of the huge numbers of blackbirds that accumulated in areas in the southern United States, causing respiratory ailments in man through their droppings. Toxoplasmosis is found in several species of animal, though the only evidence we have of direct transmission to man has been from the cat, in which the organism causing the disease is carried in the intestinal tract and passed through the feces. Authorities believe that the disease is widespread, especially in children, and poses a threat to pregnant women because it may cause fetal brain damage or even death if there is no immunization. The disease has many possible symptoms and varying degrees of severity, and anyone who is pregnant and owns a cat should handle feces with extreme caution

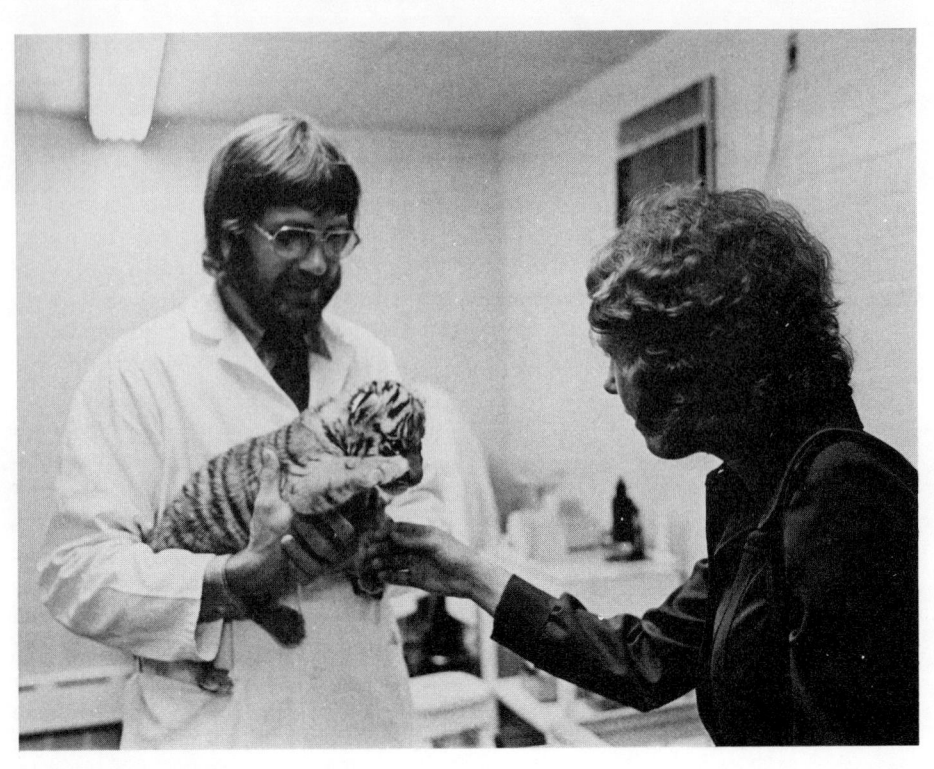

THE AUTHORS WITH A BABY SIBERIAN TIGER, IRRESISTIBLE
BUT IMPOSSIBLE TO RAISE AND KEEP IN CAPTIVITY
WITHOUT PROFESSIONAL CARE.

or not at all. It is possible for a veterinarian to determine whether an animal has toxoplasmosis by means of a simple blood test, a precaution recommended for all pregnant pet owners.

Happily, the United States is relatively free of these diseases and reports of infection are rare or sporadic, but zoonoses (as these animal-transmitted diseases are called) are far more frequently found in other parts of the world, and anyone who handles animals with regularity should be aware of them and see that rules of cleanliness are maintained, not only for the health of the animal but also for the health of the owner.

9 GROWING YOUR OWN

Anyone who owns a pet that is not neutered is likely to face the problem of breeding at some point in the animal's life, whether it takes the form of making a decision—to breed or not to breed—or of coping with a *fait accompli*. If you have a mouse and you want a whole bunch of mice, simply get yourself another mouse of the opposite sex, put them together in a breeding box, and let them go to it. If you don't stop letting them go to it soon, you'll probably end up with more mice than you can possibly care for, so what didn't seem like much of a problem at first has suddenly taken on new dimensions. If you have a cat or dog, the complications are even greater and not just because the size of the offspring is greater; most people—no matter how determined they are to have a litter "for the kids" or for themselves—do not intend to keep all the babies their pets produce. And because there is already a massive overpopulation crisis, which involves the death of over 13 million unwanted animals a year in American humane societies, the problem is no longer just yours but everyone else's. So before we go to it ourselves in the discussion of breeding and raising young animals, let's consider the alternative of not breeding at all.

Not Breeding

It's no good for an owner to feign surprise when Puss suddenly delivers a new litter in the closet; if Puss was unspayed, then it was inevitable, unless she were never allowed out of the house, that she would become pregnant. Even people who live in remote areas, far away from any other cats, would be astonished at how quickly a male cat (or a whole collection of them) can sense that some female somewhere is in heat. And it's the same with dogs, as almost everyone who has lived through an estrus season with a bitch can tell you; suddenly your peaceful front yard is filled with male dogs you've never seen before, scratching at the door and at each other. Some of these males have strayed far from home and some may have trouble finding their way back again, a problem that every owner of an unneutered free-roaming male dog has had to deal with at one time or another.

When the subject of neutering animals comes up in conversation, a few pet owners will always resist the idea for various reasons, most of them not very reasonable. "The children should have the experience," I often hear. There's no getting around it, the miracle of birth is a tremendously exciting event to watch, as is the rearing of tiny animals. But how much of this do children generally see? One cat in ten will have her kittens in full sight of the children; most cats prefer dark closets in the dead of night, when they can be assured of peace and quiet, for performing their miracles. (I used to know a cat who lived on a boat and invariably had her kittens below deck way up toward the bow, so that her owners never even saw them until they were weaned.) As for the rearing process, children generally become familiar with it in one or two sessions and after that, it's back to the playroom. And you are left with six or eight kittens or puppies that will need veterinary attention, extra food, and new homes, which may not be so easy to find. For the sake of the children, therefore, we have included a dramatic photographic sequence of the birth process, and for yourself, we have included some information about what lies in store for the owner of a new animal family.

But back to neutering for a moment to answer the rest of those reasons that people give for letting their animals breed. "Neutering is expensive and, what's more, it's unnatural!" Yes, it is expensive, because surgery of any sort involves expense and expertise on the part of a veterinarian. But there are spay and neutering clinics around, many of which charge only nominal fees. There are also new birth-control drugs being developed for use in animals. Consider, too, that the cost of spaying a female dog (which is virtually the same operation as a hysterectomy in a woman) is usually far less than the boarding costs incurred by owners who are sick and tired of keeping their females cooped up, separated from all the males outside the back door. As for the argument that neutering is unnatural, surely the act of keeping a dog or cat in a house with people is not what nature intended to begin with. Wild dogs and cats are capable of keeping their own populations stabilized, but domestic animals are at the mercy of their human owners, who will often let things get out of control just out of ignorance or carelessness.

In any event, neutering an animal will probably mean that you'll have a better pet on your hands; castrated males are less likely to roam and fight, and spayed females are less likely to develop uterine cysts, infections, and breast cancer as they mature. There is no truth to the rumor that neutered animals become obese because of the surgery; obese animals get that way by being overfed. Since neutered animals aren't likely to roam in search of sexual opportunities, they may require less food and more exercise, but the prospect of having a better-mannered animal around for a longer period of time is surely to be preferred.

For those people who think that their pet is so beautiful that it would be a crime not to let it reproduce—think twice. This is what breeders are for. *You* may be willing to undertake the considerable research necessary to find out exactly what bloodlines you are working with and what results you are likely to get, but most owners don't take that trouble and are sorely disappointed. Amateurs shouldn't count on making a lot of money by selling a purebred litter, even though they have all the right papers. Some friends of mine had a beautiful pair of German shorthair pointers and decided to breed them in the hopes of having a litter they could sell. They found that only two of the four pups were good enough to command the price of $200 apiece and that the veterinary and food bills came to nearly $300, a sum that didn't take into account the long hours they spent of their own time and the unsold pups they had to raise and keep until good homes could be found.

Breeding as a money-making venture is not likely to succeed without the advice of an expert (free, if you can manage it), a good deal of knowledge about the animal (be it a rabbit, a pigeon, or a cow), and a ready market for the offspring. A lot of fun can be involved in breeding mice and similar small animals, because they are prolific and because genetic experiments in breeding crosses and developing strains may be very instructive and useful if you know how to apply the knowledge. Just remember that one of the results of the experiment is going to be many mice and that not every family can manage to keep more than a few. Breeding animals only to be forced to destroy them is not fun.

Breeding certain species that are not easily raised in captivity can be very rewarding. I know several people who have had great success in breeding exotic birds, including some rare species, but I must admit that these people were pretty experienced with raising baby birds and were able and willing to cope with all the problems that were raised at the same time.

If you do plan to go about breeding in a sensible, forewarned way, try to keep accurate records of mating times, gestation, weaning, as well as keeping track of interrelationships. There is no law against incest among animals (and, in fact, a certain amount of controlled incest can be a good thing if you want to improve a strain by emphasizing a particular characteristic), but inbreeding can be a bad thing if it results in the propagation of unwanted traits. If you are interested in developing a new strain, record keeping will help you figure out, later on, how you did it and how you can do it again.

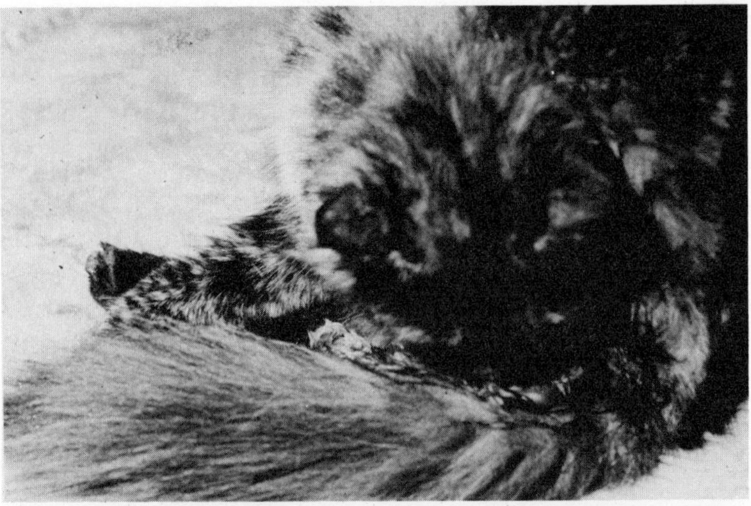

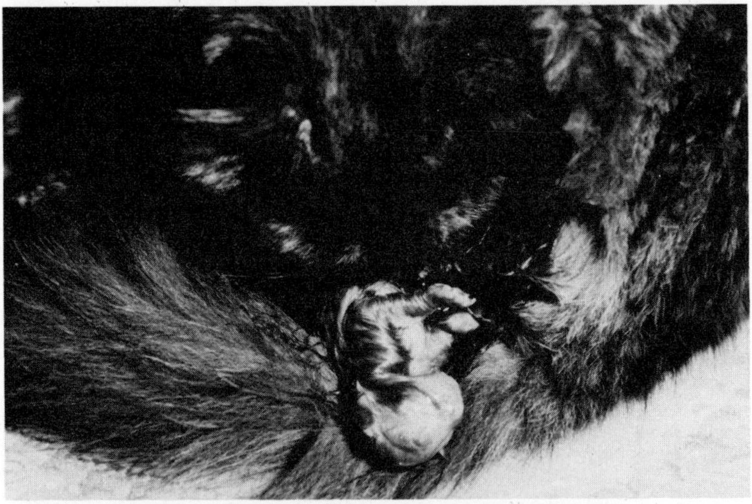

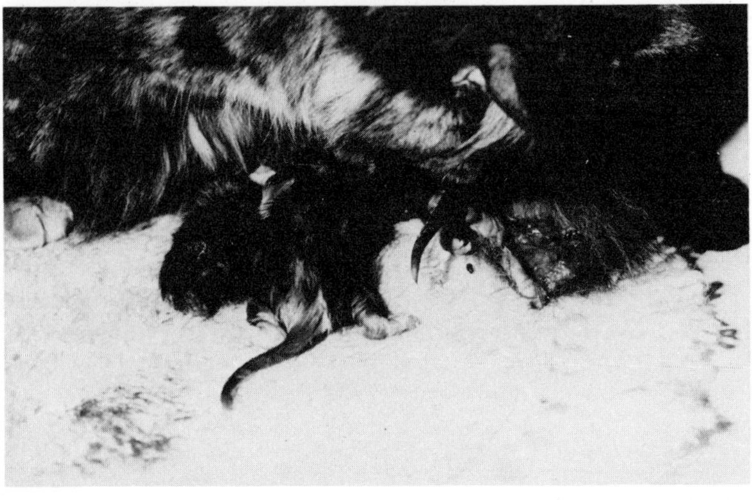

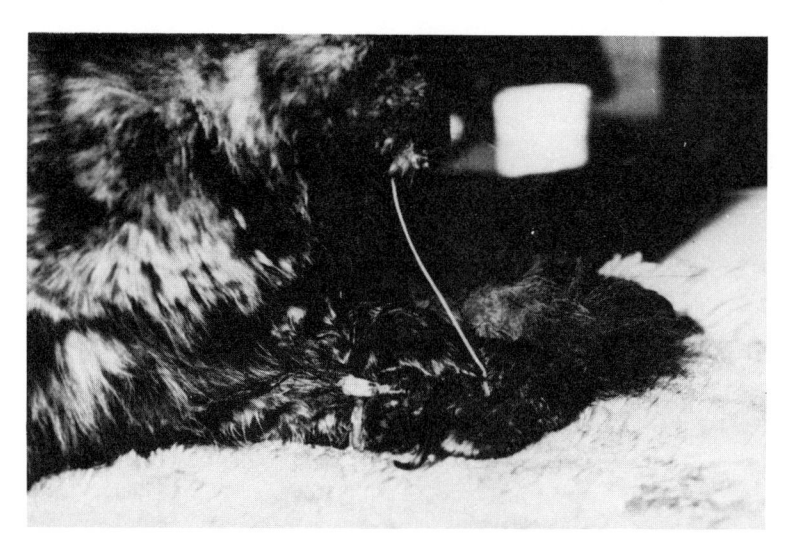

A CAT GIVING BIRTH TO KITTENS.

Breeding Mammals

THE PREGNANT FEMALE

Putting aside all questions of neutering, planned breeding, and accidents, let us assume that, for whatever reason, you have a pregnant female on your hands. Sometimes it is not at all easy to determine whether an animal is pregnant until shortly before she is due to deliver; many fat or furry females will conceal the fact effectively so that only an examination by an expert or the sudden appearance of offspring will reveal the truth. In some small mammals, pregnancy is accompanied by certain behavioral patterns; mice and other rodents will begin to build nests out of whatever they find in the cage (and if you have a breeding pair, you will have been considerate enough to provide a nesting box and cotton, grass, and other sorts of nesting materials for them). Larger mammals don't usually display unusual behavior until delivery is imminent; but physical symptoms include: swollen mammary glands, increased appetite, weight gain, and sometimes young can be seen kicking against the abdominal wall.

If you know when breeding took place and what the gestation period for the animal is (see the charts at the back of the book), you may have a pretty good idea when you can expect to be passing out cigars, but as with humans, breeding does not always guarantee pregnancy, and some species are even prone to false pregnancies, just to confuse the issue. If you mastermind the breeding yourself—as is usually done with pedigreed dogs and cats, large domestic animals, and rabbits (which should be kept in separate cages except for breeding times)—or if you know which day it was that Puss or Fifi got out when she was in heat, you should keep alert to signs of pregnancy and consult the veterinarian to see if any special prenatal care is required, such as dietary supplements, new housing arrangements, etc., and to prepare him to be on call if any emergency should arise. Prepare yourself as well by reading a good text on the reproductive patterns of your particular animal, just so that you will know what is normal and what will require professional attention.

Gestation varies considerably from one species to another; even such close relatives as the chinchilla and the hamster carry their young for very different lengths of time—111 days and 16 days, respectively. As one might expect, the chinchilla babies are quite well developed at birth and the nursing period is short; this is also true of the guinea pig, whose gestation of 63 days results in fairly sturdy little piglets. Horses, which carry their young for 11 months, produce offspring that can stand on their own feet within half an hour, whereas the gestation of an opossum—only 18 days—results in fetuslike young that need a pouch for nearly 4 months after birth before they venture out into the world.

CARE OF MOTHER AND OFFSPRING

Like gestation, the birth process and the number of young produced vary greatly depending on the species. Some animals will require little or no assistance whereas others should be observed carefully while they are in labor so that assistance can be provided if necessary. In either case, the best policy is to remain calm and unobtrusive if you are fortunate enough to witness the event. Leave the female alone when you suspect she is about to go into labor, but check on her every half hour or so; if the animal seems to be comfortable in your presence, you can stay, but be very quiet and don't make her feel any more stress than she already does. Once she has gone into the final stage of labor—when abdominal contractions are strong and she is straining—or if any part of a fetus is showing, she should deliver within an hour. If not, call the veterinarian for advice. The time between babies can vary drastically, so don't worry if they don't pop out regularly unless the female continues to strain to no avail and you are certain that there are more babies to come.

With some species, the male may remain with the female even after the babies are born and make himself useful in helping to care for them; in other species, however, the presence of the male may cause real problems, and the parents should be separated well before birth takes place. Be sure you know what the behavior characteristics are for your own animals, and don't simply count on their having humanlike feelings of pride and pleasure in having produced offspring.

Cats are usually pretty neat and troublefree about the whole business; even cats delivering their first litters always seem to know what to do and how to do it. The only precautions that you need to take are to provide her with plenty of food and water and see that her bedding is kept clean. She (like all mammal mothers except the human being) will devour her offspring's excrement and as a cat she will go one step further than other animals and train her kittens to use a litter pan. Your role in her childrearing will therefore be minimal.

One problem that often arises with cat mothers, however, is that she may select absolutely the wrong place in the house to have her babies and you may want to move them. When the delivery is finished and she is resting, purring contentedly after the exhausting task of cleaning and drying the kittens and making sure that they know where to get nourishment, you may try to approach her. If she seems willing, you can attempt to remove a baby (talking to mama the whole time) to a place where you would rather she rebuilt the nest—a box filled with clean cloth is fine. Be sure that she watches you and follows you to the new place (there's not much doubt that she will); you may even convince her to move the others for you. If not, move the whole family, one at a time (picking up each kit by the scruff of the neck, just as she would, or cradling them in a cupped hand), and sit back and wait. She may try to move them back to square one, but stay with her and encourage her not to do so, perhaps by removing whatever it was that made the first spot so attractive.

Dogs may be more difficult to raise—for both mother dog and yourself—because they take up more space and complications are more likely to set in. Make a whelping box for her in a quiet place, line it with soft material, and be sure she has access to it at all times around the time she is due to whelp. Puppies are usually born in fairly regular succession, every fifteen or twenty minutes; if her labor appears to be a difficult one and if you suspect that all the puppies have not yet appeared even after a couple of hours, call the veterinarian. Assuming that trouble does not occur, however, simply keep the mother well fed, well watered, and content with her location. Soon after the birth, call the vet and follow his advice about the next step. (If you want to have dewclaws removed—some hunting breeds may require it—or tails docked, the third day is when it should be done.) Otherwise let the female become accustomed to your presence so that you may be allowed to handle the puppies shortly after they have been dried off. Start with a very short session of praise and petting, and gradually increase the time you spend with them, praising her all the while. Some bitches are quite temperamental and do not like to have people around a lot of the time, but most pet dogs will welcome the attention if it is given in small, steady doses.

Some baby animals are born virtually helpless, hairless, and blind, unable to do much more than find mother and nourishment. The females do more than just feed these babies; they constantly lick and rub them, not simply for purposes of cleaning but also in order to stimulate their tiny digestive tracts. Some animals are born in a far more developed state; goats, sheep, and cattle, like horses, can all walk shortly after birth.

The nursing period varies considerably in length from one species to another; the rabbit, for instance, is weaned at about eight weeks (like the cat and dog), whereas the hamster is probably ready to have its own litter at that age. Most animals are weaned fairly gradually and naturally, with solid foods becoming increasingly important as the animal's digestive system becomes more developed. At the same time, the animal itself will have become larger, more active, and may be making hesitant forays into the world outside the nest. If the animals are caged, this is the time for fun—watching the babies find their way around, bumping into each other, and beginning to respond to humans as well as to their own kind. If the animals are not caged or confined in one way or another, this time of fun is also a time for caution. As little kittens and puppies become bolder and more adventurous, they can get themselves into any number of places and things, and though the mother will do her best, the owner should be careful not to make her job more difficult. (Once, when I was host to a new litter of kittens, they suddenly disappeared from the living room where they were born and simply could not be found. It wasn't until I gave up the search and collapsed on the sofa-bed that I realized—thanks to a squeaking behind my back—that they had managed to crawl up into the air space inside the sofa, all six of them.)

Because some of the smaller animals mature very quickly, it is a good idea to determine the sex of the young as soon as you can in order to know whether they should be moved to separate cages. Male hamsters and rabbits are particularly prone to fighting if left together, even at what may seem to you a very early age. With larger animals, you may have to take some role in the weaning process yourself; horses and cows, for instance, will continue to nurse their young until a new baby is about to be born, but most breeders separate mother and child much sooner, five or six months after birth when the offspring has begun to incorporate solid food into its diet. This is not necessary, of course, but professional breeders usually like to have the generations separated for human purposes, such as training the young, milking, or otherwise using the mother. Highly social animals should be allowed to remain together as long as possible, if they are to develop properly. One of the reasons that monkeys and other primates are so difficult to breed in captivity is that the young are usually removed from the adults at an early age and simply do not learn how to interact with others of their own species. Many other animals cannot learn how to fend for themselves in gathering food if they do not receive instruction from their mothers (or both parents, as is true of geese); therefore, if a person chooses to hand rear young wild animals he must take this job of education upon himself, assuming that the youngsters are to be released as soon as they are old enough.

HAND REARING BABY MAMMALS

To the inexperienced animal lover, the idea of raising orphaned or abandoned animals is very attractive; not only does it mean that a few tiny lives might be saved, but it also holds out the promise of a unique relationship between man and animal that simply caring for an adult does not. It is true that some lives have been saved, but this is usually accomplished by dedicated people who know what to do with an infant and are willing to undertake the enormous effort and spend the amount of time required. It is certainly true that a very special bond can be created between the human "mother" and the young animals, but that bond is all too often broken by the time the animals reach maturity. Like human children, animals rarely feel grateful to their parents, and sending youngsters off on their own—be it to college or to the woods or to another home—can be a heartrending experience for the ones who gave so much time and effort to their upbringing.

    I would certainly not recommend that anyone interfere with the rearing of domestic animals or go out to find orphans in the wild except in an emergency. Even then, it is best to let an expert take over, or at least to rely heavily on expert advice before taking on the chore yourself. For a chore it is, and one that requires a lot of knowledge and energy. Although it is easy enough to determine whether a domestic animal needs hand rearing if the mother has died or abandoned her offspring or can produce no milk, it is not always so simple with wild-animal babies. Just because a baby rabbit or two seem lost and alone in your backyard or in the woods does not necessarily mean that they have been abandoned. Wild mothers often find it necessary to leave their youngsters alone while they go off in search of food, so do not try to interfere unless you are sure that you have an orphan on your hands. If you find the dead mother,

HAND REARING BABY ANIMALS ISN'T ALWAYS EASY.

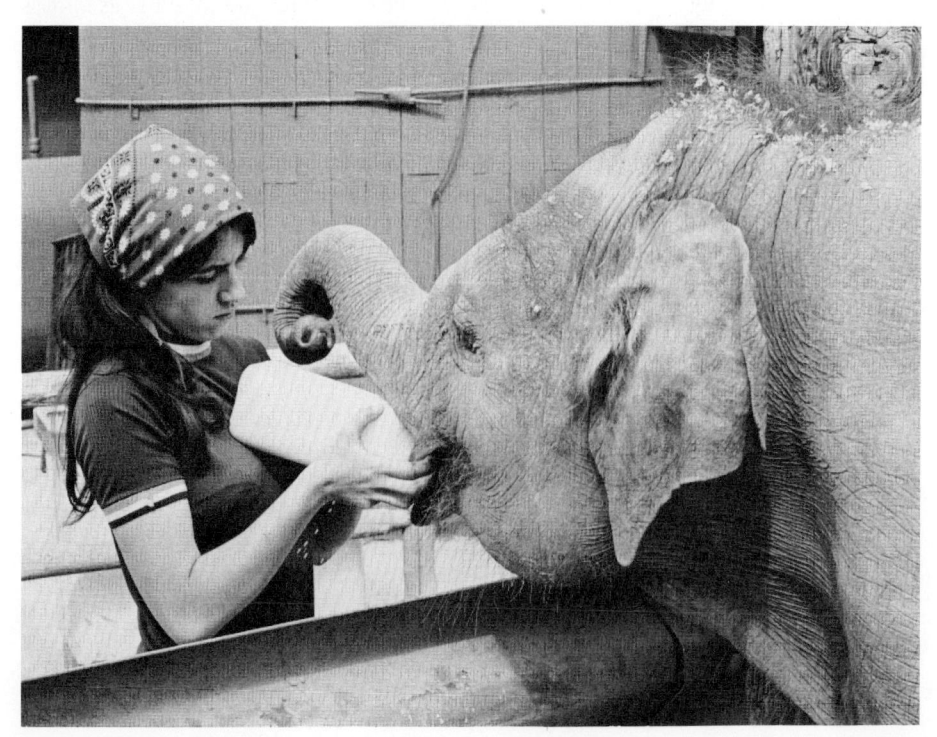

fine; if not, watch the animal from afar for at least three or four hours before you take it home. If you don't have the patience to wait that long, you won't have the patience to give it a headstart in life anyway.

Because space is limited here, I cannot describe the process of hand rearing for all of the species mentioned in the book, but I will try to outline below the general problems involved, suggest certain formulas and feeding schedules as well as other kinds of care, and refer the interested reader to a number of texts on the subject.

Warmth and food are the two most important elements in raising any young mammal, regardless of size. For small animals you will need a box lined with clean cloth (towel and flannel are soft and absorbent) and heated in some way to keep the temperature around 85°F. A heating pad or hot-water bottle (wrapped in cloth to prevent scorching) is usually the most convenient source of warmth, although some people have found that a regular light bulb or light fixture such as those used in aquarium setups will provide sufficient heat. Whatever you use, be sure that the animal can escape the source of heat if it wishes; regulate the heat if it appears to be too high or too low. A cardboard box, not too large, is fine; the animal should be made to feel as secure as possible, and darkness (afforded by a loose-fitting cover) and the comfort of fabric or facial tissues may in some way help the home provided by humans resemble the animal's original nest with mother and siblings installed. Some people find that babies rest a little easier if there is a steady noise like a clock ticking or a radio humming, something to take the place of its family.

Larger babies may not fit so conveniently into a shoe box or a carton, but a small room in a barn or in the house (or on the porch if you have one and the weather is warm) can be set aside as a nursery. A nest will still be necessary, some place with few visitors where the animal may curl up, in peace and quiet and dark, against some soft materials. Be sure the area is warm and that the nesting materials are clean and replaced regularly.

Food, for very young animals, should be made available as soon as they have settled into their new home, especially if you don't know how long they have gone without nourishment. Cow's milk is too high in lactose for most young mammals, but Esbilac, a substitute bitches milk made by the Borden Company, is, when diluted half and half with water, an excellent formula for most animals. It is available in most pet shops or through veterinarians; if you can't get it, however, evaporated (not condensed) milk will do for a short period of time. Make enough formula for one day's feeding and store it in the refrigerator, warming it up in single portions just before feeding. This formula will do very well for puppies, kittens, squirrels, rabbits, members of the weasel family, opossums, raccoons, foxes, badgers, coyotes, though each will need special foods added to their diets as they develop a taste for solid food. Deer need a special high-fat, high-solid diet; homogenized milk mixed with heavy cream and calf manna, a pelleted commercial food available from feed stores, is the best combination. They may take as much as one seventh of their body weight at each feeding. Wild felines will do best on KMR, a special cat diet also made by Borden, but Esbilac will do in a pinch.

The types of food required by young animals may be determined in part by the way they are fed in the wild. Mothers that are constantly on hand for nursing—such as opossums, primates, and cattle—will tend to produce milk that is relatively low in fat with as much as 90 per cent water content. Mothers that leave their young and return at intervals will produce concentrated milk that is high in fat. The more you know about the nursing habits of the animal in nature, the better equipped you will be to deal with the hand rearing of its young in captivity.

As a general rule, very young animals will need to be fed every two hours, if not more often, and may take very little at a time, at least until their eyes open, at which point their appetites will pick up. Tiny babies may not be able to handle pet-nurser bottles, but eye droppers will usually serve; however, take care that they are not made of glass for even baby rodents have very sharp teeth and may break the glass and injure themselves. Plastic catsup bottles are usually better than doll or baby bottles because the openings are smaller and easier for the handler to control. After each feeding, be sure to "burp" the baby and stroke its tiny stomach and abdomen (in the direction of the anus) to release gas and promote intestinal movement. Shortly after feeding, the animal should produce a tiny fecal pellet which may be picked up and removed, to save your cleaning the nest. Larger animals that are on their feet and exercising soon after birth will not need this kind of assistance for their own activity will stimulate intestinal movement. Be sure to notice the consistency and frequency of bowel movements, however, just to be sure that all is well.

Once the animal's eyes have opened, you may try to incorporate some soft food into the formula every feeding; baby oatmeal made in a thin gruel and added to the milk formula is usually best, but some animals, raccoons for instance, will tolerate strained baby foods made with meat and vegetables along with the formula; watch their stools to see how well they do with these additions. As the babies begin to eat more formula at each feeding, and if their stomachs are still tight just before feeding, you can lengthen the time between feedings and drop the night feedings at last. When the animals seem interested in chewing on things—their nest, your finger, whatever they can reach—you can begin letting them try out solid food—seeds, dog biscuits, rabbit pellets, canned dog food, nuts, bits of apple, toast, whatever they seem to like. Do not let the pieces of perishable food stay for very long in the box or cage and remove uneaten portions periodically. Members of the weasel family will crave meat very quickly; when their eyes open, kill a baby mouse and put it in with the weasel (or mink or ferret), and as soon as it is eaten, start feeding live young mice or rats and taper off the formula. Opossums, on the other hand, are very slow to develop; very young ones are difficult to raise, and few survive outside their mother's pouch, but furred opossum babies may be fed dog food and chopped hardboiled egg along with the Esbilac formula and will probably pull through (if they don't escape before you've had a chance to release them). Larger animals take a long time to be weaned and may not even be interested in solid food for two or three months; just keep offering calf manna and handfuls of grain or hay and they'll decide if they want it or not.

When the young animal no longer needs the bottle, it will simply reject it and suddenly you will have a self-feeder on your hands. At this stage, you may begin giving bits of chopped or ground meat or dog food to the meat eaters and different kinds of vegetables and seeds and nuts to the vegetarians (not too much of anything at first or you'll cause diarrhea). Fresh water should be made available to all, either in a sturdy (unspillable) dish or in a water feeder such as those used for domestic rodents. The feeding periods will vary: three times a day for some animals and a constant supply for others, depending on the species. Until animals become nearly full grown, the amount of food they take in should be determined by how much they will eat; give them as much as they want—unless you have rabbits and hares, which will overeat until they become sick. The diet should be varied according to their tastes but do not suddenly introduce new foods in large quantity; do it gradually and try to stick to the foods recommended in the charts for the adult animals. Raccoons, for instance, will eat almost anything, but avoid a steady diet of table scraps and try to provide fresh food whenever possible.

By this time you should start thinking about a larger cage or enclosure, for the babies will have become very active and far messier than a box lined with cloth (or than you, the cleaner-upper) can tolerate. Animals that you are preparing for release may be put outside, weather permitting, either on a screened-in porch, in a metal cage, or in a fenced-in area. Allow them to forage for themselves if possible or increase the number of natural items in their diet. Then, one day, you can simply leave the door or gate open and let them take their own time about setting out on their own. It may be necessary to release your adolescents in some area away from your house, in which event be sure that you select the right spot (where other animals of the species are native, where food is abundant, and where humans are rare) and give the animals a trial run if desirable before you abandon them forever. You might wish to leave a supply of food for the first few days, just to be sure that the transition to life in the wild is made without unecessary trauma.

Now is the time when you can sit back (or lie back, for you'll be pretty exhausted after those weeks of feedings every two and three hours) and congratulate yourself for having accomplished something that only another mother could understand.

Breeding Birds

Although chickens and other kinds of domestic fowl seem to lay eggs and breed with incredible regularity under human supervision, most birds do not, and, if anything, human interference has often given them a good deal of trouble. Our use of DDT, for instance, managed to endanger a number of species by reducing the amount of calcium in their food, thereby ensuring that the shells of their eggs would not be strong enough to allow their young to mature until hatching time. And many birds have simply not been able or willing to produce eggs in captivity. Nevertheless, a number of cage birds will lay eggs and even incubate them naturally if the proper conditions are provided, and for any bird owner this event is one to be welcomed. Now that it has become difficult to import foreign birds, the fact that several popular species will breed readily has encouraged cage-bird fanciers into hoping that sooner or later some of the parrots and other beautiful exotics can be raised in this country, just as canaries and budgies are.

One of the problems facing hopeful bird-raising amateurs (and some professionals) is a basic one: differentiating between the sexes. There's not much one can expect from two well-suited companionable males except for two well-suited companionable males, after all. Yet in many species, it is impossible to detect sexual distinctions except by medical methods. Sometimes there may be behavioral differences (male canaries will sing; females won't), and occasionally there are small but distinct differences in coloration (as seen with parakeet ceres for instance). But usually owners simply have to trust to luck or to an expert.

Even if the right sexes have been placed together and are compatible, breeding may not occur, for reasons best known to the birds themselves. Pairs that have been known to breed are usually far more expensive than untried specimens, and for good reason. Someone has spent a lot of patience and probably a lot of praying to achieve success. As with mammals, species and individuals exhibit many differences in terms of behavior, habitat requirements, and—once the eggs are laid—incubation and care of the young. But there are some useful generalizations that will at least get you started in the right direction.

If you wish to encourage your correctly sexed pair of birds to begin breeding, introduce them gradually, first in separate but adjacent cages and then, once they are used to each other, in a larger breeding cage outfitted with a nesting box. These are usually simple boxes made of wood (see Chapter 7); size will vary according to the size of the bird, and the box should have an entry hole, just large enough for the adult to pass through, placed about one-third of the way down from the top. A concave bottom so that the eggs won't roll, a perch inside the box just opposite the entry, and some nesting material, and you're in business. Maybe. Budgies, half-moon parrots, and cockatiels don't seem to care much about nesting material, and may even throw it out of the cage if it is provided. Some birds like wood chips and will chew on their nesting box until they have enough in the bottom; canaries use their own feathers and nesting hair (a commercial product); cedar or pine shavings, cat litter, dried grass, and shredded rope are also good materials. If you don't know which your bird prefers and can't find out from an expert, try one or a combination of these and see whether the female allows it to stay. Some of the small finches will make their own nests out of stringy material without requiring a breeding box; occasionally people like to hang strawberry baskets for these birds just for the decorative value the birds give them.

When the female has laid her eggs, it is best to leave them undisturbed in the nest, although people who raise chickens, for instance, prefer to collect the eggs from all the hens in one day and place them under a brooding hen or hens so that they will all hatch at the same time. With less cooperative birds, however, the best policy is to leave well enough alone. If the parent birds desert the nest for some reason, or if one of them becomes ill, the eggs should be removed to an incubator before they become too chilled. The temperature of the incubator, which need be no more elaborate than an insulated wooden box with a heating element and dish of water to maintain humidity, should be kept at a constant 103°F., and each egg should be marked with the date it was laid (a felt pen is good for this purpose). If the eggs do not hatch when you expect them to, they may be dead or unfertilized; leave them two or three days longer and then discard them. If they do hatch, your troubles have only begun, for you must provide adequate warmth and appropriate food if they are to survive.

The chicks of pheasants, quail, ducks, geese, swans, chickens, and a few others are born well covered with down and able to feed themselves. Provide them simply with a warm (85°F. at first and then room or barn temperature as they develop) environment, plenty of water, and some chick starter, which is available at feed stores.

THE EGGS OF VARIOUS SPECIES OF BIRDS
IN A HOMEMADE INCUBATOR;
NOTE THE FIGURES MARKED ON THE EGGS
TO INDICATE THE DATE THEY WERE LAID.

Because they will peck at anything, they will soon pick up bits of food and eventually get the idea that pecking is what gets food into their bills. Some chicks may need help; pheasant babies may require the addition of some greenish material if their attention is to be directed toward the food, but for the most part, these precocial chicks, as they are called, will learn to feed themselves promptly.

The chicks of most aquatic birds are semiprecocial, in that they are covered with down when they hatch but require some parental care or hand feeding. Sugared water is a quick source of nourishment, but, because all young birds need a great deal of protein, vitamins, and minerals in their diet, another formula should be substituted fairly quickly. Cooked baby cereal or farina mixed with honey, chopped hard-boiled egg yolk, and powdered milk blended with water to a relatively thin consistency is a good diet for baby birds, and can be fed either with a dropper if the bird can manage it or placed on a finger and rubbed against the tiny bill until the baby learns to peck it off. Force feeding is not usually necessary, but if a baby refuses to eat, you may try jiggling it in your hand gently as you open its beak by applying gentle pressure to the sides of its head. There are many other formulas that will work; combinations of strained baby foods made with meat, egg, and vegetable together with milk and a vitamin-mineral supplement (see Chapter 7) are also satisfactory for most nestlings.

Altricial species, such as pigeons, parrots, owls, hawks, hummingbirds, woodpeckers, and finches, are hatched more or less naked and cannot leave their nests or feed themselves without parental care for at least five or six weeks. If they are hatched and dried in the incubator, the temperature may be lowered to 95°F. where it should stay for about two weeks; then give them another week at 90°F. and a fourth at 85°F. By this time the birds should be fully feathered and able to survive at room temperature. During those early weeks, however, they must be hand fed, of course; the formulas discussed above will be sufficient, but the timing of feedings will be enough to exhaust even the most dedicated bird lover. Adult birds feed their babies about every fifteen minutes in nature, and because so little nourishment can be taken in at each feeding, human parents must feed them as often as humanly possible, at least every two hours.

Some birds feed their young insects or fruits but others will predigest food and regurgitate it. Pigeons have a milky crop secretion which they feed to their chicks; it is impossible to reproduce this substance and so a special formula of baby cereal mixed with strained-beef baby food, together with vitamins, will have to suffice for orphaned birds. All these formulas should be cooked and served at a relatively warm temperature. Be sure that the baby bird maintains its body temperature during the feeding process; it will take only a few moments to feed the baby, but removal from the incubator every fifteen or twenty minutes during the day (no night feedings; adult birds have to sleep sometime!) can bring on chills if the babies aren't insulated. As soon as the chicks are able to take more than a few drops at a time, the period between feedings may be lengthened. By the time they are fully feathered, they should be given items from the adult menu and finally they will become entirely self-feeding.

Obviously it is better to let the parent birds do the rearing of their young if they can, although this isn't always possible. Some birds will reject their young by killing them, throwing them out of the nest, or picking at them. If a couple of eggs or more hatch, and the parents destroy the first fledging, don't remove the others, for sometimes the parents will manage to pull themselves together sufficiently to raise them. Sometimes even before hatching occurs, a brooding bird will remove eggs from the nest; although you may try to hatch them yourself in an incubator, chances are that the eggs are not good and that the female somehow sensed this while she was sitting.

Wild birds that have been orphaned after hatching are extremely difficult to raise by hand, if only because cold and shock have usually set in before the birds are rescued and nourishment has not been given in time. Nevertheless, some dedicated people have been successful, often after a long trial-and-error period of experimenting with different foods. Several good books on the subject are listed in the bibliography; in addition to supplying useful information they also give encouragement and moral support to anyone who tries to undertake the massive job of bringing up baby birds.

The subject of breeding animals in captivity is a vast and complex one, involving many more species than mammals and birds. As I have indicated in earlier chapters, it is highly possible to breed reptiles, insects, and fish under appropriate conditions, and the process is almost always a fascinating one. A great many animals—even under what seem like more natural conditions—may never breed in captivity, for their demands on an environment will be far more complicated than we can determine. Valuable studies have been made, and these are worthy of exploration by the interested pet keeper, but success is not always possible even for experts. Animals in captivity, particularly those with wide natural ranges, may settle into a life of relative inactivity—sexual inactivity included—and no amount of correct food, temperature, and having animals of the opposite sex around may stimulate them to reproduce their own kind. But when it does happen—whether we expect it or not—we can be sure that we have done something extraordinary and possibly valuable in terms of the species; at least we can congratulate ourselves on having created an environment in which the animal has felt enough at home to produce and rear its young.

10 THE END OF THE AFFAIR

It would be nice if we didn't have to include a chapter on the subject of losing pets, but giving this kind of book a happy ending would be both unrealistic and irresponsible. Because most animals have a lifespan far less than half our own, sooner or later every pet owner must face the loss of an animal—whether through death or removal from the household. The death of a pet can be a very sad occasion, particularly if the animal has played an important role in the life of its owner. People react to the situation in many different ways: some are inconsolable, at least for a while, and refuse to consider the possibility of obtaining a new pet, whereas others rush right out to get a new puppy or kitten to distract themselves or their children from the sense of loss and feeling of grief. Some will spend lavish amounts of money on burials and memorials in a pet cemetery; others will simply allow their veterinarian to dispose of the animal with no ceremony at all. Some parents may regard the death of an animal as a valuable experience for the children who must eventually learn to face the inevitable fact that life ends, others may try to conceal the truth in the hope of sparing the children's feelings. In short, people react to the death of a pet in as many different ways as they react to the death of a human being.

Death caused by old age, illness, or accident is only part of the story, however. Sometimes pets will simply disappear, having escaped their enclosures or having been allowed to roam freely; in some instances they may be recovered, but usually they are not, because they have died, been taken in by some individual or organization unable to trace the owner, or been stolen (a rare occurrence but possible). Although the loss of an animal in any of these ways is usually inadvertent, an owner can take precautionary measures either to prevent straying or to improve the chances of recovery.

Undoubtedly the most difficult way to end a relationship with a pet is to be forced into making the decision yourself either to find the animal another home or to put an end to its life. Presumably if you have read this far through the book, you are not the sort of person who would take such a decision lightly, but it is possible that you are not aware of the various alternative ways in which the disposal of an animal may be handled. In this chapter, therefore, I will cover briefly a number of the ways in which animals may be lost to their owners and the most humane, practical methods of coping with the various situations.

Death

The best way to prepare yourself—and your children—for the death of a pet animal is to be aware of the animal's natural lifespan and to be knowledgeable about the diseases and accidents that may terminate life before the maximum age is reached. If one knows that a gerbil is likely to live only three or four years, its death will not come as a shock, though it may be a sad event for everyone who has been fond of the animal during its lifetime. If one knows that rabbits, which may well live until the age of eight or ten years, are susceptible to certain kidney ailments that may cause premature death, one will be better able to accept the fact that four or five years may be as long as the rabbit will spend with you. Even within the same species, lifespans vary considerable. A breed of large dogs, such as the Saint Bernard or great Dane, may not live more than ten years, because of its great size and the strain that is put on its skeletal system, whereas a small terrier or beagle can be expected to live fifteen years or more with proper care. Many conditions may encourage premature illness and death; congenital defects are, of course, out of the owner's control, although they may be observed in a young animal by expert eyes or become evident through a knowledge of the animal's genetic background; information from both kinds of study should accompany the selection of the animal in the first place. I am frequently asked to look at young puppies and kittens to determine their general health and condition before owners make the commitment to acquire them, and often it is possible to predict that a certain puppy, for instance, might be likely to suffer from a malfunction caused by a defect in conformation. An owner's lack of knowledge about proper care may also bring about early death; obesity caused by overfeeding can make even a basically healthy animal susceptible to arthritis or other kinds of dysfunction. The omission of certain vaccines and preventive medicine—as for rabies, distemper, internal parasites, etc.—will also lessen an animal's chances to live a full life, as will improper diet, inadequate exercise, and other kinds of neglect.

Although many accidents may be prevented, too often they just simply happen and the owner need feel no real guilt; his general feelings of sadness, however, may be compounded by the desire to blame someone (including himself) or by the kind of shock for which no one can ever be adequately prepared.

Nevertheless, reasons for death aside, there are some practical matters that will need attention, most notably that of disposing of the animal's body. If the animal can be easily carried, of course, the simplest method is simply to place the body in a plastic bag or some other container and take it to the local dump or leave it for the sanitation department to pick up. Or you can take the body to the local humane society or to your veterinarian for cremation. If you have a larger animal or for some reason cannot transport it yourself, there will probably be a pickup charge; and if you wish to have your veterinarian perform a post-mortem examination (necropsy), there will be a nominal charge for that also. Another simple method—if you live in an area where there is some land and no zoning restrictions—is to bury the animal yourself. When I was a child I had the habit of performing elaborate burials in the backyard for every dead mouse, mole, and rabbit I found, complete with ceremonies and gravestones; after a couple of summers, however, my parents put a stop to it when they began to find rows of tiny stones in the vegetable garden, each marked with a faint but lovingly inscribed "R.I.P." together with the animal's name (bestowed posthumously) and date of demise. After some family discussion, my parents managed to make me understand that these small carcasses would probably have been better off left where I found them, not only because handling them could potentially cause me some trouble but also because even in a state of decomposition, the animals served a natural purpose that was not required in the vegetable garden.

A rather more expensive method of disposal, but a popular one, particularly for city dwellers, is to have the animal interred at one of the more than four hundred pet-burial grounds throughout the country. This form of burial can cost as little as $15 for a bird or as much as several thousands of dollars. The services may include provision of a simple container and a plot, with burial and maintenance thrown in, or an elegant casket (complete with silk pillow and mattress), an engraved stone marker, a burial ceremony, and seasonal flowers and decorations. Some people even go so far as to have their animals restored to some semblance of their former selves by animal undertakers (or restorers) and, of course, some pets are not buried but preserved by taxidermists (Roy Rogers's Trigger is probably the most famous example). All of that, naturally, costs money. As long ago as 1924, a woman in Westchester County spent $13,000 on a mausoleum for her two pet poodles, so you can imagine what it is possible to spend in this day and age for a similar show of devotion and bereavement.

If you know that the death of your pet was caused by someone because of negligence or deliberate violence, you may find you are eligible for financial recompense for your loss. Animals can be insured against loss or death if they are considered valuable property by an insurance company; breeding, racing, or show stock are often insured. Although I hesitate to mention it, malpractice suits are filed occasionally against veterinarians, and some boarding kennels may also be liable for damages when owners have proof that a death or injury was caused by negligence or mistreatment on their premises. (One court even decided in favor of a woman whose prize chihuahua was "raped" by an intruding male dog, though the result in that case was not death but a litter of unsalable crossbreeds; the story does show, nevertheless, how sympathetic courts may be toward an offended pet owner.) If an animal dies shortly after purchase, the seller may be forced (if there has been a written agreement) or persuaded to replace the animal or repay the owner.

But in a less formal way, owners may also get some satisfaction (if that's really what they want) by having the person who caused the animal's death cover at least the cost of veterinary bills (if any) and burial arrangements. When an animal is killed by a car, for instance, many drivers—even if the accident has not been their fault—will feel enough responsibility to find the owner, explain what has happened, and offer to help. The law is not usually on the owner's side, however. In most states, the driver is not only free of legal responsibility for hitting a dog or a horse but also can find the owner liable for damages or injuries that may have resulted to the car or its occupants. (A driver who hits a cow or a pig or other farm animal, however, is required to reimburse the owner for the loss of the animal.)

Legal status aside, most of us react angrily to hit-and-run situations, where the driver kills or injures an animal and then drives off. It should be pointed out, however, that sometimes the driver may try unsuccessfully to find the owner and then be unwilling or unable to take the trouble to do much more than move the body to the side of the road. If you do hit an animal with a car, and that animal is obviously someone's pet, it is always the humane thing to do to stop the car, first to see if the animal is dead and then to see if it has any identification tags. Even if you do not care to handle the animal yourself (which may be dangerous if the animal is alive and in pain), you can always report the accident at a nearby house or service station. Someone will be grateful for your trouble, even if the news is unpleasant and unwelcome.

Lost or Stolen

In some ways the loss of an animal that has run away or strayed, never to return, is more difficult to accept than known death, if only because so many questions about its fate cannot be answered. Was the loss my fault, and could I have done anything to prevent it? Will the animal die of exposure or be killed? Has it been stolen or picked up, and is it still alive though perhaps uncomfortably so? Has it found a good home with someone who tried but failed to find me? Everyone who loses a pet asks himself these questions and must cope with emotional responses far more complicated than a sense of loss. It is true that in most cases an animal's disappearance can be prevented by the owner. The use of proper enclosures, adequately secured, or other forms of restraint (leashes, runs, tethers, etc.) are part of the responsibility of any pet owner. All too often, dogs and cats are allowed to roam free, and though many pets will stick close to home, most will stray at one time or another—whether for the sake of sexual adventure, or because of encouragement from strange animals or people, or simple curiosity. In spite of all the moving stories we hear about Lassie's coming home and incredible journeys through terrible weather and places, many animals, once they get beyond their home territory into unknown regions, cannot find their way back. If you choose to allow the animal its freedom having faced all the risks involved, at least you can be certain that it wears identification of one sort or another. There is always the chance that collars will be broken or rubbed off in the woods and the tags lost, and several organizations now promote the use of tattooed identification marks on dogs (it has been used on race horses for years), but even this precaution is not foolproof. The tattoos are relatively simple for a veterinarian to apply (usually on the animal's inside hind leg), but the code numbers (often the owner's social security number) are very difficult to trace. The real purpose of them in any case is not to ensure recovery but to make positive identification possible when the animal is found by the owner.

Aside from restricting the animal's territory in some sure, practical way and providing it with identification, an owner can do little to prevent the loss of an animal, although there are some ways to make recovery more likely. A photograph of the animal is a valuable asset in any search, for it can be reproduced and distributed to humane societies, veterinarians, and local stores. Accurate descriptions are also important, and many radio stations will run "lost" ads free of charge. Enquiries in person are also important, for many organizations that handle a large turnover in stray animals may not treat your notice with as much attention as you feel it deserves. This is understandable considering that the place may get well over a dozen such notices a day, and many more animals than that. A humane society may hold on to any unclaimed animal for a period of time to enable owners to make recovery, but in some areas, depending on local laws, this is only a matter of days. After that time, the animal is put up for adoption (to individuals or laboratories) or destroyed. Often the animal may not even get to the humane society—if it has been lucky enough to run into someone who is willing to give it a new home. I know many people who acquired their pets in this way, though I would not recommend the method, at least not until efforts have been made to find the original owner.

A lot has been written (and rumored) in recent years about animal theft and in some areas there may in fact be a certain amount of traffic in stolen animals. Nevertheless, animals that disappear are rarely stolen, no matter how much the owner may believe this to be true. Laboratories do need animals for their experiments, but almost all of them obtain dogs and cats through dealers and other legitimate channels if they do not breed their own. Some ten years ago, it was estimated that about 50 per cent of the animals used in laboratory experiments were originally stolen pets, but legislation passed since that time, putting pressure not only on unsavory animal "collectors" but also on the laboratories themselves, has drastically reduced that percentage. (This pressure was brought about not only because of the theft involved but also because of the extreme cruelty and negligence suffered by the animals.) In addition to the more stringent laws, the tremendous increase in the number of unwanted, abandoned animals available through pounds and shelters has caused the market in stolen pets for laboratory use to dwindle considerably. Valuable animals may be stolen, but this is rare since the value of breeding or show stock is usually as much in the pedigree as in the animal itself, and it's no easy trick to coax a piece of paper into your car. And people who want a pedigreed dog as a pet and don't need the papers can usually get them from humane societies without going to the trouble or risk of stealing one. Spokesmen for the Humane Society of New York City say that if one dog in ten thousand is stolen a year, that's a lot; in suburban and rural areas, however, some thefts do occur, and thieves have been known to use any number of devious schemes for stealing animals. The most common method of rounding up dogs is to bring a female in estrus into a neighborhood and collect all the males that collect around her. One accomplished thief drove a panel truck around to suburban areas and explained to children with animals in their yards or on leashes that he was picking up all local dogs for rabies tests.

There are ways of preventing loss even to professional burglars who employ clever methods of luring animals away from their homes, most of them involving the common sense that you probably apply in protecting your home and family. If you have children, you have undoubtedly told them not to talk to strangers; if you make certain that they do not walk their animals far from home or listen gullibly to people who ask for the animal, so much the better. If you keep the animal confined, it will be less likely to be caught by someone who is not authorized to catch it. Don't discourage any animal from barking when strangers approach (though do guard against aggressive behavior); this, of course, will serve to protect your property as well as your pet.

If you have good reason to believe that your animal has been stolen (and it had better be pretty good if you want to be taken seriously by the authorities), report the incident to the police, or to the newspaper if the theft was not of a nature to require criminal action. Dogs are considered personal property in most states, as are horses and other farm animals, and anyone committing the theft of a dog may be charged with burglary. Cats and many small housepets are not so considered, and of course wild pets—especially if you have no permit to keep them—will simply bring the law back on yourself. If reports to the authorities result in little or nothing, you can pursue your own search—at local laboratories and pet dealers, as well as at the humane societies and pounds—but unless you have a way of making a positive identification the time and effort involved may be wasted. If you find an individual (either through neighborhood inquiry or other sources of information) who has taken your animal in, you may of course demand it back, though often your legal leg may not be strong enough to stand on. Because the line between theft and adoption in these cases is very thin indeed, your best approach is one of persuasion (perhaps by means of a reward) rather than coercion.

Getting Rid of a Pet

FINDING A NEW HOME

Up to this point we have talked only about the loss of an animal when it is beyond the owner's control and not at all the result of his wishes. But many pet-owner relationships have come to an unhappy end because the owner has decided that for one reason or another he can no longer keep the animal. Often this decision is made for good reasons (moving to a location that is unsuitable; inability to provide sufficient care and attention; and so on), but sometimes it is not given enough consideration and the animal is made to suffer as a result. Many people come to me for advice about animals that have become unruly or simply too much trouble to keep, and I can sometimes convince them that there are ways in which their problems can be alleviated or even eliminated without exiling the pet from the household. A dog that has never been housebroken, for example, can be a real nuisance, but there may be a number of reasons for this, not all disciplinary. If you—with professional help—have had no success in training the animal, perhaps the problem is a medical one, such as internal parasites or low estrogen levels. An animal that constantly chews the furniture or pieces of clothing can also be difficult to live with, but this habit may be caused by anything from vitamin deficiency to nervousness and may also be cured with appropriate medical treatment. Or one can simply prevent trouble by keeping the animal and the valuable chewables separated and giving the animal some toys of its own. This may not always be possible in an apartment, but it is worth trying. It is also worth trying to accept the animal's behavior and to learn to love beat-up furniture.

Although one expects to have some animals adapt themselves well to living with humans, on human terms, some can never learn and their behavior will be a constant irritation unless the owner does some adapting. Skunks and squirrels will bite, as we have pointed out earlier, and anyone who tries to keep them in captivity should understand this and not blame the animal for what is entirely natural behavior on its part. One might expect a domestic animal, with centuries of living in captivity bred into it, to conform somewhat to human ways, but some house cats are quite apt to prefer their own ways, in spite of all pleas and special treats. And any animal that has been born and bred in the wild is likely to remain wild in most respects; it is simply unfair to blame it for not respecting human possessions and manners.

There are not quite so many ways of getting rid of pets as there are reasons for getting them, but if the decision has been made, it is up to the owner also to decide how it is to be carried out. Too many people are too quick to decide that putting an animal to death is the only viable solution. I have been asked more often than I like to think to euthanize a perfectly healthy animal in the prime of its life simply because it is "too much trouble to keep." Although some veterinarians will kill the animal rather than risk having it mistreated or deliberately "lost," my own personal experience is that a discouraged pet owner, even one desperate to be free of the responsibility, can usually be talked out of such a drastic measure, especially when I refuse to do the job and give them some useful advice on how to remedy what is obviously a bad relationship. Suggestions about training methods for unruly animals, different kinds of living arrangements, or even declawing operations (for cats) have often led to workable solutions for what had seemed impossible situations. And if the owner is still determined to get rid of the animal, I have sometimes been able to persuade him to find another home—a warm-hearted person (or organization) that will take on his troubles. Nobody can count on such warm hearts being around at the right time, of course, but at least it's an avenue worth exploring. The local humane society is always around at the right time, but this alternative is usually the same as a death sentence; because of the hundreds of thousands of animals taken in each year, less than 10 percent are placed and the rest are destroyed.

If you decide that you, too, must dispose of your pet, analyze your reasons very carefully and consider every possible alternative before taking a step that will be fatal for the animal. If the problem can be solved without killing the animal—even at the expense of effort and money—you will undoubtedly find yourself feeling a whole lot better about the situation.

SELLING

Because the opportunities for reselling an animal that has proven unsuitable as a pet are so limited, and the market is so glutted, the subject of selling pets needs only a few sentences. Sometimes, if the animal you have is valuable enough to sell or young enough to adapt readily to a new owner, you can find someone willing to lay out money to take the animal off your hands. Raising animals for sale is a commercial venture and has no real place in this book, since the kinds of animals, the reasons for their value in the market place, and the ways of selling them are so varied and complicated. But if you have a well-bred, well-trained domestic animal and a buyer, you can sometimes manage to make a deal. Some people believe that if they charge something, even a nominal sum, the new owner will treat the animal with more respect, but my personal feeling about this attitude is that if you even suspect the new owner of not showing sufficient respect to the animal, you shouldn't consider his a good home, no matter how much he is willing to pay. Also, if you have accepted money for an animal, you must always be willing to pay it back if the new owner finds the animal unsuitable, unhealthy, or otherwise unacceptable within a certain period of time.

For some expensive, exotic animals, pet dealers may sometimes be persuaded to offer a trade or a credit for the animal they originally sold you, but this is obviously a subject for negotiation and depends on your good relationship with the dealer. In any event, the resale value is usually far less than the price you paid to begin with, and most shops or dealers will be interested in buying, swapping, or giving credit only if they know the animal can be placed easily for a larger sum than they have to pay for it. A good deal is uncommon except where there is a market for mature animals of certain species (snakes or parrots, say). In any case, be sure to check local and state laws governing the resale of exotic animals, because the restrictions are sometimes quite stringent or even prohibitive.

GIVING AWAY

This is undoubtedly the most common way of getting rid of an animal that can no longer be kept, though it is no longer the easiest. As I have said elsewhere, many more puppies and kittens are in need of good homes than there are good homes; and adult animals are even more difficult to place. Sometimes the humane society is the only place that will take an animal, and they may even charge you a small sum for accepting it. Word-of-mouth or paid advertising and notices left in shops or in veterinary clinics may have good results, although I believe that it is the owner's responsibility to follow up on the animal and its welfare, if possible, and see that the new home is a good one. Rescue shelters that have been set up in some areas to take in unwanted animals may promise that even if the animals are not adopted they will not be destroyed; some of these shelters are good, some not so good. Check them out for yourself. Occasionally a pet shop will take in a "give-away" animal if they feel it is easy to place, though they will probably charge you, the giver, for the service and insist that your animal has had proper medical attention and requisite inoculations before they take it.

No matter who decides to take the animal, however, you must always be prepared for questions as to why you are disposing of it, and you should always be honest in giving the answers—for the sake of the animal as well as to avoid trouble with the new owner. It is important to pass along the animal's medical history, and it is also helpful to give the name of the animal's veterinarian, especially if you are giving away an animal other than a dog or cat for which a new doctor may not be easy to find.

If you have a wild animal—exotic or native—do not assume that a zoo will be a ready recipient for your gift. Most big-city zoos are forced to decline gifts of pet animals, although if you are in the possession of a rare species, a breeding specimen, or a healthy exhibit animal that the zoo has only in small numbers, it may be worth asking the zoo administration whether it might be interested. In any event, admission requirements are fairly stiff, and pet animals are usually not sufficiently well qualified to pass them. Even an unneutered, fully equipped, perfect specimen may prove unadaptable to a zoo environment—as is true of many pets reared in the luxury of a private home—and most zoos now obtain their stock from breeders, dealers, or other zoos rather than private individuals.

Nevertheless, smaller zoos or nature centers are occasionally willing to accept a gift of an unusual animal and these are worth exploring as are schools with animal-care courses and conservation groups where the animals may be made part of education programs. Many of these organizations have little or no budget for acquisitions (because they put their money into maintenance) and must rely on donors or students or generous science teachers for their animals. If you care anything about your animal, however, do check over the premises before you make a gift; although most educational centers do not inflict cruelty deliberately, the management may not have sufficient information about the animal's requirements and conditions may be inadequate, if not downright bad. If the animal is likely to become the subject of experimentation or unsupervised handling, you should find yourself another beneficiary.

RELEASING

A friend of mine who lives in a New York City apartment has a small basil plant on her kitchen window sill which regularly produces aromatic leaves that are important additions to her excellent salads. Once in a while the plant also seems to produce a tiny green bug, a creature obviously bent on making basil leaves a regular part of its own diet. Because the plant is not large, my friend does not feel that she can afford to share it with the bug, and so she ends up having to throw the bug out with the trash. Being warm-hearted, however, she can't bear the thought of coldly evicting it into regions unknown, and she always picks off one basil leaf to throw out with the bug, hoping that it will have at least a small chance to survive in the wilds of the city's sanitation system.

Most people, I suppose, would not consider such a pest worthy of thoughtful release, but the story does have a message, since most people who consider release into nature as a logical way of getting rid of wild-animal pets do not take enough care to see that the job is done properly. Many wild animals raised in captivity do not make good candidates for a life in the wild, and even the adaptable species need some preparation. Therefore release, although it might seem like a good way to restore the balance of nature as well as an easy way of disposing of a pet that has proven difficult to keep, is not in fact as simple as it sounds. I have covered the subject in some detail in the sections of earlier chapters devoted to individual species, but a general warning and some guidelines seem to be in order here.

Release is only possible if the creature is equipped to defend itself and to care for itself without human support. Certain species are not difficult to release; raccoons and squirrels can, after a short transitional period, become readapted to their native habitats, although there is always the risk that their tameness may prove to be a danger to themselves or a nuisance to other people. Some animals are even easy to release; snakes, opossums, turtles, and others will take to a life on their own with little or no transitional period required. It is usually best to remove any about-to-be-released animal to a relatively rural area so that its chances of surviving will be improved; some state and local parks will allow release, but permission should be obtained ahead of time from the supervisory warden, since the park may already have too many of a particular species (or none), and the balance may be upset by your erstwhile companion.

Any animal that is not native to an area should not be released at all, unless one goes to the trouble of returning it to its original environment. Some animals may not be able to survive in a climate or geographical terrain that is hostile in one way or another; other animals may be able to adapt too well and interfere with the natural ecology. It is, moreover, illegal to release certain exotic species into areas where they are not native; monk parakeets, for instance, are hunted in New York State because in adapting to the area they learned to feed on certain crops that farmers were saving for other species, namely their own. The regulations governing the release of non-native animals are complex and inconsistent, but they are for the most part justified and should be taken seriously. Although we would never have been able to enjoy the English sparrow or even the horse if they had not originally been imported into the United States, we would also not have had the problems caused by the overpopulation of German carp (at the expense of many now rare native fish) or the much-publicized Asian walking catfish in Florida, or the millions of starlings that the Army declared war on early in 1975.*

Even if an animal is native, it should not be released if it has in any way lost its means of self-defense through physical or psychological alteration by its human captors. Declawing, descenting, and neutering all make an animal unfit for life in the wild, and some hand-reared creatures never learn to feed themselves properly in order to survive on their own. One couple I know had to teach their pet raccoons how to pick berries and how to find nice, juicy grubs under logs and rocks. Raccoons learn quickly, which is lucky for them, but even certain birds of prey are not so lucky and, without the natural training they receive from their parents and peers, must be taught by humans how to catch living prey. If you are considering the release of any wild native animal, therefore, make sure the animal knows how to do more than amble up to a supper dish and back to its pillow; otherwise it would be a cruel and probably fatal act to thrust it back into a world in which it has become ill equipped to survive. In addition to learning about local laws, therefore, be sure you know the animal's capabilities before you decide to release it.

It should not be necessary to point out that any domestic animal is, by virtue of its breeding, incapable of living on its own in a nonhuman environment. Although many animals do become feral and are able to survive on their own (mustangs, for example, were originally domesticated Spanish horses), most of them do not, and the ones that are successful are often the cause of many problems. Thousands of feral dogs and cats now live on the periphery of human civiliza-

---

*The starling, incidentally, was originally brought from Europe in the 1890s by a New York businessman who wanted to establish here all of the species of birds mentioned in Shakespeare; the starling, mentioned once in *Henry IV, Part I,* immediately took hold and now well over 300 million of them are damaging crops, causing disease, and otherwise making pests of themselves.

tion, and they are usually destructive and even dangerous, to say nothing of being unhealthy and generally miserable. Anyone who "releases" a domestic animal is, of course, simply abandoning it, and there is no getting around the fact that this is one of the cruelest acts that humans can inflict on animals. In many states, it is now illegal and the abandoner is liable for prosecution.

Euthanasia

This is a subject nearly as replete with controversy and confusion as that of abortion. Any owner may put any animal that belongs to him to death (or cause it to be killed), as long as the method of killing is humane, without running the risk of breaking the law; and unfortunately euthanasia is too often selected as the easiest way of disposing of an animal one no longer wants. For most animal lovers, of course, the decision is never easy to make, but sometimes it is necessary, most often for reasons of health. If an animal is terminally ill, aged and suffering from a number of irreversible ailments that cause it pain, or has suffered injuries from which no successful recovery can be expected within a reasonably short period of time, euthanasia is unquestionably the best and most humane solution, when performed humanely, of course, by an expert. Because "terminal," "successful recovery," and "reasonably short period of time" are all difficult for someone with little or no experience to define, I would always recommend that a veterinarian be consulted. He is usually the best judge of an animal's condition, and one should follow his advice, allowing him to do the job of destroying the animal if it is necessary; he will use the quickest and least painful methods of putting the animal to death, usually by using intravenous drugs that produce anesthesia, then death. Humane societies, whose main responsibility these days seems to be the destruction of unclaimed animals, will also perform euthanasia on privately owned pets, either with drugs, decompression chambers, or gas, such as carbon monoxide.

Most people, even the fiercest defenders of animal rights, would not argue with the medical reasons given above. But there are some other reasons that owners give for having their animals destroyed, and this is where the controversy enters the picture. I myself, like some other veterinarians, will not undertake to euthanize (or recommend euthanasia for) any animal for any reason other than a medical one, unless (and this is a big "unless," I admit) that animal has proven itself to be dangerous and cannot otherwise be disposed of. If the animal is considered dangerous by others (whether it actually is or not), its fate is often decided by authorities rather than by the owner himself. For instance, it is illegal in New York City according to the

Health Code to harbor any wild animal that is considered dangerous by law. Many local laws in other states also prohibit the keeping of animals that are capable of injuring domestic animals and farm crops as well as human beings, except in zoos, laboratories, or by people with special permits. Sometimes, even where laws do not exist or are not regularly enforced, public pressure will cause authorities to step in; escaped skunks or boa constrictors will send police departments and entire neighborhoods into immediate and noisy action, often creating headlines and causing more trouble than the animals ever could.

When an owner himself decides that an animal is vicious the question becomes somewhat more complicated. (The word "vicious," by the way, is often misused, for few animals are full of vice; what is usually meant is "aggressive" or simply "fierce.") It is, of course, perfectly natural for most animals to react aggressively when frightened or threatened, and an animal fully equipped with claws and teeth can cause serious injury, even without intending to do so. The owner of a perfectly tame lynx once told me that his pet, even in play, would sometimes get carried away and that what was at first enjoyable roughhousing would suddenly become the real thing. But as any owner of a wild animal should know, this is to be expected in an adult no matter how responsive or affectionate the animal may have been as a youngster or how tame it is with its owner even after sexual maturity.

The question of a "vicious temperament" in a domestic animal is far more difficult to handle. For some animals, euthanasia is the only logical solution, both to remove a source of potential danger and to prevent the continuation of the strain in the animal's offspring, should it be given the opportunity to breed. But the decision to put an animal to death, like that facing a judge who is about to sentence a criminal, should not be made without a careful analysis of the situation. If aggressive and dangerous behavior is suddenly and inexplicably displayed by an animal with no previous history of it, some explanation may be found that has nothing to do with temperament at all. Children are occasionally bitten by dogs because they have teased an otherwise good-natured animal to the point of complete frustration, pain, or panic. In such a case, death to the animal is further unnecessary cruelty, and the real offender goes undisciplined. By all means remove the pet if the child's behavior cannot be altered, but don't assume you are getting rid of it because the animal is "vicious." Very few animals are so good natured that they will allow themselves to be tortured. A headline story appeared some time ago concerning a Saint Bernard which suddenly and without apparent provocation attacked and killed a small boy; the dog was killed immediately before the reason for the attack was determined, and it was not until a post-mortem was performed that a ball-point pen was found lodged deep in the animal's ear. Although it is not always easy to make a small child understand about gentle handling (especially when what is gentle to him can be terrifying to a creature half his size), this aspect of pet owning is as important as proper feeding and housing. A hamster that is cuddly and well mannered when held in the hand may bite readily if that same hand is thrust suddenly into its cage; the nip may be painful, but it is an excellent way for a child to begin to learn about animal territories and even the importance of privacy.

Although the reason for aggression in an animal that has caused harm to a human being is not always easy to determine, it is usually unwise to risk a wait-and-see approach. But a certain amount of common sense should be applied to the situation. A guard dog that has been trained to display ferocious behavior may be perfectly trustworthy when properly controlled by its master, but such a dog should not under any circumstances be considered a pet animal. As a veterinarian, I have been bitten by many animals—even by cats and dogs that are normally the most gentle and well mannered of creatures. Often they bite because they are suffering pain which is compounded by the fear of being handled by a stranger, especially when that handling is forceful or unpleasant. Even owners themselves administering to animals that are ill or have been injured may encounter a surprising hostility and be forced to muzzle or otherwise restrain their normally loving pet.

Sometimes the presence of fear alone or the memory of a painful experience will elicit erratic behavior; many a stout-hearted dog has been known to shake in the reception room of a veterinary clinic, though I find that this is often because the owner is nervous and has transmitted his own fear to the animal. I know a city-dwelling cat that turns into a fierce scratcher and biter whenever it is picked up and carried near the door of the apartment, and many a dog has been known to turn on a beloved owner when it is interrupted at dinner or during a chewing session of an equally beloved bone, interpreting the interference as a threat. One female cat which belongs to some friends of mine behaves ferociously with anyone who tries to play with her using his hands, although she is a perfect lady when you put your face right in front of hers as long as your hands are behind your back. The owners believe this is because they used to play with her rather roughly when she was a kitten and may have inadvertently caused her an injury with their hands. But they do not consider this vicious behavior on her part, and give due warning to all guests who might be tempted to pat her. Because they know what to expect and are willing to grant the animal a reason for acting unpleasantly, the cat is a congenial companion and gives them no particular problems. In any similar situation, of course, the presence of strangers may easily complicate matters, and anyone owning an animal with peculiar habits like this should anticipate trouble and avoid it before it has a chance to occur.

Obviously, any domestic animal that bites or scratches or kicks or whatever indiscriminately and at the drop of any old hat is not to be considered a safe or trustworthy pet. If precautions cannot be taken (by training, muzzling, caging, or tying on a lead—some of which may aggravate the animal to further frustration and rage) and the animal is truly dangerous, one should not keep the animal, and euthanasia is often the only answer. In my experience as a veterinarian, however, this extreme action has rarely been necessary, and when it has been unavoidable, I have always felt that some measures could have been taken to prevent it, most of them having to do with the selection of the pet in the first place and with proper care and handling. Which is, of course, what this whole book has been about. As I have tried to point out in these pages, the experience of owning a pet should be and usually is one of the most enjoyable we can have, and, like anything worth doing, it takes thoughtfulness and a certain amount of dedication, as well as knowledge and effort. The wonderful thing about having an animal share your life is that the experience is different with each relationship. Although I have lived through, heard, and read about hundreds of unusual animal stories, each time I meet a new owner or see a new book on the subject, I can only conclude that the number of animal stories is as unlimited as the number of individual pets and their owners.

The best of these stories, of course, focus on situations where both animal and human have given the best of themselves to each other. Although there is as much cruelty in the world today as there ever was—most of it practiced by human beings on all species including their own—it is still possible for us to learn to avoid this kind of behavior in ourselves (or prevent its development in our children) by learning to respect the right of every other being to a full life. It is my belief that one of the fundamental ways in which we can learn to achieve this respect for life is by understanding what is involved in living with other animals—not by "possessing" an animal and forcing it to conform to our own ways, but by allowing it to reach its full potential within our care. Pet keeping is only one aspect of this learning to live with animals, since it can involve only a very few species, but it is one of the richest and most rewarding of experiences and one that can give us a unique opportunity to understand, accept, and protect the rights of other living creatures.

AFTERWORD

A little information can be a dangerous thing, as we all know, and though I would be pleased to learn that a reader had actually read and absorbed every word of this book, I would be irresponsible indeed if I did not point out again that it represents only a fraction of the information that exists about the animals I have discussed. The charts and bibliography that follow will supplement the book's text by giving further specific data or sources for additional reading, and I would advise every animal owner to take advantage of those that relate to his pet. There is, however, plenty of information around that cannot easily be fit into any single book or series of books. The knowledge and experience of experts—veterinarians, zoologists, animal breeders, or anyone who has proved successful in the fine art of animal keeping—can be invaluable sources of help for all amateurs. When you find yourself needing advice or assistance, do not draw your own conclusions or make your own diagnoses without trying to obtain aid from someone qualified to give it. If, in spite of all your best efforts, you simply cannot manage for one reason or another to keep your animal well, don't blame yourself unrealistically but get the animal another home and leave its care to someone else.

Many animal lovers I know have no pets of their own because they cannot or will not change their lives sufficiently to suit the needs of the animals they love. Rather than do a bad job, they prefer to enjoy animals from afar and restrict their own activities to raising houseplants or tending gardens. Their impulse to care for a bit of nature is satisfied, and everyone involved is undeniably better off. As I have tried to point out, some animals are very easy to keep and may require only a little more attention than a flowering begonia to remain healthy, but no animal can tolerate being ignored for very long and no pet owner worth his salt would tolerate keeping an animal whose demands were more troublesome than rewarding. Selecting and obtaining an animal—or a plant—involves taking on the responsibility for another living individual—a responsibility that must continue for the rest of that individual's life. Understanding and undertaking that responsibility, however, is not enough unless it also involves a certain amount of research into the best ways of making that life as long and as healthy as possible. The acquiring of that information need not be a chore; in fact, it can be exciting and rewarding for its own sake, especially when you are able to relate your own experiences to those of other people. It is in that spirit that this book has been written.

REFERENCE CHARTS

The following charts are arranged alphabetically by the common name of each animal discussed at any length in this book (with the exception of insects and fish), whether it is to be considered an easy, difficult, or impossible pet. After the common name appears the taxonomic name of the species discussed, including genus and species (e.g., *Rattus norvegicus; rattus* = genus; *norvegicus* = species), or simply the genus name if the chart applies to more than one species (e.g., *sciuris spp.* refers to various species of squirrels). Each animal's domestic status is noted where it applies; if the animal has not been domesticated, its native habitat is given. The animal's natural lifespan, which may vary considerably from one individual or breed to another, is listed; for wild animals, this range generally refers to lifespan in captivity.

Because the information relating to living arrangements must be brief and because the appropriate cage size or environment varies even within the same species, the reader is encouraged to consult more detailed sources, such as those listed as references. Remember that the space requirements given are to be considered minimal rather than ideal, and that the dimensions are given for animals kept singly, unless otherwise noted.

The suggested adult diets are geared to life in captivity, so that wild-animal diets are only suggested substitutes for natural foods eaten in the wild. In raising a young animal for release, every effort should be made to offer natural food items to make the animal's adjustment to the wild habitat an easier one. Commercial diets may be obtained through pet shops, veterinarians, feed stores, supermarkets, or directly from the manufacturer; special multivitamins, mineral supplements, and formulas may also be obtained at pharmacies. Fresh food should be just that, unblemished, washed, and unseasoned. Do not allow fresh food to sit uneaten for very long; remove anything that becomes stale or wilted or soiled, and be sure to dispose of debris, such as fruit rinds and shells, on a regular basis. Table scraps, when they are allowed, should be of good quality (no gristle or bone bits) and not spicy or greasy. Avoid bones that may splinter or get caught in an animal's digestive tract (chicken, pork, lamb, and fish, particularly).

Water is necessary for all species and is therefore not specified in each chart. It should be made available at all times (except for equines immediately following heavy work) and changed daily or more often if necessary. Use only containers that may not be tipped or destroyed by the animal.

In addition to the type of food recommended as a basic diet or as supplementary food, the amount to be consumed daily by each animal is given, as well as the timing of feeding periods. Keep in mind that old, young, pregnant, lactating, hard-working, and diseased animals will have special requirements; veterinary advice is recommended for diets fitting individual needs. "Free choice" means that an animal may have food present at all times or in whatever quantity the animal desires.

Chapter 9 contains general guidelines to the feeding of unweaned animals, but because these are not repeated in each chart in the section on infant diet, they deserve some space here as well. All young animals should be kept warm (80° to 95°F., depending on the animal, and tapering off to normal adult tolerance levels gradually as the animal develops), and formulas must be warmed to body temperature before feeding. Formulas may be fed to very young animals with droppers or nipple bottles, but care should be taken that glass is not used where it might be broken by the animal's teeth. Avoid overfeeding; when the stomach or crop feels firm to the touch, stop feeding. The digestive tracts of many young animals require manual stimulation after each feeding (rubbing the body from the stomach toward the rectum) if the animal is to defecate and urinate properly. This practice may be discontinued as soon as the animal is self-feeding or moving around vigorously.

Any change in diet—in content or frequency of feeding—should be brought about gradually for adults as well as for young animals; a close watch should be kept on the consistency and regularity of the stool. If it is loose or watery, the formula should be reduced; diarrhea for extended periods will require a veterinarian's attention. Failure to eliminate and refusal to eat should also be considered serious signs, as they may be caused by any number of conditions.

Following the sections on diet is information about breeding where it is currently available: the age at which the animal becomes sexually mature (puberty); the period during which the animal may be fertile (breeding season or frequency of estrus); the length of time the animal carries its young (gestation) or incubates its eggs; and the number of young born at one time. Normal body temperature is also listed where known, as well as recommended vaccines or other normal medical needs that require periodic attention. Charts for most animals designated as "easy" pets also include a listing of common ailments and symptoms; veterinarians may not always be willing to treat these animals, and so I have included some recommendations for treatment. Special notes about each animal's behavior, its suitability as a pet, or its unsuitability, are given, but these are only brief summaries of the descriptions appearing earlier in the book. Readers are also advised to consult the references listed in the charts or in the bibliography at the back of the book.

ALLIGATOR, North American

Alligator mississippiensis
Southeastern United States
LIFESPAN: 50 years or more
ADULT WEIGHT RANGE: c. 125 pounds at 6 years
LIVING ARRANGEMENTS: sturdy tank at least twice as long as animal, as high and wide as animal's length; sand or gravel floor; enough water for animal to submerge itself; hollow log or box for privacy; temperature range 80° to 95°F.; 30 to 60 per cent humidity
ADULT DIET: whole fish, raw beef, beef liver, frogs, with supplements of bonemeal; feed once or twice a week; free choice
INFANT DIET: small whole fish, insects, mealworms, cut-up raw fish or beef, with supplements of bonemeal; feed at least three times a week; free choice
PUBERTY: 8 to 10 years
CLUTCH SIZE: 10 to 120 eggs
INCUBATION: 9 to 10 weeks

Comments

Although about 9 inches long at hatching, the alligator grows about a foot a year and soon becomes difficult for the average pet owner to keep; will become aggressive without constant handling. Endangered species. IMPOSSIBLE

References

Neill, Wilfred T.: *The Last of the Ruling Reptiles: Alligators, Crocodiles, and Their Kin.* New York: Columbia University Press, 1971

Vogel, Zdenek: *Reptiles and Amphibians* (see Bibliography, "Books on Animal Care")

ANOLE (or American Chameleon)

Anolis carolinensis
Southeastern United States
LIFESPAN: 3 years
ADULT SIZE: 6 to 8 inches

LIVING ARRANGEMENTS: wooden or glass cage at least 1 foot square with lid; sleeping box; newspaper or wood flooring; twigs or branches for climbing; water container; temperature range: 75° to 82°F. by day; 64° to 68°F. by night; high humidity

ADULT DIET: live mealworms, flies, moths, cockroaches, spiders, and small crickets; feed every other day free choice; offer lettuce and other greens sprinkled with water daily

PUBERTY: 2 to 3 months

CLUTCH SIZE: 1 egg

INCUBATION: 8 weeks

COMMON AILMENTS: 1. Symptoms—deformity of limbs, softness of bones. Cause—calcium deficiency. Treatment—place on adequate diet; administer Neocalglucon orally 2 drops per 100 gr. of body weight for 20 to 30 days

2. Symptom—mucous discharge from nostrils. Cause—bacterial pneumonia. Treatment—administer Gentamycin (injection) 1 mg. per 100 gr. of body weight every 3 days for 15 days

3. Symptoms—weight loss and voracious appetite. Cause—intestinal parasites. Treatment—administer Thiabendazole orally 5 mg. weekly for 3 weeks

Comments

This lizard (not a true chameleon) is a common pet and relatively easy to keep, though it may not breed in captivity; males are territorial but fights are not usually harmful. EASY

References

Vogel, Zdenek: *Reptiles and Amphibians* (see Bibliography, "Books on Animal Care")

ARMADILLO, Nine-Banded

Dasypus novemcinctus

South and Central America, southern United States

LIFESPAN: 4 to 7 years

ADULT WEIGHT RANGE: 12 to 15 pounds

LIVING ARRANGEMENTS: strong wire cage (minimum 6-foot × 6-foot floor space, 3 feet high) with sleeping box and 6 inches depth of rag, straw, or cedar-chip flooring; temperature range: 72° to 85°F.

ADULT DIET: canned dog food or raw meat mixed with evaporated milk and baby cereal; supplements of egg yolk, bonemeal, codliver oil, and multivitamins; feed 10 per cent of body weight once a day in evening

INFANT DIET: Esbilac formula every 3 hours; at 6 weeks add ground meat, raw egg, vitamin supplement, codliver oil; weaned at 2 months

PUBERTY: 6 months

BREEDING SEASON: late summer

GESTATION: about 4 months (delayed implantation)

LITTER SIZE: 4 (identical)
BODY TEMPERATURE: 84° to 92°F.

Comments

Not very responsive and unlikely to breed in captivity. DIFFICULT

References

Crandall, Lee S.: *Management of Wild Mammals in Captivity* (see Bibliography, "Books on Animal Care")

Mathews, Dick: *Wild Animals as Pets* (see Bibliography, "Books on Animal Care")

BADGER

Taxidea taxus

North America

LIFESPAN: 10 to 20 years

ADULT WEIGHT RANGE: 15 to 20 pounds

LIVING ARRANGEMENTS: sturdy wire cage with strong latch (6-foot × 6-foot floor space and 3 feet high); concrete flooring with sand bedding; sleeping box; temperature range varied

ADULT DIET: whole rats, chicken necks, raw beef, canned dog food, dog kibble, with supplements of bonemeal and codliver oil; feed once a day; free choice

INFANT DIET: Esbilac formula five or six times a day until eyes open; gradually incorporate a good canned dog food during second or third week; introduce live mice or rats after third week; ready for release at 4 weeks

PUBERTY: 1 to 2 years

BREEDING SEASON: August to September

GESTATION: about 60 days (delayed implantation)

LITTER SIZE: 1 to 4, average 2

VACCINES RECOMMENDED: feline distemper and canine distemper (killed vaccines only)

Comments

Will grow aggressive with age; unsatisfactory housepet after maturity (odor, nocturnal behavior, temperament). IMPOSSIBLE

References

Burkett, Molly: *The Year of the Badger*. Philadelphia: Lippincott, 1974

Crandall, Lee S.: *Management of Wild Mammals in Captivity* (see Bibliography, "Books on Animal Care")

BEAR, American Black

Euarctos americanus

North American forests

LIFESPAN: 20 to 30 years

ADULT WEIGHT RANGE: 200 to 600 pounds

LIVING ARRANGEMENTS: steel cage (25-foot × 70-foot floor space with 9-foot walls or 14-foot moats); sleeping den; temperature range varied

ADULT DIET: whole fish, raw meat, frogs, lizards, rodents, bread, with supplements of vegetables (celery, carrots, etc.) and fruit; about 5 per cent of body weight once a day (3 pounds fish, 4 pounds meat, 3 loaves bread plus vegetables)

INFANT DIET: warm cow's milk every 3 hours, gradually increasing size of feeding as more is taken at each feeding; introduce solid food at 2 to 3 months, such as chopped meat, canned dog food, with bonemeal and codliver oil; free choice three times a day

PUBERTY: 4 to 5 years

BREEDING SEASON: June to July

GESTATION: 7 months (delayed implantation)

LITTER SIZE: 1 to 4

Comments

Aggressive, dangerous, and destructive; requires large quantities of food; highly susceptible to mange and parasites; permit (if obtainable) required, even for cubs. IMPOSSIBLE

Reference

Crandall, Lee S.: *Management of Wild Mammals in Captivity* (see Bibliography, "Books on Animal Care")

BEAVER, American

Castor canadensis

North American forests

LIFESPAN: 15 to 20 years

ADULT WEIGHT RANGE: 35 to 80 pounds, average 40 pounds

LIVING ARRANGEMENTS: wire cage (6-foot × 6-foot floor space with 3-foot walls) with water tank, allowing total submersion; temperature range varied

ADULT DIET: maple and willow branches, bread, grain (corn), potatoes, apples, celery, carrots, greens; feed once a day 10 per cent of body weight

INFANT DIET: Esbilac formula every 3 to 4 hours for 2 weeks; decrease number of feedings to five daily and introduce solid food during third week; usually weaned at 4 months

PUBERTY: 2 to 2½ years

BREEDING SEASON: January to February

GESTATION: 105 to 120 days

LITTER SIZE: 2 to 7, average 4

Comments

Beavers are best as free-roaming pets, if they are to be pets at all; can be tamed with food and petting but do not do well when confined. IMPOSSIBLE

REFERENCE CHARTS

References

    Crandall, Lee S.: *Management of Wild Mammals in Captivity* (see Bibliography, "Books on Animal Care")

    Rue, Leonard Lee: *The World of the Beaver*. Philadelphia: Lippincott, 1964

BOA CONSTRICTOR

Boa constrictor

Central and South America

LIFESPAN: up to 20 years

ADULT SIZE: up to 18 feet (13 to 17 inches at birth; 27 to 30 inches at 5 months; 38 to 46 inches at 1 year)

LIVING ARRANGEMENTS: terrarium or vivarium setup with glass sides and lid, measuring at least one and one-half times length of snake in one direction and half its length in other; newspaper or wooden flooring; water container allowing for total submersion; brick for scraping sloughed skin, and branches for climbing and shelter; temperature range about 78° to 86°F. by day and 74°F. by night; moderate humidity

DIET: live, fresh-killed, or frozen (and thawed) whole rodents and small birds; feed adults once a week, young snakes, free choice

PUBERTY: 3 to 4 years

CLUTCH SIZE: 10 to 60

INCUBATION: young born alive

COMMON AILMENTS: see Garter Snake

Comments

    These imported snakes are becoming increasingly expensive; large adults may be difficult to keep but small snakes are relatively undemanding, though they must be kept impeccably clean and have proper diet. EASY

References

    Smith, Hobart M.: *Snakes as Pets* (see Bibliography, "Books on Animal Care")

    Vogel, Zdenek: *Reptiles and Amphibians* (see Bibliography, "Books on Animal Care")

BOBCAT

Lynx rufus

North America, extinct in eastern states

LIFESPAN: 15 to 25 years

ADULT WEIGHT RANGE: 15 to 25 pounds

LIVING ARRANGEMENTS: see Ocelot; however temperature range can be varied

ADULT DIET: raw meat, canned dog food, dry dog food, or combination (one part dry dog food to one part raw meat, with multivitamin and calcium lactate, ¾ teaspoon of each for each cup of dry food) with supplements of milk, eggs, cooked vegetables, multivitamins, calcium lactate; 5 per cent of body weight, feed once daily

INFANT DIET: KMR or Esbilac formula with small amount strained baby-food meat five times daily (once during night) until eyes open; increase strained meat and vegetables in third week and reduce formula slightly; at 4 weeks add dry dog food (small pellets); at 5 weeks introduce food from adult diet. If preparing for release, offer live rodents or rabbits

PUBERTY: 1 year

BREEDING SEASON: late winter, early spring

GESTATION: 50 days

LITTER SIZE: 1 to 4, average 2

VACCINES RECOMMENDED: feline distemper (killed vaccine only)

Comments

Although tractable when very young, bobcats become extremely aggressive as they reach maturity. IMPOSSIBLE

References

Crandall, Lee S.: *Management of Wild Mammals in Captivity* (see Bibliography, "Books on Animal Care")

Mathews, Dick: *Wild Animals as Pets* (see Bibliography, "Books on Animal Care")

Van Wormer, Joe: *The World of the Bobcat*. Philadelphia: Lippincott, 1964

BUDGERIGAR

Melopsittacus undulatus

Domestic (originally Australian)

LIFESPAN: 6 to 15 years

ADULT SIZE: 7½ inches

LIVING ARRANGEMENTS: wire cage 24 inches long, 12 inches wide, 18 inches high (sufficient for two birds); two or more wooden perches; nesting box; temperature range 60° to 75°F. (no sudden changes or drafts)

ADULT DIET: canary seed, millet, rape, sesame seed, oats in combination, with supplements of greens, vegetables, "condition food" containing vitamins, minerals, and protein; cuttlebone and grit; free choice (about 6 grams daily for each bird)

INFANT DIET: commercial canary-rearing diets; mashes of egg yolk, wheat germ, yeast, pediatric vitamins, milk protein, parsley flakes, alfalfa meal; free choice until fully feathered and self-feeding (4 to 5 weeks)

PUBERTY: 2 to 3 months

CLUTCH SIZE: 4 to 8 eggs

INCUBATION: 18–21 days

Comments

Well adapted to cage life; breeds readily in captivity. EASY

References
> Bates, Henry, and Busenbark, Robert: *Parrots and Related Birds* (see Bibliography, "Books on Animal Care")
> Hart, E. H.: *Budgerigar Handbook.* Jersey City: TFH Publications, n.d.
> Petrak, Margaret L., ed.: *Diseases of Cage and Aviary Birds* (see Bibliography, "Books on Animal Care")
> Rogers, Cyril H.: *Parakeet Guide.* Garden City, N.Y.: Doubleday, 1971

CACOMISTLE (Ringtail or Civet Cat)

> *Bassariscus astutus*
> North America, southern and western states
> LIFESPAN: 10 to 15 years
> ADULT WEIGHT RANGE: 3 to 6 pounds
> LIVING ARRANGEMENTS: wood-and-wire cage at least 5 feet square and 4 feet high with lid; sleeping box; branches for climbing; temperature range varied
> ADULT DIET: ground horsemeat, beef, chicken necks, mice, nuts, vegetables (not carrots or celery), fruits, with vitamin and mineral supplements, bonemeal, codliver oil; 6 to 10 per cent of body weight once daily
> INFANT DIET: see Raccoon
> PUBERTY: 2 years
> BREEDING SEASON: fall
> GESTATION: 73 to 74 days
> LITTER SIZE: 1 to 4, average 3
> VACCINES RECOMMENDED: see Raccoon

Comments
> Nocturnal, can be affectionate if hand reared, but very shy; males caged together may fight. DIFFICULT

References
> Crandall, Lee S.: *Management of Wild Mammals in Captivity* (see Bibliography, "Books on Animal Care")
> Mathews, Dick: *Wild Animals as Pets* (see Bibliography, "Books on Animal Care")

CANARY

> *Serinus canarius*
> Domestic (originally Canary Islands)
> LIFESPAN: 7 to 10 years or more
> ADULT SIZE: 5 to 5½ inches
> LIVING ARRANGEMENTS: see Budgerigar
> ADULT DIET: canary seed, rape, millet with supplements of greens, egg

biscuits, vegetables, condition food (see Budgerigar), free choice, about 3 to 4 grams daily; cuttlebone and grit; breeding birds may take breadcrumbs soaked in water, hard-boiled egg, wheat germ, bran, peanut and codliver oils; boiled milk for diarrhea; toast in raw milk, lettuce for constipation; molting—egg yolk (cooked), 2 tablespoons breadcrumbs, ½ teaspoon paprika, 3 drops olive oil

INFANT DIET: commercial canary-rearing diets with supplements of mashed egg; feed every half hour (except at night) until self-feeding (4 to 5 weeks)

PUBERTY: 1 year

CLUTCH SIZE: 1 to 6 eggs, average 3

INCUBATION: 12–14 days

NORMAL BODY TEMPERATURE: 106.2° to 106.4°F.

Comments

Well adapted to cage life; breeds readily in captivity; only the males are singers. EASY

References

Petrak, Margaret L., ed.: *Diseases of Cage and Aviary Birds* (see Bibliography, "Books on Animal Care")

Canaries, Their Care and Breeding. Alhambra, Calif.: Borden, n.d.

CAT

Felis catus
Domestic

LIFESPAN: 14 to 20 years

ADULT WEIGHT RANGE: 8 to 20 pounds

LIVING ARRANGEMENTS: cats may be allowed freedom of house (freedom outdoors at owner's risk; releasable collar recommended); sleeping box or area; constant access to water; temperature range varied; if cage used, minimum dimensions: 30 inches high, 16 inches wide, 18 inches high

ADULT DIET: combination of meat or fish and vegetables, minerals and vitamins to provide balanced diet of approximately 70 per cent water, 14 per cent protein, 10 per cent fat, 5 per cent carbon, 1 per cent ash, 0.6 per cent calcium (some commercial diets, canned, soft moist, or dry may be satisfactory if palatable; fresh food two to three times weekly recommended); ½ ounce canned food per pound of body weight, or 4 per cent of body weight in dry food; feed once or twice daily

INFANT DIET: KMR or Esbilac formula up to 10 to 15 per cent of body weight in four to six daily feedings; weaned at 5 to 7 weeks; introduce solid food at 3 to 4 weeks; feed weaned kittens 1 ounce canned or fresh food per pound of body weight or 6 to 8 per cent of body weight in dry food daily in three feedings

PUBERTY: 5 to 9 months

BREEDING SEASON: spring to fall with 3 to 5 cycles of 10 to 14 days

GESTATION: 52 to 69 days, usually 63

REFERENCE CHARTS

LITTER SIZE: 1 to 6

NORMAL BODY TEMPERATURE: 101.5°, range: 100.5° to 102.5°F.

VACCINES RECOMMENDED: feline infectious enteritis (distemper), rabies, rhinotracheitis, pneumonitis

Comments

Very responsive to humans, more difficult to train than dogs but possible; will use litter box by choice; may claw furniture, and will shed. EASY

References

Fox, Michael: *Understanding Your Cat.* New York: Coward McCann, 1974

McCoy, J. J.: *The Complete Book of Cat Care.* New York: Putnam, 1968; paperback, New York: Berkeley, 1974

McGinnis, Terri: *The Well Cat Book.* New York: Random House, 1973

CHEETAH

Acinonyx jubatus

Northern Africa and Middle East

LIFESPAN: 5 to 15 years

ADULT WEIGHT RANGE: 105 to 150 pounds

LIVING ARRANGEMENTS: should be allowed wide running area; 8-foot × 10-foot minimum cage with 9-foot walls; sleeping box; varied temperature range

ADULT DIET: raw meat with supplements of bonemeal, codliver oil; 3 to 4 pounds in one feeding daily

INFANT DIET: KMR or Esbilac formula every 3 hours until eyes open; then gradually incorporate solid food and decrease number of feedings as amount taken at each feeding increases

PUBERTY: 2 to 3 years

BREEDING SEASON: throughout year

GESTATION: 92 to 95 days

LITTER SIZE: 2 to 4

VACCINES RECOMMENDED: see Cat

Comments

May be aggressive if not constantly handled from birth; endangered species. IMPOSSIBLE

References

Crandall, Lee S.: *Management of Wild Mammals in Captivity* (see Bibliography, "Books on Animal Care")

Eaton, Randall L.: *The Cheetah: Biology, Ecology, and Behavior of an Endangered Species.* New York: Van Nostrand, 1974

CHICKEN

Gallus gallus

Domestic

LIFESPAN: 8 to 10 years

ADULT WEIGHT RANGE: 4 to 10 pounds, depending on breed

LIVING ARRANGEMENTS: allow 3 square feet of floor space for each bird, with litter cover of shavings, peat, or straw; one nesting box for every four hens; enough roosting space and room at feeder for all; temperature range 55° to 70°F.; humidity c. 55 per cent

ADULT DIET: commercial grains, table-scrap supplements, poultry grit; free choice (a laying hen will eat about 7 pounds a month)

INFANT DIET: chicken starter (23 per cent protein); free choice to 6 weeks; then pullet mash or pellets to 18 weeks; then adult diet

PUBERTY: 18 to 24 weeks

CLUTCH SIZE: 5 to 20 eggs

INCUBATION: 21 days

NORMAL BODY TEMPERATURE: 106.5°F.

Comments

No marked responsiveness to humans; roosters may be aggressive; may be cannibalistic if not enough space or adequate conditions provided; avoid drafts, noise, wetness; zoning permit may be required in some areas.
DIFFICULT

References

Ewing, William Raiford: *Poultry Nutrition.* Pasadena, Calif.: Ray Ewing, 1963

Senevitatna, P., ed.: *Diseases of Poultry.* 2nd ed. Baltimore: Williams and Wilkins, 1969

CHIMPANZEE

Pan troglodytes
Africa

LIFESPAN: 25 to 40 years

ADULT WEIGHT RANGE: 100 to 200 pounds

LIVING ARRANGEMENTS: should be confined as little as possible, though needs constant supervision; minimum cage size: 10 × 10 feet with shelves, branches, a swinging tire; concrete floor and a shelter box; temperature range of 75° to 90°F.

ADULT DIET: monkey pellets, potatoes, carrots, celery, lettuce, bread, raisins, apples, milk, with vitamins and minerals; average 3000 calories daily in two or three feedings

INFANT DIET: human milk formula every 3 hours; at 4 to 6 weeks add baby cereal; gradually introduce mashed vegetables, reducing feedings to three or four daily until end of first year; ready for adult diet at about 2 years

PUBERTY: 9 years

BREEDING SEASON: throughout year, 35-day estrus cycle

GESTATION: 231 days

NUMBER OF YOUNG: usually 1

NORMAL BODY TEMPERATURE: 98°, range: 96° to 100°F.

VACCINES RECOMMENDED: polio, tetanus

Comments

Easily trained and docile while young, but at 4 to 5 years may become quite aggressive and dangerous. IMPOSSIBLE

References

Bourne, Geoffrey Howard, ed.: *The Chimpanzee.* 5 vol. Baltimore: University Park Press, 1970–71

Hayes, Catherine: *The Ape in Our House.* New York: Harper, 1951

Yerkes, Robert: *Chimpanzees: A Laboratory Colony.* New Haven: Yale, 1943

CHINCHILLA

Chinchilla laniger

Domestic (originally South America)

LIFESPAN: 6 to 10 years

ADULT WEIGHT RANGE: 1 to 2 pounds

LIVING ARRANGEMENTS: wire mesh cage (3-foot × 2-foot floor space) with 2-foot-high sleeping box, straw flooring with dust bath; temperature range varied

ADULT DIET: commercial chinchilla pellets, timothy hay with supplements of rolled oats, greens, lawn trimmings, yellow corn, raw vegetables, bread, apples, sunflower seeds, carrots, or twigs; 10 per cent of body weight in one daily feeding or self-feeding

INFANT DIET: see Rat; weaned at 60 days

PUBERTY: 8 months to 1 year

BREEDING SEASON: December and March

GESTATION: average 111 days

LITTER SIZE: 1 to 4, average 2

COMMON AILMENTS: see Rat

Comments

These are larger and livelier than the guinea pig; should be kept in separate cages to avoid fighting and hair pulling; may be expensive. EASY

Reference

Chinchilla Breeders. (A twelve-page pamphlet published under the auspices of Ralston Purina; available through Fur Trade Journal, Play Publishing Co., Bewdley, Ont., Canada.)

COATI-MUNDI

Nasua spp.

South and Central America

LIFESPAN: 10 to 15 years

ADULT WEIGHT RANGE: 6 to 30 pounds

LIVING ARRANGEMENTS: wood-and-wire cage as large as possible (minimum 5-foot square, 4-foot height) with sleeping box, logs or shelves for climbing; temperature range of 60° to 80°F.

ADULT DIET: chopped meat, dog food, canned or dry, with supplements of apples, fresh greens, and an occasional egg, multivitamins, bonemeal, calcium lactate; feed once daily 6 to 10 per cent of body weight
INFANT DIET: see Raccoon
PUBERTY: 6 to 10 months
BREEDING SEASON: fall
GESTATION: 72 to 77 days
LITTER SIZE: 3 to 4
NORMAL BODY TEMPERATURE: 100° to 102°F.
VACCINES RECOMMENDED: see Raccoon

Comments

Affectionate, trainable when young but gradually becomes aggressive and destructive. DIFFICULT

Reference

Mathews, Dick: *Wild Animals As Pets* (see Bibliography, "Books on Animal Care")

COCKATIEL

Nymphicus hollandicus
Australia/Asia
ADULT SIZE: 12 inches

Care

See Lovebird

COW

Bos bovis
Domestic
LIFESPAN: 15 to 20 years
ADULT WEIGHT RANGE: 800 to 2800 pounds
LIVING ARRANGEMENTS: will use 5-acre grazing pasture; shelter should be provided; temperature range varied
ADULT DIET: hay and grain or pelleted feeds; amount varies with breed and quality of feed
INFANT DIET: calf should receive colostrum (mother's milk) during first 3 days; then whole cow's milk (1 pound for every 10 pounds of body weight a day) every two hours; offer grain or calf starter or manna after 1 week; introduce hay at 3 weeks; discontinue milk at 2 months and permit free-choice grain or calf starter (up to 4 or 5 pounds daily) and hay
PUBERTY: 8 to 14 months
BREEDING SEASON: throughout year, 21-day estrus cycle
GESTATION: 260 to 280 days
NUMBER OF YOUNG: 1 to 4

NORMAL BODY TEMPERATURE: 100.4° to 102.8°F.

VACCINES RECOMMENDED: tetanus, brucellosis

Comments

May be responsive if hand reared; males become aggressive at maturity; zoning permit may be required in some areas. DIFFICULT

References

Bailey, J. W.: *Veterinary Handbook for Cattlemen.* New York: Springer, 1972

Davis, Richard F.: *Modern Dairy Cattle Management.* New York: Prentice Hall, 1962

Ensminger, M.: *Beef Cattle Science.* 4th ed. Danville, Ill.: Interstate, 1968

Reaves, Paul M., and Henderson, H. O.: *Dairy Cattle Feeding and Management.* New York: Wiley, 1963

COYOTE

Canis latrans

North and Central America

LIFESPAN: 10 to 15 years

ADULT WEIGHT RANGE: 50 to 100 pounds

LIVING ARRANGEMENTS: should be allowed wide running range; wire-cage minimum 10 feet × 25 feet with high (6-foot) walls; sleeping box; temperature range varied

ADULT DIET: see Dog

INFANT DIET: see Dog

PUBERTY: about 1 year

BREEDING SEASON: early spring

GESTATION: 60 to 65 days

LITTER SIZE: 1 to 11, average 5

VACCINES RECOMMENDED: canine distemper, rabies

Comments

Although tractable and docile as pups, coyotes are very high strung and unpredictable as adults; permit required. IMPOSSIBLE

References

Ryden, Hope: *God's Dog.* New York: Coward McCann, 1975

Van Wormer, Joe: *The World of the Coyote.* Philadelphia: Lippincott, 1964

DEER, White-Tailed

Odocoileus virginianus

North American woodlands

LIFESPAN: 14 to 20 years

ADULT WEIGHT RANGE: 80 to 320 pounds

LIVING ARRANGEMENTS: half-acre pasture minimum, with high (4- to 5-foot) fence of material other than wire; temperature range varied

ADULT DIET: hay (free choice); 2 pounds of daily commercial dairy grain in addition to pasture grazing or corncobs supplemented by corn, soybeans, linseed, and alfalfa meal

INFANT DIET: whole cow's milk mixed with heavy cream and calf manna (1 quart milk to ½ cup each cream and calf manna); 4 ounces four times daily to fawn up to 5 pounds in weight; increase to 5 ounces per feeding up to 10 pounds and introduce dry food (hay, dried leaves, calf manna); at 2 months reduce to two feedings daily and increase solid food

PUBERTY: 1 to 3 years

BREEDING SEASON: late summer, early fall

GESTATION: 205 to 210 days

NUMBER OF YOUNG: 1 to 4

NORMAL BODY TEMPERATURE: 99° to 101°F.

VACCINE AVAILABLE: tetanus

Comments

Hand-reared and hand-fed deer may learn to come when called and may tolerate handling; bucks become aggressive and unpredictable when mature, particularly during mating season; protected in most states and permits required for confinement. IMPOSSIBLE

References

Stadtfeld, Curtis K.: *Whitetail Deer: A Year's Cycle.* New York: Dial, 1975

Taylor, Walter Penn: *The Deer of North America: The White-Tailed, Mule, and Black-Tailed Deer, Genus Odocoileus, Their History and Management.* Harrisburg, Pa.: Stackpole, 1956

DOG

Canis familiaris

Domestic

LIFESPAN: 12 to 20 years

ADULT WEIGHT RANGE: 2 to 250 pounds, depending on breed

LIVING ARRANGEMENTS: may be allowed freedom of house (outdoor freedom at owner's risk, collar required); sleeping quarters and constant access to water recommended; cage size depends on breed; temperature range varied

ADULT DIET: combination of meat, vegetables, minerals, and vitamins to provide balanced diet of approximately 2.3 grams protein, 0.6 gram fat, 7 grams carbohydrate for every pound of body weight plus vitamins and minerals (some commercial diets—canned, soft-moist, or dry—can be recommended if complete and palatable; dry foods will require supplement of some fat and meat); ½ pound of food for every 10 pounds of body weight up to 50 pounds of body weight; less for larger or older dogs, more for pregnant or lactating bitches, in one or two daily feedings

INFANT DIET: Esbilac formula up to 10 to 15 per cent of body weight in four to six daily feedings; weaned at 5 to 7 weeks; solid food may be introduced at 3 weeks

WEANED PUPPY DIET: four feedings daily (or self-feeding), all they will consume in 20 minutes up to 3 months; three feedings daily (or self-feeding) all they will consume in 20 minutes up to 5 months; two feedings daily, 15 per cent of body weight, up to 10 months

PUBERTY: 6 to 12 months

BREEDING SEASON: twice yearly in most breeds, three times yearly in small breeds, once in Basenji; season lasts 21 to 28 days; fertile for 10 to 16 days of cycle

GESTATION: 63 days

LITTER SIZE: 1 to 16, usually 3 to 6

NORMAL BODY TEMPERATURE: 100.5° to 102°F.

VACCINES RECOMMENDED: canine distemper, canine hepatitis, leptospirosis, rabies; heartworm—test yearly, tablets or liquid prophylaxis daily during mosquito season

Comments

Very tractable and trainable; must be exercised and trained to a moderate degree; requires permit (license) and regular rabies inoculation. DIFFICULT

References

American Kennel Club: *The Complete Dog Book.* New York: Howell, 1972
Ensminger, M. E.: *The Complete Book of Dogs.* Philadelphia: Barnes, 1974
Fox, Michael: *Understanding Your Dog.* New York: Coward, 1974
Lorenz, Konrad: *Man Meets Dog.* Baltimore: Penguin, 1965
McGinnis, Terri: *The Well Dog Book.* New York: Random House, 1974

DONKEY

Equus asinus

Domestic

LIFESPAN: 20 to 30 years

ADULT WEIGHT RANGE: average 200 pounds for miniature donkeys; up to 1000 pounds for large asses

LIVING ARRANGEMENTS: 1 to 3 acres of grazing pasture; shelter or stall at least 5-foot square with straw or other bedding, salt block, access to water; fencing and stall latches must be secure

ADULT DIET: commercial grains, timothy hay; about 1 pound of grain and 1 flake hay daily for small donkeys; two daily feedings

INFANT DIET: Foal-Lac formula (Bordens) or skimmed cow's milk with added sugar every hour for first 3 days; then allow to drink from pail; introduce grain as soon as possible

PUBERTY: 2 years

BREEDING SEASON: throughout year, 21-day estrus cycle

GESTATION: 365 days

NUMBER OF YOUNG: usually 1

NORMAL BODY TEMPERATURE: 99°F.

VACCINE RECOMMENDED: tetanus, encephalitis

Comments

Intelligent and tractable with regular, gentle handling; permit may be required in some areas; regular care of hooves and parasite control required. DIFFICULT

Reference

De Wesselow, M. R.: *Donkeys: Their Care and Management.* Boston: Branden, n.d.

DUCK, Northern Mallard

Anas platyrhnychos

LIFESPAN: 10 to 15 years

ADULT SIZE: 20 to 28 inches

LIVING ARRANGEMENTS: pond or stream with predator-proof fence if confined; pen for duckling 30 × 30 inches with 18-inch wall including pan of water ½ inch deep and wire roof; temperature range varied

ADULT DIET: game-bird feed, or equal parts turkey starter and whole wheat, with supplements of crushed oyster shell during breeding season; poultry grit, some greens, free choice (wet food will cause illness)

INFANT DIET: turkey starter, supplements of greens beginning on tenth day; at 3 weeks gradually add whole wheat, vitamin supplement, and poultry grit; may be released after 3 weeks when self-feeding

PUBERTY: 8 months

CLUTCH SIZE: 8 to 10 eggs

INCUBATION: about 28 days

Comments

Wild ducks may not be confined without a permit, but many will remain as free-roaming pets during breeding season. DIFFICULT

Reference

Hyde, Dayton O., ed.: *Raising Wild Ducks in Captivity.* New York: Dutton, 1974

DUCK, White Peking

Anas spp.

Domestic

LIFESPAN: 10 years

ADULT WEIGHT RANGE: 7 to 9 pounds

LIVING ARRANGEMENTS: 4-foot × 4-foot pen with 2-foot walls; water container (or pond access) and shelter box; temperature range varied

ADULT DIET: commercial duck pellets or a combination of cornmeal and bran with rolled oats, dry milk, salt, codliver oil, and table scraps; free choice; poultry grit

INFANT DIET: duck or turkey starter or mash of corn, bread soaked in water or milk, cornmeal, and ground oats; free choice for two weeks; then duck-grower pellets; introduce grit at 3 weeks; introduce adult diet at 6 weeks

PUBERTY: 7 to 8 months

CLUTCH SIZE: 5 to 10 eggs

INCUBATION: 28 days

Comments

Can be messy and noisy in confinement and not particularly responsive except to food; permits may be required in some areas. DIFFICULT

Reference

Ewing, William Raiford: *Poultry Nutrition.* Pasadena, Calif.: Ray Ewing, 1963

FALCONS

See Owl

References

Freeman, Gage E., and Salirn, Francis H.: *Falconry: Its Claims, Its History and Practice.* Golden, Colo.: Falcon Head Press, 1972

Fleming, Arnold: *Falconry and Falcons: The Sport of Flight.* London: Country Life, 1934; reprint ed. 1974

FERRET

Mustela pertorius furo

North America and Europe

LIFESPAN: 10 to 15 years

ADULT WEIGHT RANGE: 300 to 2000 grams

LIVING ARRANGEMENTS: wood-and-wire mesh cage minimum 6 feet × 3 feet with 18-inch wall; sleeping box; temperature range varied

ADULT DIET: canned dog and cat foods, chicken parts, milk, bones, mink pellets, with supplements of multivitamins, codliver oil; feed once daily 4 to 5 ounces

INFANT DIET: Esbilac formula four to six times daily until eyes open; gradually introduce solid food, first adding high-protein baby cereal to formula, and then adult food until self-feeding

PUBERTY: 8 to 9 months

BREEDING SEASON: twice yearly

GESTATION: 36 to 42 days

LITTER SIZE: 5 to 13

NORMAL BODY TEMPERATURE: 101.6° to 102.4°F.

VACCINES RECOMMENDED: canine distemper, feline distemper, rabies

Comments
    Very affectionate though may bite in play; must be kept impeccably clean: permits required in some areas. DIFFICULT

References
    Crandall, Lee S.: *Management of Wild Mammals in Captivity* (see Bibliography, "Books on Animal Care")
    Mathews, Dick: *Wild Animals As Pets* (see Bibliography, "Books on Animal Care")

FINCH, Zebra

Taeniopygia castanotis

LIFESPAN: 2 to 3 years

ADULT SIZE: 3 to 6 inches

LIVING ARRANGEMENTS: wire cage or aviary 2-foot × 2-foot floor space with 18-inch walls; perches placed near top of cage; sleeping boxes; temperature range 65° to 80°F.

ADULT DIET: 1 part red millet, 1 part yellow millet, 3 parts whole millet, 3 parts canary seed; grit and cuttlebone, with supplements of "condition food"; free choice

INFANT DIET: see Canary

PUBERTY: 6 months

CLUTCH SIZE: 3 to 6 eggs

INCUBATION: 18 to 20 days

Comments
    These colorful little birds (like other finches, such as the waxbill and Java sparrow) do not have good singing voices but they are interesting to watch; may be kept in groups, though fighting (territorial) should be avoided if possible. EASY

References
    See Canary

FOX, Red

Vulpes fulva

North America

LIFESPAN: 10 to 15 years

ADULT WEIGHT RANGE: 8 to 20 pounds

LIVING ARRANGEMENTS: wire cage, 15-foot square with 4-foot walls; sand over earth flooring; sleeping box and litter box; temperature range varied

ADULT DIET: see Dog; if preparing for release, include live mice and chicken necks in diet; 4 ounces of food per pound of body weight once daily

INFANT DIET: Esbilac formula every 4 hours until eyes open; five feedings daily until 3 or 4 weeks when a good dog-food diet may be introduced;

present live mice and rats as soon as formula ceases, and encourage animal to kill prey; release during third month

PUBERTY: 1 year

BREEDING SEASON: December to February

GESTATION: 51 to 52 days

LITTER SIZE: 1 to 11, average 4

VACCINES: canine distemper, rabies

Comments

Although tractable as pups if hand reared, foxes will become nervous and aggressive as adults; permit required. IMPOSSIBLE

References

Crandall, Lee S.: *Management of Wild Mammals in Captivity* (see Bibliography, "Books on Animal Care")

Rue, Leonard Lee: *The World of the Red Fox*. Philadelphia: Lippincott, 1969

FROG, Gray Tree

Hyla versicolor

North American ponds and streams

LIFESPAN: up to 10 years

ADULT SIZE: 2 to 2½ inches

LIVING ARRANGEMENTS: 5- or 10-gallon aquarium tank with water container (less spacious than for the leopard frog); perforated lid; branches, leaves; earth flooring; temperature range 65° to 75°F.

ADULT DIET: houseflies, live crickets, mealworms

INFANT DIET: see Leopard Frog

PUBERTY: 3 years

BREEDING SEASON: late spring

CLUTCH SIZE: up to 1000 eggs (in water)

INCUBATION: 2 to 3 days; tadpoles begin metamorphosis by second month

COMMON AILMENTS: see Leopard Frog

Comments

The genus *Hyla* also includes spring pepper, squirrel tree frog. EASY

References

Vogel, Zdenek: *Reptiles and Amphibians* (see Bibliography, "Books on Animal Care")

Zappler, George and Lisbeth: *Amphibians As Pets* (see Bibliography, "Books on Animal Care")

FROG, Leopard

Rana pipiens

North American ponds and streams

LIFESPAN: up to 10 years
ADULT SIZE: 2 to 4 inches
LIVING ARRANGEMENTS: for 2 to 3 adult frogs, 10-gallon aquarium tank with sizable water area and earth; perforated lid; plants and logs for shelter; temperature range varied (65° to 75°F. ideal); tadpoles will want complete water environment
ADULT DIET: moths, cockroaches, grasshoppers, crickets, mealworms, with supplements of bonemeal and multivitamins; feed twice weekly
INFANT (TADPOLE) DIET: algae scraped from pond, ground cooked lettuce; when limbs appear (at a month or so), add small bits of meat to diet or cooked egg white
PUBERTY: 2 years
BREEDING SEASON: spring
CLUTCH SIZE: 400 to 500 eggs
INCUBATION: 2 to 4 weeks
COMMON AILMENTS: 1. Symptom—reddening on inside and ventral surface of rear leg and abdomen. Cause—bacteria (red leg). Treatment—Tetracycline orally; 1 mg per 10 grams body weight 2 to 3 times a day for 5 to 7 days
2. Symptom—swelling of rear legs. Cause—tumor or fungus infection. Treatment—none effective
3. Symptoms—paralysis of rear legs and convulsions. Cause—calcium deficiency. Treatment—add Neo Calglucon to regular diet

Comments

The genus *Rana* also includes carpenter, pickerel, and bull frogs. EASY

References

Vogel, Zdenek: *Reptiles and Amphibians* (see Bibliography, "Books on Animal Care")

Zappler, George and Lisbeth: *Amphibians As Pets* (see Bibliography, "Books on Animal Care")

GECKO

Gekko spp.

Southeast Asia, India, Australia, East Indies

LIFESPAN: 10 years or more
ADULT SIZE: 5 to 11 inches
LIVING ARRANGEMENTS: wooden or glass cage at least 2 feet long, 1 foot wide, 18 inches high with lid; branches and bark arranged for climbing; water pan and newspaper or sand (thin layer) flooring; dry warm climate (70° to 85°F.)
DIET: see under Anole
COMMON AILMENTS: see under Anole

Comments

Unlike the anoles, the geckos are nocturnal naturally and may not be as interesting to watch during the day; handling difficult as tails break off and skin tears easily; they also bite. DIFFICULT

References

See Anole

GERBIL, or Clawed Jird

Meriones mongoliensis

Domestic (originally Asia)

LIFESPAN: 2 to 5 years

ADULT WEIGHT RANGE: 60 to 190 grams

LIVING ARRANGEMENTS: wire cage 2-foot square with cotton or wood-shavings as bedding (clean once daily); sleeping box and wood for gnawing; temperature range 60° to 75°F.; low humidity

ADULT DIET: barley, oats, sunflower seeds, commercial mouse pellets, with supplements of fresh greens and carrots; free choice

INFANT DIET: evaporated milk diluted one to one with water plus 1 drop pediatric vitamin; feed every 3 hours until weaned at 3 weeks; introduce solid food when eyes open (during third week)

PUBERTY: 10 to 14 weeks

BREEDING SEASON: throughout year, 10-day estrus cycle

GESTATION: 21 days

LITTER SIZE: 1 to 7, usually 4

COMMON AILMENTS: see Rat

Comments

Should be handled frequently; will bite when startled. EASY

References

How to Raise and Train Gerbils. Jersey City: TFH, n.d.

Pet Library Ltd.: *Know Your Gerbil.* Garden City, N.Y.: Doubleday, n.d.

GOAT

Capra hircus

Domestic

LIFESPAN: 12 to 25 years

ADULT WEIGHT RANGE: 80 to 250 pounds, depending on breed

LIVING ARRANGEMENTS: pen should be minimum 24-foot square or 4-foot × 6-foot pen with outdoor pasture; fences should be at least 5 feet high; tethering (inorganic tether) often preferable; temperature range varied but indoor shelter required in cold weather

ADULT DIET: commercial pellets (14 to 16 per cent protein), hay; 1 pound of pellets to 100 pounds of body weight daily; free choice hay or grass or browse (watch out for toxic plants); occasional raw vegetables

INFANT DIET: orphaned kids may often be "grafted" to another nanny; if not, feed whole goat's or cow's milk three to four times daily, as much as animal will take; introduce solid food as soon as possible

PUBERTY: 1 year to 18 months

BREEDING SEASON: September to March, 21-day estrus cycle

GESTATION: 140 to 160 days

NUMBER OF YOUNG: 1 to 4

NORMAL BODY TEMPERATURE: 102° to 103°F.

Comments

May be affectionate, even demanding of attention; males will butt and be aggressive and odorous during breeding season; some areas may require permits. DIFFICULT

References

Ensminger, M.: *Animal Science*. 6th ed. Danville, Ill.: Interstate, 1969

MacKenzie, Donald: *Goat Husbandry*. London: Faber, n.d.

Walsh, Helen: *Starting Right with Milk Goats*. Charlotte, Vermont: Garden Way Publishing, 1972

GOOSE, Canada

Branta canadensis

North America

LIFESPAN: about 20 years

ADULT WEIGHT RANGE: 8 to 12 pounds (36 to 40 inches)

See Greylag Goose

Comments

Canada geese are noisier and will be more aggressive than domestic geese; permit must be obtained for confinement of wild geese. DIFFICULT

References

Dill, Herbert H., and Lee, Forrest B., eds.: *Homegrown Honkers*. Washington D.C.: Bureau of Sport Fisheries and Wildlife, 1970

Wild Waterfowl and Its Captive Management. Salt Lake City: Wildlife Publications, 1974

GOOSE, Greylag

Anser anser

Domestic

LIFESPAN: up to 50 years

ADULT WEIGHT RANGE: 7 to 10 pounds (25 to 39 inches)

LIVING ARRANGEMENTS: may be free roaming with access to grasses and pond; breeding pen 3 feet × 3 feet × 2 feet on bare-earth flooring

REFERENCE CHARTS

ADULT DIET: commercial chicken feed, alfalfa pellets, or mixture of grains (corn, wheat, barley, oats) with greens (lawn trimmings) or forage (grass, clover, etc.); poultry grit; free choice

INFANT DIET: chicken starter until 2 or 3 weeks old, or mash of bread soaked in water or milk, cracked corn, cornmeal, and vitamin-mineral supplements; self-feeding at 7 to 10 days when grains and grit should be made available; free choice

PUBERTY: 3 to 4 years

CLUTCH SIZE: 4 to 7 eggs

INCUBATION: 27 to 28 days

Comments

Geese can be aggressive, noisy, and messy; permits may be required in some suburban areas. DIFFICULT

Reference

See Canada Goose, previous page

GUINEA PIG (Cavy)

Cavia porcellus

Domestic (originally South American)

LIFESPAN: 5 to 8 years

ADULT WEIGHT RANGE: 600 to 1000 grams, 700 grams average

LIVING ARRANGEMENTS: wire cage 3-foot square for each pair (clean twice weekly); corncob or peatmoss or commercial bedding; temperature range 60° to 80°F.

ADULT DIET: greens, hay, commercial pellets with vitamin C added (0.1 per cent per 100 grams ascorbic acid); free choice up to 10 per cent body weight

INFANT DIET: evaporated milk mixed half and half with water every 2 hours for 10 days with added pediatric vitamins (1 drop at each feeding); at 10 days introduce solid food and reduce formula feedings to every 3 hours; weaned at 4 weeks

PUBERTY: 5 to 10 weeks for female (when weight is 400 grams); 8 to 10 weeks for male

BREEDING SEASON: throughout year, every 13 to 20 days

GESTATION: 59 to 67 days, usually 63

LITTER SIZE: 1 to 6

COMMON AILMENTS: 1. Symptoms—stiffness of the hocks, swollen joints, lethargy, poor hair coat, loss of weight. Cause—vitamin C deficiency. Treatment—add 5 mg ascorbic acid (vitamin C) to diet daily for 2 weeks; change diet to guinea-pig pellets containing vitamin C

2. Symptoms—bilateral hair loss from shoulders to tail or baldness in young animals. Cause—excessive grooming by individual or parents. Treatment—make roughage (hay) available

3. Symptom—overgrowth of incisor teeth. Cause—insufficient roughage.

REFERENCE CHARTS

Treatment—trim teeth to allow for normal wear and add roughage to diet; also give animal a wooden block for chewing

4. Symptoms—stunted growth, gradual loss of body condition. Cause—calcium-phosphorus imbalance. Treatment—change diet to guinea-pig pellets

5. Symptoms—acute diarrhea, sudden death in colony. Cause—salmonella bacteria. Treatment—administer Gentamycin 2 mg. per 100 gr. of body weight daily (injection) for 5 to 7 days; clean cage thoroughly

6. Symptom—head tilt. Cause—middle-ear infection. Treatment—administer Gentamycin (injection) 2 mg. per 100 gr. body weight daily for 5 to 7 days

7. Symptom—chronic diarrhea. Cause—coccidia or other intestinal parasites. Treatment—if coccidiosis, add sulfa-dimethoxine to drinking water; if intestinal nematodes, administer Thiabendazole (injection) 5 mg. per 100 gr. of body weight once weekly for 3 weeks

8. Symptom—death of female late in pregnancy. Cause—pregnancy toxemia and insufficient food quality

Comments

Not very trainable but docile; will whistle for food and should be handled frequently; may bite if startled; pregnant females should be isolated from males. EASY

References

Roberts, Mervin F.: *Guinea Pigs for Beginners*. Jersey City: TFH, 1972

The UFAW Handbook on the Care and Management of Laboratory Animals (see Bibliography, "Books on Animal Care")

HAMSTER, Syrian or Golden

Mesocricetus auratus

Domestic (originally Syria)

LIFESPAN: 1 to 4 years

ADULT WEIGHT RANGE: 100 to 140 grams

LIVING ARRANGEMENTS: wire cage at least 2-foot square with bedding of wood chips; sleeping box with nesting material; wooden stick for gnawing; exercise wheels, etc.; temperature range 70° to 75°F. with moderate humidity

ADULT DIET: mouse or rat pellets, sunflower seeds, with supplements of fresh greens, bits of carrot; free choice

INFANT DIET: evaporated milk mixed one to one with water, with 1 drop pediatric vitamin added for a daily portion; feed at 2-hour intervals, and wean at 21 days; introduce solid food during second week

PUBERTY: 6 to 10 weeks

BREEDING SEASON: fertile throughout year

GESTATION: 15 to 18 days

LITTER SIZE: 1 to 12, usually 6

NORMAL BODY TEMPERATURE: 96.8°F.

COMMON AILMENTS: see Rat

Comments

Should be handled daily to keep tame; may bite; antisocial and should be kept singly in cages; nocturnal in habits; separate male and female following breeding. EASY

References

Pet Library, Ltd.: *Know Your Hamster.* Garden City, N.Y.: Doubleday, 1973

Roberts, Mervin F.: *How to Raise Hamsters.* Jersey City: TFH, n.d.

The UFAW Handbook on the Care and Management of Laboratory Animals (see Bibliography, "Books on Animal Care")

HORSE

Equus caballus

Domestic

LIFESPAN: 20 to 35 years

ADULT WEIGHT RANGE: 500 to 1400 pounds, depending on breed

LIVING ARRANGEMENTS: 3 to 5 acres of grazing pasture; stalls should be 1½ times length squared (i.e., 12 feet × 12 feet for horses; 8 feet × 8 feet for ponies); straw or other bedding; salt block; temperature range varied

ADULT DIET: commercial grains, oats (½ to 1 pound grain per 100 pounds body weight for lightly worked horses, 1 to 3 hours daily), and timothy hay, free choice; growing, pregnant, lactating, and hard-working horses may need 1 to 2 pounds of grain daily per 100 pounds of body weight; feed twice daily

INFANT DIET: Foal-Lac formula (Bordens) or sweetened cow's milk; about ½ cup every hour for first 3 days; increase intervals as amount taken at each feeding increases; introduce grain as soon as animal will take it; usual weaning time: 6 months

PUBERTY: 12 to 15 months

BREEDING SEASON: throughout year in 21-day cycles of 4 to 6 days

GESTATION: 336 days

NUMBER OF YOUNG: 1, rarely 2

NORMAL BODY TEMPERATURE: 99° to 100.8°F.

VACCINES RECOMMENDED: tetanus—2 injections 4 to 8 weeks apart during first year, yearly boosters; equine influenza—2 injections 4 to 12 weeks apart and yearly boosters; equine encephalitis—2 injections yearly; strangles (where prevalent)—3 injections at weekly intervals; rhinopneumonitis—for pregnant mares: first injection 60 days after breeding; second during 5th month; (for other horses: 2 injections 4 to 8 weeks apart with yearly boosters; equine infectious anemia: no vaccine available but yearly Coggins test recommended, or more frequently if animal shipped

Comments

Trainable, docile if worked with frequently; caution against overfeeding; must be groomed frequently and wormed regularly. DIFFICULT

References

Davidson, Joseph B.: *Horsemen's Veterinary Advisor.* Columbus, Ohio: Horse Publications, 1966

Devlin, C. B.: *Horseman's Dictionary: Medical and General.* Philadelphia: Barnes, 1974

Greeley, R. Gordon: *The Art and Science of Horseshoeing.* Philadelphia: Lippincott, 1971

Johnson, Patricia, and Hayes, Marcia: *A Horse around the House.* New York: Crown, 1972

Prince, Eleanor F., and Collier, Gaydell M.: *Basic Horsemanship: English and Western—a Complete Guide for Riders and Instructors.* Garden City, N.Y.: Doubleday, 1974

Stratton, R. C.: *A Horse Owner's Vet Book.* Philadelphia: Lippincott, 1973

IGUANA, Green

Iguana iguana

Central and South America

LIFESPAN: up to 25 years

ADULT SIZE: 6 feet

LIVING ARRANGEMENTS: wooden or glass cage at least 4 feet long, 2 feet wide for adults; newspaper, linoleum or wooden flooring; branches for climbing; water dish; temperature range 78° to 88°F.

ADULT DIET: cabbage, clover, fruit, dry dog food, tomatoes, mealworms; occasional lettuce and chopped fruits; free choice every other day sprinkled with powdered vitamins and minerals

PUBERTY: 4 to 6 years

INCUBATION: 6 weeks

CLUTCH SIZE: 6 to 45 eggs, average 35

COMMON AILMENTS: see under Anole

Comments

Iguanas have sharp claws and teeth and may injure handlers, so handling not recommended. EASY

References

See Anole

JAGUARUNDI

Felis jaguarundi

See Ocelot

KINKAJOU, or Honey Bear

Potos flavus

South and Central America

REFERENCE CHARTS

LIFESPAN: 20 to 22 years
ADULT WEIGHT RANGE: 3 to 8 pounds
LIVING ARRANGEMENTS: cage minimum 4-foot square, 5 feet high, with logs for climbing; sleeping box near top of cage; temperature range 65° to 80°F.
ADULT DIET: eggs, meats, canned or dry dog food, some fruits; multivitamins once daily; feed 5 to 10 per cent of body weight daily
INFANT DIET: see Raccoon; add a bit of honey to formula
PUBERTY: 1 year
BREEDING SEASON: fall
GESTATION: not known
NUMBER OF YOUNG: 1 or 2
NORMAL BODY TEMPERATURE: 100° to 101.5°F.
VACCINES RECOMMENDED: see Raccoon; rabies not necessary

Comments

Nocturnal, affectionate and tractable; inquisitive and may be destructive but not likely to be as aggressive as raccoon or coati-mundi with regular handling; may be trained to leash; reacts poorly to change. DIFFICULT

References

Crandall, Lee S.: *Management of Wild Mammals in Captivity* (see Bibliography, "Books on Animal Care")

Vandivert, William: *Barnaby.* New York: Dodd Mead, 1962

LIZARD—see Anole, Gecko, Iguana, Monitor Lizard,

LLAMA

Lama glama
Domestic
LIFESPAN: 20 to 25 years
ADULT WEIGHT RANGE: 250 to 500 pounds
LIVING ARRANGEMENTS: see Sheep
ADULT AND INFANT DIETS: see Sheep
PUBERTY: 2 to 3 years
BREEDING SEASON: spring to early fall
GESTATION: 11 months
NUMBER OF YOUNG: 1, occasionally two
VACCINES RECOMMENDED: tetanus

Comments

Easily trained when young; need pastureland. DIFFICULT

Reference

Crandall, Lee S.: *Management of Wild Mammals in Captivity* (see Bibliography, "Books on Animal Care")

LYNX

Lynx canadensis
North America
LIFESPAN: 15 to 20 years
ADULT WEIGHT RANGE: 25 to 50 pounds

Care

See Mountain Lion

LOVEBIRD

Agapornis spp.
Africa, Madagascar
LIFESPAN: up to 20 years
ADULT SIZE: 6 to 7 inches

Care

See Budgerigar but cage should be larger, and sunflower seeds should be added to diet

---

MACAW

Ara spp.
Central and South America
LIFESPAN: up to 50 years
ADULT SIZE: average 3 feet

LIVING ARRANGEMENTS: steel-wire cage large enough to allow bird to spread wings fully or do not confine (do not chain to post either); temperature range 60° to 75°F.; wooden block or stick for gnawing

ADULT DIET: two parts canary seed, one-half part white millet to equal parts sunflower seeds, hemp, yellow millet, unsalted peanuts, with supplements of apples, greens, mealworms, toast or crackers, earthworms; cuttlebone and grit; free choice

PUBERTY: 1 year
CLUTCH SIZE: 2 to 4 eggs
INCUBATION: 24 to 26 days

Comments

Very large and dangerous if aggressive and not frequently handled; good talkers, long lived, and expensive. DIFFICULT

Reference
>   Bates, Henry, and Busenbark, Robert: *Parrots and Related Birds* (see Bibliography, "Books on Animal Care")

MARGAY

Felis weidii
See Ocelot

MARMOSET

Hapala spp., *Saguinus* spp., *Calithrax* spp.
South America
LIFESPAN: 5 to 10 years
ADULT WEIGHT RANGE: 1 to 2 pounds
LIVING ARRANGEMENTS: wire cage 4 inches by 4 inches by 3 inches with climbing equipment and sleeping box; temperature range 70° to 80°F.
ADULT DIET: marmoset diet (high protein commercial diet with Vitamin D); raw meat, insects, baby chicks, with supplements of raw vegetables (yams, carrots, etc.); 2 ounces twice daily for every pound of body weight
INFANT DIET: Enfamil, Simulac, or other human baby formula every 3 hours; gradually increase intervals between feedings; free choice; weaned at about 6 to 8 months; introduce solid foods (strained baby meats and vegetables) at 2 months
PUBERTY: about 2 years
BREEDING SEASON: throughout year in 28-day estrus cycle
GESTATION: 134 to 140 days
NUMBER OF YOUNG: 1 to 3, average 2
NORMAL BODY TEMPERATURE: 100° to 101°F.
VACCINES RECOMMENDED: tetanus; tuberculin test annually

Comments
>   Frighten easily and then bite. IMPOSSIBLE

Reference
>   National Research Council: *Non-Human Primates: Standards and Guidelines for the Breeding, Care, and Management of Laboratory Animals* (see Bibliography)

MARTEN

Martes americana
North America
LIFESPAN: 5 to 15 years

ADULT WEIGHT RANGE: 2 to 4 pounds (14 to 17 inches)

LIVING ARRANGEMENTS: pen or cage 4-inch cube; sleeping box and climbing equipment; temperature range varied

ADULT DIET: live mice, insects, frogs; canned dog food, with supplements of berries, unsalted nuts; feed once daily up to 10 per cent of body weight

INFANT DIET: see Ferret

PUBERTY: 1 year

BREEDING SEASON: July to August

GESTATION: 220 to 297 days (delayed implantation)

LITTER SIZE: 1 to 5

VACCINES RECOMMENDED: Feline distemper (killed-vaccine only); canine distemper

Comments

Difficult to handle as maturity approaches; will bite seriously if provoked. IMPOSSIBLE

Reference

Crandall, Lee S.: *Management of Wild Mammals in Captivity* (see Bibliography)

MONITOR LIZARD

Varanus spp.

Asia, Australia, India, Africa, Malaya, New Guinea

LIFESPAN: 10 to 50 years

ADULT SIZE: 1 to 10 feet

LIVING ARRANGEMENTS: see Iguana

ADULT DIET: mice, rats, chicks, canned dog food, large insects once a week, squash, etc.) every 2 or 3 days

COMMON AILMENTS: see under Anole

Comments

May be aggressive if not handled frequently; expensive. DIFFICULT

Reference

Vogel, Zdenek: *Reptiles and Amphibians* (see Bibliography)

MONKEY, Capuchin (or Sapajou or Ringtail)

Cebus spp.

South and Central America

LIFESPAN: 10 to 25 years

ADULT WEIGHT RANGE: 5 to 7 pounds

LIVING ARRANGEMENTS: wire cage 6-×-6-inch floor space with floor-to-ceiling walls; climbing equipment and sleeping box; temperature range 70° to 80°F.; humidity up to 50 per cent

ADULT DIET: monkey pellets, canned primate diet, sunflower seeds, dry dog food, raw meat or fish, unsalted peanuts, greens, evaporated milk, codliver oil; feed free choice three times daily (as much as will be taken in half an hour)

INFANT DIET: see Marmoset

PUBERTY: 2 to 3 years

BREEDING SEASON: throughout year, 28-day cycle

GESTATION: 6 months

NUMBER OF YOUNG: 1 or 2

VACCINES RECOMMENDED: tetanus; tuberculin tests annually

Comments

This is the familiar "organ-grinder" monkey, but will survive well only in groups; will bite readily. IMPOSSIBLE

References

See Rhesus monkey

MONKEY, Rhesus

Macaca mulatta

Africa

LIFESPAN: 15 to 20 years

ADULT WEIGHT RANGE: 20 to 25 pounds

LIVING ARRANGEMENTS: wire cage 6-×-6-inch floor space with floor-to-ceiling walls; climbing equipment and sleeping box; temperature range 60° to 85°F.

ADULT DIET: monkey pellets with supplements of vegetables, hard-boiled eggs, unsalted nuts; 4 per cent body weight in two daily feedings

INFANT DIET: see Spider Monkey; weaned at 3 to 6 months, when weight reaches 2 pounds

PUBERTY: 5 years female; 6 years male

BREEDING SEASON: throughout year in 28-day estrus cycles

GESTATION: 150 to 180 days, 165 days, average

NUMBER OF YOUNG: 1

NORMAL BODY TEMPERATURE: 101.8°F.

VACCINE RECOMMENDED: tetanus

Comments

Like all monkeys, these become impossible as housepets after maturity. IMPOSSIBLE

Reference

Valaris, David Allen, et al.: *Macaca Mulatta: Management of a Laboratory Breeding Colony.* New York: Academic Press, 1969

MONKEY, Spider

Ateles spp.

South and Central America

LIFESPAN: 4 to 20 years

ADULT WEIGHT RANGE: 10 to 20 pounds

LIVING ARRANGEMENTS: wire cage with 4-×-4-inch floor space; floor-to-ceiling walls; climbing equipment and sleeping box; temperature range 70° to 80°F.

ADULT DIET: monkey pellets, canned primate diet, mealworms, raw vegetables (carrots, kale, yams, etc.), hard-boiled eggs; with oranges as supplement (one or two slices daily); 4 ounces for every pound of body weight in 2 or 3 daily feedings

INFANT DIET: see Marmoset

PUBERTY: 5 to 6 years

BREEDING SEASON: throughout year, 28-day cycle

GESTATION: 139 days

NUMBER OF YOUNG: 1 or 2

VACCINES RECOMMENDED: tetanus; tuberculin tests annually

Comments

These relatively large monkeys may inflict serious bites as they approach sexual maturity. Like all other monkeys, they should be kept only in social groups. IMPOSSIBLE

References

See Rhesus monkey

MONKEY, Squirrel

Saimiri sciurens

South and Central America

LIFESPAN: 3 to 20 years

ADULT WEIGHT RANGE: 2 to 3 pounds

LIVING ARRANGEMENTS: see Marmoset

ADULT DIET: see Capuchin monkey

INFANT DIET: see Marmoset

PUBERTY: 2 to 3 years

BREEDING SEASON: throughout year, 28-day cycle

GESTATION: 6 months

NUMBER OF YOUNG: 1

NORMAL BODY TEMPERATURE: 99° to 99.8°F.

VACCINES RECOMMENDED: tetanus; tuberculin tests annually

Comments

These highly social monkeys must be kept in groups if they are to do well in captivity; will bite if frightened. IMPOSSIBLE

References

See Rhesus monkey

MONKEY, Woolly

Lagothrix lagotricha

South America

LIFESPAN: 4 to 20 years

ADULT WEIGHT RANGE: 15 to 20 pounds

LIVING ARRANGEMENTS: see Rhesus monkey

ADULT DIET: see Rhesus monkey

INFANT DIET: see Marmoset

PUBERTY: 4 to 5 years

BREEDING SEASON: throughout year, 28-day cycle

GESTATION: 139 days

NUMBER OF YOUNG: 1

NORMAL BODY TEMPERATURE: 98.6°F.

VACCINES RECOMMENDED: tetanus toxoid; tuberculin tests annually

Comments

These large monkeys should be kept at least in pairs; will bite if provoked; these are the most amiable of the New World monkeys but at 4 to 5 years they usually become difficult to handle. IMPOSSIBLE

References

See Rhesus monkey

MOUNTAIN LION (Cougar, Puma, Panther, or Catamount)

Felis concolor

North and South America

LIFESPAN: 10 to 20 years

ADULT WEIGHT RANGE: 80 to 225 pounds

LIVING ARRANGEMENTS: run at least 10 feet × 20 feet with wire fence; sleeping box and logs or platform for climbing; temperature range varied

ADULT DIET: Zu/Preem Feline diet or raw meat or chicken necks with bonemeal and codliver oil supplements; 1½ pounds of food for every 50 pounds of body weight once daily

INFANT DIET: see Ocelot

PUBERTY: 2 to 3 years

BREEDING SEASON: anytime

GESTATION: 90 to 97 days

LITTER SIZE: 1 to 6

VACCINES RECOMMENDED: feline distemper (killed virus only) and rabies (killed virus only)

Comments

Hand-reared mountain lions can be affectionate but their adult size and temperament make them unsuitable as house pets. IMPOSSIBLE

References

Crandall, Lee S.: *Management of Wild Mammals in Captivity* (see Bibliography, "Books on Animal Care")

Mathews, Dick: *Wild Animals As Pets* (see Bibliography, "Books on Animal Care")

MOUSE

Mus musculus

Domestic

LIFESPAN: 2 to 4 years

ADULT WEIGHT RANGE: 20 to 25 grams

LIVING ARRANGEMENTS: wire cage (or glass or plastic tank) allowing at least 1-foot-square floor space, with 18-inch walls for each mouse; nest box with bedding and exercise wheel; temperature range 65° to 75°F.

ADULT DIET:/   commerical mouse pellets; free choice

INFANT DIET: evaporated milk mixed one to one with water fed with dropper every 2 hours until eyes open; increase intervals as more food is taken at each feeding; introduce solid food when mouse begins to move around and nibble on bedding

PUBERTY: 6 to 8 weeks

BREEDING SEASON: throughout year, 4- to 5-day cycle every 5 days

GESTATION: 17 to 21 days

LITTER SIZE: 1 to 20, average 10

NORMAL BODY TEMPERATURE: 96.8° to 99°F., average 97.7°

COMMON AILMENTS: see Rat

Comments

Should be handled daily; may bite if startled. EASY

References

Hirschhorn, Howard: *All about Mice.* Jersey City: TFH, 1974

Lauber, Patricia: *Of Man and Mouse.* New York: Viking, 1971

The UFAW Handbook on the Care and Management of Laboratory Animals (see Bibliography, "Books on Animal Care")

MYNAH, Indian Hill

Gracula religiosa

Asia

LIFESPAN: up to 20 years

ADULT SIZE: 11½ inches

LIVING ARRANGEMENTS: wire cage 4-foot square and 24 inches high with

REFERENCE CHARTS

348

perches and nest box; temperature range 60° to 75°F. (no drafts or sudden changes)

ADULT DIET: commercial mynah diet or a moist mixture of ground raw meat, hard-boiled egg, milk, bread, cooked vegetables with supplements of chopped raw fruit, multivitamins or bonemeal; grit and cuttlebone; free choice

INFANT DIET: same as adult diet

PUBERTY: 1 to 2 years

CLUTCH SIZE: 2 to 3 eggs

INCUBATION: 14 to 18 days

Comments

Excellent talkers and responsive, but messy and do not breed readily. DIFFICULT

Reference

Bates, Henry, and Busenbark, Robert: *Guide to Mynahs.* Jersey City: TFH, n.d.

OCELOT

Felis pardalis

Central and South America

LIFESPAN: 6 to 10 years

ADULT WEIGHT RANGE: 20 to 65 pounds

LIVING ARRANGEMENTS: wood-and-wire cage (or room) with 6-foot × 10-foot floor space and 4-foot walls with sleeping box or layers of fabric for bedding; toilet area (box with high sides and litter); logs, shelves; temperature range 60° to 80°F.

ADULT DIET: Zu/Preem Feline diet; canned dog food; or combination of chopped beef, lamb, chicken necks and hearts, beef kidney, some cooked vegetables, with supplements of codliver oil, bonemeal, and multivitamins; 10 per cent of body weight daily in one or two feedings

INFANT DIET: KMR or Esbilac formula four or five times daily; free choice until eyes open (17 days); introduce solid food finely ground at 55 days in two or three daily feedings

PUBERTY: about 1 year

BREEDING SEASON: late fall, early winter

GESTATION: 75 days

LITTER SIZE: 1 to 3, average 2

BODY TEMPERATURE: 99.5° to 101.5°F.

VACCINES RECOMMENDED: feline distemper (killed virus only)

Comments

Docile when young and may be trained to leash/or allowed supervised run of house; but becomes aggressive with maturity if not handled constantly and can be very destructive of property and self; endangered species. IMPOSSIBLE

Reference

Sisin, Catherine: *Especially Ocelots*. Amagansett, N.Y.: Sisin, 1967

OPOSSUM

Didelphis marsupialis
North America
LIFESPAN: 3 to 5 years
ADULT WEIGHT RANGE: 5 to 15 pounds
LIVING ARRANGEMENTS: cage 3 feet × 3 feet × 3 feet with sleeping box, bedding; temperature range varied
ADULT DIET: chopped meat, liver, canned dog food, eggs, vegetables, fruits (apple, banana, oranges, grapes), with supplement of table scraps; 8 to 10 per cent of body weight daily in single evening feeding
INFANT DIET: Esbilac formula every 3 hours if animal is furred (if very young, probably cannot be saved, but try using syringe of formula directly into stomach); when eyes open, mix canned dog food and hard-boiled egg with formula and feed five or six times daily; when self-feeding, introduce solid food (live insects or rodents if you plan to release it); may be released when about 12 inches long
PUBERTY: 6 to 8 months
BREEDING SEASON: winter
GESTATION: 12 to 13 days (babies stay in pouch for 4 to 6 weeks)
LITTER SIZE: 5 to 13, average 7
REGULAR WORMING RECOMMENDED

Comments

Can be handled if hand reared; solitary as adults and unresponsive to humans except at feeding time; may become aggressive after 3 to 6 months. DIFFICULT

References

Collett, Rosemary K.: *My Orphans of the Wild* (see Bibliography, "Books on Animal Care")

Crandall, Lee S.: *Management of Wild Mammals in Captivity* (see Bibliography, "Books on Animal Care")

Keefe, James J. *The World of the Opossum*. Philadelphia: Lippincott, 1967

OTTER, America

Lutra canadensis
North America
LIFESPAN: 10 to 15 years
ADULT WEIGHT RANGE: 6 to 20 pounds
LIVING ARRANGEMENTS: cage or run at least 10-foot square with 4- to 5-foot fence and pool of water; sleeping box and hay for burrowing; temperature range varied

REFERENCE CHARTS

ADULT DIET: meat (raw fish, horse meat, canned dog food, chicken necks) with supplements of eggs, rolled oats, bonemeal, vegetables; table scraps acceptable (not greasy or spicy) and also mink pellets; 10 to 25 per cent of body weight in one or two daily feedings

INFANT DIET: Esbilac formula every 3 hours until eyes open; decrease number of feedings as amount taken increases at each feeding; introduce solid food gradually (in ground or mashed form) as soon as eyes open (5 weeks)

PUBERTY: 2 years for female; 5 to 6 years for male

BREEDING SEASON: December to April

GESTATION: 9 to 12 months (delayed implantation)

NUMBER OF YOUNG: 2 to 4

NORMAL BODY TEMPERATURE: 102°F.

VACCINES RECOMMENDED: canine distemper (killed virus), feline distemper (killed virus), rabies (killed virus), hepatitis, and leptospirosis

Comments

Can be affectionate if handled frequently, but likely to bite; very lively and demanding; unpredictable after maturity; expensive; permit required. IMPOSSIBLE

References

Crandall, Lee S.: *Management of Wild Mammals in Captivity* (see Bibliography, "Books on Animal Care")

Harris, C. J.: *Otters: A Recent Study of the Recent Lutrinae.* London: Weidenfeld and Nicolson, 1968

Mathews, Dick: *Wild Animals As Pets* (see Bibliography, "Books on Animal Care")

Maxwell, Gavin: *Ring of Bright Water.* New York: Dutton, 1961

Wisbeski, Dorothy: *The True Story of Okee the Otter.* New York: Farrar Straus, 1967

OWL, Great-Horned

Bubo virginianus

North America

LIFESPAN: 15 to 30 years

ADULT SIZE: 18 to 23 inches

LIVING ARRANGEMENTS: large aviary with branches for perching and cover

ADULT DIET: live or fresh-killed rodents, day-old chicks, free choice daily; ground meat or beef heart occasionally

INFANT DIET: feed cut-up rat babies ("pinkies") during first week, head and stomach removed; during second and third weeks use older rats, head and stomachs and skin removed; after fourth week present whole mice or day-old chicks at least three times daily or 3 ounces raw beef heart with multivitamin supplement; when preparing for release introduce live rodents or small birds, and encourage bird to kill prey

PUBERTY: 2 to 3 years
CLUTCH SIZE: 2 to 4 eggs
INCUBATION: 5 weeks

Comments

Like other birds of prey, owls cannot be confined without a permit; nocturnal. IMPOSSIBLE

References

Austin, G. Ronald: *The World of the Great-Horned Owl.* Philadelphia: Lippincott, 1966

Service, William: *Owl.* New York: Knopf, 1961

Walden, Lewis Wayne: *The Book of Owls.* New York: Knopf, 1974

PARROT, African Gray

Psittacus erithacus

Africa

LIFESPAN: up to 50 years

ADULT SIZE: 14 to 15 inches

LIVING ARRANGEMENTS: wire cage large enough to allow flying; several perches; nest box; temperature range 70° to 80°F. (no drafts or sudden changes)

ADULT DIET: see Macaw

PUBERTY: 2 to 3 years

CLUTCH SIZE: 2 to 4 eggs

INCUBATION: 28 to 29 days

Comments

Good talkers but expensive; difficult to breed in captivity. DIFFICULT

References

Bates, Henry, and Busenbark, Robert: *Parrots and Related Birds.* Jersey City: TFH, n.d.

Petrak, Margaret L., ed.: *Diseases of Cage and Aviary Birds* (see Bibliography, "Books on Animal Care")

PEACOCK, Blue or Indian

Pavo cristatus

India and Ceylon

LIFESPAN: 15 to 20 years

ADULT SIZE: 30-inch body, 60-inch tail

LIVING ARRANGEMENTS: may be allowed to roam freely; shelter required in cold weather; temperature range varied

ADULT DIET: see Chicken

INFANT DIET: see Chicken

PUBERTY: 1 year

Comments
    CLUTCH SIZE: 4 to 8 eggs
    INCUBATION: about 28 days

    If free roaming must be introduced to area as chicks; may be very noisy. DIFFICULT

PHEASANT, Common Ringneck

Phasianus colchicus
Domestic (originally Asia)
LIFESPAN: 10 to 15 years
ADULT SIZE: 21 to 25 inches for females; 30 to 35 inches for males
LIVING ARRANGEMENTS: may be allowed to roam freely; if confined, allow 20-foot square floor space for each bird, with 4-foot walls; 1 cock to 6 hens; will require shelter in cold weather
ADULT DIET: chicken or turkey pellets; poultry grit, free choice
INFANT DIET: see Chicken
PUBERTY: 1 year
CLUTCH SIZE: 8 to 15 eggs
INCUBATION: 22 to 27 days

Comments
    Permit required for confinement; noisy. DIFFICULT

Reference
    Delacour, Jean: *Pheasants of the World.* New York: Scribner, 1951

PIG

Sus domestica
Domestic
LIFESPAN: 12 to 20 years
ADULT WEIGHT RANGE: 100 to 1000 pounds, depending on breed
LIVING ARRANGEMENTS: pen should be two to four times length of animal; sleeping box; temperature range 60° to 80°F. best, higher for young animals
ADULT DIET: commercial pig or hog feeds, table scraps; 1 pound for every 30 pounds of body weight once daily
INFANT DIET: cow's milk formula (with codliver oil, brewers' yeast, and minerals added) at 100°F. every hours for first 2 days; increase intervals thereafter and put on starter ration at one week; wean at 6 to 8 weeks to adult diet
PUBERTY: 4 to 7 months
BREEDING SEASON: throughout year, 18- or 24-day cycle
GESTATION: 112 to 115 days
LITTER SIZE: 4 to 12

NORMAL BODY TEMPERATURE: 102° to 103.6°F.
VACCINE RECOMMENDED: erysipelas

Comments

As housepets, pigs can be trained to perform simple commands; can be affectionate; grow very large. DIFFICULT

References

Ensminger, M.: *Swine Science.* Danville, Ill.: Interstate, 1970

National Research Council: *Swine Standards and Guidelines for the Breeding, Care, and Management of Laboratory Animals.* Washington, D.C.: National Academy of Science, 1971

PIGEON

Columba livia domesticus
Domestic
LIFESPAN: 5 to 15 years
ADULT SIZE: 8 to 14 inches
LIVING ARRANGEMENTS: in loft allow 3 cubic feet for each bird with nest boxes, perches, wood or cement flooring; temperature range varied
ADULT DIET: commercial pigeon grains, hulled seeds, cereal grains (wheat, yellow corn, peas); pigeon grit; salt; free choice (½ pound a week average)
INFANT DIET: pigeon "milk" regurgitated by adult birds cannot be replaced by substitutes; use evaporated milk mixed one to one with water and mix with equal parts of baby cereal or cooked arrowroot (1 heaping teaspoon boiled in 1 cup of water); feed with syringe every half hour; at 10 days introduce warmed mash or seeds and grains with milk until 5 weeks old; pigeons will consume about ½ pound every 4½ days until 8 weeks; consumption will decrease gradually at about 6 months
PUBERTY: 150 days (female)
CLUTCH SIZE: 2
INCUBATION: 17 to 19 days
NORMAL BODY TEMPERATURE: 107°F.

Comments

A good bird for hobbyists to show or race, but messy as a housepet. DIFFICULT

References

Allen, William H., Jr.: *How to Raise and Train Pigeons.* New York: Sterling, 1972

Levi, Wendell M.: *The Pigeon.* Sumter, S.C.: Levi, 1974

PORCUPINE, North American (or Quill Pig)

Erethizon dorsatum
North America
LIFESPAN: 5 to 10 years

ADULT WEIGHT RANGE: 20 to 35 pounds (29 inches long, minus tail)

LIVING ARRANGEMENTS: 4-foot-cube wire cage with sleeping box, bedding, and branches for climbing, shelves for resting; temperature range varied

ADULT DIET: nuts, grains (especially corn and crushed oats), celery, potatoes, lettuce, berries, bread, green bark-covered sticks, salt brick, and a small portion of chopped meat or canned dog food mixed with codliver oil; feed once daily 5 per cent of body weight

INFANT DIET: see Guinea Pig

PUBERTY: about 1 year

BREEDING SEASON: fall

GESTATION: about 7 months (delayed implantation)

LITTER SIZE: 1 to 4

Comments

Baby porcupines may be raised in captivity, with permit, but adults cannot be confined satisfactorily as pets. IMPOSSIBLE

References

Costello, David F.: *The World of the Porcupine.* Philadelphia: Lippincott, 1966

Crandall, Lee S.: *Management of Wild Mammals in Captivity* (see Bibliography, "Books on Animal Care")

Rood, Ronald: *How Do You Spank a Porcupine?* New York: Trident, 1969

Vandivert, Rita: *The Porcupine Known as J.R.* New York: Dodd Mead, 1959

PRAIRIE DOG, Black-Tailed

Cynomys ludovicianus

Western United States

LIFESPAN: 5 to 10 years

ADULT SIZE: 12 to 17 inches

LIVING ARRANGEMENTS: as large a cage or enclosure as possible with deep sand or earth for burrowing, series of nest boxes; sticks for gnawing; temperature range varied

ADULT DIET: raw vegetables, greens (grass trimmings, clover, alfalfa), crushed oats, canned dog food; 5 per cent of body weight once daily

INFANT DIET: see Woodchuck; weaned at 7 weeks, eyes open 33 to 37 days

PUBERTY: 1 year

BREEDING SEASON: spring

GESTATION: 27 to 33 days

LITTER SIZE: 5 to 10

Comments

Very difficult to keep successfully under home conditions; endangered species. IMPOSSIBLE

References

Costello, David F.: *The World of the Prairie Dog.* Philadelphia: Lippincott, 1970

Crandall, Lee S.: *Management of Wild Mammals in Captivity* (see Bibliography, "Books on Animal Care")

PYTHON, Reticulated

Python reticulatus

Southeast Asia

LIFESPAN: up to 20 years

ADULT SIZE: up to 30 feet

LIVING ARRANGEMENTS: see Boa Constrictor

ADULT DIET: see Boa Constrictor

PUBERTY: 4 to 5 years

CLUTCH SIZE: 12 to 100+ eggs

INCUBATION: 3 months at 77° to 86°F. (pythons will brood their eggs)

COMMON AILMENTS: see Garter Snake

Comments

Increasingly expensive to obtain because imported; grow very large. DIFFICULT

References

Smith, Hobart M.: *Snakes As Pets* (see Bibliography, "Books on Animal Care")

Vogel, Zdenek: *Reptiles and Amphibians* (see Bibliography, "Books on Animal Care")

RABBIT

Oryctolagus cuniculus

Domestic

LIFESPAN: 5 to 10 years

ADULT WEIGHT RANGE: 2 to 20 pounds, depending on breed

LIVING ARRANGEMENTS: wire hutch with 2-foot × 3-foot floor space and 18-inch walls for medium-size rabbit, with bedding or wire floor; nest box; temperature range varied

ADULT DIET: commercial pellets, alfalfa hay, greens, with treats of dry bread, carrots, ungreasy table scraps; free choice up to 10 per cent of body weight daily, with multivitamin supplements once a week in winter

INFANT DIET: Esbilac formula every 3 hours until eyes open, free choice (8 to 12 days); reduce feedings to four to five times daily and gradually introduce greens, apple, baby-rabbit pellets; taper off formula as rabbit starts self-feeding

PUBERTY: 5 to 6 months for female; 6 to 7 months for male

BREEDING SEASON: throughout year, at any time; ovulation follows mating

GESTATION: 30 to 32 days

LITTER SIZE: 1 to 16

NORMAL BODY TEMPERATURE: 100.6° to 103.4°, average 102.8°F.

COMMON AILMENTS: 1. Symptom—chronic diarrhea. Cause—coccidia or other intestinal parasites. Treatment—if coccidiosis, add sulfa-dimethoxine to drinking water; if intestinal nematodes, administer Thiabendazole (injection) 5 mg. per 100 gr. of body weight once weekly for 3 weeks

2. Symptom—overgrowth of incisor teeth. Cause—insufficient roughage. Treatment—trim teeth to allow for normal wear; add roughage to diet; add wood block to cage for chewing

3. Symptom—head tilt. Cause—trauma or middle-ear infection. Treatment—if trauma, none; if middle-ear infection, administer Gentamycin (injection) 5 mg. per 1000 gr. of body weight daily for 5 to 7 days

4. Symptoms—weight loss or poor weight gain, loss of strength or stiffness in rear legs. Cause—Vitamin E deficiency. Treatment—add vitamin E to diet 1 mg. per 1000 gr. of body weight orally until symptoms disappear

5. Symptoms—purulent nasal discharge and sneezing. Cause—bacterial infection. Treatment—administer Ampicillin orally 10 mg. per 1000 gr. of body weight twice daily for 7 to 10 days

6. Symptoms—protruding, reddened eye. Cause—abscess below eye. Treatment—lance and drain abscess; administer Gentamycin (injection) 5 mg. per 1000 gr. body weight daily for 5 to 7 days

7. Symptom—large growth or growths on body surface. Cause—abscess or insect larvae. Treatment—if abscess, lance and drain and use suitable antibiotic; if insect larvae, carefully remove with forceps and treat open wound

8. Symptom—grayish or yellowish crust on nose, face, ears, possibly in circular patterns. Cause—mange or fungus infection. Treatment—if mange, apply Benzylbenzoate lotion to ⅓ of body surface daily until whole body has been treated; repeat weekly for 2 to 3 weeks; if fungus, remove scales and crust and paint with iodine or Tresaderm solution

9. Symptom—lack of stool. Cause—impaction of colon. Treatment—feed only moist greens for 2 to 3 days

Comments

Will become very tame; may be taught to use litter box; affectionate but can scratch or bite if roughly handled; do not lift by ears; nocturnal. EASY

References

Committee on Animal Nutrition: *Nutrient Requirements of Rabbits.* Washington, D.C.: National Academy of Science, 1966

Hirschhorn, Howard: *All about Rabbits.* Jersey City: TFH, 1974

Templeton, George S.: *Domestic Rabbit Production.* New York: Scribners, 1975

RACCOON

Procyon lotor
North America
LIFESPAN: 10 to 13 years
ADULT WEIGHT RANGE: 12 to 30 pounds
LIVING ARRANGEMENTS: cage minimum 10-foot-square floor space; 8-foot walls; nest box, branches for climbing, toys; temperature range varied
ADULT DIET: balanced diet of dry dog food, vegetables, fruits, table scraps (not greasy or spicy), live rodents, breads, with regular codliver-oil supplements; feed twice daily no more than 10 per cent of body weight
INFANT DIET: Esbilac formula every 3 to 4 hours until eyes open; then five times daily until 4 weeks old; at 3 weeks introduce strained baby meats and strained vegetables to formula; at 4 weeks introduce crackers, egg, bran as solid food, reduce to 4 daily feedings; after 5 weeks gradually reduce amount of formula and increase solid food; feed three times daily as much as will be taken in ½ hour. Weaned at about 5 months
PUBERTY: 1 year or later
BREEDING SEASON: January to March
GESTATION: 63 days
LITTER SIZE: 1 to 6
NORMAL BODY TEMPERATURE: 100.6° to 102°F.
VACCINES RECOMMENDED: canine distemper, feline distemper, rabies (killed vaccines only)

Comments
Affectionate and responsive when young; may be trained to use litter pan; very inquisitive; be careful not to overfeed; becomes aggressive with maturity; seldom kept as pet after 1 or 2 years. DIFFICULT

References
Mathews, Dick: *Wild Animals As Pets* (see Bibliography, "Books on Animal Care")
North, Sterling: *Rascal.* New York: Dutton, 1963
———: *Raccoons Are the Brightest People.* New York: Dutton, 1966
Rue, Leonard Lee: *The World of the Raccoon.* Philadelphia: Lippincott, 1964

RAT

Rattus norvegicus
Domestic
LIFESPAN: 3 to 6 years
ADULT WEIGHT RANGE: 250 to 660 grams
LIVING ARRANGEMENTS: wire cage, minimum 2-foot square, 18-inch walls; wire floor, nest box with bedding, exercise equipment; temperature range 65° to 80°F.; 45 to 50 per cent humidity best
ADULT DIET: commercial pellets; free choice (12 to 15 grams daily)

REFERENCE CHARTS

INFANT DIET: evaporated milk mixed one to one with water and 1 drop pediatric vitamin every 3 hours until eyes open; four to five feedings daily until weaned at 21 days; introduce solid food at 12 days

PUBERTY: 90 to 100 days

BREEDING SEASON: throughout year

GESTATION: 20 to 22 days

LITTER SIZE: 8 to 12

NORMAL BODY TEMPERATURE: 98.6° to 100.6°, average 99.1°F.

COMMON AILMENTS: 1. Symptom—head tilt. Cause—middle-ear infection. Treatment—administer Gentamycin (injection) 1 mg. per 50 gr. of body weight daily for 5 to 7 days

2. Symptoms—runny nose, loss of hair on chin. Cause—pneumonitis. Treatment—administer Chloromycetin orally 2 mg. per 100 gr. of body weight 3 times daily for 5 to 7 days

3. Symptoms—dark eyes, crust around nose, diarrhea. Cause—bacterial infection. Treatment—administer Gentamycin (injection) 2 mg. per 100 gr. of body weight daily for 5 to 7 days; clean cage thoroughly

4. Symptom—swelling on any part of body. Cause—possible tumor. Treatment—surgical removal with Ketamine or gas anesthesia

5. Symptom—red and swollen tail or gangrene of tail. Cause—insufficient humidity. Treatment—amputation of tail anterior to constricted portion and increase humidity to 50 per cent; remove drafts

6. Symptom—overgrowth of incisor teeth. Cause—insufficient roughage. Treatment—trim teeth to allow for normal wear and add roughage to diet; add wood block to cage for chewing

7. Symptom—scaly patches on skin or gray warty lesions on tail, ears, nose. Cause—mange from mites. Treatment—administer Benzylbenzoate lotion or Ronnel dip; clean cage thoroughly

8. Symptom—chronic diarrhea. Cause—coccidia or intestinal parasites. Treatment—if coccidiosis, add sulfa-dimethoxine to drinking water; if intestinal nematodes, administer Thibendazole (injection) 5 mg. per 100 gr. of body weight once weekly for 3 weeks

Comments

Will become very tame if handled frequently; curious, trainable, affectionate; will bite if provoked. EASY

References

The Rat: A Study in Behavior. Chicago: Aldine Press, 1963

The UFAW Handbook on the Care and Management of Laboratory Animals (see Bibliography, "Books on Animal Care")

SALAMANDER, Tiger

Abystoma spp.

North America

LIFESPAN: 10 to 30 years

ADULT SIZE: 8 to 10 inches

LIVING ARRANGEMENTS: 5-gallon "woodland" aquarium tank (200 square inches for each adult) with several inches of "aged" water and rocks or earth and leaves, branches; temperature range 60° to 75°F. (will hibernate at 46° to 50°F.)

ADULT DIET: earthworms, crickets, mealworms

INFANT (TADPOLE) DIET: algae scraped from pond, cornmeal, mealworms, aquatic insects

PUBERTY: 1 year to 16 months

BREEDING SEASON: April to May

CLUTCH SIZE: 250 to 600 eggs

INCUBATION: 14 to 18 days

COMMON AILMENTS: see Frog

Comments

Fun to watch; not particularly responsive to humans except at feeding time. EASY

References

Bishop, Sherman Chauncey: *Handbook of Salamanders*. Ithaca, N.Y.: Comstock, 1943

Vogel, Zdenek: *Reptiles and Amphibians* (see Bibliography, "Books on Animal Care")

Zappler, George and Lisbeth: *Amphibians As Pets* (see Bibliography, "Books on Animal Care")

SHEEP

Ovis aries

Domestic

LIFESPAN: 15 to 20 years

ADULT WEIGHT RANGE: 100 to 200 pounds, depending on breed

LIVING ARRANGEMENTS: 10-foot-square indoor pen with bedding; or outdoor pasture, minimum ½ acre; temperature range varied

ADULT DIET: alfalfa hay, grain concentrate; 1 to 2 pounds of grain per 100 pounds of body weight daily; free choice hay

INFANT DIET: whole cow's milk with 1 egg yolk for every 8 ounces of body weight three or four times daily as much as animal will take; introduce solid food as soon as possible

PUBERTY: 5 to 7 months

BREEDING SEASON: throughout year, 14- to 20-day cycle

GESTATION: 144 to 152 days, average 148

NUMBER OF YOUNG: 1 to 3

NORMAL BODY TEMPERATURE: 100.9° to 103.8°F.

VACCINES RECOMMENDED: tetanus and clostridium

Comments

Lambs can be affectionate; adults tractable. DIFFICULT

References

Diggins, Donald V., and Bundy, Clarence E.: *Sheep Production.* New York: Prentice-Hall, n.d.

Jensen, Rue: *Diseases of Sheep.* Philadelphia: Lea & Febiger, 1974

SKUNK, Striped

Mephitis mephitis
North America
LIFESPAN: 5 to 6 years
ADULT WEIGHT RANGE: 3 to 10 pounds
LIVING ARRANGEMENTS: wire cage 5-foot × 4-foot floor space with 3-inch walls; wire floor; sleeping box with bedding; temperature range varied
ADULT DIET: canned or dry dog food, chicken necks, supplements of table scraps (ungreasy), fruits, and vegetables, codliver oil, and an occasional raw egg; feed once daily as much as skunk will consume in about 15 minutes
INFANT DIET: Esbilac formula five or six times daily until eyes open (about 3 weeks); introduce solid food (cereal mixed with formula) during fourth week and gradually increase solids, including meat, in three or four daily feedings; wean at 2 months; feed twice daily until 6 months; can be released at 3 months
PUBERTY: 1 year
BREEDING SEASON: late winter, early spring
GESTATION: 62 to 72 days
LITTER SIZE: 3 to 8
NORMAL BODY TEMPERATURE: 100° to 101°F.
VACCINES RECOMMENDED: canine distemper (killed virus), feline distemper (killed virus), and rabies

Comments

Skunks are relatively docile and may even become lethargic if allowed to overeat during fall months; can be kept intact but if scent glands are to be removed, surgery must be done before 6 weeks of age; descented skunks may not be released; permit required. DIFFICULT

Reference

Crandall, Lee S.: *Management of Wild Mammals in Captivity* (see Bibliography, "Books on Animal Care")

Mathews, Dick: *Wild Animals As Pets* (see Bibliography, "Books on Animal Care")

Verts, B. J.: *The Biology of the Striped Skunk.* Urbana, Ill.: University of Illinois Press, 1967

SNAKE, Common Garter

Thamnophis sirtalis
North America

LIFESPAN: 6 to 10 years

ADULT SIZE: 18 inches to 4 feet

LIVING ARRANGEMENTS: wooden or glass enclosure at least 1½ times the snake's length in one direction and half the snake's length in the other; 2 feet high with cover; shelter of rock or log and branches; water container large enough for complete immersion; temperature range 70° to 88°F.

ADULT DIET: earthworms for young snakes (15 inches or less); minnows, frogs, toads, salamanders, occasional small mice, strips of raw fish or raw meat every other day; larger snakes need feeding every 3 or 4 days; supplements of codliver oil or multivitamin once weekly

PUBERTY: 1½ to 2 years

CLUTCH SIZE: 3 to 85, average 15, young born alive

COMMON AILMENTS: 1. Symptom—purulent exudate in mouth and reddened sores around teeth. Cause—bacterial infection (mouth rot). Treatment—administer Gentamycin (injection) 1 mg. per 100 gr. of body weight every 3 days for 15 days; clean and flush mouth gently every 3 days and apply antibiotic liquid to sores

2. Symptom—gurgling, mucous discharge from nose or mouth. Cause—bacterial pneumonia. Treatment—administer Gentamycin (injection) 1 mg. per 100 gr. of body weight every 3 days for 15 days

3. Symptom—blistering or sores on ventral scales. Cause—bacterial skin infection. Treatment—administer Chloromycetin (injection) 5 mg. per 100 gr. of body weight daily for 14 days

4. Symptom—bloody diarrhea. Cause—usually amoebic dysentery. Treatment—administer 250 mg. Flagyl orally once; administer Gentamycin (injection) 1 mg. per 100 gr. every 3 days for 15 days

Comments

Once adjusted to confinement, these common small snakes can be easily kept. Will readjust readily if released in appropriate area. EASY

References

Smith, Hobart M.: *Snakes as Pets* (see Bibliography)

Vogel, Zdenek: *Reptiles and Amphibians* (see Bibliography)

SQUIRREL, Gray

Sciuris spp.

North America

LIFESPAN: 5 to 12 years

ADULT WEIGHT RANGE: 1 to 3 pounds

LIVING ARRANGEMENTS: cage with 3-foot × 3-foot floor space; 5 feet or room high with logs and branches for climbing; sleeping box with bedding; temperature range varied

ADULT DIET: nuts (unsalted, unshelled), corn, oats, greens, vegetables, eggs, sunflower seeds, oranges and grapes, dry dog food in milk; free choice (about a pound a week)

INFANT DIET: Esbilac formula every 2 hours during day with 1 nighttime feeding until eyes open, then every 2 to 3 hours during day; when eyes open (about 16 days) increase formula at each feeding and include baby cereal (high protein) and introduce solids—fruits, lettuce; as solid food taken, decrease formula feedings to once daily and increase solids until squirrel rejects formula. Can be released when it cracks a nut by itself

PUBERTY: 12 months
BREEDING SEASON: December to January, March to June
GESTATION: 40 to 44 days
LITTER SIZE: 1 to 4

Comments

Young squirrels can be very affectionate but gradually become aggressive as maturity approaches and will bite if startled; older squirrels may be tame as free-roaming pets. DIFFICULT

References

Collett, Rosemary L.: *My Orphans of the Wild* (see Bibliography, "Books on Animal Care")

Fairbairn, Douglas: *A Squirrel Forever*. New York: Simon & Schuster, 1974

SWAN, Mute

Cygnus olor
Domestic

LIFESPAN: 15 to 20 years
ADULT SIZE: 58 inches
LIVING ARRANGEMENTS: 6-foot × 12-foot minimum pond, 2 to 4 feet deep, with 4-foot-square nesting boxes; temperature range varied, but shelter required when water frozen
ADULT DIET: game-bird diet or turkey pellets with supplements of greens (lawn trimmings, lettuce); poultry grit; free choice
INFANT DIET: chicken starter, with supplements of hard-boiled egg yolk, chopped lettuce; may be put outside at 2 to 3 weeks and grit introduced
PUBERTY: 3 years
CLUTCH SIZE: 3 to 8
INCUBATION: 35 to 37 days

Comments

These are the white swans commonly seen in parks; although they are graceful to watch, they are quarrelsome and may kill ducklings and other waterfowl; may also be aggressive toward humans, especially children. DIFFICULT

Reference

Scott, Peter: *The Swans*. London: Michael Joseph, 1972

TERRAPIN, or Water Turtle

Chrysemys spp., *Pseudemys* spp.
New world

LIFESPAN: up to 50 years

ADULT SIZE: 5 to 10 inches

LIVING ARRANGEMENTS: 3- to 5-gallon tank for 2 young turtles with 1 or 2 inches of "aged" water and gravel and rocks for islands; temperature range 75° to 90°F.

ADULT DIET: live crickets, earthworms, mealworms, canned or semi-moist dog food, with supplements of aquatic plants, calcium, vitamins; free choice twice a week (feed in water and do not let uneaten food remain more than a few hours)

INFANT DIET: mash of 1 tablespoon of chopped fish, beef, lettuce leaves every other day

PUBERTY: 5 to 6 years

CLUTCH SIZE: 4 to 12 eggs

INCUBATION: 45 to 75 days at 85°F.

COMMON AILMENTS: 1. Symptom—swollen eyes. Cause—usually vitamin A deficiency. Treatment—administer vitamin A palmitat orally 1000 to 2000 units daily for 1 week; change to proper diet

2. Symptom—soft or deformed shell. Cause—calcium deficiency. Treatment—add calcium to diet

3. Symptom—shell rot or reddened shell with open lesions. Cause—bacterial infection. Treatment—administer Gentamycin (injection) 1 mg. per 200 gr. of body weight every third day for 15 days; sanitize cage and maintain cleaner conditions

4. Symptom—large swelling on neck. Cause—usually iodine deficiency (goiter). Treatment—place on adequate diet

Comments

The painted turtle *(Chrysemys picta)* and red-eared terrapin *(Chrysemys scripta elegans)* are common American varieties in this category of chelonians; turtles under 4 inches in diameter can no longer be sold commercially. EASY

References

Burt, Charles E., and Landry, Walter D.: *My Baby Turtle: The Biology and Care of the Young Terrapins of the United States.* Topeka: Quiriva, 1954

Carr, Archie Fairly: *Handbook of Turtles.* Ithaca, N.Y.: Comstock, 1952

Ernest, Carl H., and Barbour, Roger W.: *Turtles of the United States.* Lexington, Ky: University of Kentucky, 1972

Pope, Clifford H.: *Turtles of the United States and Canada.* New York: Knopf, 1939

Pritchard, Peter Charles Howard: *Living Turtles of the World.* Jersey City: TFH, 1967

TOAD, Common American

Bufo americanus

LIFESPAN: 20 to 30 years

ADULT SIZE: 4 to 4½ inches

LIVING ARRANGEMENTS: 5- or 10-gallon tank with woodland climate; sizable water container, shelter of leaves, logs; temperature range 68° to 78°F.

ADULT DIET: live earthworms, mealworms, canned dog food (rarely), crickets, grasshoppers, any large insects

INFANT (TADPOLE): DIET: see: Leopard Frog. Also high-protein cereal

PUBERTY: 3 to 4 years

BREEDING SEASON: spring

CLUTCH SIZE: 4000 to 12,000 eggs laid in long jelly-like tubes

INCUBATION: 5 to 12 days; metamorphosis in 2 months

COMMON AILMENTS: see Leopard Frog

Comments

EASY

References

Vogel, Zdenek: *Reptiles and Amphibians* (see Bibliography, "Books on Animal Care")

Zappler, George and Lisbeth: *Amphibians As Pets* (see Bibliography, "Books on Animal Care")

TORTOISE, or Land Turtle

Geochelone spp.

Worldwide, warm countries

LIFESPAN: up to 100 years

ADULT SIZE: varies according to species

LIVING ARRANGEMENTS: 3- to 5-gallon "woodland" tank for 2 young turtles with leaves, branches, bark, and enough water to allow turtle to submerge itself; temperature range 77° to 85°F.

ADULT DIET: canned dog food, lettuce, cabbage, dandelions, clover, grass, chopped carrot and cauliflower, chopped liver and earthworms; free choice every other day when young, twice a week when more than 4 inches in diameter; supplements of calcium and multivitamins

PUBERTY: 7 to 20 years

CLUTCH SIZE: 6 to 10 eggs

INCUBATION: 90 to 120 days at 85°F. (Some require up to 300 days.)

COMMON AILMENTS: see ailments 1, 2, and 4 under Terrapin

1. Symptom—swelling at side of neck from ear canal. Cause—abscess or insect larvae. Treatment—if abscess, lance and drain and administer Gentamycin (injection) 1 mg. per 200 gr. of body weight every 3 days for 15 days; if insect larvae, remove and treat open wound

2. Symptom—loss of body weight. Cause—malnutrition. Treatment—place on proper diet

Comments

Baby turtles under 4 inches in diameter may no longer be sold commercially; grown turtles may behave as free-roaming pets if fed regularly. EASY

References

See Terrapin

TOUCAN

Ramphastos spp.

Central and South America

LIFESPAN: 10 to 14 years

ADULT SIZE: 12 to 18 inches

LIVING ARRANGEMENTS: wire cage large enough to allow bird to spread wings; perches and ladders for exercise; temperature range 60° to 80°F.

ADULT DIET: commercial feed, Mellins food (dried mix available at health stores), evaporated milk mixed with honey; sweet fruit

INFANT DIET: mash of adult-diet food with supplements of mealworms and mashed hard-boiled egg

PUBERTY: 2 to 3 years

CLUTCH SIZE: 2 to 4 eggs

INCUBATION: 16 days

Comments

These beautifully beaked birds are colorful but messy to keep; they do not talk but will make considerable noise. DIFFICULT

Reference

Petrak, Margaret L., ed. *Diseases of Cage and Aviary Birds* (see Bibliography, "Books on Animal Care")

WOLF

Canis lupis

Worldwide

LIFESPAN: 12 to 16 years

ADULT WEIGHT RANGE: 50 to 125 pounds

LIVING ARRANGEMENTS: as large a run as possible; sleeping house or box with bedding; temperature range varied

ADULT DIET: raw meat, chicken necks, dry dog food, with supplements of bonemeal and codliver oil; feed once daily up to 5 per cent of body weight

INFANT DIET: Esbilac formula every 4 hours; when animal begins to lap (at about 4 weeks), add egg and baby cereal to formula; at 2 months introduce raw meat and reduce formula, adding multivitamins and calcium lactate, feeding three times a day; at 4 months reduce to two feedings until full grown

PUBERTY: 2 years

BREEDING SEASON: January to March

GESTATION: 60 to 63 days

LITTER SIZE: 1 to 13, average 3

NORMAL BODY TEMPERATURE: 100° to 102°F.

VACCINES RECOMMENDED: canine distemper and rabies

Comments

May be very responsive as cub if hand reared but can never be completely predictable as maturity approaches; requires daily handling to remain tame; endangered. IMPOSSIBLE

References

Mech, David L.: *The Wolf: Ecology and Behavior of an Endangered Species.* Garden City, N.Y.: Natural History Press, 1970

Mowat, Farley: *Never Cry Wolf.* Boston: Little, Brown, 1963

Mutter, Russell J., and Pimlott, Douglas H.: *The World of the Wolf.* Philadelphia: Lippincott, 1968

WOODCHUCK (Groundhog)

Marmota monax

Eastern North America

LIFESPAN: 5 to 10 years

ADULT WEIGHT RANGE: 10 to 40 pounds

LIVING ARRANGEMENTS: very strong cage (chain-link) with concrete walls and floor; straw bedding and sleeping box; temperature range varied

ADULT DIET: rabbit pellets, vegetables, fruit, bread, milk, nuts (unsalted, unshelled); feed up to 10 per cent of body weight once daily

INFANT DIET: Esbilac formula every 4 hours except at night until eyes open (at about 4 weeks); reduce feedings to 5 a day, and at 6 weeks introduce cereal into formula (animal should lap from a bowl at this point) and gradually offer solid food at about 2 months; eliminate formula at 3 months

PUBERTY: 1 year

BREEDING SEASON: early spring

GESTATION: 1 month

LITTER SIZE: 2 to 5

BODY TEMPERATURE: 99° to 100°F.

Comments

Not particularly responsive; may be aggressive as an adult; naturally sluggish in winter. IMPOSSIBLE

References

Crandall, Lee S.: *Management of Wild Mammals in Captivity* (see Bibliography, "Books on Animal Care")

Schoonmaker, Walter J.: *The World of the Woodchuck.* Philadelphia: Lippincott, 1966

BIBLIOGRAPHY

General Books

Altmann, Stuart A., ed.: *Social Communication among Primates.* Chicago: University of Chicago Press, 1967, 1974.

Bates, Marston: *A Jungle in the House: Essays in Natural and Unnatural History.* New York: Walker, 1970.

Bellairs, Angus: *The Life of Reptiles.* 2 vols. London: Weidenfeld, 1969.

Borror, Donald J., and White, Richard E.: *A Field Guide to the Insects of America North of Mexico.* Boston: Houghton Mifflin, 1974.

Bourliere, Francois: *The Natural History of Mammals: A Field Outline.* 3rd ed. New York: Knopf, 1961.

Burt, William Henry, and Grossenheider, Richard P.: *A Field Guide to the Mammals: Field Marks of All Species Found North of the American Boundary.* Boston: Houghton Mifflin, 1964.

Caras, Roger: *Dangerous to Man.* 2nd ed. New York: Holt, 1976.

Carr, Archie Fairly: *The Reptiles.* New York: Time, Inc. 1963.

Carson, Gerald: *Men, Beasts, and Gods: A History of Cruelty and Kindness to Animals.* New York: Scribners, 1972.

Case, Marshall T.: *Look What I Found!* Riverside, Conn.: Chatman, 1971. (Junior.)

Chrystie, Frances: *Pets.* Rev. ed. Boston: Little, Brown, 1974. (Junior.)

Cochran, Doris Mabel: *Living Amphibians of the World.* Garden City, N.Y.: Doubleday, 1961. (Junior.)

Cohen, Daniel: *Watchers in the Wild.* The New Science of Ethology. Boston: Little, Brown, 1971. (Junior.)

Conant, Roger: *A Field Guide to Reptiles and Amphibians.* Boston: Houghton Mifflin, 1958.

Crook, John H., ed.: *Social Behavior in Birds and Mammals.* New York: Academic Press, 1970.

Dembeck, Hermann: *Animals and Men.* Garden City, N.Y.: Natural History Press, 1965.

Dorst, Jean: *The Life of Bird.* 2 vols. New York: Columbia University Press, 1974.

Durrell, Gerald: *My Family and Other Animals.* New York: Viking, 1957.

———: *Birds, Beasts, and Relatives.* New York: Viking, 1969.

———: *Catch Me a Colobus.* New York: Viking, 1972.

———: *A Bevy of Beasts.* New York: Simon & Schuster, 1973.

Eisenberg, J. F., and Dillon, Wilton S., eds.: *Man and Beast: Comparative Social Behavior.* Washington, D.C.: Smithsonian, 1971.

Fitch, Henry S.: *Reproductive Cycles in Lizards and Snakes.* Lawrence: University of Kansas Museum of Natural History, 1970.

Forshaw, Joseph M.: *Parrots of the World.* Garden City, N.Y.: Doubleday, 1973.

Fox, M. W., ed. *The Wild Canids: Their Systematics, Behavioral Ecology and Evolution.* Princeton: Van Nostrand, 1975.

Goin, Coleman, J. and Olive B.: *Introduction to Herpetology.* 2nd ed. San Francisco: W. H. Freeman, 1971.

Heidiger, H.: *Wild Animals in Captivity.* New York: Dover, 1964.

Hughes, John: *The Animals Came In.* New York: Taplinger, 1971.

Hunt, John: *A World Full of Animals.* New York: McKay, 1969.

Leslie, Robert Franklin: *Wild Pets.* New York: Crown, 1970.

Levinson, Boris M.: *Pets and Human Development.* Springfield, Ill.: C. C. Thomas, 1972.

Lorenz, Konrad: *King Solomon's Ring.* New York: Crowell, 1952, and New American Library, 1972.

———: *Studies in Human and Animal Behavior.* 2 vols. Cambridge, Mass.: Harvard University Press, 1970.

Marshall, Alan John: *Biology and Comparative Physiology of Birds.* 2 vols. New York: Academic Press, 1960, 1961.

Matthiessen, Peter: *Wildlife in America.* New York: Viking, 1959.

Oliver, James A.: *The Natural History of North American Amphibians and Reptiles.* Princeton: Van Nostrand, 1955.

Palmer, Ralph S.: *Handbook of North American Birds.* 2 vols. New Haven: Yale University Press, 1962.

Peterson, Roger Tory: *A Field Guide to the Birds.* Boston: Houghton Mifflin, 1947, 1969.

Pope, Clifford H.: *The Giant Snakes: The Natural History of the Boa Constrictor, the Anaconda, and the Largest Pythons.* New York: Knopf, 1961.

Porter, Kenneth R.: *Herpetology.* Philadelphia: W. B. Saunders, 1972.

Robbins, C. S. et al.: *Birds of North America: A Guide to Field Identification.* New York: Golden Books, 1966.

Rood, Ronald: *Animals Nobody Loves.* Brattleboro: Stephen Greene Press, 1971.

Schmidt, Karl P., and David, D. Dwight: *Field Book of Snakes of the United States and Canada.* New York: Putnam, 1941.

Schmidt, Karl P., and Inger, Robert F.: *Living Reptiles of the World.* Garden City, N.Y.: Doubleday, 1957.

Southwick, Charles H. *Animal Aggression.* Princeton: Van Nostrand, 1970.

Stebbins, Robert Cyril: *A Field Guide to Western Reptiles and Amphibians.* Boston: Houghton Mifflin, 1966.

Szasz, Kathleen: *Petishism: Pet Cults of the Western World.* New York: Holt, 1969.

Terres, John K.: *Songbirds in Your Garden.* 2nd ed. New York: Crowell, 1968.

Tinbergen, Niko, and the Editors of Life Magazine: *Animal Behavior.* New York: Time, 1965.

Van Tyne, J., and Berger, A. J.: *Fundamentals of Ornithology.* New York: Dover, 1971.
Von Frisch, Karl: *The Dancing Bees: An Account of the Life Senses of the Honeybee.* New York: Harcourt, 1966.
Wilson, Edward Osborne: *The Insect Societies.* Cambridge, Mass.: Belknap Press of Harvard University, 1971.
Zeuner, F. E.: *A History of Domesticated Animals.* New York: Harper, 1964.

Books on Animal Care

American Game Bird Breeders Cooperative Federation: *Wild Waterfowl and Its Captive Management.* 2 vols. Salt Lake City: Wildlife Publications, n.d.
Animals in the Classroom: A Guide for Teachers. New York: McGraw-Hill, 1970.
Arbib, Robert: *Hungry Bird Book.* New York: Ballantine, 1972.
Asdell, Sydney Arthur: *Patterns of Mammalian Reproduction.* Ithaca, N.Y.: Comstock, 1964.
Axelrod, Herbert, and Burgess, Warren: *Finch and Soft-Billed Birds.* Jersey City: TFH Publications, n.d.
Axelrod, Herbert, and Schultz, Leonard P.: *Handbook of Tropical Aquarium Fishes.* Jersey City: TFH Publications, 1970.
Axelrod, Herbert, and Shaw, Susan: *Breeding Aquarium Fishes.* Jersey City: TFH Publications, 1971.
Bates, Henry, and Busenbark, Robert: *Finch and Soft-Billed Birds.* Jersey City: TFH Publications, n.d.
———: *Parrots and Related Birds.* Jersey City: TFH Publications, n.d.
Beveridge, W. I., ed.: *Breeding Primates.* White Plains, N.Y.: Phiebig, 1972.
Brown, Vinson: *How to Make a Miniature Zoo.* Rev. ed. Boston: Little, Brown, 1957. (Junior.)
Christopher, William Miller, and West, Geoffrey P.: *Encyclopedia of Animal Care.* 7th ed. Baltimore: Williams and Wilkins, 1964.
Cole, H. H., and Cubs, P. T., eds.: *Reproduction in Domestic Animals.* New York: Academic Press, 1969.
Collett, Rosemary K.: *My Orphans of the Wild.* Philadelphia: Lippincott, 1974.
Conalty, M. L., ed.: *Husbandry of Laboratory Animals.* New York: Academic Press, 1967.
Crandall, Lee. S.: *Management of Wild Mammals in Captivity.* Chicago: University of Chicago Press, 1964.
Crawford, M. A., ed.: *Comparative Nutrition of Wild Animals.* London: Zoological Society, 1968.
Current Veterinary Therapy: *Small Animal Practice.* Philadelphia: W. B. Saunders, 1975.
Davis, John W., et al., eds.: *Infectious and Parasitic Diseases of Wild Birds.* Ames: Iowa State University Press, 1971.
Delacour, Jean: *The Waterfowl of the World.* 4 vols. New York: Arco, 1974.
Dennis, John V.: *A Complete Guide to Bird Feeding.* New York: Knopf, 1975.

De Rochemont, Richard: *The Pets Cookbook: A Layman's Comprehensive Guide to the Feeding of Dogs, Cats, Bird, Fish, and Odd Animals Around the House.* New York: Knopf, 1964.

Ensminger, M. E.: *Animal Science.* 6th ed. Danville, Ill.: Interstate, 1969.

Ensminger, M. E.: *Poultry Science.* Danville, Ill.: Interstate, 1971.

Frye, Frederic L.: *Husbandry, Medicine, and Surgery in Captive Reptiles.* Santa Barbara: American Veterinary Publications, 1974.

Guthrie, Esther L.: *Home Book of Animal Care.* New York: Harper, 1966.

Hafez, E. S. E.: *Reproduction in Farm Animals.* 3rd ed. Philadelphia: Lea and Febiger, 1974.

Hafez, E. S. E., ed.: *Animal Growth and Nutrition.* Philadelphia: Lea and Febiger, 1969.

Hafez, E. S. E., ed.: *The Behavior of Domestic Animals.* Baltimore: Williams and Wilkins, 1969.

Harris, Robert S. *Feeding and Nutrition of Non-Human Primates.* New York: Academic Press, 1970.

Heinz Handbook of Nutrition. New York: McGraw-Hill, 1965.

Hickman, Mae, and Guy, Maxine: *Care of the Wild Feathered and Furred: A Guide to Wildlife Handling and Care.* Santa Cruz, Calif.: Unity Press, 1973.

Hofstad, M. S., ed.: *Diseases of Poultry.* Ames: Iowa State University Press, 1972.

Johnson, A. A., and Payne, W. H.: *Ornamental Waterfowl: A Guide to Their Care and Breeding.* London: Witherby, 1957.

Kauffeld, Carl F.: *Snakes: The Keeper and the Kept.* Garden City, N.Y.: Doubleday, 1969.

Kingsbury, John M.: *Deadly Harvest: A Guide to Common Poisonous Plants.* New York: Holt, 1965.

Kramer, Jack: *Pets and Plants in Miniature Gardens: How to Create Woodland, Desert, Marshland, or Tropical Worlds.* Garden City, N.Y.: Doubleday, 1973.

Low, Rosemary: *Aviary Birds.* South Brunswick, N.J.: A. S. Barnes, 1970.

Manual for Laboratory Animal Care. St. Louise Ralston Purina, 1961.

Marshall, A. J.: *Biology and Comparative Physiology of Birds.* 2 vols. New York: Academic Press, 1960-61.

Martin, Alexander; Zim, Herbert S.; and Nelson, Arnold L.: *American Wildlife and Plants: A Guide to Wildlife Food Habits.* New York: Dover, 1951.

Mathews, Dick: *Wild Animals as Pets.* Garden City, N.Y.: Doubleday, 1971.

McCoy, Joseph J.: *Our Captive Animals.* New York: Seabury, 1971.

McDonald, Peter, et al.: *Animal Nutrition.* 2nd ed. New York: Hafner, 1973.

Merck Veterinary Manual. 4th ed. Rahway, N.J.: Merck, 1973.

Merne, Oscar J.: *Ducks, Geese, and Swans.* New York: St. Martin's, 1974.

Morse, Roger, ed.: *The Complete Guide to Beekeeping.* New York: Dutton, 1974.

National Research Council: *Amphibians—Standards and Guidelines for the Breeding, Care, and Management of Laboratory Animals.* Washington, D.C.: National Academy of Science, 1974.

National Research Council: *Non-Human Primates—Standards and Guidelines for the Breeding, Care, and Management of Laboratory Animals.* Washington,

D.C.; National Academy of Science, 1973.

National Wildlife Federation: *Gardening with Wildlife: A Comprehensive Guide to Attracting and Enjoying Fascinating Creatures in Your Backyard.* Washington, D.C.: National Wildlife Federation, 1974.

Petrak, Margaret L., ed.: *Diseases of Cage and Aviary Birds.* Philadelphia: Lea and Febiger, 1969.

Pillsbury, Ernest Walker: *First Aid and Care of Small Animals.* New York: Animal Welfare Institute, 1955.

Poultryman's Manual: Flock Management and Chicken Diseases. New York: Springer, 1957.

Reichenback-Klinke, H., and Elkan, E.: *The Principal Diseases of the Lower Vertebrates: Fishes, Amphibians, and Reptiles.* 3 vols. Jersey City: TFH Publications, 1972.

Riccuitti, Edward R.: *Shelf Pets; How to Take Care of Small Wild Animals.* New York: Harper, 1971. (Junior.)

Rogers, H. Cyril H.: *Encyclopedia of Cage and Aviary Birds.* New York: Macmillan, 1975.

Rood, Ronald: *May I Keep This Clam, Mother? It Followed Me Home.* New York: Simon and Schuster, 1973.

Rutgers, Abram, and Norris, K. A., eds.: *Encyclopedia of Aviculture.* 2 vols. London: Blandford, 1971.

Simon, Seymour: *Pets in a Jar.* New York: Viking, 1975. (Junior.)

Smith, Hobart M.: *Snakes as Pets.* Jersey City: TFH Publications, 1965. (Junior.)

Snediger, Robert: *Our Small Native Animals: Their Habits and Care.* New York: Dover, 1963.

Spotte, Stephen M.: *Fish and Invertebrate Culture: Water Management in Closed Systems.* New York: Wiley, 1970.

———: *Marine Aquarium Keeping: The Science, the Animals, and the Art.* New York: Wiley, 1973.

Stroud, Robert: *Stroud Bird Disease.* Jersey City: TFH Publications, 1943.

The UFAW Handbook on the Care and Management of Laboratory Animals. Edinborough and London: E. & S. Livingstone, 1966.

Van Duijn, C.: *Diseases of Fish.* 3rd ed. Springfield, Ill.: C. C. Thomas, 1973.

Villiard, Paul: *Insects as Pets.* Garden City, N.Y.: Doubleday, 1973. (Junior.)

Villiard, Paul: *Birds as Pets.* Garden City, N.Y.: Doubleday, 1974. (Junior.)

Vogel, Zdenek: *Reptiles and Amphibians: Their Care and Handling.* New York: Viking, 1964.

Ward, Peter, and Batt, Bruce D. J.: *Propagation of Captive Waterfowl.* Washington, D.C.: Delta Waterfowl Research Station, North American Wildlife Foundation, 1973.

Weber, William, D.V.M.: *Wild Orphan Babies: Mammals and Birds. Caring For Them/Setting Them Free.* New York: Holt, 1975. (Junior.)

Weideger, Paul, and Thorsten, Geraldine: *Travel with Your Pet.* New York: Simon and Schuster, 1973.

Whitney, Robert A.; Johnson, Donald J.; and Cole, William C.: *Laboratory Primate Handbook.* New York: Academic Press, 1973.

Zappler, George and Lisbeth: *Amphibians as Pets.* Garden City, N.Y.: Doubleday, 1973.

Journals and Periodicals

MAMMALS

American Cat Fanciers Association Bulletin (5395 South Miller, Littleton, Colo. 80123).
American Dairy Goat Association Bulletin (P.O. Box 186, Spindale, N.C. 28160).
American Goat Society (1606 Colorado, Manhattan, Kan. 66502).
American Horseman (257 Park Avenue South, New York, N.Y. 10016).
American Kennel Club Gazette (51 Madison Ave., New York, N.Y. 10010).
American Rabbit Journal (Warrenton, Mo. 63383).
Cats Magazine (2900 Jefferson Ave., Washington, Pa. 15301).
Chinchilla Breeders Journal (Coarsegold, Calif.).
Chronicle of the Horse (Middleburg, Va. 22117).
National Association of Animal Breeders A.I. Digest (512 Cherry, P.O. Box 1033, Columbia, Mo. 65201).
Popular Dogs (1 Park Avenue, New York, N.Y. 10016).
Practical Horseman (Philadelphia, Pa.).
Sheep and Goat Raiser (San Angelo, Tex.).
Simian (510 Lowell St., Wakefield, Mass. 01880).
Western Horseman (3850 N. Nevada, Colorado Springs, Colo. 80901).

BIRDS

American Birds (Audubon), (950 Third Ave., New York, N.Y. 10022).
American Cage-Bird Magazine (3449 North Western Ave., Chicago, Ill. 60618).
American Pigeon Journal (Warrenton, Mo. 63383).
American Racing Pigeon News (2421 Old Arch Rd., Norristown, Pa. 19401).
Avicultural Bulletin (4729 Norwich Ave., Sherman Oaks, Calif. 91403).
British Ornithologists Club Bulletin (Hon. Treasurer P. Tate, c/o Messrs Stockton & Lazarus, 3 London Wall Buildings, London EC 2, England).
Cage Birds (Dorset House, Stamford St., London, England).
Canary Journal (Rollers Fanciers Corp., 2002 South 17th St., East Salt Lake City, Ut.).
Canary World and Cage Bird Digest (Lecanto, Fla.).
Game Bird Breeders, Pheasant Fanciers and Aviculturists Gazette (Allen Publishing Co., 1328 Allen Park Drive, Salt Lake City, Ut.).
Modern Game Breeding (300 Front Street, Boiling Springs, Pa. 17007).
National Pigeon News (Rte. 4, P.O. Box 83, Watertown, Wisc.).

REPTILES AND AMPHIBIANS

COPEIA (American Society of Ichthyoloists and Herpetologists, Division of Reptiles and Amphibians, U.S. National Museum, Washington, D.C., 20560).
Herpetologica (The Herpetologists League, Frederick B. Turner, Laboratory of Nuclear Medicine and Radiation Biology, University of California, Los Angeles, Calif. 90024).
Journal of Herpetology (Museum of Natural History, University of Kansas, Lawrence, Kan. 66044).

FISH

The Aquarium (87 Route 17, Maywood, N.J. 07605).
The Marine Aquarist (P.O. Box 362, Bayside, N.Y. 11361).
Tropical Fish Hobbyist (TFH Publications, 245 Cornelison Ave., Jersey City, N.J. 07002).
Tropical Fish World (Tropical Fish Publishing Co., 509 Fifth Ave., New York, N.Y. 10017).

INDEX

Abyssinian cat, 35
Abyssinian guinea pig, 26
Accessories, grooming, 249–251
Adamson, Joy, 147
Additives, food, 233–234
Adjustment and responsibility, 190–210:
 to the animal, 190–193; care and attention, 190–191; with other animals, 192–193; with other humans, 192; space arrangements, 191–192, 213–214
 in the household, 193–207; surgical alteration, 205–207; taming, 193–197; training, 197–203; training equipment, 203–205
 for special occasions, 207–210; boarding kennels, 209; care with another person, 209–210; when traveling, 208–209
 See also Living with pets
Adult wild animals, 139–140
Affection (between man and animal), 210–212: behavioral changes and, 212; special relationship of, 210–211; withdrawal of, 209–210
African gray parrot, 131
Amazon parrot, 132–133
American canary, 47
American chameleon, 62
American domestic flight pigeon, 108
American Kennel Club, 84
American Society for the Prevention of Cruelty to Animals (ASPCA), 90, 176, 270
Amphibians: easy kinds of, 53–68; feeding, 236; living quarters for, 222–225; water requirements, 238
Anaconda snake, 59
Andersen, Hans Christian, 188
Angora cat, 35
Angora goat, 97
Angora rabbit, 29
Animal bites, 272–274: diseases transmitted by, 273–274; first-aid treatment for, 272
Anoles, 62
Anthrax, 274
Ants, 69–70
Aquaria and vivaria, 222–225: covering top of, 223; gallon glass jar, 223; glass tanks, 222; lights and lighting, 222–223; plants, 75–76; simulating environment in, 223–225; size of, 223
Aquatic frogs, 66
Araucana chicken, 101
Argentine pygmy horse, 94
Armadillo, 115–117
Asian walking catfish, 306
Asses, 94
Attack dogs, 84
Australian parrot, 138
Aviaries, indoor or outdoor, 220–221

INDEX

375

Badger, 145
Bantam chicken, 101
Bathing and grooming, 248–249
Bears, 157
Beavers, 143–144
Bee Bee parrot, 52–53
Bees, 110–112
Belgian hare, 29
Bengalese finch, 48
Bird cages, 219–222: fixtures in, 219; indoor or outdoor, 220–221; privacy area, 219; sizes of, 219–220
Birdhouses, 169
Birdman of Alcatraz (Robert Strond), 50
Birds: breeding, 290–294; difficult kinds of, 101–110; as easy pets, 40–53; feeding (free-roaming), 167–169, 238–241; grooming, 251; impossible kinds of, 164–169; injured, caring for, 165–167; living quarters for, 219–221; oil-damaged, 166–167; wild species, 130–134
Bishop finch, 49
Black bear, 157
Black tegu lizard, 62–63
Black-footed ferret, 138, 144, 145
Black-tailed prairie dog, 144
Blake, Amanda, 135
Boa constrictor, 58–59
Boarding kennels, 209
Bobcats, 150–151
Born Free (Adamson), 147
Box turtle, 57
Brahma chicken, 101
Brazilian woolly monkey, 138
Breeders, 178–180: buying from, 178–180; organization for, 178–179; types of, 179; *see also* Pet shops
Breeding, 277–294: birds, 290–294; mammals, 282–290; reptiles, insects, and fish, 294; versus neutering, 277–279
Brine shrimp, 78–79
British blue cat, 35
Brucellosis, 269, 274

Budgerigars, 50–51
Burial grounds, 297
Burmese cat, 35
Burmese python, 58
Butterflies, 71–72

Cacomistles, 127–130
Cadillac Pet Foods, 234
Cages, 217–221: for birds, 219–221; for small mammals, 217–219
Caiman, 163–164
Canaries, 47–48
Canine distemper, 268
Canned pet foods, 233–234
Capuchin monkey, 160
Caras, Roger, 140
Cardinal finch, 49
Cardinals, 167
Care of pets, 213–256: exercise, 252–256; food and feeding, 225–241; grooming, 241–252; in health and sickness, 257–276; living quarters, 213–225
Caribbean finch, 138
Carolina anole, 62
Caterpillars, 72
Cats, 33–40: domestication of, 34; species of, 34–36; superstitions about, 34; training process, 202
Cat-scratch fever, 273
C/D (cat food), 234
Chameleon, 62
Cheetahs, 149
Chickadees, 167
Chickens, 101–103
Chimpanzees, 159, 162–163
Chinchilla rabbit, 29
Chinchillas, 25–26
Chinese pheasant, 138
Chipmunk, 118–120
Chlorine in water, 238
Choking, first-aid treatment for, 272
Civet cat, 127
Coati-mundis, 126
Coats, for pets, 204
Cochin chicken, 101

INDEX

376

Cockatiels, 51–52
Cockatoos, 132
"Cold-blooded," 54
Combing or brushing, 245–246, 247, 248
Commercial pet foods, 232–234: canned, 233–234; dry packaged, 232–233
Communication, animal: gestures, 185–186, 187; imprinting theory of, 188; instinct theory of, 188–189; laboratory research in, 186; social interaction, 187–188; tone of voice, 187; words and concepts, 186
Coops, chicken, 102–103
Copperhead snake, 62
Cordon blue finch, 49
Corn snake, 59
Cosmetic surgery, 207
Costa Rican spider monkey, 138
Cottonmouth snake, 62
Cougar, see Mountain lion
Cows, 99–100
Coyotes, 153–155
Cremation, 297
Crickets, 70
Crows, 164
Cutthroat finch, 49

Damselfish, 74
Dangerous animals, 140–142
Dealers, see Breeders; Pet shops
Death, 296–298: killed by a car, 298; methods of disposal, 297; by negligence, 297–298; reasons for, 296–297
Declawing or defanging, 205–206
Deer, 156–157
Dentistry, 247–248
Diamondback turtle, 57
Diet supplements, 227, 237
Difficult pets, types of, 80–134: domestic species, 81–112; wild species, 112–134
Diseases, animal-transmitted, see Zoonoses
Doberman pinscher, 84
Dog collars, 203–204

Dog litter, 88, 214
Dogs, 82–92: domestication of, 3; training process, 198–203; in the wild, 152–156
Domestic shorthair cat, 34–35
Donkey, 93–96
Doves, 108
Dry pet foods, 232–233; with water, 238
Dry shampoos, 249
Ducks, 103–105
Dutch rabbit, 29
Dwarf hamster, 22

Eagles, 164
Ear problems, first-aid treatment for, 271
Ear trimming, 207
Earthworm, 71
Eastern chipmunk, 119
Eastern indigo snake, 59
Easy pets, types of, 12–79: birds, 40–53; fish, 74–79; insects, 68–74; mammals, 13–40; reptiles and amphibians, 53–68
Egyptian cobra, 140
Endangered Species Act of 1973, 113, 147
Endangered wildlife, 137–139
English guinea pig, 26
English sparrow, 306
Equine encephalitis, 269, 275
Equine infectious anemia, 269
Esbilac (substitute bitches milk), 287, 288
European polecat, 90
Euthanasia, 307–310
Exercise, 252–256: area for, 253–255; individual requirements, 252–253; supervised freedom and, 255–256
Eye problems, first-aid treatment for, 271

Fairbairn, Douglas, 119–120
Falconry, 164–165
Feline infectious enteritis, 269
Feline pneumonitis, 269–270
Ferrets, 90–93
Field cricket, 70
Fighting fish, 74

Finches, 48–49
First-aid treatment, 270–272
Fish, 74–78: aquaria, 75–76, 222–225; breeding, 294
Fish and Wildlife Service (U.S. Department of the Interior), 137
Fish-eating birds, 239
Flea powder, 246–247
Fleas, first-aid treatment for, 271
Flemish rabbit, 29
Food and feeding, 225–241: animal dependency on, 225; for baby birds, 292–293; carnivores, 226–227; commercial foods, 232–234; diet supplements, 227, 237; dietary changes in, 229–230; free-roaming pets, 238–241; fresh food and table scraps, 235–236; health care and, 230; misconceptions about, 226; nutritional diet, 228–229, 230; pet-food industry and, 225–226, 228; routine, time, and amount of, 230–232; specific requirements for, 226; in stall area, 216–217; for taming, 195; vegetarians, 227–228; water requirements, 237–238; young animals, 287–288
Foot problems, first-aid treatment for, 271–272
Fox, 153
Fracture, first-aid treatment for, 270
French Alpine goat, 97
Fresh foods, 235–236
Frizzle chicken, 101
Frogs, 65–68
Furballs, 37

Garter snake, 59, 60–61, 62
Geese, 105–106
Gerbil, 23–25
German carp, 306
German shepherd, 84
Getting a pet (and how not to), 173–183: from breeders, 178–180; expert advice for, 174–175; factors to consider, 173–174; gift from friends, 181; from humane societies, 180–181; from pet shops, 176–178; strays and beggars, 181–183; veterinarian check-up and, 175
Giant boa constrictor, 59
Giant hamster, 22
Gila monster, 62
Goats, 96–98
God's Dog (Ryden), 152
Golden hamster, 21–23
Golden retriever, 84
Goldfish, 74
Goodall, Jane, 163
Goshawk, The (White), 139
Grass parakeet, 50–51
Gray squirrel, 119
Grooming, 241–252: birds, 251; mammals, 243–250; preventive measures, 242; regularity in, 241–242; reptiles, 251–252
Groundhog Day, 144
Groundhogs (woodchucks), 144
Groupers, 74
Guinea fowl, 103
Guinea pig, 26–28
Guppies, 74

Hamsters, 21–23
Hares, 29–30
Harness, use of, 204
Harvest mouse, 17
Havana brown cat, 35–36
Hawks, 164
Health care, 257–276: diseases (that man can catch), 272–276; first-aid treatment, 270–272; food and feeding, 230; handling animals in trouble, 262–267; preventive medicine, 267–270; veterinarians and, 257–262
Heartworm, 269
Heat stroke, first-aid treatment for, 272
Henry IV (Shakespeare), 306
Hepatitis, 159
Hills Packing Company, 234

Himalayan cat, 35
Histoplasmosis, 275
Hognose snake, 59
Homer pigeon, 108
Hooded rat, 21
Hookworms, 275
Horses, 93–96
House cricket, 70
Housebreaking a puppy, 198–199
Household adjustments, *see* Adjustment and responsibility
Humane societies, 180–181

Iguanas, 62
Impeyan pheasant, 106
Impossible pets, types of, 135–169: adult wild animals, 139–140; birds, 164–169; cat family, 147–151; dangerous animals, 140–142; endangered wildlife, 137–139; mammals, 142–163; primates, 157–163; reptiles, 163–164; rodent family, 142–144; weasel family, 144–147; ungulates, 156–157; wild dogs, 152–156
Imprinting, theory of, 188
Indigo snake, 59
Infectious hepatitis, 269
Injured animal, handling, 262–267
Injured bird, caring for, 165–167, 239
Insect-eating birds, 239
Insects: breeding, 294; difficult kinds of, 110–112; diseases carried by, 274–275; easy kinds of, 68–74; living quarters for, 225
Intestinal blockage, first-aid treatment for, 272
Irish rat, 21

Jackets for pets, 204
Java green peacock, 106
Jefferson salamander, 64

Ken-L-Ration Blue Label Dog Food, 234
King snake, 59
Kinkajous, 126–127

KMR (special cat diet), 288
Kodiak bear, 157

Laboratory Welfare Act, 176
Lacey Act of 1900, 177
Lady Gouldian finch, 49
Land turtle, 56
Leashes, types of, 204
Least chipmunk, 119
Leptospirosis, 269, 273–274
Lice, 275
Living with pets, 184–212: adjustment and responsibility of, 190–210; affection between man and animal, 210–212; communication, 185–190
Lizards, 62–64
Lockjaw, 269
Loneliness, 209–210
Lop rabbit, 29
Lorenz, Konrad, 105, 188
Loriinaes (lorikeets), 50
Loss of an animal, 295–310: abandoning and chances of survival, 305–307; through death, 296–298; euthanasia, 307–310; by finding a new home, 301–303; by giving away, 303–305; lost or stolen, 298–301; by reselling, 303
Lovebirds, 51
Lymphocytic choriomeningitis, 275

M Diet (brand), 234
Macaw, 49, 131–132
Maine coon cat, 35
Mammals: breeding, 282–290; difficult kinds of, 82–92, 115–130; as easy pets, 13–40; grooming, 243–250; impossible kinds of, 140–163; living quarters for, 213–219
Mannikin finch, 49
Manx cat, 35
Marbled salamander, 64
Margay, 147
Marmoset, 160
Marten, 146–147

Masked-bandit raccoon, 123
Maxwell, Gavin, 145
May I Keep This Clam, Mother? It Followed Me Home (Rood), 61
Medakas, 74
Medication, 263–264
Mexican beaded lizard, 62
Mice, 17–19, 142–143
Migratory Bird Treaty Act, 164
Mikado pheasant, 106
Mites, first-aid treatment for, 271
Mole salamander, 64
Mongolian pheasant, 106
Monitor lizard, 62–63
Monkey-bite encephalitis, 273
Monkeys, 157–163
Morris Animal Foundation, 258
Moths, 71–72
Mountain lion, 149–150
Mowat, Farley, 152
Mud turtle, 57
Mules, 94
Musk turtle, 57
Muzzles, 204–205
Mynah bird, 133

Nectar-eating birds, 239
Neon goby, 74
Neutering operation, 180–181, 206–207, 277–279
Never Cry Wolf (Mowat), 152
New Zealand rabbit, 29
Newcastle disease, 40, 113
Newts, 64–65
North, Sterling, 123
North American Falconers Association, 165
North American Peregrine Falcon Foundation, 165
Norway rat, 19
Norwich canary, 47
Nubian goat, 97

Obesity, 206–207
Ocelot, 147–149
Opossum, 117
Ornithosis, 40, 108
Otter, 145–146
Owls, 164
Owning a pet, 3–11: in ancient times, 3; children and, 6–7; factors involved in, 8–11; reason for, 4–8

Paar, Jack, 147
Painted turtle, 57
Parakeets, 50–51
Parrots, 49–50, 130–133
P/D (brand), 234
Peacocks, 106–107
Peking duck, 104–105
Peregrine falcon, 138
Persian cat, 35
Peruvian guinea pig, 26, 176
Pet shops, 176–178: buying from, 176–178; health bill of sale, 177; importers, 177; veterinary certificates, 176
Pets: breeding, 277–294; care of, 213–256; difficult kinds of, 80–134; easy kinds of, 12–79; getting (and how not to), 173–183; health of, 257–276; impossible kinds of, 135–169; living with, 184–212; loss of, 295–310; owning, 1–11; *see also* types of pets
Pet-Tabs (diet supplement), 237
Pheasants, 106–107
Pigeons, 107–110
Pigs, 99–100
Pills, how to give, 267
Pinworms, 275
Poisoning, first-aid treatment for, 271
Polecats, 90
Polish chicken, 101
Polish rabbit, 29
Ponies, 93–96
Poodles, 84, 85
Porcupines, 142
Powders and dressings, 246–247
Prairie dogs, 144
Praying mantises, 72
Preventive medicine, 267–270
Primates, 157–163
Psittacosis, 40, 113, 275
Puma, *see* Mountain lion
Puppy mills, 176
Pythons, 58

Quaker Oats Company, 234
Queen bee, 111
Quills, porcupine, 142

Rabbits, 28–33
Rabies, 159, 267–268, 273
Raccoon family, 123–130
Raccoons, 123–126
Racing pigeons, 107–109
Rascal (North), 123
Rat-bite fever, 273
Rats, 19–21, 142–143
Red factor canary, 47
Red squirrel, 119
Repellent sprays and lotions, 202
Reptiles: breeding, 294; easy kinds of, 53–68; feeding, 236; grooming, 251–252; impossible kinds of, 163–164; living quarters for, 222–225
Reticulated python, 58
Rex rabbit, 29
Rhesus monkey, 158
Rhinotracheitis, 270
Rhode Island chicken, 101
Ring of Bright Water (Maxwell), 145
Ringworm, 275
Rogers, Roy, 297
Roller pigeon, 109
Rood, Ronald, 60
Round worms, 275
Runaway pets, how to prevent, 298–300
Russian blue cat, 35
Ryden, Hope, 152

Salamander, 64–65
Salmonellosis, 274
Sapajous, 160
Satin rabbit, 29
Scent glands, removal of, 206
Science (food brand), 234
Scissors, grooming with, 246
Scurvy, 176
Sea basses, 74
Seed-eating birds, 239
Self-mutilation, 210
Self-watering devices, 218
Seton, Ernest Thompson, 145
Shedding, 246

Sheep, 96–98
Shock, first-aid treatment for, 270
Shots, *see* Preventive medicine
Shrimp, 78–79
Siamese cat, 35
Sicilian (or Sardinian) donkey, 94
Silver fox rabbit, 29
Skin problems, first-aid treatment for, 271
Skunks, 120–123
Snakes, 58–62
Snapping turtle, 57
Song canaries, 47
Songbirds, training, 203
South American cardinal finch, 49
Spider monkeys, 160–161
Spiders, 73–74
Spotted salamander, 64
Spotted turtle, 57
Squirrel Forever, A (Fairbairn), 119–120
Squirrel monkey, 161
Squirrels, 118–120
Stalls, 215–217: bedding and ventilation, 215–216; feeding in, 216–217; fencing, 216; size of, 215
Star finch, 49
Starlings, 133–134, 306
Ste-Med (diet supplement), 237
Stolen animals, 298–301: traffic in, 300; ways of preventing, 300–301
Strays and beggars, 181–183
Surgery, kinds of, 205–207
Swans, 105–106
Swordtails, 74

Table scraps, feeding, 235–236
Tadpoles, 67–68
Tail docking, 207
Taming process, 193–197: caged animals, 194–197; care in, 193–194
Tapeworms, 275
Tarantula, 73
Tattoos, 299
Taxidermists, 297
Terrapins (water turtles), 56
Terriers, 84

Tetanus, 269, 273
Theralin (diet supplement), 237
Tick fever, 275
Tick powder, 246–247
Ticks, 275; first-aid treatment for, 271
Tiger salamander, 64
Timber wolf, 138
Tippler pigeon, 109
Toads, 65–68
Toggenburg goat, 97
Tooth problems, first-aid treatment for, 271
Tortoises, 56
Tortoiseshell cat, 36
Toucans, 134
Toxoplasmosis, 275–276
Tracheobronchitis, 270
Training process, 197–203: basic approach to, 199; equipment for, 203–205; mature animals, 200–201; reward-and-punishment system, 197–198, 199–200
Traveling with pets, 208–209
Trichinosis, 275
Tropical fish, 74–78
Tuberculosis, 159, 274
Tumbling pigeon, 109
Turtles, 56–58

Umbrellas that attach to collars, 204
Under the Shadow of Man (Goodall), 163
Ungulates, 156–157
U.S. Department of Agriculture, 176
U.S. Department of the Interior, 137

Venom, 140–141
Veterinarians, 175, 257–262: handling the animal, 262–267; house (or barn) calls, 258–259; owner's responsibilities and, 259–262; selecting, 257–259
Veterinary Services Division (U.S. Department of Agriculture), 176

Vet-Nutri (diet supplement), 237
Vionate (diet supplement), 237
Vivaria, *see* Aquaria and vivaria

Warbler finch, 49
Water, importance of, 237–238
Water snake, 62
Water turtles (terrapins), 56
Watling, Thomas J., 50
Waxbill finch, 49
Weaver finch, 49
Whipworms, 275
White, T. H., 139
White Animal Farm rat, 20
White-tailed prairie dog, 144
Whydah finch, 49
Wild animals, 112–130: adult, 139–140; birds, 130–134; feeding, 238–241; mammals, 115–130
Wild dogs, 152–156
Wild mice, 17, 142–143
Wild rabbit, 30
Wild rats, 142–143
Wings, pinioning, 207
Wolves, 139, 155–156
Wood turtle, 57
Woodchucks (groundhogs), 144
Woodland salamander, 64
Woodpeckers, 167
Woolly monkey, 161–162
Worms, first-aid treatment for, 271

Yellow fever, 159
Yellow rat snake, 59
Yokohama chicken, 101
Yorkshire canary, 47
Young animals, rearing, 285–290

Zebra finch, 48
Zoo animals, foods for, 234
Zoo Wildlife Division (Morris Animal Foundation), 258
Zoonoses, 272–276: bites, 273–274; external parasites, 275; internal parasites, 275–276; viral infections, 274–275
Zoos, 205, 304
Zu/Preem (food brand), 234
Zymadrops (diet supplement), 237